CHAMPIONSHIP CHESS

By

P. W. SERGEANT

Edited and modernized by

FRED REINFELD

Dover Publications, Inc.
New York

Published in Canada by General Publishing Company, Ltd., 30 Lesmill Road, Don Mills, Toronto, Ontario.

Published in the United Kingdom by Constable and Company, Ltd., 10 Orange Street, London WC 2.

This new Dover edition, first published in 1963, is an unabridged republication of the work first published by the Sterling Publishing Co., Inc., in 1960, to which have been added two new games, especially prepared for this edition by Fred Reinfeld.

International Standard Book Number: 0-486-21012-X
Library of Congress Catalog Card Number: 63-4620

Manufactured in the United States of America

Dover Publications, Inc.
180 Varick Street
New York 14, N.Y.

CONTENTS

PART I—THE WORLD CHESS CHAMPIONSHIP

PART II—ILLUSTRATIVE GAMES

PART III—MODERN DAY CHESS

PREFACE

THE Chess Championship of the World was said to have been "invented" by Steinitz, who was credited also at Simpson's Divan in the old days with the invention of chess itself. But, jesting apart, it was certainly that Bohemian-Jewish genius, of the squat figure, dominated by a tremendous head, who brought the term Chess Championship of the World into currency in this language of ours which he learnt to use—not to say abuse—so fluently. He had a firm conviction of the importance of chess among the activities of the human brain, and a still firmer conviction of the glory of being the best player at it. "Here am I, Wilhelm Steinitz," he is alleged to have said, "the youngest child of a poor rabbi; and I am Steinitz, the Chess Champion of the World!"

With his acquisition of the English language he acquired also (or was it inborn in him?) a journalist's appreciation of the value of terms; and the title which he made for himself was destined to stay, and to be taken up all over the world. Why no previous journalist had thought of popularising the title it is difficult to imagine, for the wording of it is not far-fetched, and the idea behind it was familiar enough in the days of Howard Staunton, who was not backward in asserting his claim to anything that he thought was his. He was content to be called "the best player in the world," as he was until 1851.

Staunton would have agreed no doubt—since he liked classical quotations—that *vixere fortes ante Agamemnona*, that there were "best players" before him. But there had been, and there still was, no recognised method of establishing the pretension. Then came the first International Masters' Tournament, in London in 1851, which Adolf Anderssen, from Breslau, won, beating among others Staunton, who was under handicap of having to manage the tournament. In consequence of his victory, Anderssen was now commonly regarded as the world's best player. Staunton pressed for a match to decide the question, but it was not found possible to arrange one.

The rivalry between tournament and match-play as deciding supremacy at chess is discussed in Chapter I, and need not be further considered here. We must give Steinitz the credit of making a title to fit that supremacy. He did not claim any title when he defeated Anderssen in a match in 1866. But twenty years later he definitely set up to be played for by himself and Zukertort "the Chess Championship of the World," and the name has remained ever since. Nowadays not merely the chess-player, but even the man in the street, unless he is very restricted in his reading of newspapers, must be aware that there is such a person as the World Champion of Chess. The late champion, had he retained his title, might even have found his name a household word, mispronounced no doubt; for an Euwe is under a disadvantage compared with a Capablanca, for instance.

The plan of this book is simple enough to require little or no explanation. It begins with the history of the World Championship; then deals with the makers of that history, and with their influence upon chess; and ends with the presentation, in Part II, of fifty-two examples illustrating the play of the masters, mostly taken from matches in which the Championship title was definitely at stake.

In Part II I have tried to give due credit to previous annotators of the games when it has been possible to trace suggestions or detailed analysis to one particular source. Where, however, a note on the move is, if not exactly obvious, at least "in the common domain," I have treated it as such, without specifying where I found it first put forward in print. In all cases I have used such analytical powers as I may myself possess to test any line of play which I have mentioned. Only those who have ventured to challenge their fate by publishing chess analysis can know what labour is involved in the task. That I have made errors I am prepared to hear; but at least I hope that they are not too many nor too serious.

P.S.—My original intention was to produce this book before the recent match for the World Championship. I was induced to include a notice of that match in it; but I must ask indulgence for my inability, in the circumstances, to give more space to the match than would have been possible if I had longer time at my disposal.

I desire to acknowledge the kind help of Mr. W. Henderson in reading the proofs of the book.

PHILIP W. SERGEANT.

7, Brunswick Square,
London.

For a long time I have wanted to bring Sergeant's classic account of the World Championship contests up to date. The old struggles deserve to be remembered, but the contemporary ones clamor for our attention too. As part of the new edition the number of games has been raised from 52 to 64. I have tried as far as possible to maintain the style of my distinguished predecessor.

FRED REINFELD.

Berkeley Street,
London.

July, 1960.

PART I

THE WORLD CHESS CHAMPIONSHIP

CHAPTER I

THE ORIGIN OF THE WORLD CHAMPIONSHIP

THE attempt has often been made to set back the beginning of the Chess Championship of the World to an early date, usually to the second half of the Sixteenth Century, when the title is bestowed upon the Spaniard Ruy Lopez, of Segura. Following that romantic chess-writer George Walker, many have called Ruy Lopez a bishop, but, though he undoubtedly was an ecclesiastic, there is no evidence that he ever obtained such high preferment. As a player, however, he reached proficiency in his own country before he went to Rome on Church business about 1560, and there he made a point of meeting the leading Italian experts of the day.

Italy was at the time the main centre of chess activity, having been probably the introducer of the modern game,* even if the capture of a Pawn " in passing " was not yet recognised, nor the method of castling systematised. The Portuguese Damiano had published his book on the game in Italian in 1512; and this had reached its seventh edition when Ruy Lopez visited Rome, and, noting Damiano's insufficiency as an instructor, was inspired to produce something better. Returning to Spain he published in 1561 his *Libro de la invencion liberal y arte del juego del Axedrez*. He was now recognised as the foremost Spanish player. But when some thirteen years later Giovanni Leonardo di Bona, of Cutri in Calabria, whom Lopez had met and defeated as a youth in Rome, came to Spain, he beat both Lopez and his nearest rival, Alfonso Ceron of Granada, playing in the presence of that royal patron of chess, Philip II. Soon after the Syracusan Paolo Boi, who had shown himself Leonardo's equal in Italy, also visited Spain and beat the same two Spanish players.

There is in this no substantial basis for the claim that the first World Champions at chess were Ruy Lopez and Leonardo di Bona. Nor is there more ground for conferring the visionary title in the Seventeenth Century upon Gioachino Greco, *il Calabrese*, or upon Philip Stamma, who came originally from Aleppo. Their works on chess made them known; and that must suffice for their fame.

The pretensions of François-André Danican Philidor to be

* H. J. R. Murray in his *History of Chess* puts the invention of this no earlier than 1485.

regarded as champion are a little more firm, as chess was now growing as a medium of intercourse between nations. Philidor, who as a boy in Paris used to take the odds of a Rook from the somewhat shadowy but reputedly great Légal, at the age of seventeen was too strong to receive any odds from his master, and when he came to London in 1747 had already a reputation as a fine player, which he enhanced when he met Stamma in a match, conceding the odds of the draw, and beat him easily. Returning to France he beat Légal in a match. No other set encounters of his are recorded, but he found no one who could defeat him until his death in 1795, so that, in the difficult international conditions of his day, he may be allowed to have been an uncrowned king of the game.

The two Frenchmen who succeeded him, A. Le Breton Deschapelles and L. C. Mahé de Labourdonnais, imposed their sway on the chess world in Paris, which was in their times the centre of the game beyond a doubt, by sheer merit. Deschapelles, the master, met no one to equal him until he considered that his pupil was on a level with him, and retired from chess to devote himself to whist. Labourdonnais ventured his skill outside France when, in 1834, he came over to London and engaged in a long match-series with Alexander M'Donnell, beating him by 44-27, with 13 draws. M'Donnell being recognised as the strongest player on this side of the Channel, and no country outside France and Great Britain having anyone competent to challenge their best, Labourdonnais was not excessively praised, on his death in 1840, as having been the first chessplayer in the world.

The Labourdonnais-M'Donnell games, however, can hardly be regarded as part of an encounter, even virtually, for the World Championship. Labourdonnais had come to London expressly to challenge the best player there, obviously meaning M'Donnell; and there were stakes. But a series of 84 games (which it was intended to continue, had not Labourdonnais been obliged to return to Paris, and M'Donnell fallen ill and died) is not to be put on the same level with a set match of so many games, in which a fixed number of points decides the victory. For that reason it was decided not to include any of the Labourdonnais-M'Donnell games in this book, and to defer the start of the championship record until we came to a match between two masters under conditions more or less resembling those which prevail today.

We reach such a point in 1843. It is true that the match between Howard Staunton and P. C. F. de Saint-Amant was never claimed, in so many words, as being for the Chess Championship of the World. Staunton, in his magazine *The Chess Player's Chronicle*, was content to call it " The Grand Chess Match between

England and France," and Saint-Amant, in his magazine *Le Palamède*, headed the scores of the games simply "France et Angleterre." As there were still only two countries eminent for chess at the time, and Saint-Amant, pupil of both Deschapelles and Labourdonnais, was beyond dispute the best French player, while Staunton's supremacy in England was not seriously challenged, it is rather curious that the claim was not made. When the match was over, however, Staunton's friend Captain H. A. Kennedy wrote of him in *The Brighton Guardian* as having "achieved, by right of conquest, the sceptre of Philidor, the first time, if we mistake not, that it has ever been wielded by a Briton."

Staunton had a special incentive to strive for victory in this match. Earlier in 1843, on one of his subsequently frequent visits to London in connection with his business as wine-merchant, Saint-Amant met Staunton at the St. George's Chess Club in a series of six games for a small stake, and beat him by 3—2, with one draw. When he returned to Paris Saint-Amant described this encounter as a match. Staunton was fully justified in retorting that it was no match. Saint-Amant had come to London on business, not for chess; and he himself had only recently recovered from illness. On August 8 he issued a challenge to Saint-Amant, "or any other player in the field," to a formal match of twenty-one or forty-one games, for a stake of fifty or a hundred guineas a side. Saint-Amant agreed to play in Paris for the first eleven games won by either, with a stake of £100 or 2,500 francs; and the other conditions were soon arranged. Four games were to be played a week, from 11 a.m. each day, without a break. No time-limit was imposed for a move. (Even "the innovation of timing" by sand-glasses had to wait eighteen years before it was introduced in a short match between Anderssen and Kolisch in London.) We hear of the strain upon the players in this match; but nothing is said of the effect on the numerous spectators at the Cercle d'Échecs, though the partisans of each combatant accused the other of having been very slow. In those spacious days no little wits made jests about slow-motion chess.

In another respect than the absence of clocks the circumstances of the match differed from those of today. There was no protection of the players. Marlet's well-known picture gives some idea perhaps of the scene in the Paris clubroom; but it does not reproduce the noise which was bound to arise from a crowd of onlookers. *The Chess Player's Chronicle* complains that this was specially unfavourable to Staunton, as his opponent was accustomed to play in the Café de la Régence.

Nevertheless, when the match started on November 4, the English champion showed himself in far better form than the French. He won the first 2 games, drew the 3rd, and won 5 more in succession before Saint-Amant scored his first win. A hollow victory appeared probable, and indeed was anticipated by the English commentators on the match. Staunton took the 10th game, Saint-Amant the 11th, and Staunton the 12th; and then Saint-Amant produced the most brilliant effort of the match, which is given, with one of Staunton's wins, in Part II. The 14th game was drawn, but Staunton won the 15th, making the score 10—3 in his favour. At this point Captain Harry Wilson, the chief of Staunton's two seconds, was compelled by serious indisposition to leave Paris, and as the other, J. Worrell, had been obliged to go a few days earlier, Staunton had, as he complains, to " bear the brunt alone." It is possible that R. B. Brien, who was in Paris at the start of the match, was still with him; but Staunton was undoubtedly upset, and having to make but one more point took 6 games to get it. He lost the 16th game, drew the 17th and 18th, lost the next 2, and finally won the 21st, making his full score 11—6, with 4 draws.

The margin of victory was sufficiently large to make natural the English exultation over it; but it is also natural, especially when the games are examined, that Saint-Amant and his supporters should have been dissatisfied with his form. With the controversy which followed we are not concerned. Neither player was at his best throughout, indeed but rarely; and the games suffer in consequence. The same, however, may be said of practically every Championship match. The perfect game—that is, a game in which neither player makes any slip—should theoretically end in a draw, unless and until it can be shown that the first move gives a winning advantage, which no competent judge of the game believes. The approach to perfection which results in an early " agreed " draw is extremely unpopular with the followers of chess. So perhaps we may call the ideal game one in which a slight slip by one side is finely taken advantage of by the other. The best example of this in Part II is Game 38 (Capablanca-Alekhine), though there White slips more than once.

It is of no small interest to look at the openings in the Staunton-Saint-Amant match, particularly in view of its having been played ninety-four years ago. When Labourdonnais and M'Donnell had their long encounter in 1834 the openings included the *Evans Gambit* twenty-two times, various *King's Gambits* eleven times, and *M'Donnell's Double Gambit* once. As against this, Labourdonnais opened with 1 **P—Q4** sixteen times, and M'Donnell once.

Now in 1843 Staunton, in 10 games, opened with 1 **P—QB4** six times, with 1 **P—Q4** twice, and with 1 **P—K4** twice—being met with the *Sicilian Defence.* Saint-Amant opened with 1 **P—K4** thrice, being also met by the *Sicilian,* which was enough for him, as he only succeeded in drawing 1 of the 3 games. He then played 4 games each at the *Queen's Pawn* and *Queen's Gambit.* There was not, therefore, one so-called "open" game in the whole match. "The era of close games," which R. B. Wormald later declared to have culminated in the London Tournament of 1851, had set in strongly. But what do we find when Anderssen met Steinitz in 1868? Anderssen played 6 *Evans Gambits* and 1 *Ruy Lopez;* Steinitz 4 *Salvio Gambits* and 1 *King's Gambit* (*Declined*), while twice his 1 **P—K4** was met by the *Sicilian Defence.*

Superficially the Staunton-Saint-Amant match might be considered as being, in its openings, an interlude of "modernity," or the close game, in a long run of the open game; but that would be entirely wrong. The main weapon of Labourdonnais was 1 **P—Q4.** Staunton established the vogue of that move and of 1 **P—QB4** in England. Anderssen, when he met Steinitz, was fifty, and a firm supporter of 1 **P—K4,** while Steinitz was only thirty and had yet to become, with the help of his English practice, the great exponent of the Modern School—which was far from involving the abandonment of 1 **P—K4,** as we shall see in his match with Zukertort in 1886.

After his defeat Saint-Amant pressed for a return match, which Staunton promised before he left Paris; and negotiations went on, constantly on the point of being wrecked by the acrimony in print of supporters of the two masters. Staunton's attitude was not unreasonable, irritated though he was by Saint-Amant's claim that they had won a match each. He consented to go again to Paris in the autumn of 1844; but a chill on the journey developed into pneumonia, and he was too ill to play even after convalescence. No further meeting therefore took place.

Staunton remained virtual chess champion until 1851, when Adolf Anderssen came over from Breslau to London, and won the first International Masters' Tournament, thus introducing a new country into the Championship arena. Staunton, who had competed in the tournament under the serious handicap of having to manage it, was knocked out by Anderssen in the third round by a score of 4—1. When Anderssen took the first prize, Staunton at once challenged him to a match. Anderssen agreed, but could not stay in England to play it. It was arranged that it should be played later in Germany.

At a dinner in Manchester in 1853 a challenge was issued on Staunton's behalf to any player in the world to a match of 21 games, for a stake of £250 if the player should be from abroad; and Staunton let it be known that the challenge was particularly addressed to Anderssen. No one took it up, though there was much talk of its acceptance by Daniel Harrwitz. That this too came to nothing was certainly not Staunton's fault. Staunton now retired from chess; and Paul Morphy, coming over from America in 1858 especially to meet him, failed to persuade him to return to match-play. The story has been too often told to need repetition. Morphy while in Europe beat Harrwitz by 5—2, with one draw, and Anderssen by 7—2, with two draws.

On the strength of the latter victory the Championship of Chess has been claimed for Morphy from 1858 to 1859, or perhaps 1860, when he definitely declined a match with Louis Paulsen. The date might even be extended to 1861, when he replied to a challenge on behalf of Ignaz Kolisch that he might, "as a special exception," break the rule he had adopted to play no matches in future, but positively declined playing for any stake whatever; which made the match impossible for Kolisch, then still a professional player, who apart from chess had only his pen to rely upon.

Now Morphy undoubtedly deserved the Chess Championship of the World, and did his best to win the title. But, strictly, his right to it was based on his defeat of Anderssen, apart from what right was conferred by his unbeaten record. Had he only accepted Louis Paulsen's or Kolisch's challenge, and won again, his position would have been secure. He did not care to do so, and consequently the question of the Championship was left in an unsatisfactory position.*

Anderssen's chess was obviously rusty when he met Morphy; but he was still only forty, and he soon recovered his form. On a visit to England in 1861 he won the match against Kolisch in which sand-glasses were used for the first time; and next year came out at the head of the first Masters' Tournament on modern lines, in which each of the fourteen competitors played every other. His score was 12 against the 11 of Louis Paulsen, the 10 of the Rev. John Owen, the 9 each of the Rev. G. A. MacDonnell and Serafino Dubois, and the 8 of Wilhelm Steinitz. With 4

* It may be asked why no game of Morphy's against Anderssen has been included in this book. The answer is that I have dealt with the great American master so fully in my *Morphy's Games of Chess* and *Morphy Gleanings*, not to mention a short section in *A Century of British Chess*, that I was reluctant to use old matter over again. The choice of a game would have been difficult. Perhaps the 5th game might have been selected, though Anderssen's conduct of it was much criticised.

points only the young J. H. Blackburne was well out of the prize-list.

This tournament restored Anderssen to the position formerly assigned him as the world's best chessplayer, omitting now the retired Morphy. His successor was as yet unsuspected; for the Austrian Steinitz at the age of twenty-six had made no great impression in the London Tournament; and his victory in a match arranged soon after against Blackburne, though achieved by 7—1, with two draws, was explained by the immaturity of his opponent, chiefly noted as yet for brilliant blindfold play. But Steinitz, settling in London, rapidly became one of the most prominent figures in chess circles there.

The year 1866 gave Steinitz the chance of proving himself something more. The British Chess Association in January had shown an access of vigour after three years of inactivity, and it was determined to hold a congress in London in June. The principal event was to be a Grand Challenge Cup competition for British players only; and the programme issued gave no hint of a match in London between Anderssen and Steinitz. The credit for arranging this belongs to the three clubs, the St. George's, the London, and the Westminster (a new foundation under an old name), the sum of £100 being put up for the winner, with another £60 for the loser. In *The Transactions of the British Chess Association for* 1866 *and* 1867 the encounter is simply called "Match between Anderssen and Steinitz"; it is not claimed as a World Championship match.

The rules of the contest laid down that twenty moves should be completed on each side in two hours, the time being measured by sand-glasses, and that all games should be played at one sitting, without adjournments except for an interval of a quarter of an hour for rest and refreshment after four hours' play. The first 8 wins to either party were to decide the match.

Anderssen could not come to London before the second half of July. He is reported to have arrived full of confidence, in spite of his handicap of eighteen years—forty-eight against thirty—and his much less recent practice. He started well on July 18 with an *Evans Gambit*, in which he maintained his Pawn-majority; but it was a blunder by Steinitz on the 32nd move that gave him a win. Steinitz retorted two days later with a *Salvio Gambit*, against which Anderssen was guilty of an extraordinary slip as early as the 9th move, from which he never recovered.

The openings in this match have already been mentioned, the *Evans* and *Salvio* continuing to be the favourites, though Anderssen introduced two *Sicilian Defences*, both of which he won. Steinitz won the third (see Part II, Game 3), fourth, and fifth games. Then Anderssen in his turn had a run of four wins, including one against the *Salvio* (Game 4), which made his score 5—4. With the tenth and eleventh games Steinitz recovered the lead, and, after Anderssen had scored the twelfth, he went on to win the thirteenth (Game 5) and the fourteenth, giving him the match by 8—4. The last game was a very obstinate affair, running to 85 moves and was marked by Anderssen's fine resistance after judiciously sacrificing the Exchange in his 41st move to restrain his opponent's menacing Pawns.

The contemporary comments on the match scarcely did justice to Anderssen; at least, not those from Staunton's pen. In his new and short-lived magazine, *The Chess World*, we read that in the first five games Anderssen hardly sustained his high and well-earned reputation, winning the first rather by an accident than by superiority of play, while in the following four " there are few indications of the depth, the comprehension, and the daring enterprise which distinguish his play in former times." At the end of the match Staunton wrote: " The vicissitudes were so remarkable . . . and the play of Mr. Anderssen so variable that lookers-on were prepared for any termination. To those who were not present, however, the defeat of the Prussian champion by an antagonist scarcely recognised among the magnates must have appeared incredible. . . . The real cause of it, we believe, is not hard to seek. Mr. Anderssen was beaten because his day for match-playing is over. . . ." In the October issue of *The Chess World*, however, a discursive article on " Laurels and Ashes " speaks of " the invidious manner in which many persons who ought to have known better carp at the play of Anderssen since his defeat by Steinitz, and also the unjust elevation which they would assign to the latter, undoubtedly a very skilful athlete at the game "—though his claim to be placed in the first rank rests on this match alone.

There is, of course, something in what Staunton says; but those who were so much impressed by Steinitz's feat may be credited with foresight in guessing that it was a portent of greater triumphs to come.

In the meantime the amateurs of the Westminster Club were anxious to see Steinitz engaged in a test of skill with some English player. The champion selected was H. E. Bird, who at the age of just under twenty-one had made a promising entry into the higher grade of chess at the London Congress of 1851, and since then had never looked back. Bird was about to pay a visit to the United States (on business, as far as chess would allow him to attend to that), and the match had to be arranged quickly. When the score stood at 7—5 against him, with 5 draws, he resigned, having no more time to spare. *The Chess World* speaks of this as " the little match " between Steinitz and Bird. It certainly was not to be included among Championship encounters, even if the idea of such had become definite in those days.

So far was that from being the case yet that the period which succeeded was one of big tournaments, after each of which there was a tendency to acclaim the victor as the world's best player. In 1867 the Paris International Masters' Tournament brought Kolisch to the top, with 21 points in 24 games, against the 19½ of Simon Winawer and Steinitz, the 19 of G. R. Neumann (who in the previous year had in vain challenged Steinitz to a match), etc. In 1870 came the Baden-Baden Tournament, organised by Kolisch, who had retired from master-chess to devote himself most successfully to business, while remaining a generous supporter of the game. Here Anderssen triumphantly proved that his tournament days at least were not over by taking the first prize, with 11 points in 16 games, against Steinitz's 10½, Blackburne's and Neumann's 10 each, etc.

In 1872 the British Chess Association attempted to emulate foreign rivals, announcing an International Masters' Tournament at the Crystal Palace; but for some reason it failed to attract. Apart from Steinitz, who was a London resident, and one newcomer, there were no non-British competitors, and Blackburne, the Rev. G. A. MacDonnell, Cecil de Vere, and John Wisker were alone of master-strength among the six home players.

The new foreign player gave no little interest to the tournament. This was Dr. Johann Hermann Zukertort, born in Russian Poland just under thirty years previously, and winner of a short match with Anderssen in 1871. The story of his introduction to London was curious, it being said that it was due to some people who did not like Steinitz and wished to see him beaten. If that was true, Zukertort's sponsors were disappointed. He drew a game indeed with Steinitz, but by the rules of the tournament this had to be replayed, when Steinitz won. The Austrian finished with a clean score of 7 wins, Blackburne scored 5, and Zukertort, MacDonnell, and De Vere 4 each, Zukertort after a play-off taking third prize.

Zukertort made a good impression, however, and soon had a number of English friends who were anxious to see him pitted against Steinitz in a match. The money was forthcoming, £20 for the winner and £10 for the loser; and on August 8, 1872, the match began, being played at the St. George's and Westminster Clubs alternately. Steinitz's victory was hollow, 7—1, with

4 draws. There was no question of any Championship being involved, and the affair had little publicity.

Next year Steinitz had the opportunity of confirming his position, for in the Vienna Masters' Tournament, to which he went over from England with Blackburne and Bird, he gained first prize. The system under which the tournament was arranged was peculiar, each competitor playing for the best of 3 games against the 11 others. Steinitz scored 20 points, though he lost 2 games and drew 1 against Blackburne; but he lost to no one else. Blackburne also scored 20, but he lost 7 games, so that Steinitz was ranked above him. Anderssen was third with 17 points.

Steinitz was now both Anderssen's conqueror in their match and the winner of the last great International Tournament, and his claim as all-round champion would have been hard to dispute. Bird issued a fruitless challenge for a match with him in the autumn of 1874; but Steinitz was not to be tempted to engage in a serious individual encounter until early in 1876, when the ambitious young West End Chess Club persuaded him to meet Blackburne for a stake of £60, though Steinitz at first pressed for more. The match was to be for the first 7 wins to either side, and the time-limit thirty moves in the first two hours, fifteen an hour afterwards. It was originally arranged to have sand-glasses, but when the match began " alarum time-pieces " were substituted for the first time in the history of chess.

Blackburne's supporters, remembering what he had done in the Vienna Tournament, were terribly disappointed with what happened in the match. Steinitz won 7 games in succession, without even conceding a draw. It was poor consolation that Blackburne in the 2nd game was offered but refused a draw, and then lost; or that in the 3rd (see Part II, Game 6) he obtained a winning position but, running short of time, threw it away, and after the adjournment blundered so badly that he lost again.

Wisker wrote judiciously of the match in *The City of London Chess Magazine* that there might be reasons far Blackburne's collapse, but the public would look at results only, and they were right, " public form " being the only safe guide. Another critic, in *The Chess Player's Chronicle* (a kind of illegitimate descendant of Staunton's original magazine), was far less discreet. He stated that Blackburne's play after dinner, when the games were resumed, was affected by " the cuisine, or the wine, or the salmon, or—can you suggest any other obfuscating agency ?"

Steinitz's book of the match, reprinted with additions from his column in *The Field*, ridicules any plea that Blackburne held winning positions up to the dinner-hour, and " played heedlessly after, and in consequence of, the adjournment for refreshment." He points out that the adjournment could take place only after 30 moves a side had been made, and fairly proves that Blackburne's apologists were incorrect.

It came to be recognised later that Blackburne was emphatically a magnificent tournament player, whose temperament match-play against the greatest masters did not suit. Some of his finest tournament successes were to come very soon, notably at Wiesbaden in 1880 and Berlin in 1881. But in the latter year he had just lost a match to Zukertort by 7—2, with 2 draws, proceeding to come out 3 points ahead of him in the tournament.

Steinitz, after his match with Blackburne, remained comparatively quiet as far as serious play was concerned. As chess editor of *The Field*, however, he was exceedingly active, and his controversies with *The Chess Monthly*, founded in 1879 by Zukertort and Leopold Hoffer, were marked by extreme bitterness. The chess-rivalry of Steinitz and Zukertort was partly the cause of this, but it was fanned by a mutual antipathy which the extravagances of their admirers were constantly aggravating. Zukertort's tournament successes—equal second at Leipzig, 1877; first after a tie with Winawer, at Paris, 1878; and second at Berlin, 1881—showed that he was approaching the top of his form. At last in 1882 Steinitz decided to return to tournament play, entering for the great Vienna Tournament, which was the most important of international tournaments held so far. Lasting six weeks, it was a double-round affair of eighteen competitors. At the end Steinitz and Winawer had scored 24 points each; and after winning 1 game each in the tie-match they agreed to divide first and second prizes between them. The third fell to the Irishman James Mason, who, after spending his early years in the United States and learning his chess there, at the age of twenty-eight had made his first European appearance in the Paris Tournament of 1878, and had done well in the subsequent Wiesbaden and Berlin Tournaments. But his position now, with 23 points, next to Steinitz and Winawer (whom he beat twice), was a startling surprise.

Zukertort divided fourth and fifth prizes with Captain G. A. Mackenzie, $22\frac{1}{2}$ points each, Zukertort having the satisfaction of scoring $1\frac{1}{2}$-$\frac{1}{2}$ against Steinitz. Blackburne ($21\frac{1}{2}$) took the sixth and last prize.

It was felt that some match ought to be the outcome of this tournament; and at the time England was the most likely country to provide the stakes. Steinitz was the obvious choice as one of the players. For an opponent in London, where Winawer was unknown, Zukertort had many advocates, but it would be almost impossible to bring the two men together. After Mason's performance at Vienna, though he had been regarded as an American when he first came to London, he soon found people desirous of putting him up against Steinitz. But even this proposal came to nothing. Steinitz declined to play unless during the match there was to be a cessation of what he considered a Press campaign—"literary hooting," he called it—against him. Then came an invitation to him from Philadelphia to visit the United States, offering him very favourable terms for at least one match and numerous exhibitions, etc. He decided to accept the offer, resigned his post on *The Field*, and left England on October 25. So a match with Mason was out of the question.

Steinitz had not definitely severed his connection with England yet. Before he left there had been talk of an International Masters' Tournament in London in 1883, on lines similar to those of the recent Vienna Tournament. The fact that the British Chess Association was at this period dormant did not prevent the London clubs, aided by the exertions of the wealthy Robert Steel, home on leave from Calcutta, making a splendid effort to supply its place in the organisation of a congress, which was a great success and incidentally paved the way for the institution of a World Chess Championship.

With fourteen players, of whom at least eleven, headed by Steinitz and Zukertort, were in the front rank of masters, meeting one another twice, the struggle in the principal event was bound to be arduous; and, to make it more so, a rule provided that draws should be replayed twice if necessary, only a third draw counting half a point to each player.

Zukertort achieved the most striking of all his successes. In twenty-three rounds he scored 22 points, his only loss being 1 of his 2 games with Steinitz. Then, utterly exhausted, he lost his remaining 3 games; but he had made sure of the first prize before doing so! Steinitz took second prize with 19 points (7 losses), followed by Blackburne (16½), Tchigorin (16), B. Englisch, Mackenzie, and Mason (15½), S. Rosenthal (14), Winawer (13), Bird (12), etc.

Steinitz had been a sufferer under the rule about the replay of draws, for he had to play 6 games in all with the young American, A. G. Sellman, before he could score 2 wins. But Steinitz at this period was "hard," not even a prolonged series of exhibitions across the Atlantic having tired him out. The far less robust Zukertort, on the other hand, constantly drawing on his nervous energy to keep him going, was a wreck before the end of the tournament, and was told by his doctor that he must take a rest from chess. He professed himself willing to do so.

He had already received an invitation to visit Canada and the United States—which boded ill for his rest from the game.

For the present, however, Zukertort felt justified in declining a challenge he received from Steinitz at the end of the tournament to play him a match. Steinitz relied on the backing of Robert Steel.* That he should issue the challenge was not so strange as it may appear in the light of future developments. There was no recognised World Championship yet, especially not one decided by match-play only. The tendency was, after the London Tournament, to look on Zukertort as the world's best player, regardless of the fact that seventeen years ago Steinitz had conquered Anderssen, previously the "world's best," and that since he had won matches against Zukertort himself and other less important players, while losing to none. Steinitz believed that match-play was the true test of superior skill at chess; and he succeeded, from 1886 onwards, in converting the chess world to his view, though in 1907 the question again rose of the claim of a Tournament Champion to dispute the World Championship title. Lasker, by his defeat of Tarrasch in the following year, established the case for match-play. But even now we have advocates of "Grand International Masters' Tournaments" as at least equal tests with Championship matches.

The fair solution seems to lie in the proposal of the Dutch Chess Federation at Stockholm in 1937, to hold a tournament of players with outstanding qualifications to challenge the holder of the World Championship, who is to play a match with the winner. The Dutch proposal was not a new one, except that it specified a double-round tournament of eight players. Unfortunately the International Chess Federation did not favour this proposal, but took another course, which will be referred to later on. It is impossible to regard the question as closed.

Both Steinitz and Zukertort had left England for America before the end of 1883, and Steinitz was piqued to find that his rival was greeted when he reached the United States as Champion of Chess. He still pressed for a match, even with no stake;† but negotiations made no headway owing to the incompatibility of the principals, which their agents failed to overcome. In June, 1885, six months before the match actually began, Thomas Frere, Steinitz's second, wrote that Steinitz had on three separate

* A letter from Thomas Frere to J. I. Minchin on June 22, 1885, speaks of Steinitz having issued his challenge "through the kind offices of Mr. Steel"; and it appears that Steel was in correspondence with Minchin about the matter in 1883.

† Zukertort could not afford this. When Cuba offered $1,000 towards a match, if played in Havana, he declined the offer.

occasions within the last three years opened and carried on negotiations with Zukertort through the medium of seconds. But it is evident that Zukertort had returned to England towards the end of 1884 in no conciliatory mood, since we find him writing soon after: " It is beyond the limits of decorum and parliamentary language to enter into a discussion with an opponent who prides himself on the scurrility of his speech and his writings. Past experience has taught me that any direct negotiations with Mr. Steinitz would exhaust human patience and finally prove barren" (*Chess Monthly*, March, 1885). With Zukertort and Hoffer heaping coals on the fire from their magazine, and Steinitz from his new *International Chess Magazine*, a settlement looked impossible. But at last the tact of the seconds, J. I. Minchin for Zukertort, and Frere for Steinitz, brought about an understanding. The last difficulty to be removed was the question as to who should be considered the challenger. Steinitz admitted that, as " a great concession," he had challenged in 1883, but " obviously such a concession cannot be demanded again as a right." Finally Frere wrote to Minchin on July 21 that Steinitz was willing to leave the point entirely an open question.

It was now agreed that the match, which was definitely for the World Championship, should go to the winner of 10 games, draws not counting; but if the score should reach 9—9 the match should be drawn. It was to be played in the United States—up to the winning of 4 games by either side, at the Manhattan Chess Club, New York; up to the winning of 3 more games by either, at the Chess, Checker and Whist Club, St. Louis; and for the remaining games at the club of the same name in New Orleans. Three games were to be played a week. After the first section of the match there was to be a week's interval, after the second two weeks'. The time-limit was two hours for the first 30 moves and an hour for each subsequent 15. The stakes were $2,000; and Charles F. Buck, of New Orleans, was appointed stakeholder and referee.

It may be noted that, though the match was played in the United States, Steinitz (who had brought his wife and daughter to his new home) declining to come to London, most of Zukertort's backing was English, and much of Steinitz's was from England or, through Robert Steel, from India.

Zukertort sailed from Liverpool on December 5, and on January 11 the first game began in New York, with Zukertort as White. In a *Queen's Gambit Declined* Steinitz adopted what is now known as the *Slav Defence*, and won in 46 moves. Zukertort then had a wonderful run of success. After winning the second (see Part II, Game 7), he won also the next 3 games, 2 of them being against the *Slav Defence*, which Steinitz abandoned for the rest of the match, though it was his subsequent errors, not the defence, that caused his losses.

The New York series thus ended in Zukertort's favour by 4—1. The story was very different in St. Louis, for Steinitz won the 6th game in 61 moves, and the 7th (see Game 8), drew the 8th in 22, and won the 9th (see Game 9). He was now only 1 point down, and Zukertort seemed to be flagging after his great start.

The final series began on February 26 with a restful draw in 21 moves, but Steinitz took the next 2 games fairly quickly, being helped by his opponent in both. The 13th was a tremendous struggle, which ran to 86 moves and over eight hours' play before Zukertort could win it, with some assistance from his opponent. Two draws followed, and then another win for Steinitz, in 49 moves. With the score now 7—5 against him, Zukertort made a supreme effort and should have won, but missed his way and only drew (see Game 10). From this point his play is described by the American critic G. Reichhelm as "painfully feeble and purposeless." The truth was that he was worn out, and New Orleans was a bad climate for him. He lost the 18th game in 40 moves and the 19th in 29. The 20th was to have been played on March 26, but he was down with fever, and could not play until three days later, when Steinitz, having White, ventured on his own *Steinitz Gambit*. Zukertort overlooked the loss of his Queen, and resigned on the 19th move, each player having taken thirty minutes only. The score was 10—5, with 5 draws.

It was a sad ending to a match of which so much had been expected. Steinitz is reported to have said that a great chess-player has no right to be ill, though whether he said it now, or about himself later when his health broke down, is uncertain. Zukertort undoubtedly was ill in the third section of this match, and he never recovered from the strain which he had put upon himself in New Orleans. It is true that he lived on until June 20, 1888, when he died from the rupture of a blood-vessel on the brain. He was, however, but a shadow of himself after his defeat for the World Championship by a man he esteemed so little. Zukertort, says Dr. Lasker, could never understand *why* Steinitz beat him. "It puzzled him so much that it lost him his mastery and hastened his death."

Some statistics concerning the match may be of interest. We have seen what was the time-limit agreed. Steinitz had originally asked for twelve moves an hour, which Zukertort refused. The divergence of wishes is explained by what actually happened in the play. The whole time measured by the clocks in the match was 80 hours 6 minutes, of which Steinitz took 48 hours 27 minutes, Zukertort 31 hours 39 minutes. In no game except the last did Zukertort take as long as his opponent, and frequently he took over an hour less.

As for the openings, Steinitz, adhering to the King's side, played the *Ruy Lopez* eight times (winning 4 games and drawing 3), the *Scotch Game* and the *Steinitz Gambit* once each (losing the first and winning the other). Zukertort played 9 *Queen's Gambits*, all declined (winning 3 and drawing 2), and one *Four Knights'* (lost). The critics complained of " the monotony of the openings." They should have lived today!

A more considerable complaint was about the fewness of victories after good play on both sides, and " the number of cases of weak play, almost to be classed as blunders " (*Times-Democrat*, New Orleans). This complaint has some justification. We may refer back, however, to what we wrote of the Staunton-Saint Amant match on p. 14: " Neither player was at his best throughout; and the games suffer in consequence. The same, however, may be said of practically every Championship match." High tension, in fact, does not tend to produce a uniformly high standard of play. There is no better example of this than the 17th game of the match under review. Zukertort had to make a great effort, in view of the score. He made it, but on his 28th move forced the pace too much, and on his 33rd made a more serious slip, leaving himself no more than a draw. His strength was spent; and the last 3 games of the match may be disregarded. It is harder to explain Steinitz's poor show in the New York series, after he had won the 1st game. In the 5th he was simply outgeneralled by a supreme tactician. Speculation is useless as to what might have happened, had the whole of the match been played in New York. There is little to be said in favour of perambulating chess matches—except that they bring in more money.

In New Orleans Zukertort challenged his conqueror to a return match, and Steinitz agreed. But there never was a chance of its coming off. Zukertort was not fit to face the task. Just before his death he was beaten 5—1 in a match with Blackburne, whom seven years previously he had beaten by 7—2. His glorious day was over.

CHAPTER II

THE WORLD CHAMPIONSHIP, 1886-1927

STEINITZ, after his victory over Zukertort, was destined to hold the World Championship for another eight years: from the age of not quite fifty till he was just fifty-eight. But his total reign was twenty-eight years, beginning with his defeat of Anderssen in 1866. His successor, Lasker, approached his record with a reign of twenty-seven years. No modern master is likely to be able to rival these figures, because of the ever-increasing competition, which it would require a super-man to defy. All great chess masters, perhaps, are super-men in their way. The more there are, however, in one period, the less the chance of a long rule. For the game this is well; for the World Champion of the day, not so well, unless he can acquiesce in briefer glories than the first two holders of the title won.

Steinitz was not a man to rest on his laurels, nor, in spite of his asperities of character, did he attempt to stall off challenges. But from whom, with Zukertort removed, was a challenge to come? Recent big master-tournaments suggested some names. Winawer had won at Nuremberg in 1883, soon after the London Tournament of that year; Isidor Gunsberg at Hamburg in 1885; Captain Mackenzie at Frankfurt in 1887; Gunsberg again at Bradford in 1888. Nevertheless, it was to the Russian, M. I. Tchigorin, that Steinitz accorded the privilege of a match.* Tchigorin had tied for third prize at Berlin in 1881, and taken the fourth in London in 1883; but his reputation, especially in his own country, was much higher than his actual achievements so far. It was Steinitz himself who made the choice. Visiting Havana early in 1888, he was asked by the local chess enthusiasts whether he would play a Championship match there, provided that they supplied the stakes and paid all expenses; and if so whom would he prefer to play.

Steinitz agreed to play, and selected Tchigorin as his opponent. It is not unlikely that he was influenced by the conviction that against the Russian he could make experiments in the openings, such as he delighted in, and could still win. Anyhow that was what actually happened. A contest was arranged of 20 games,

* The match which Steinitz played in 1888 with Celso Golmayo, champion of Cuba, was only of the nature of an exhibition. Steinitz won by 5—0.

draws counting half a point, and began on January 20, 1889. Tchigorin, having the move, characteristically opened with an *Evans Gambit*, confident that Steinitz's theories on the defence were unsound. He won this game; and, as in 7 more *Evans Gambits* in the course of the match he scored 3—3, with one draw, he had no reason to be dissatisfied with the opening. He also won the 3rd game, a *Ruy Lopez*. Steinitz, however, when he had the move and relied on Queen's side games entirely, made the overwhelming score of 7—1. (For one of these see Part II, Game 11.) Consequently the match never ran to the 20th game. After 16 Steinitz had scored 10—6, and when the 17th ended in a draw there was no need to play on, as even a series of three wins could give Tchigorin no more than 9½ points.

An outcome of this match was that the two masters agreed to have 2 games by cable, in one of which Tchigorin should play the *Evans Gambit*, while in the other he should take Black in the *Two Knights' Defence*, on which also Steinitz had peculiar views. These games were played in 1890-91, and were both won by Tchigorin.

Steinitz had agreed to a return Championship match with Tchigorin. But first he accepted a challenge from another quarter. The great New York Tournament of 1889 brought about a tie for first and second places between Tchigorin and Max Weiss of Vienna, who in a double-round affair of twenty players scored 29 points each; but Gunsberg was only half a point behind, which gave him too a claim to be considered a potential challenger for the Championship. This naturalised British subject, born at Budapest near the end of 1854, was very unjustly criticised by Hoffer. He had made a good name for himself as a player since coming to England, and a match which was arranged between him and Tchigorin was a natural outcome of their close struggle in the New York Tournament. The match was played at Havana in January and February, 1890, and ended with the score 9—9, with 5 draws. When Gunsberg came back to London and was said to have pretensions to the title of the leading British player, Hoffer in *The Chess Monthly* stated that Gunsberg had been lucky in the match with Tchigorin, and that he had no right to call himself better than Mason or Blackburne—both of whom, by the way, had come out below him at Bradford two years ago as well as at New York.

Gunsberg, however, on his way back through New York from Havana, had met Steinitz and persuaded him to accept a challenge for the World Championship. Having ventured to say in one of his chess columns that the interest in such a match was considerable, he drew on himself fresh wrath from Hoffer, who declared that its interest was far from considerable, and that a provision of the match, that one-third of the stakes should go to the loser, was contrary to English ideas of sport. When the encounter came off he wrote of it as a mere exhibition affair, which Steinitz took lightly.

The match had every appearance of seriousness, however. It was played at the Manhattan Chess Club, New York, between December 9, 1890, and January 22, 1891, with a time-limit of fifteen moves an hour. After a draw, a win for Steinitz and another draw, Gunsberg won 2 games running (for the 2nd see Part II, Game 12). Steinitz won the 6th and 7th (see Game 13), and kept the lead from that point. But of the remaining 12 he could only win 3 (one of which is Game 13) against Gunsberg's 2, while 7 were drawn. The score was thus 6—4 in his favour, with 9 draws.

Possibly Steinitz was not " all out " in this match; but he took no liberties in the openings, unless defending 4 *Evans Gambits* be considered such; of these he won 1, and drew 1, against 2 losses. As first player he invariably began with 1 **P—Q4,** or else with 1 **Kt—KB3,** leading to a Queen's-side game. On figures Gunsberg fared better than Tchigorin in his first match with the champion, and as well as he did in the second, to which we shall come soon. Nor can it be said that the Steinitz-Gunsberg games are of poor quality, though some of the draws are rather dull.

This match marked the highest point in Gunsberg's chess career. Perhaps the physical inertia which characterised him at the board in his later years was already beginning to set in. Anyhow his great tournament successes, of which the last had been his share in the fifth prize at Manchester in 1890, came to an end. He seldom competed again, though his chess journalism kept him in intimate touch with the game.

Steinitz did not wait long before engaging in another match in defence of his title, his opponent being for the second time Tchigorin, whom he met again at Havana in the first two months of 1892. The conditions were much the same as before; and once more Steinitz exploited his opening fads in a way that gave his opponent opportunities. Tchigorin won the 1st game, an *Evans* (see Part II, Game 15), and he led by a point again after the 8th game, by 2 after the 12th. Two wins to Steinitz levelled matters, but alternate wins made the score after 20 games 8—8, with 4 draws. It was agreed to continue until one side should have ten wins. The 21st game was drawn, and then with 2 successive wins Steinitz made the final score 10—8, with 5 draws.

Even to a greater extent than in the first match Steinitz had allowed his adversary rope in the second. He had accepted 8 *Evans Gambits* again, and in addition he had four times allowed the *Two Knights' Defence* to be played against him. At the former opening Tchigorin had scored 4—1, with 3 draws; at the latter 3—1. The extent of the handicap which Steinitz imposed on himself can be judged by these figures. With the *Ruy Lopez*, however, he scored 3—0, with 1 draw; with Queen's-side openings 3—0. He was right, therefore, if he thought that he could concede Tchigorin odds and win. Where he erred was that such matches were not good for his play against a great master who disdained eccentricities; and this he was soon to find out. A match with Max Weiss, had it been possible (for Weiss had retired from master-chess since 1889), would have been far better training than those Steinitz had played since his match with Zukertort. Doubtless it might have been less entertaining

During the period while Steinitz was successfully defending his title against Tchigorin and Gunsberg there was gradually arising a new star destined to outshine him in an almost incredibly short space of years. Emanuel Lasker, born at Berlinschen on December 24, 1868, and therefore Steinitz's junior by thirty-six years, had in 1889 gained his mastership at the Breslau congress where Dr. Tarrasch won the first of his magnificent series of International Tournaments. Lasker followed this up with second prize in a tournament of nine players at Amsterdam in August. Amos Burn was first with 7 points, Lasker scoring 6 (losing a game to L. Van Vliet), Mason 5½, Van Vliet 5, Gunsberg 4, etc.

Thus when Lasker paid his first visit to London in the spring of 1890 his reputation was still in the making, and he failed to secure a match with Blackburne or Gunsberg. He could only meet Bird, whom he beat by 7—2, with 3 draws. Returning to the Continent, he proceeded in Vienna and played a match with Englisch, which he won by 2—0, with 3 draws. He also took part in a small tournament at Graz, in which he was only third to G. Makovetz (who beat him in their individual game) and J. H. Bauer.

A second visit to London in 1891 secured him no more than an engagement for a series of simultaneous displays at the German Exhibition; for the hopes of a masters' tournament in London that year were unfulfilled. Still persevering, however, he came back again next spring; and now, receiving a chance, established his reputation in this country. At the last congress of the British Chess Association in March he won by the margin of a point and a half from Mason, his only loss in 11 games being 1 to Bird.

Invited then to take part in a double-round tournament with Blackburne, Mason, Gunsberg, and Bird, he took first prize, with 5 wins and 3 draws, two of which were with Mason. He beat Blackburne twice; but Blackburne served Mason the same way and came out only half a point behind Lasker.

An individual match with Blackburne followed, which Lasker won crushingly by 6—0, with 4 draws. Later in the year he beat Bird at Newcastle by 5—0. It was not only the figures of his successes, however, which impressed the chess world in this country, but still more the style in which he achieved them. He obtained here the appreciation which his own country had so far failed to give him.

It appears that Lasker had intended to enter for the Dresden Tournament this year; but for some reason he changed his mind. While it was in progress he wrote to Hoffer, who was in Dresden, as to the chances of a match with the winner of it, which Tarrasch already seemed likely to be. Hoffer approached Tarrasch, whose reply, he asserts, was so unsatisfactory that he did not communicate it verbatim to Lasker. At this date Tarrasch clearly saw no comparison between their records.

Lasker remained in England until towards the end of 1892, when, having nothing more to conquer here, he set out for America. It is possible that he already had a secret ambition of being able to persuade Steinitz to grant him a match, for, whatever Tarrasch might think of what he had done already, he himself was confident of what it was in him to do. He was an immediate success in the United States, and also in Canada. In October, 1893, a tournament was arranged in New York for him to meet a number of strong players, native or visiting. This Lasker won with a clean score of 13, beating Albin, Delmar, Lee, Showalter, Hanham, the youthful Pillsbury, etc.

Steinitz, engaged on the second volume of his *Modern Chess Instructor*, had not been inclined to listen to suggestions on Lasker's behalf for a Championship match. But he could not afford to disregard the appeal of good stake-money; and after Lasker's latest success he could hardly say that he was not a challenger worthy of respect. So at last the match was arranged, for the Championship title and two thousand dollars, victory to go to whoever should win 10 games. Three games were to be played a week, at 15 moves an hour. The first 8 were to be at the Union Square Hotel, New York; the next 3 at the Franklin Chess Club, Philadelphia; and the remainder at the Cosmopolitan Club, Montreal.

Play began on March 15, 1894, Lasker opening with a *Ruy Lopez*, and Steinitz answering with his own defence. Lasker won on the 60th move the following day. Steinitz, playing the *Lopez* in his turn, made still shorter work of Lasker's *Berlin Defence*, and won in 42 moves. A third *Lopez* went to Lasker (see Part II, Game 18); and then Steinitz, changing to the *Giuoco Piano*, won in 60 moves. As the next 2 games were drawn the match was a good fight so far. Lasker, however, won the 7th (see Game 19) and the 8th, though it took him 77 moves to do so, and thus stood 2 up on the New York series.

The Philadelphia games were disastrous to Steinitz, who lost all 3. He varied his defence to the *Lopez* in the 1st, following 3.., **P—Q3** with 4.., **P—QR3,** producing by transposition a *Steinitz Defence Deferred*, but lost in 49 moves. In the 10th game he opened with a *Queen's Gambit* (*Declined*), as did Lasker in the 11th (see Game 20). Both games were short.

Though Lasker's score was now 7—2, with 2 draws, considerable enthusiasm was shown for both players when they started again at Montreal on May 3. Steinitz was popular in Canada, and when, after a draw he proceeded to win twice (Games 21 and 22), his effort raised his supporters' hopes. But Lasker dashed them by winning a *Queen's Gambit Declined*, first for White, in 44 moves, and then for Black (see Game 23). Steinitz was not quite done with, as he won the 17th game in 51 moves, and drew the next in 61. Then Lasker finished off the match against a wearied opponent, winning a *Queen's Gambit Declined* in 51 moves. The score in his favour was 10—5, with 4 draws.

There were no freak openings. The *Queen's Gambit Declined* was played 8 times, the *Ruy Lopez* 7, the *Giuoco Piano* 3, and the *French Defence* once.

So, at the age of not yet twenty-six, Emanuel Lasker was Chess Champion of the World. His visit to America, however, brought him bad luck as well as success, for he contracted typhoid fever and was dangerously ill. Though his health was still poor when he returned to England, he entered for the great Hastings International Tournament, and on August 5, 1895, started on three weeks' arduous play. In the circumstances his third prize, with 15½ points in 21 games, after the new chess comet from the United States, Harry Nelson Pillsbury, and the comparatively veteran Tchigorin, was an excellent achievement. Tarrasch, hero of four international first prizes, and Steinitz were the next below him in the table.

Chess enthusiasm ran high now, and at the end of this year there was staged at St. Petersburg a contest unique in the history of the game until the Ostend Championship Tournament of 1907. The World Champion; his predecessor Steinitz; Pillsbury, the winner of the last International Masters' Tournament; and

Russia's greatest player, Tchigorin—these four were invited. Dr. Tarrasch's professional duties prevented him from coming to St. Petersburg.

Each player met his opponents six times, so that there were practically six short matches among them. Lasker won with a total of 11½ points in 18 games. His score against Pillsbury was unfavourable, 1 win, 3 draws, and 2 losses. But Pillsbury lost 4 games to Steinitz, and only drew 2; while Steinitz in turn had only 2 wins against Tchigorin's 3, with 1 draw. Steinitz's total point-score was 9½, Pillsbury's 8, and Tchigorin's 7.

The Nuremberg Tournament followed in the summer of 1896, when Lasker took first prize, with 13½ points in 18 games, though losing to Pillsbury. The Hungarian Geza Maróczy, in his first masters' tournament, was second with 12½ points, followed by Pillsbury and Tarrasch with 12 each. After Pillsbury's return to the United States his compatriots began to urge his right to a match with Lasker. But for the present the Champion had another matter in hand. He had to fulfil his promise to Steinitz of a return match, for which facilities were offered at Moscow at the end of 1896. Hastings had previously offered hospitality, but Moscow's terms were better.

Steinitz had made a claim that, as Lasker had been slow in naming a date for their second match, the Championship title should revert to himself. This was manifestly absurd, but now that the match was arranged it only remained to fight it out. Steinitz was advised by his doctor to take a " cure " in Germany first. This, however, he refused to do, being pathetically anxious to regain his title, and on November 7 play began.

It soon became obvious that the older master had no chance at all. Lasker won the first 4 games off the reel. Then in the 5th Steinitz as White, abandoning the *Giuoco Piano*, at which he had lost 2 games, and changing to the *Queen's Gambit Declined*, obtained what should have been a winning position, but let it deteriorate into a draw. The 6th game went to Lasker, who chose the *Giuoco Piano* for once only in the match. Three draws in succession were followed by 2 more wins for Lasker, making his score 7—0.

Now, whether on account of a slight indisposition, or because he relaxed his efforts, Lasker lost both the 12th and 13th games. But he won the 14th, and, after a draw, the 16th. Only one point more was required for the match. The last game (which is given in Part II, Game 24) was a fine effort on Steinitz's part, in spite of eccentricity in the opening; but Lasker's skill prevailed. On January 14, 1907, the Champion won the match by 10—2, with 5 draws, a result that was absolutely conclusive. Apart from the 5th game Steinitz had missed no opportunity, except perhaps a draw in one of his lost games.

Lasker had opened with the *Ruy Lopez* in 7 of his games as White, the exception being, as mentioned, a *Giuoco Piano.* He could point to the fact that with the *Lopez* he scored 5—1, with 1 draw; and the *Steinitz Defence* against it came off badly, leading to its disfavour among players for a long while. Steinitz played the *Queen's Gambit Declined* seven times, winning once as against three losses, and the *Giuoco Piano* twice.

After the match Steinitz fell ill, and was very unfortunate in being in a foreign country, where he had no close friends. His excitable disposition was misunderstood, and he was sent to the Morosoff Clinical Hospital in Moscow as mentally afflicted. He was actually reported as having died on February 22; but so far was this from the truth that he was very shortly set at liberty. Undoubtedly he felt his defeat badly, and in consequence exhibited curious mental symptoms. Leaving Russia, however, and going to Vienna, he soon showed that he was himself again by playing a number of games with Carl Schlechter, with about even results, after which he gave a simultaneous display against twenty-two opponents at the New Vienna Chess Club; scoring 17—2, with 3 draws. There was no question of his sanity now !

A very long interval in the Championship series followed the return match between Lasker and Steinitz ; no less than ten years indeed. There were many rumours of matches, and some negotiations. In the autumn of 1898 it was said that Tarrasch was anxious to challenge for the title and a stake of £1,000. He had just won the very important Vienna International Tournament after a tie with Pillsbury for first place, below them being Janowski, Steinitz, Schlechter, Burn, Tchigorin, etc. But it was always difficult to bring Lasker and Tarrasch together, and no formal challenge was issued. Nor did the fervour for Pillsbury on his return to the United States succeed in bringing about a match for him against the Champion, though no doubt financial support would have been found for him if convenient arrangements could be made.

In the double-round London International Tournament of 1899 Lasker himself competed, and came out a triumphant first with 22½ points, Janowski, Maróczy, and Pillsbury being bracketed next to him with 18 points each, and Schlechter being fifth with 17, while Steinitz was low down in the list. Janowski promptly challenged Lasker to a match for £400. The Champion did not decline, but as Janowski was about to visit America there was no chance of such a contest yet.

For a time Lasker was engaged otherwise than in chess, taking his degree of Ph.D. at the University of Erlangen early in 1900. In the summer of that year, however, as Dr. Lasker now, he won his second big tournament in succession, the Paris International. He was 2 points ahead of Pillsbury, who was just above Maróczy and the new American player Marshall. When Lasker subsequently visited the United States there was renewed talk of a match between him and Pillsbury, but again nothing came of it. Pillsbury, marrying early in 1901, confined himself for a while to chess near home. But at the end of the year, before setting out for Europe, he issued a formal challenge for the Championship—with no result.

There was soon a rival challenger from the United States; for in 1903 Frank Marshall, who was already well known in England, challenged Lasker to play him here for a stake of £100. Lasker, though he considered that Marshall would do better to play Janowski first, did not decline the challenge, but was unwilling to play for a less stake than £400, while stating that the place of the encounter must be decided by himself as title-holder. Marshall found the stake of £400 too high, and negotiations dropped.

Towards the end of 1903 it really looked as if a Lasker-Tarrasch match were at last coming off. Discussions reached such a point that the date was fixed as the autumn of 1904, the stakes at £400 a side, the number of games to be won at 8, and the time-limit at 14 moves an hour. Unluckily Tarrasch had a serious skating accident this winter, and a postponement of the date of the match was announced.

In 1904 Marshall sprang his surprise on the chess world by winning the Cambridge Springs International Masters' Tournament without losing a game, Lasker and Janowski tieing for second place, 2 points below him. Pillsbury was now a very ill man, though he succeeded in winning his game against Lasker here; and in little more than two years he was dead. Among potential challengers for the World Championship he must always be remembered. Yet it may be doubted whether, even in more favourable circumstances, he could ever have been in match play anything like what he was in tournaments—which is, of course, to judge him by an exceeding high standard.

After his Cambridge Springs victory Marshall's name came into discussion again as a challenger for the Championship, and a provisional agreement was reached, fixing the date of commencement at January 14, 1905, the number of games to be won by either player at 8, and the stakes at £400 a side. At the last moment, however, negotiations broke down, and Marshall instead played first Janowski in the United States, and then

Tarrasch at Nuremberg, beating the former, and losing heavily to the latter.

The next aspirant was Maróczy, who established a strong claim in July, 1905, when he won the double-round tournament at Ostend, Janowski and Tarrasch being bracketed next to him, Schlechter fourth, and Marshall only equal seventh; and followed this up by tieing for first place with Janowski at Barmen in August, half a point above Marshall. In the spring of 1906 it seemed as if, through the exertions of a committee in New York, definite agreement had been reached, on terms similar to those suggested for Marshall. It was proposed that the match should be played in three parts; at Vienna until one side had won 3 games, at Havana up to 2 more won games for either, and finally at New York. It was expected to start on October 1; but a hitch arose, which at the time seemed rather mysterious. First it was stated that Maróczy had neither deposited £100 as forfeit-money, nor notified Lasker that he found himself unable to play. Then G. Marco announced on Maróczy's behalf from Vienna that he was prevented by "political conditions" from playing—the reference being apparently to a threatened revolution in Cuba. Later it came out that the Vienna Chess Club was dissatisfied with the proposed division of the match, and wanted all the games to be played in Vienna. To this Lasker was unable to agree, as the original proposal had come from New York.

Thus one more challenge had come to nothing, and the chess public was beginning to wonder whether there was a prospect of any match for the Championship within a reasonable period. The chess enthusiasm of New York prevailed, and Lasker was induced to accept Marshall as his opponent. A variation was made in the financial terms, £200 being allotted to the winner, while the remainder of whatever should be subscribed was to be equally divided between the two players. January 26, 1907, was fixed as the date of commencement of play.

Of the match with Marshall Hoffer wrote* that, while it was advertised as for the Championship of the World, it was nothing of the sort. "In sporting parlance it amounted to a good thing for Dr. Lasker, and in a minor degree also for Marshall. . . . The Americans being willing to provide a purse for Marshall, Dr. Lasker consented to give him a 'run' for a consideration which he deemed adequate—adequate because the purse was in reality a minor matter compared with the financial possibilities, such as gate-money and Press returns."

In Hoffer's view a better choice of antagonist for Lasker would have been Tarrasch, Maróczy, Schlechter, Teichmann, or

* *Year-Book of Chess*, 1908, p. 3.

Janowski; though he admitted that negotiations with the first two had proved abortive. Therefore the fact that Tarrasch had beaten Marshall in a match in 1905 by 8—1, with 8 draws, was not to the point. As for Janowski, Marshall had beaten him, in the same year 1905, by 8—5, with 4 draws; and what was very much to the point was that at Cambridge Springs Marshall, unbeaten, had come out well ahead of Lasker and Janowski; while in the Paris Tournament of 1900 Marshall had been the only player to take a game from Lasker. The present match might be a foregone conclusion, but Marshall, having the backing in the United States, was certainly entitled to his chance.

New York was the scene of the first six games, and in the first, played on January 26, Lasker showed himself in daring mood against Marshall's *Ruy Lopez*. He missed a speedy win, but ultimately prevailed (see Part II, Game 25). In the 2nd game Marshall had a chance of winning at one stage, which he did not grasp, with the result that he lost again. In the 3rd Marshall sacrificed, and was defeated by play both careful and ingenious. Three draws completed the New York series, not very interesting in character. Two games followed in Philadelphia, the first drawn, the second running strongly in favour of Marshall, but, after he had failed at a critical point, being beautifully turned to a win by his opponent. The next 3 games, at Washington, Baltimore, and Chicago, were all drawn. Then at Memphis Lasker won the 12th, 13th, and 14th games. In the 15th, at New York on April 6-8, Marshall played a *Queen's Gambit Declined* in indifferent fashion, and was beaten in 37 moves. He had lost the match by 8—0, with 7 draws. Towards the end he seemed, in the words of the annotators, demoralised.

There was not much of the variety in the openings so craved for always by the critics. Lasker invariably played 1 **P—K4,** being met each time by the *French Defence* (the McCutcheon variation in 4 of the games, 3 of which were drawn). Marshall played one *Ruy Lopez*, and six times the *Queen's Gambit Declined*, while in one game his 1 **P—Q4** was met by the *Dutch Defence*.

After this match the chief interest of the year centred in the second great Ostend Congress, which was even more ambitious than its predecessor, and was designed by its promoters to throw light upon the question of the World Championship. The principal tournament was to include only winners of recognised first-class international tournaments, and it was hoped that Lasker would compete. The actual Champion, however, perhaps not unnaturally, did not feel called upon to enter for a contest called a "Championship Tournament," when he already held the title by right of conquest. Nor would he agree that he should be called upon to meet the winner of the tournament in a match for the title. He declined, in fact, to recognise a distinction between Match Champion and Tournament Champion, who must settle the question of their relative strength before either could be styled Champion of the World.

Nevertheless, the Ostend committee continued with their programme of a Championship Tournament, in addition to a general Masters' Tournament and other competitions. Six entries were received for the Championship, all qualified as winners of " first-class " international tournaments in the past. These were, in alphabetical order, Burn, Janowski, Maróczy, Marshall, Schlechter, and Tarrasch. Maróczy withdrawing at the last moment, it was agreed among the players themselves that Tchigorin should be invited, on his record, although it did not qualify him according to the rule.* Then the tournament started on May 16. Each player was to meet every other four times, and the prize-money was ten thousand francs, to be divided on the Tietz system.

After four weeks' play the result was a narrow victory for first place by Tarrasch over Schlechter—12½ points against 12. The result might have been different had not Schlechter, most amiable of players, in the tenth round agreed to draw his game with Tarrasch on the 23rd move, Tarrasch pleading indisposition and asking for a draw. Janowski, who after seven rounds had led the field, and Marshall, who in the last round defeated Janowski, finished with 11½ points each. Burn scored 8, and Tchigorin 4½.

After he had won this tournament, Tarrasch was not long in intimating his willingness to meet Lasker in a match, provided that arrangements could be made by the president of the German Chess Association. But it was over a year before the long-desired encounter actually took place. At that time the two masters had only met twice in their lives over the board; at Hastings in 1895, when Tarrasch won, and at Nuremberg next year, when Lasker won. Personal relations had not been cordial.

The terms arranged by the German Chess Association were for a match for the World Championship, to be decided by the winning of 8 games by either player, draws not counting. The victor was to receive four thousand, the loser two thousand five hundred marks, while Lasker as title-holder was to have an

* So it is usually stated, though it is hard to see why Budapest, 1896, should not be considered a first-class international tournament. There Tchigorin tied with Charousek for first place, and beat him in the play-off. Among others Pillsbury, Janowski, Schlechter, Walbrodt Winawer, and Tarrasch were competing.

honorarium of seven thousand five hundred. The time-limit was 15 moves an hour, and 4 games were to be played a week, for six hours each day, either player having the right to a day off five times during the match. Düsseldorf was to be the scene of the first 4 games, Munich of the rest.

Play began on August 17 with a long game in which Lasker, opening with the Exchange variation of the *Ruy Lopez*, gradually built up a position leading to an endgame which he won on the 55th move. In the 2nd game, also a *Ruy Lopez*, Lasker went wrong early, but outplayed his opponent later and won. He experimented in the 3rd game with a Pawn-sacrifice on the 13th move, but did not continue correctly, and lost in 44 moves. In the last of the Düsseldorf games the struggle was very interesting and complicated until on his 25th move Tarrasch made a grave error, leading to resignation after 16 more moves.

Lasker thus went to Munich with the score 3—1 in his favour, which he immediately increased with another win (see Game 26), improving on his play in the 3rd game. In the 6th he adopted the *French Defence*, and should have lost, but ultimately drew. In the 7th he was met by the *French Defence* and, playing better than Tarrasch, won in 76 moves. Tarrasch was somewhat lucky to draw the 8th game, but the 9th was an even struggle, which came to a draw on the 72nd move.

Then at last Tarrasch scored a second win, in which he was helped by Lasker's difficulties with his clock, but himself played admirably. In the 11th game Lasker made short work of his opponent's inferior conduct of the McCutcheon variation of the *French Defence*, and won in 28 moves. In the next, however, he made an oversight in the opening, defending a *Four Knights'*, and though he lasted to the 65th move he never had a chance of recovering. He was himself again in the 13th game, whereas Tarrasch weakened and lost on the 44th move. A tremendous game of 119 moves followed, in which Tarrasch vainly tried to fight against a fairly obvious draw. The 15th game was also a draw, in 54 moves. Then the match came to an end on September 30. As Black in a *Four Knights'* Lasker introduced a new move. Both players got short of time, and it was Tarrasch that "cracked," losing a piece (see Game 27).

Lasker had won by 8—3, with 5 draws. A closer result was certainly anticipated, and Tarrasch's supporters pointed to the mistakes that he made as indicating that he was playing below his form. No doubt he was. But to disparage his conqueror's merit for that reason would be absurd. Lasker did more than was necessary for him to attain success. A score of 8—3 cannot be explained away.

As to openings, Lasker played the *Ruy Lopez* three times, and was met by the *French Defence* three times; he played one *Queen's Gambit Declined* and one *Queen's Pawn Game*. Tarrasch played the *Ruy Lopez* five times, the *Four Knights'* twice, and was once met by the *French Defence*. 1 **P—K4** was therefore the fashion, leading most often to the *Ruy Lopez*.

As far as master-chess was concerned, Lasker now took a rest until February, 1909, when he competed in the first of the great St. Petersburg tournaments, his first international tournament since 1900. Though a number of the older masters, notably Tarrasch, were missing here, he had to face the opposition of the newer stars, A. K. Rubinstein and O. S. Bernstein, who had made such an impression at Ostend in 1906-7, of O. Duras, whose brilliant successes began in the same period, and of R. Spielmann. Against these four he had a hard struggle, in which he did not come off best, but his superior play against the remaining fourteen competitors enabled him to tie with Rubinstein at the head of the table, each scoring 14½ points, against the 11 of Duras and Spielmann, the 10½ of Bernstein and Teichmann, etc. The tournament committee were anxious for Lasker to play a tie-match with Rubinstein, but he did not see his way to do this.

In Paris on his way back from St. Petersburg, Lasker met the wealthy chess patron M. Nardus, who pressed him to grant a match for the World Championship to the French master by adoption, David Janowski. Nardus even enquired upon what terms he would play such a match. According to Hoffer, Lasker's reply was that he would only play, as he had already announced in print, for a prize of 5,000 francs or a stake of 10,000; adding that the match could not be until two years hence. Ultimately, however, he yielded so far as to consent to play an exhibition match of 4 games now for 2,500 francs.

This match was accordingly played in Paris between May 12 and 21, 1909. Lasker won the 1st game, Janowski the 2nd and 3rd (see Game 28), and Lasker the 4th; and the prize-money was divided. The contest was both hard and interesting, though it cannot be supposed that the Champion felt as much concern about the result as if his title had been at stake.

Nardus was persuasive, and at last obtained a promise for a Championship match of 10 games in Paris in the autumn. The result was very different then. On October 19 and 20 the match started off with a draw in 48 moves, Janowski as Black in a *Ruy Lopez* recovering from an inferior position early. In the 2nd game Lasker's play was altogether too good for his opponent (see Game 29); and in the 3rd and 4th he also scored wins, in 37 and 50 moves respectively. Janowski should not have lost the 5th, but he declined a draw when there was clearly nothing better, and Lasker proceeded to win on the 61st move. In the 6th game Lasker went astray, enabling Janowski to score his only success, in 33 moves. The 7th was an obstinate struggle, which took Lasker 63 moves to win; the 8th an interesting draw though short; and the 9th another long fight, in spite of Janowski making an early mistake, after which he held out to the 60th move. The 10th game, which is given in Part II (Game 30), made the score in Lasker's favour 7—1, with 2 draws.

Lasker in this match confined himself to the *Ruy Lopez*, as he had done in the exhibition match; and with it, in the two encounters, he had five wins against 1 draw. Janowski played the *Four Knights'* six times (twice in the exhibition match), securing 1 win and 1 draw; and once he was met by the *Sicilian Defence*, losing.

One of the doubtful privileges of the Chess Champion of the World is that he shall persistently be confronted with suggestions that he ought to play a match with this, that, or the other aspirant to his title. The question of ability to secure the backing usually rules some of the claimants out. But this is an unjust method of discrimination sometimes, which prevented more than one great master from ever having his chance of a challenge-match. Schlechter was not thus handicapped, for he could obtain what backing he needed in Vienna.

Ever since Lasker's match with Tarrasch Schlechter's claims had been urged, and a tie with Duras at the head of the Prague International Tournament in the year of that match had strengthened them. Negotiations were slow, however. There was talk of a contest of 30 games, with London as the suggested place. But unfortunately the requisite money was not forthcoming, and a great opportunity was lost. Then the proposed number of games was reduced to 15, and finally to 10 only, draws counting, at which point agreement was reached, the 10 being divided between Vienna and Berlin. The time-limit was 15 moves an hour.

Shorn of the great importance which it might have had, the match began at Vienna on January 7, 1910, and soon showed that the Champion had the hardest task set him since he had won his title. Schlechter, one of the most eminent exponents of the *Ruy Lopez*, opened with this, and obtained a slight advantage, which only a very skilful defence enabled Lasker to bring to a draw after 69 moves. In the 2nd game Lasker also adopted the *Lopez*, and was met by an unexpected continuation on the 8th move, against which he lost a Pawn, but succeeded in drawing after 35 moves. The 3rd game, and third *Lopez*, was uneventful, a draw coming about early by repetition of moves. Another *Lopez* in the 4th game led to a much severer struggle, in which Lasker, refusing an offer of the Exchange, won a Pawn, but had to agree to a draw in the end.

Now came a shock for the Champion's supporters, for which see Part II, Game 31, and with Schlechter leading play was transferred to Berlin. In the 6th game Lasker gained a Pawn on the 28th move, but could do nothing with it and 19 moves later agreed to a draw. For the first time in the match the *Ruy Lopez* was not seen in the 7th game, Lasker adopting the *Sicilian Defence.* On the 18th move Schlechter sacrificed a Bishop for two Pawns and later he won a third, but after 38 moves he was content with a draw by perpetual check. The 8th game is given in Part II (Game 32). On the 9th, another *Sicilian Defence*, Lasker obtained for the first—or perhaps second*—time in the match a definite advantage, but missed what was afterwards claimed to be a win for him, and later also a probable win, a draw finally being agreed on the 65th move.

Nine games had therefore been played, and still the Champion was without a win to set against Schlechter's. He abandoned the *Ruy Lopez*, and opened with 1 **P—Q4,** a *Queen's Gambit Declined* resulting. The game lasted three days, February 8, 9, 10, and ran to 71 moves, when Schlechter was beaten. It was characteristic of his chivalrous disposition that he did not play for a draw, which would have sufficed him, but on the contrary sought adventure. Lasker retorted in the same spirit, and a game of extraordinary enterprise came about. On his 35th move Schlechter made a faulty combination, overlooking a simpler and stronger line. Four moves later he erred again, and missed a probable draw. So ended the match, with the score of 1—1 and 8 draws, otherwise 5 points all; leaving to the chess world mainly regrets that there had not been a full Championship contest with a definite number of wins prescribed. But how many drawn games might there not have been then? It is noteworthy that when Schlechter met Tarrasch in a match at Cologne in the following year the score was 3—3 with 10 draws, when play ceased owing to an arrangement not to go beyond a certain date.

Gunsberg, in one of his chess columns, questioned, with apparent seriousness, whether after the drawn match with Schlechter, Lasker should be considered to retain the World Championship. This, of course, was illogical on Gunsberg's part. A champion, unless he declines to consider reasonable challenges, is entitled to claim the name until he is beaten or decides to retire.

* See Game 31, last note.

The arrangement that drawn games should count in the score contributed not a little to the result—Schlechter being Schlechter. Lasker wrote during the course of the match that his opponent was inaugurating a new and altogether modern fashion in chess. " How," he asked, " can one beat a man who meets offers of success and threats of apparent attack with equal calm ?" And Schlechter's imperturbability remained until the last game, when, as he admitted himself, he played for a win. Behind that face of his, in which onlookers could never see a trace of excitement, there was a spirit hidden which perhaps prevented him from becoming Champion of the World. In 1910 the anxiety to witness him matched again with Lasker was great, and already efforts were being made to raise funds. But somehow the project faded out. The War prevented its revival, and a month after the end of the War Schlechter was dead, still only in his forty-seventh year.

Lasker engaged in another match of a far less arduous character than that with Schlechter in the winter of the same year. This was a return encounter with Janowski, who was certainly lucky in being able to secure substantial backing, when others who had good claims to a trial could not do so. On this occasion the scene of play was Berlin, between November 8 and December 8. From the result, 8—0, with 3 draws, in Lasker's favour, the match might be regarded as a fiasco. It is juster to say that it was not up to Championship standard. Janowski made a bad blunder on the 19th move of the 1st game, and resigned 3 moves later. In the 2nd game he was always attacking, but could do no more than draw. The 3rd ran to 101 moves, when with careful play in the ending Janowski obtained another draw. In the 4th, as the result of a serious oversight, he lost in 31 moves.

The 5th game showed the challenger in better form, and it was claimed that he ought to have won, but Lasker later disputed this. Eventually it was Lasker who won (see Part II, Game 33). Then followed the last draw, not a very good game on either side. Lasker won the 7th game in 46 moves, but in the 8th it took him 87 before he could add another point, Janowski throwing away drawing chances. Three more wins for Lasker concluded the match. In the last Janowski was guilty of an error which again cost him chances of a draw.

In this last game Lasker ventured on a *King's Gambit*, which Janowski declined with 2.., **B—B4.** Otherwise the openings were more normal, but, in contrast to the recent Championship matches, nearly all Queen's side. Lasker played the *Queen's Gambit Declined* thrice, the *Queen's Pawn Game*, and the *Ruy Lopez* once each; Janowski the *Queen's Pawn Game* all through.

With this match Lasker closed his match-playing career until his encounter with J. R. Capablanca eleven years later. There was much public desire for a match in the interval between 1910 and the War, and in particular after Capablanca's astonishing victory in the first San Sebastian Tournament in the spring of 1911, when he came out ahead of Rubinstein, Vidmar, Marshall, Nimzovitch, Schlechter, Tarrasch, etc., were the new Cuban wonder's claims urged. Later in the year a formal challenge was issued.

Lasker announced his willingness to meet Capablanca. The conditions which he proposed for the match, however, offered little chance of agreement. Six wins to either player were to decide the issue, with a maximum of 30 games. If the score should be 6—6 when the 30 games were completed, the match was to be a draw; and also if either player should then lead by 1 point only. The winner was to be World Champion and take all the stake-money. But in the event of a drawn match the holder was to retain his title, and the stakes were to be returned to the backers. The holder was to decide the time and place of the match, and also the amount of the stakes, which must in any case be higher than in previous matches. The challenger must deposit $2,000 forfeit-money. The time-limit was to be 12 moves an hour.

There were some suggestions which mitigated the apparent hardness of these conditions, for instance, that if the match were drawn, the holder should pay the challenger $250 for such games as he might win, and $75 for each drawn game. On the other hand, all the publication rights in the games were to be the title-holder's.

Capablanca sent his answer to Lasker's proposal on December 20, 1911, with unfortunate effect. While maintaining his challenge, he took exception to some of the terms offered. In particular, he wrote that the limit of 30 games would increase the likelihood of a drawn match, in which case the holder was to retain his title, and added, " The unfairness of this condition is obvious." He also claimed that the scores of the games must be the joint property of both players, that the amount of the forfeit-money prescribed for him was excessive, and that the time-limit ought to be 15 moves an hour, which custom had established, as in Lasker's previous title-matches.

Lasker's reply to this was not by letter, but by statements published in the *Berliner Zeitung* and later in the *New York Evening Post*. In both he treated the words, " The unfairness of this condition is obvious," as offensive and insulting. Capablanca, he said, overrated himself, and must now cede the place he had usurped to more worthy aspirants to the World Championship. After his words he could not expect the title-holder to sit down at the same board with him again.

Once more the fatality of direct dealing between claimants to the Championship had been illustrated. We shall not venture to express any opinion on the rights of the controversy; but it should perhaps be said that popular sympathy, particularly in America, was inclined to Capablanca's side. What was certain was that a match between Lasker and Capablanca was at present impossible.

Lasker's hint that another aspirant to the World Championship must now be looked for was soon taken, and there was little doubt as to who had the best claim to a match. Since he had flashed into prominence in the Ostend Tournaments of 1906-7, and followed this up by tieing with Lasker for first place at St. Petersburg in 1909, Rubinstein had never fallen back; and his achievements in 1912 were particularly brilliant. In February-March he won the second San Sebastian Tournament, in May-June the Pistyan Tournament, and in July-August, jointly with Duras (who had been below him at San Sebastian and Pistyan), the Breslau Tournament. As tournament-player, in the absence of Lasker and Capablanca, he had at the moment no rival.

After winning at Breslau Rubinstein went to Berlin in the hope of arranging a match with Lasker, and negotiations only proceeded slowly on account of the necessity of finding sufficient financial backing. Rubinstein was unfortunately not a man with the commanding personality that compels others to support with their money his efforts to secure his due. Nevertheless, it was at last agreed that a match of 20 games should be contested early in 1914, which it was left for various clubs in Germany, Poland, and Russia proper to finance.

First, however, in 1914 there was an International Masters' Tournament at St. Petersburg, in which the Champion made a glorious reappearance in chess of the highest grade. He had every inducement to put forth his best, since among the competitors were Capablanca and Rubinstein, as well as Tarrasch, Marshall, Janowski, etc. This " etc." included the as yet unsuspected World Champion of the future, Alexander Alekhine.

The St. Petersburg Tournament of April-May, 1914, was conducted on the system of a single-round competition of eleven players, followed by a double-round pool of the five leaders in that. Capablanca triumphed in the preliminary play, April 8-23, scoring 8 points in 10 games, without a loss. Lasker and Tarrasch, each losing 1 game, but drawing with Capablanca and with one another, scored 6½. Alekhine and Marshall, with

6 points each, completed the final pool, in which Bernstein, Rubinstein, and Nimzovitch failed to get a place.

The preliminary scores being carried forward, play started again on April 27. Capablanca appeared likely to continue his triumph, for in the first half of the final pool he added 3 points, bringing his score up to 11. Lasker added 3½ points, making his score 10, while Alekhine came into 3rd place with another 2½ points. But the second half of the final was unlucky for Capablanca, who, after missing a draw with Lasker, blundered against Tarrasch in the next round, and so had two consecutive losses. Lasker, with another 3½ points in this half, finished with a total of 13½ against Capablanca's 13. Alekhine was a bad third with 10, and Tarrasch and Marshall scored 8½ and 8 respectively.

After the St. Petersburg Tournament a reconciliation was brought about between Lasker and Capablanca, and fresh negotiations for a match between them were actually in progress when the War came to put an end to international chess in Europe. It nearly stopped all master-chess, except for the New York Tournament of 1915, which Capablanca won, and some less important events in the United States; but in 1916 Berlin was the scene of a short match between Lasker and Tarrasch, which the Champion won by 5—0, with one draw.

If we exclude the Hastings Victory Congress of 1919, chess was not started again in earnest until 1920, and the bitterness left by the War made its re-establishment on an international basis slow for a long while. There was no serious obstacle, however, to a renewal of negotiations between Lasker and Capablanca. Indeed as early as 1919 Capablanca had been approached by the Dutch Chess Federation on the subject; and in the following January he and Lasker met at The Hague, and came to a provisional agreement to play a match at whatever chess-centre should offer the best terms. Capablanca went home to Cuba, where the Havana Chess Club made a good offer. In the meantime, however, because the public, or at least the writers on chess affairs, were of opinion that Lasker's conditions for the match (which Capablanca had accepted) were still too favourable to the title-holder, Lasker announced that he resigned his title to his challenger.

This gesture was not accepted. No one was prepared to recognise a Champion by nomination, and if Lasker resigned the title then for the time it lapsed. Capablanca himself refused the gift, and in August visited Holland again for another meeting with Lasker. The Havana Chess Club had made a generous offer for the match, and terms now suggested by Lasker for a contest for the first 8 wins to either side, a maximum of 24 games, and a time-limit of 15 moves an hour, met with no objection from Capablanca. So after ten years negotiations had come to a successful end.

Perhaps of no match for the World Championship was there ever so much expected as of that between Lasker and Capablanca. Over none can there have been so much disappointment—partly, no doubt, on account of too high expectations. The holder of the title was giving twenty years to his challenger, and the advantage of playing on his own soil, in a climate to the heat of which he had been accustomed. Possibly, too, the Champion's equanimity had been the more ruffled by the long controversy over the challenge.

The match began regularly enough, however, on March 15, 1921, when Capablanca, having the move, opened with a *Queen's Gambit Declined*, which was drawn in 50 moves. Lasker retorted with the same opening, and another draw resulted (see Part II, Game 34). Capablanca then changed his openings to 1 **P—K4**, a *Four Knights'* transposing into a *Ruy Lopez* variation. In 62 moves this game was drawn, as also was the 4th game, another *Queen's Gambit Declined*, in 30 moves only.

So far critics complained that the games, though perhaps models of accuracy, were dull—" incredibly dull," said one of them. The 5th game, yet another *Queen's Gambit Declined*, saw a change, for Lasker made a sad blunder in the ending (!) of an interesting struggle and resigned on the 46th move. In the 6th game Lasker played a *Ruy Lopez*, and in 43 moves a draw was agreed. The 7th, *Queen's Gambit Declined* again, was a perfunctory draw in 23; and not much more can be said of the next 2 games, at the same opening, which took 31 and 24 moves respectively. The 10th game, however, produced a stirring fight, which is given in Part II (Game 35). It went over three days, April 8-10, before Capablanca scored his 2nd win. Writing of the game immediately after—for he was contributing a weekly letter on the match to the Amsterdam *Telegraaf*—Lasker said that in it he committed errors of judgment and obvious mistakes. He also complained of the heat and glare of the April sun in Cuba; but he allowed that Capablanca's style of play had been " beyond reproach."

In the 11th game, the 9th *Queen's Gambit Declined*, Lasker was obviously out of form, made a serious error, and resigned on the 48th move. The 12th was postponed at his request to the evening of April 16, when he opened with a *Ruy Lopez* which was drawn in a position where much play still remained (see Game 36). The 13th, the last at the favourite opening of the match, was a much less interesting draw in 23 moves. Then in the 14th Lasker again resorted to the *Ruy Lopez,* but went wrong, and on April 21 resigned after 56 moves.

At this point he asked the Havana committee to be allowed to resign the match also, on the plea of ill-health, which they could not refuse. At the same time he stated his conviction that he could not have beaten Capablanca. It is probable that in 1921 no one believed that either Lasker or anyone else could accomplish this feat against the "chess machine," as some of his American admirers called him.

The score was 4—0 in Capablanca's favour, with 10 draws. He was justified in a claim that he made, that no one could say that he had been lucky; and he asserted further that in no single game had he been in a losing position. As for the monotony of his openings, all but one the *Queen's Gambit Declined,* he said the score explained it; he could see no reason to change when he was doing so well. By this match the rule of the "*Q.G.D.*" was firmly established over Championship play, only to be slightly affected by other forms of the Queen's Pawn opening in the Alekhine-Euwe match of 1935.

On the conclusion of the Lasker-Capablanca encounter Rubinstein issued a challenge to the winner, and it was understood that Capablanca would play him, provided that financial arrangements were satisfactory. But again Rubinstein was disappointed. Alekhine, in 1921, won 3 master-tournaments, of varying strengths, in the third of which, at The Hague, Rubinstein competed and came out 3rd. Then at Pistyan in April, 1922, a tournament of nineteen players was won by another Russian, E. D. Bogoljuboff, with 15 points, Alekhine and Spielmann scoring 14½ each, Rubinstein not competing.

It was the London International Tournament of July-August, 1922, however, which pointed most to the probability of a new challenger for the World Championship. Capablanca, Alekhine, Dr. Milan Vidmar, Rubinstein, and Bogoljuboff were all entered, and came out in that order at the head of the prize-list, Alekhine like Capablanca being undefeated, though he drew 3 more games, to score 11½ against Capablanca's 13.

While so many of the masters were together in London, certain conditions were drawn up among them, which were to regulate future World Championship matches. These London Rules provided that such a match must be for the first 6 games won by either player, draws not counting; but no fixed total number of games was prescribed. The time-limit must be 40 moves in two hours and a half. The Champion must play within a year of the receipt of a challenge for the title, but was not bound to accept any challenge from an acknowledged international master for a purse of less than $10,000—of which 20 per cent. was to be a fee for the title-holder, the remaining $8,000 to be divided between the winner and the loser of the match in the proportions of 60 and 40 per cent. There were numerous additional rules, among them being that a challenger on acceptance of his challenge must deposit $500 as a guarantee of good faith, and three months before the beginning of the match another $500; while, should the Champion for reason of illness be unable to play the match, the title was to pass to the challenger.

These London Rules had the authority only of the masters who drew them up, since there was no higher authority to which they could be submitted. The *Fédération Internationale des Échecs* (F.I.D.E.) was not constituted until next year, at Zürich. This body at The Hague in 1928 took cognizance of the Rules, but only agreed to them as applying to the proposed return match between Alekhine and Capablanca.

A serious objection to the London Rules was that the only qualification for a challenger (so long as he was an acknowledged international master) was his ability to fulfil the financial conditions as to the provision of the purse and the making of the deposits as guarantee. There was no provision for elimination in the case of more than one claimant, indeed several claimants, to the right to challenge the Champion. What the Dutch Chess Federation proposed at Stockholm in 1937 was an excellent suggestion for an eliminating tournament among candidates; and it is exceedingly to be regretted that it did not find favour with the international governing body.

The position in 1922 was that Capablanca must accept a challenge for his title, provided that the stringent terms of the London Rules were complied with. Rubinstein's challenge was still in the air; but unhappily financial support seemed impossible to obtain, even when near the end of the year he won first prize in the Vienna Tournament, where Alekhine had to be content with a share in fourth to sixth prizes, and Bogoljuboff was outside the prize-list.

However, at Carlsbad in April-May, 1923, Alekhine tied with Bogoljuboff and Maróczy for the top three prizes, while Rubinstein was only twelfth out of eighteen players. Then Lasker complicated the position by returning to tournament play at Mährisch-Ostrau in July and winning first prize, among those below him being Bogoljuboff and Rubinstein.

In November, 1923, Alekhine went to America with the part-view of obtaining support for a challenge to Capablanca, which he was able to do early in 1924. Then a tournament was organised at New York in March, which helped a little to clarify the situation, though it brought Lasker to the top of a double-round contest of eleven masters. His score was 16 points, Capablanca's 14½, Alekhine's 12, Marshall's 11, Réti's 10½, Maróczy's 10, Bogoljuboff's 9½, etc. In important European tournaments there was a gap until 1925, when Alekhine won at Baden-Baden, above Rubinstein, Bogoljuboff, etc.; Aron Nimzovitch and Rubinstein tied at Marienbad; Bogoljuboff won at Breslau, above Nimzovitch, Rubinstein, etc.; and finally at Moscow in November-December Bogoljuboff gained his most brilliant success.

The field at Moscow was tremendously strong, for though it lacked Alekhine, it included Lasker, Capablanca, Rubinstein, Spielmann, Richard Réti, Dr. S. G. Tartakover, a meteoric young Mexican named Carlos Torre, and the cream of those Russian players who had hitherto been cut off from intercourse with the rest of the chess world by political difficulties. Bogoljuboff, still a Russian, went through 20 games with only 2 defeats, by Capablanca and Réti, and scored 15½ points. Lasker scored 14, Capablanca 13½, Marshall 12½, Tartakover and Torre 12 each, Réti and P. Romanovsky 11½ each, etc. After this Bogoljuboff's claim to a challenge match had to be considered seriously; and Lasker suggested that a quadrangular tournament, on the lines of that at St. Petersburg in 1895-6, between Capablanca, Bogoljuboff, Alekhine, and himself, would be the best solution of the Championship question.

This suggestion was not taken up, and 1926 brought further puzzles. First at Semmering Spielmann finished half a point above Alekhine, with Vidmar third, and Nimzovitch and Tartakover bracketed next. Then at Dresden Nimzovitch took first prize, above Alekhine, Rubinstein, etc. After Dresden Nimzovitch sent a formal challenge to Capablanca.

The Argentine Chess Club of Buenos Aires came forward with an offer of a $10,000 purse for a match between Capablanca and Alekhine in 1927. But Capablanca said that, as Alekhine had not followed up his challenge in 1924 by depositing the forfeit-money required by the London Rules, he must consider Nimzovitch as having the prior claim to a match. He gave Nimzovitch until January 1 to deposit the requisite $500, in default of which he would take up Alekhine's challenge. As Nimzovitch did not comply with the formality, his claim failed.

Alekhine in the meanwhile, as though to get in training for his attempt on the Championship, had engaged in a match for 10 games over the year-end 1926-27 against the young Dutch Champion Max Euwe. This was played in Amsterdam, under the new time-limit of 40 moves in two hours and a half, which Alekhine admitted to finding strange at first, and a cause of trouble with his clock ! Partly through this he only gained a victory by the odd point—3—2, with 5 draws. Euwe had to wait nearly nine years for his revenge; and who could have guessed that he would have it even in that time ?

New York was the scene of another very interesting Grand Masters' Tournament in February-March, 1927. It had been hoped to secure Capablanca, Lasker, Alekhine, and Nimzovitch, as well as the United States Champion Marshall and another; but unfortunately Lasker's acceptance was delayed; and places were given to Dr. Vidmar and Spielmann to make six players for a four-round contest. The result seemed to indicate Capablanca's supremacy. He scored 14 points out of a possible 20, losing no game and winning each separate encounter with his rivals. Alekhine, who lost a game each to Capablanca and to Nimzovitch, was second with 11½ points,* Nimzovitch third with 10½, and Vidmar fourth with 10, while Spielmann scored 8 and Marshall 6.

Alekhine had substantiated his challenge for the World Championship by the deposit of his forfeit-money; and, while awaiting the beginning of the match, he visited Hungary to take part in the Kecskemét Tournament in July and August. This he won fairly easily, out of 16 games winning 8 and drawing 8. Nimzovitch and Lajos Steiner were close behind him with 11½ points; but Alekhine had had no special reason to exert himself in the final pool of a tournament arranged on a sectional basis.

* It appears that it was vital for Alekhine to take at least second place in this tournament to establish his right to a match for the Championship; but I have not been able to trace when Capablanca laid down this condition, if he did so. It could not be considered as an unfriendly gesture, however, in view of Nimzovitch's claim.

CHAPTER III

THE WORLD CHAMPIONSHIP, 1927-1937

THE long-expected Capablanca-Alekhine match began at Buenos Aires on September 16, 1927, being the first contest fought under the London Rules. It was anticipated that, in the absence of any stipulation for a fixed total of games, the struggle to obtain the 6 wins necessary for victory would be a long one, and expectations were fully realised. Twenty-five draws prolonged it to a total of 34 games.

The 1st game, however, produced a definite result. Capablanca opened with 1 **P—K4** and had to deal with the *French Defence*, against which he failed to make the best moves in the early middle-game and lost a Pawn, though he fought on to the 43rd move. The 2nd game was a very short draw, and then in the 3rd Capablanca, being given chances in the opening, went on to a very fine ending (see Part II, Game 37), and levelled the score. Three draws followed, of which the second was a good fight, while the third was marred by errors on both sides. In the 7th game Capablanca took the lead for the only time in the match, playing much the sounder chess. After 2 more well-fought draws and a 3rd of 20 moves, which requires no comment, Alekhine made an effort that was one of the turning-points of the match. The 11th game was exceptionally difficult, causing both players to run short of time. Capablanca, after an earlier advantage in position let it slip, recovered, and then erred again, though Alekhine could not force resignation until the 67th move. In the 12th game both were early at fault, but Capablanca compromised his game entirely on his 34th move, and resigned 7 moves later. The challenger's score now stood at 3—2.

The next 8 games were drawn, though the 17th was one of vicissitudes and full of interest, while the 20th, marked by extreme time-pressure on both sides towards the end of the first period (five hours in all), was not unfairly rewarded with half a point to each player. The 21st game (see Part II, Game 38) was a fine win for Alekhine. Then the draws began again, and mounted up to another 7. Alekhine made a spirited attempt in the first of them, with the sacrifice of a piece on his 32nd move, and should have won but for an error 10 moves later. In the 27th game Capablanca should have won, on his opponent's own showing, but threw his advantage away. In the 28th the draw only came about on the 60th move.

The 29th was a long game—70 moves—in which Alekhine made his worst mistake of the match, when, though a Pawn down, he could still have saved a loss. As he was now only 1 point ahead, 4—3, the match looked open. But 5 more games sufficed to end it. The 30th was a model draw in 40 moves, of which 19 had occurred two games previously. In the 31st Alekhine gave up a Pawn, for which he got no compensation, but two subsequent errors by Capablanca threw away his chances of a win. This was serious for the Champion, who, in the next game found his challenger, in spite of one slip, in his best fighting form (see Part II, Game 39). One more draw, of a very conventional pattern, paved the way for the 34th and last game. In this Alekhine, in his own opinion, gave his best display of the match, though so stubborn was Capablanca's resistance that resignation only came at the 82nd move (see Game 40).

Alekhine had won by 6—3, with 25 draws, and was World Champion. That he won on his merits cannot be denied. He owed very little to luck, for if he ought to have lost the 27th game he ought equally to have won the 22nd. Perhaps other games, too, may be said to have gone otherwise than as they should have gone—if only the first mistake counted. But the match was more free from grave errors than almost any of its predecessors in the Championship series. As against its general interest as an exposition of chess it has been urged that there were too many draws. Of 9, or perhaps 10, of these it may be said that they showed little sign of severe effort on either side to force a different result. Some were obviously so conducted as to allow the players to take a rest in a struggle that might become exhausting. And, after all, the object of the match was not "brighter chess," but the decision of the World Championship.

Another complaint of the critics was that of the whole 34 games all but 2 began with the *Queen's Gambit Declined*, and, up to a point, one particular form of that opening. (The only variety, apart from the one *French Defence*, was in the 3rd game, when Alekhine defended a Queen's side opening with a *Queen's Indian*). Well, we may conclude that both players were of opinion that 1 **P—Q4, P—Q4;** 2 **P—QB4, P—K3;** 3 **Kt—QB3, Kt—KB3;** 4 **B—Kt5, QKt—Q2** is the soundest way of beginning a game of chess. Those who would dispute the view of such great masters have to produce some stronger argument than the cry of monotony. In the highest chess the fight does not rage in the preliminary moves.

It was generally understood that a return match between

Alekhine and Capablanca would follow in due course. As a matter of fact, though there were " negotiations," as we shall see, they met next, for a single game only, at Nottingham ten years later !

In the meanwhile, in the very year of the match, the International Chess Federation circularised its constituent units, stating that the conditions of the World Championship " need very considerable modification for the benefit of chess generally," and asking for the units' views. The difficulties of the situation, though this was not mentioned, were two: that the holder of the Championship title could not be dispossessed of it against his will, without being beaten, and that the F.I.D.E. was not possessed of funds sufficient to take over the management of the Championship. Private enterprise must still be looked to if matches were to be played.

Chess activity in 1928 was mainly confined to tournament play, from which the new Champion stood aside. The most important tournaments were at Kissingen in August and Berlin in October. Bogoljuboff (who about this time acquired German nationality) won the former, with Capablanca second, Euwe and Rubinstein bracketed third, and Nimzovitch fifth; Capablanca the latter, with Nimzovitch second, Spielmann third, and Tartakover fourth. During the year and early in the next, Bogoljuboff played two practice matches with Euwe, winning each by the margin of 1 point, and making a total score of 5—3, with 12 draws.

Bogoljuboff had already before the end of 1928 issued a challenge for a title-match, to which Alekhine replied that he accepted it " in principle "; and hopes were strong that some time in 1929 a match might actually be arranged. Capablanca undoubtedly would have been the popular choice as opponent for Alekhine; and Buenos Aires was anxious again to secure them as guests. But it was in the United States that the first definite offer was made. Alekhine was in New York in March, having promised to play in a tournament at Bradley Beach (which he went on to win easily against moderate opposition); and the promoters of that tournament offered a guarantee for a return encounter between him and Capablanca at Bradley Beach.

Alekhine, however, could not agree to the offer, and returned to Europe. At Wiesbaden in July he had a meeting with Bogoljuboff, and definitely arranged a match with him for the World Championship, to be played in Germany and Holland, beginning at Wiesbaden on September 6. The terms were much the same as laid down by the London Rules, except that a limit was fixed at 30 games, or as many as should be required to give one player 15½ points, draws counting, but at least 6 won games to be included in the points.

Capablanca's chance of a match was therefore put on one side. Yet his retention of form was definitely proved at the Carlsbad and Budapest tournaments in August and September this year. At Carlsbad, though he came out half a point below Nimzovitch, he was 3 points above Bogoljuboff, and at Budapest he was first, his chief opponent being Rubinstein.

Nevertheless, it was Bogoljuboff who was the accepted challenger. Now, while it could not be denied that Bogoljuboff's tournament record, particularly his first prizes at Moscow in 1925 and Kissingen in 1928, gave him a claim to a match against Alekhine, it cannot be said that any but one result was expected. The question was by how much Alekhine would win.

Yet on the mere results of the first 6 games there was not much in it. Alekhine, with the move, won the 1st in 26 moves, which showed that Bogoljuboff, though he made no absolute blunder, played some inferior moves. Two draws, considerably longer games, followed, and then Bogoljuboff displayed very good form to win the 4th game in 38 moves. Alekhine took the 5th, and Bogoljuboff the 6th game, both in 48 moves.

The 7th game was important in that Alekhine's lead from this point was never disputed. Bogoljuboff went wrong on his 20th move, and lost on the 35th. He also lost the 8th (see Part II, Game 41), and, after an intervening draw, the 10th, where he disdained drawing chances and lost. The 11th game was a very hard fight, drawn after 60 moves. In the 12th Bogoljuboff did not make the best of his opening, but lasted for 56 moves. In the 13th, however, he scored a win (see Game 42), and in the 14th another, conducting a well-played ending to success on the 71st move. A draw followed, and then two more wins for Alekhine, one in 60 moves, the other quickly finished.

The two players now went to Holland, Alekhine leading by 8—4, with 5 draws. In the 18th game, for the first time a *French Defence*, Alekhine erred, and Bogoljuboff scored his last success in the match. In the 19th, which was very long, Bogoljuboff blundered on his 70th move and resigned in 7 more. The 20th was drawn. Alekhine won the 21st game in good style, and the 22nd (see Game 43) in better still. He had now little reason to exert himself, and the match finished with 3 draws, of which the 3rd, however, played at Wiesbaden on November 11-12, was of considerable interest, Bogoljuboff claiming afterwards that he had winning chances.

So the final score was 11—5 in Alekhine's favour, with 9 draws, giving him the necessary 15½ points to win the match, against Bogoljuboff's 9½. Expectations had been fulfilled, and now the question which mainly troubled the commentators on the match was whether the Champion had played his hardest in it, whether he had not rather taken undue risks, confident in his ability to win in spite of doing so. The suggestion was not altogether unjustified. A comparison of Alekhine's games in this match with those in his match with Capablanca is sufficient to show that he did treat his two opponents very differently. A significant point is the proportion of drawn games in the two matches; at Havana 25 in 34, here 9 in 35. But, of course, it takes two to make a draw, and Bogoljuboff on several occasions rejected drawing chances.

There was nothing speculative in the openings, as far as the first few moves were concerned. Alekhine played the *Queen's Gambit Declined* nine times, including once with a transposition, and the *Queen's Pawn Game* four times—or five if we disregard the transposition. Bogoljuboff played the *Queen's Gambit Declined* and the *Queen's Pawn* four times each, and the *Ruy Lopez* twice, while twice his 1 **P—K4** was countered by the *French Defence.* A feature of the match was the number of times in the *Queen's Gambit Declined* in which Black adopted 2.., **P—QB3,** Bogoljuboff invariably, and Alekhine four times. In 4 of these games a "Cambridge Springs Defence" came about, with each player Black twice. Some new light was thrown on this variation by the match.

Whom would the Champion play next? Once more hopes were raised at the end of 1929 by the report that he had accepted Capablanca's challenge for a return match. But before long it became known that negotiations were not proceeding harmoniously, and about the middle of 1930 they were suspended. The question of financial guarantees was one obstacle. Another, still more serious, was that the two masters conducted their own correspondence. Past history of the World Championship should have provided lessons that direct communications between champion and challenger were dangerous. But the principals were not to be dissuaded from writing to each other; and the F.I.D.E. had not the power to take the matter out of their hands. At last on February 20, 1931, Capablanca wrote to Alekhine, demanding that he should play the match during the following winter, failing which he would claim the Championship title. He pointed out that twenty-nine months had elapsed since he had sent a formal challenge.

Again, by a report from New York, it was asserted that Alekhine was willing to play. It became obvious that this report was not based on knowledge of letters passing between him and Capablanca. In the summer of 1931 it came out that Alekhine had stated that he considered the challenge formally annulled through Capablanca having failed to deposit with the agreed treasurer the sum of $500 required by the London Rules. And so the matter ended.

The whole controversy was unedifying, and prejudicial to the best interests of chess. It has only been mentioned here because of the impossibility of ignoring it entirely. No attempt will be made to apportion the blame for it. What emerges clearly is the necessity for the arrangement of Championship matches to be taken out of the hands of champion and challenger, and vested in a governing body of the chess world. This, indeed, at one time seemed likely to happen; since the late Champion, after gaining the title in 1935, intimated that, should he retain it in a return match with his predecessor, he would submit to the control of the F.I.D.E. But Fate has decided otherwise.

While the two great masters had been busy with their pens an event had occurred of greater significance in chess history than was appreciated at the time. Dr. Max Euwe, at the age of twenty-nine, had won his first important tournament, at Hastings over the year-end 1930-31, and he won it by half a point over Capablanca, with whom he drew their individual game. Partly in consequence of this, Capablanca agreed to play a match of 10 games with Euwe in Holland in July. The result was 2—0 in Capablanca's favour, with 8 draws, which was a better score for the ex-champion than either Alekhine or Bogoljuboff had been able to make against a younger Euwe, as did not fail to be noticed.

Alekhine in this summer won one of his best tournament victories, at Bled (Veldes), where in a double-round contest of fourteen players he came out undefeated with 20½ points, against Bogoljuboff's 15, Nimzovitch's 14, the 13½ each of Flohr, Kashdan, Stoltz, and Vidmar, etc. Salo Flohr, though only twenty-two, had already made his mark, notably by his second prize, after Rubinstein, at Rogaska-Slatina two years earlier. But no one could have supposed in 1931 that he would be nominated by the International Chess Federation in 1937 as the most suitable challenger for the winner of the return match between Euwe and Alekhine. Some hint of future possibilities, however, was given in 1932. In February Alekhine took part in the *Sunday Referee* Tournament in London, and scored 9 points in 11 games, followed by Flohr with 8, I. Kashdan and Sultan Khan with 7½, etc. In June at Bad Sliac, in Alekhine's absence, Flohr and Vidmar divided first and second prizes, Bogoljuboff failing to get a prize. And next month at Berne, where Alekhine was first, with 12½ points in 15 games, Euwe and Flohr scored 11½ each, Sultan Khan 11, Bernstein and Bogoljuboff 10 each, etc.

The Champion then went on his world tour, though he was back in time to play, with great success, for France in the International Team Tournament at Folkestone in June, 1933. Going next to the United States, he won the Pasadena Tournament with ease, but the promoters of that had been much disappointed in their hopes of including Capablanca among the competitors. It may be added that it was by no fault of Capablanca's that he was absent. Two such stars apparently could not meet in a tournament yet, except at a cost which few tournament promoters could afford.

Nor were the optimists justified who saw in the fact that Alekhine and Capablanca were both in the United States simultaneously a chance of their coming together for discussion in New York. Their orbits did not cross. Before he left the States the Champion was induced to say whom he thought likely challengers for his title in the future. He named two Americans, Kashdan, who was favourably known in Europe already, and R. Fine, whose achievements so far were mainly in his own country, and the Czecho-Slovakian, Flohr.

It cannot be said that the announcement, early in 1934, that Alekhine's next match would be a return encounter with Bogoljuboff was anything but a disappointment to the chess world in general. It was right, no doubt, that promises of return matches should be performed. But where was the return to the match of 1927? A new Alekhine-Bogoljuboff match was a poor substitute for that.

More interest was aroused by the news that the Dutch Chess Federation was trying to promote a meeting between Alekhine and Euwe, and it became clear that it was only a question of terms, in other words of Euwe's backing being raised in Holland, as to which Dutch enthusiasm for the national Champion left little doubt.

Alekhine and Bogoljuboff began their second match at Baden-Baden on April 1, 1934, the conditions being as in 1929, that victory should go to the scorer of 15½ points in a contest of 30 games, draws counting. The 1st game was abandoned as a draw after 65 moves, though Bogoljuboff, who had for a long time had the better game, should, according to the weight of expert opinion, have continued, with a probable win. Alekhine won the 2nd game without much difficulty. The 3rd was a draw; and then Alekhine won again, this time with some difficulty. The next 4 were all drawn, but in the best of these Bogoljuboff certainly threw away good chances—as indeed had Alekhine in the first of them. The ninth game, in which Alekhine played a *Benoni Counter Gambit* and won, is given in Part II (Game 44).

Bogoljuboff made a spirited response in the 10th game, and meeting Alekhine's *Queen's Gambit Declined* with the Cambridge Springs variation, ultimately secured a win after 81 moves. But Alekhine scored the 11th, after which came 4 more draws, in the first of which Bogoljuboff missed a probable win. Alekhine took the 16th and 17th games, both in 41 moves, and now stood at 6—1, with 10 draws. The 18th was a tame draw, but in the 19th Bogoljuboff let slip a win, to allow another draw. The 20th was colourless. The 21st saw Bogoljuboff make a good effort to win and then ruin his game absolutely. After another draw, Bogoljuboff took the 23rd and 24th games in succession, Alekhine in the latter giving his weakest exhibition in the match. But the Champion made no mistake in the 25th game, outplaying his opponent completely in the middle-game, and forcing resignation after 44 moves.

Alekhine now needed but half a point to clinch the match, which, as White at Berlin on June 14, he had no difficulty in making. The final score in his favour was therefore 8—3, with 15 draws, or 15½ points against 10½.

Dr. Lasker, in his book of this match, puts forward a curious theory about the challenger's heavy defeat. "Alekhine," he says, "relying on his tremendous imagination and the accuracy of his far-sighted combinative powers, took liberties with Bogoljuboff, and Bogoljuboff failed to punish him for it, therefore Alekhine continued to take these liberties. It was a hazardous road to victory, but easy because Bogoljuboff seemed to lose his bearings in complicated positions. . . . The success [of Alekhine's strategy] is to some extent due to his opponent's belief in witchcraft."

Seriously Dr. Lasker seems to suggest that Bogoljuboff thought his bad play to be due to a spell cast by his conqueror!—or we may call it hypnotism, he says. Well, that is a suggestion, whether it is necessary or not to explain why the better player won. It may be added that the time-limit of 40 moves in two hours and a half proved much more troublesome to the loser than to the winner, Bogoljuboff being very often in serious difficulties with his clock, though he had played with the same time-limit before against the same opponent.

The constant moving about from place to place—all in Germany this time, but involving twelve journeys—was no new feature after the previous match, and presumably did not affect one player more than the other.

There was the modern sameness of the openings in this match. Alekhine played the *Queen's Gambit Declined* 7 times, the *Queen's Pawn Game* 5, and the *Ruy Lopez* once. More variety was introduced into Bogoljuboff's openings by his opponent's defences. He offered the *Queen's Gambit* 10 times, and in 7 games Alekhine accepted it. Against Bogoljuboff's 1 **P—Q4** Alekhine played the *Benoni*, the *Dutch Defence*, and the *Queen's Indian Defence* once each. The frequent occurrence of the *Queen's Gambit Accepted* gave its chief theoretical value to the match. White won once, Black twice, and 4 games were drawn.

On the conclusion of the match Euwe, while telegraphing his congratulations to Alekhine, announced that he accepted his terms for a match between them for the World Championship in the autumn of 1935. So now the chess world was promised the spectacle of the Champion defending his title against a player whose full possibilities were as yet unknown—though the case had been somewhat similar with Steinitz and Lasker in 1894.

As if to show that he had not been in any way exhausted by his recent match, Alekhine in the following month went to Zürich and won a mixed tournament there, with a score of 13 points in 15 games. The opposition was furnished by Euwe, Flohr, Bogoljuboff, Lasker (who three years previously had announced his determination to take no further part in master-chess, but had happily changed his mind), O. S. Bernstein (who had been out of tournaments, with one exception, since the War), Nimzovitch, G. Stahlberg, and six Swiss players. Euwe beat Alekhine in their individual encounter, but, losing to Lasker, tied with the unbeaten Flohr at 12 points each, while Bogoljuboff scored 11½, Lasker 10, etc.

One of the most welcome signs in the chess world this year was a further dropping of the bar between Russia and other nations. Euwe went in August to a tournament at Moscow, in which Hans Kmoch from Vienna also took part. Unfortunately, through indisposition, Euwe could not do himself justice, and all four prizes fell to Russian players, headed by M. M. Botvinnik, who, though he had never yet played outside his own country, was already, at the age of twenty-three, recognised as a coming Grand Master.

After this Botvinnik was allowed by the Soviet Government to go abroad for the Hastings Tournament over the year-end 1934-35. But in totally strange conditions he was much handicapped, and among the players he came out equal fifth with A. Lilienthal, each scoring 5 points against the 6½ of Euwe, Flohr, and Sir George Thomas, and the 6 of Capablanca.

Moscow was the scene, in February and March, 1935, of another tournament, this time truly international, for the eight foreign masters who came to contend with twelve Russians included Lasker, Capablanca, Flohr, and Spielmann. Botvinnik now gave proof of his greatness by tieing with Flohr for first place, each scoring 13 points. Botvinnik lost 2 games, both to compatriots, while Flohr lost none, but drew no less than 12. Lasker was in astonishing form, coming out third with 12½ points, losing no game but drawing even one more than Flohr. Capablanca was next with 12 points, followed by Spielmann with 11, the Russians I. Kan and G. Lövenfisch with 10½ each, and seven more players with scores of 10 or 9½. Few tournaments have ever had so close a finish between fourteen competitors.

Match-play once more held the stage in the closing months of 1935, when the eagerly anticipated encounter between Alekhine and Euwe took place, for the World Championship and a stake of $10,000. The match was to be of 30 games at most, draws counting, and the scorer of 15½ points, including at least 6 won games, was to be the victor. Three games were to be played a week, and the time-limit was 40 moves in two hours and a half.

It is safe to say that Alekhine started as strong favourite when at Amsterdam on October 3 he opened with 1 **P—Q4.** He was met with a *Slav Defence*, which variation of the *Queen's Gambit Declined* was a great feature of this match. The game is given in Part II (Game 45), being won by Alekhine. Euwe played much better in the second game, and equalised the score; but in the third he adopted the *French Defence*, of which he had an unfortunate experience in this match, and against an old variation revived went astray and lost. Alekhine was in fine form in the 4th game, and profiting by an error by his opponent sacrificed a piece on the 20th move, obtaining later a winning endgame. As, after 2 draws, Alekhine won the 7th game against another *French Defence* he stood 4—1, with 2 draws; and expectations of his success seemed well justified.

The 8th game yielded a win to Euwe, but it took him 69 moves to force resignation after a hard ending. In the 9th Euwe for the last time adopted the *French Defence*, and lost. Alekhine's own explanation of what happened next must be accepted, which is that he presumed upon his lead—thinking the match was "virtually over." He played badly in the 10th game, even as early as the 8th move. Having drawn the 11th, in the 12th game he gave his worst exhibition in the series, while in the 13th he had a narrow escape (see Game 46), and in the 14th he speculated rashly in the opening and lost again. The score was now 5—5, with 4 draws.

The 15th game was a fine fight, which ended in a draw after 61 moves, though both sides had missed winning chances. A revival followed on Alekhine's part, as he won the 16th game, Euwe making errors, and after 2 short draws the 19th also. The last was a good example of the Champion's play, though he might have won more quickly, and inspired hope in his supporters that, being 2 points up again, he would now proceed steadily to victory.

But that was not what happened. In the 20th game, with a *Slav Defence*, Alekhine went wrong on his 13th move and again on his 18th, and he was unable to recover. In the 21st (see Game 47) Euwe, adopting the same defence, showed his opponent what he ought to have done, and won for the first time with the Black pieces. The score was 7—7, with 7 draws, and 3 more draws followed, the first short and of little interest, but the other 2 much more stirring affairs. In the 23rd game, Alekhine took a grave risk in attempting to win, but fought admirably to save a loss, which perhaps he should not have been able to do. The 24th is given in Part II (Game 48); in it Alekhine missed a win, was offered another chance, and missed it again by an unaccountable mistake, which left only a draw.

In the 25th game Euwe took the lead at last, playing the Cambridge Springs variation against the *Queen's Gambit Declined*, and defeating Alekhine's efforts to win at all costs. With the 26th Euwe increased his lead after a magnificent struggle (see Game 49).

Alekhine's position was all but hopeless. There could be only 4 more games, and to win the match he had to score 3 of them and at least draw the fourth. He began with a surprise, playing a *Vienna Game*, an opening which he had abandoned for eight years. As he perhaps expected, the moves ran 1 **P—K4, P—K4;** 2 **Kt—QB3, Kt—KB3;** 3 **B—B4, Kt × P**—a course recommended by himself for Black, but leading after 4 **Q—R5, Kt—Q3;** 5 **B—Kt3** to possibilities of adventure. He was rewarded, for Black soon was faced with a very difficult game and, missing an opportunity of equalising the position on the 32nd move, resigned 9 moves later.

The 28th game was momentous. Alekhine as Black met the *Queen's Gambit Declined* with an "Orthodox Defence," which he had not adopted before in the match, and got a superior position. Whether he could at one point have converted it into a win was much disputed. As a matter of fact, he only drew, though continuing the ending to the 63rd move. Two wins in the remaining 2 games would still give him the match, and he made a good attempt for the first of them, against *Alekhine's Defence* played by his opponent. By a slight slip on his 34th move, however, he allowed a draw to become inevitable; and now the match could not be won.

Still, a win in the 30th game would have enabled Alekhine to draw the match. But against the move, and Euwe's almost inevitable 1 **P—Q4,** this was a tremendous task. Alekhine chose acceptance of the *Queen's Gambit*, with an unfamiliar continuation 3.., **Kt—Q2.** It brought him no advantage, for Euwe refused to go astray, forcing his opponent to desperate measures. On the 26th move White, with a Pawn up, offered a draw, which was declined. A further attempt to complicate led to White winning another Pawn. He had then a clear win, but on the 40th move agreed to a draw, which gave him the match, with the score of 9—8, and 13 draws.

Dr. Lasker before the end of the match—in fact, while Alekhine was still leading—answering his own question, "What has happened to Alekhine?" expressed the opinion that he had had too much success, that he had got out of the habit of losing, and so had become uncritical. With still more justification might Dr. Lasker have asserted this when the match finished. Alekhine's own statement about his over-confidence confirms the judgment. He did not allude, however, as he might have done, to the effect which his second easy victory over Bogoljuboff had had on his play. That it was bad there can be no doubt.

Alekhine suffered from two handicaps to his ability to put forth his best chess. He had not trained physically as well as mentally (or "technically," as he himself expressed it) for the match, with the consequence that Euwe was much the fitter man. As early as the 4th game the Champion was reported to be showing signs of strain, and later he had to struggle against indisposition, though it did not stop him playing except for three days' rest after the 21st game. The other handicap was that the match took place entirely in Holland, beginning and ending at Amsterdam, but scattered also over a dozen other spots. There was apparently some reason to complain of excessive sympathy for the national hero, though its expression may have been confined to a small section of the Dutch Press.

Nevertheless, Alekhine readily allowed that Euwe's victory was well merited whether or not it was the superior player who won, and said that it was up to him to prove that he could play a better game when the return match came off.

It had been expected that in the match of 1935 the openings would be largely, in accordance with modern practice, Queen's side; nor were expectations upset. Alekhine, however, on seven occasions out of thirty played 1 **P—K4,** being allowed to have the *Ruy Lopez* once and the *Vienna* once, while four times he was met by the *French* and once by *Alekhine's Defence*. Altogether in these King's side openings he scored 4—0, with 3 draws. In view of this, it is permissible to wonder how he would have fared with 1 **P—K4** throughout.

Euwe only once departed from 1 **P—Q4,** to play an *English Opening* in the 18th game, in which Alekhine effectually prevented any transposition into his opponent's favourite Queen's side development. Otherwise the match provided fourteen examples of the *Queen's Gambit* (one *Accepted*), and eight of the *Queen's Pawn Game*. As has been said, the *Slav Defence* to the *Gambit Declined* was a great feature of the match. When Steinitz played 2.., **P—QB3** against Zukertort in 1886 the move was " not considered in accordance with the recognised defence " (see Part II, Game 8, first note). Now it was adopted by Euwe seven times and by Alekhine five. Needless to say, it became for a time extremely fashionable among amateurs. Yet the figures show that White scored against it 5—3, with 4 draws. The most noteworthy game at it is the 21st (Part II, Game 47), where Black won.

Altogether statistics in the match decidedly favoured the first player; White scored 13—4, with 13 draws. No undue significance must be given to this fact, though an examination of Championship matches reveals a good preponderance in White's favour,* encouraging the idea that in match-play more than in tournaments the advantage conferred by the 1st move is very considerable.

Little time was lost before arranging the next match for the World Championship. In March, 1936, Euwe and Alekhine met at Amsterdam for a preliminary discussion, and in June they met again at the same place and definitely agreed to a return match in Holland in the autumn of 1937.

In the meanwhile an International Masters' Tournament had been played at Moscow in May-June, which could not be denied significance in its bearing upon the right to challenge for the Championship. Five Russians and five foreigners met in a double-round contest, and Capablanca came out first, undefeated, with 13 points, the remaining prizes falling to Botvinnik (12), Flohr (9½), Lilienthal (9), and V. Ragosin (8½), while Lasker (8) was just outside the prize-list.

This was followed by a still more important tournament organised by the British Chess Federation at Nottingham in August, in which there participated the World Champion, three

* *E.g.*, in Capablanca-Alekhine, 1927, White won 6—3, with 25 draws, and in Lasker's various matches White's majority is large.

ex-champions, and the four leading aspirants* to a match for the Championship, Flohr, Botvinnik, and the Americans Fine and S. Reshevsky. The struggle for the seven prizes was confidently expected to be severe, and it was. Only a point and a half separated the first eight players out of the total fifteen. Botvinnik, undefeated, and Capablanca, with one loss to Flohr, tied for first place with 10 points each. Euwe, Fine, and Reshevsky tied at 9½ each, Fine losing no game; Alekhine scored 9, and Flohr and Lasker 8½ each. As to the correctness of the result, in play lasting three weeks, under a time limit of 18 moves an hour,† no opinion need be expressed. A comparatively fast time limit tends to produce errors (from which, however, slower play is very far from exempt), and luck plays a greater part. But it cannot be said that chance had a great influence on the final placings. With one round still to go only Botvinnik or Capablanca could secure the first prize outright, each having 9½ points, while the nearest scores to theirs were 8½. As neither was able to do more than draw, they remained together at the top of the table.

That the result of the Nottingham Tournament should revive the demand for Capablanca to be given the opportunity of another Championship match was not surprising. Botvinnik's youth would give him plenty of time, but Capablanca was no longer at the happy stage when he could go on waiting as he had waited for his first bid for the Championship, and as he had been compelled to wait again vainly since 1927. With a keen sense of justice the Council of the British Chess Federation at their annual general meeting in October, 1936, passed a resolution strongly recommending to the F.I.D.E. that, after the return match between Euwe and Alekhine, Capablanca's claim to challenge the winner—" which is so clear from records of recent tournament play "—should be admitted at once. Unhappily, as it seems to us, and as we think it should seem to all fair-minded judges, the international body at Stockholm last August decided, against the choice of their own sub-committee, which was for Capablanca, to nominate Flohr as the next candidate for a challenge match.

* The young Estonian Paul Keres has since, by his remarkable triumph in the double-round tournament in Austria in October, 1937, fully entitled himself to be considered among the leading aspirants. But his claim was not clear enough in 1935 for him to be invited to Nottingham.

With regard to Keres, as also to Reshevsky (the United States champion) and Fine, it must be emphasised that it has been impossible within the limits of this book to notice any but the greatest tournaments, so that the non-appearance before of some eminent young masters' names must be excused.

† 36 moves in the first two hours.

Dr. Euwe, with that fairness which has always marked his conduct, made an offer to the F.I.D.E. that, should he beat Alekhine again, he would play a match with Capablanca, on condition that the winner of it plays Flohr in 1940; and in September it was stated that Capablanca had agreed to Euwe's proposal, a match between being arranged, provisionally, for 1939.

* * * * *

Since the foregoing words were written the return match between Euwe and Alekhine has been played and a new chapter has been added to chess history, marked by an unprecedented occurrence. A " come-back " is a very rare event in any branch of athletics, bodily or mental; and in chess it has never been known before that the previous holder of the Championship title has won it again from the player who wrested it from him. This Alekhine has done, and by the convincing score of 15½ points to 9½.

The terms of the match were the same as in that of 1935; 30 games for the World Championship and a stake of $10,000, the scorer of 15½ points, including at least 6 won games, to be the victor. It was arranged, however, that the full 30 games should be played regardless of the result.

That such a margin of success as 15½-9½ was a surprise cannot be denied. Not that, as a player, Alekhine was not thought capable of achieving it, on a comparative estimate of the chess genius of the two antagonists. For sheer genius Alekhine has generally been allowed to be supreme in his own time; or even, his admirers claim, in all time. But the previous match between him and Euwe had aroused serious misgivings as to his staying-power, and the addition of two years to their respective ages—making him just on forty-five to Euwe's thirty-six—was held to be in the Dutch master's favour.

Probably what most followers of chess expected was a narrow victory for Euwe again; and the start of the match encouraged the belief that the result would be nothing less. Euwe began with a win at The Hague on October 6, opening with a *Queen's Gambit*, which Alekhine declined with a *Slav Defence*. Alekhine's handling of the game was faulty on the 16th move, after which he soon lost a Pawn, and at the adjournment he was obviously in for a defeat, which duly came about on the second day at the 50th move.

In the second game, however, Alekhine was in his best form, steadily outplaying his opponent—to such an extent that Euwe did not think it worth while to continue after the adjournment. The game is given in Part II (Game 51).

Thus the happenings of the previous match had been reversed, though the score was, as in that, one all. Now the resemblance ceased, for two drawn games followed, the earlier of them being a fine struggle, where the title-holder had a slight advantage, which he could not convert into a win, though the fight went on to the 60th move. The other was a short game, not, however, lacking in interest.

In the fifth game Euwe took the lead again. Alekhine did not play well against a vigorous attack, and on his 23rd move had to sacrifice a piece to stave off a mate, without escaping defeat. He made up for this in the sixth game, getting Euwe into a variation of the *Slav Defence* that he apparently did not know, and bringing about the shortest victory ever seen in a Championship match—in 23 moves only.

Alekhine proceeded to establish a good lead with two more wins. Of these the seventh game was daringly played by both sides, and Euwe blundered in a precarious position on the 28th move. In the eighth Euwe was again at fault, this time on his 17th move, and Alekhine finished in attractive style.

After an uneventful draw, the 10th game produced another win for Alekhine, helped by Euwe's indifferent play. The Champion was indeed disappointing his supporters' expectations, and, if there were such a thing as betting at chess, the market would now have shown odds on the challenger. Euwe had clearly to make a special effort to save the situation; and this after two not remarkable draws, he was able to do in the 13th game, securing a positional advantage early and, in spite of great ingenuity on Alekhine's part, bringing matters to a successful issue on the 68th move.

But this was only a flash in the pan. Alekhine in the 14th game seemed to puzzle his opponent with an unusual 3rd move (1 **P—Q4, Kt—KB3;** 2 **P—QB4, P—K3;** 3 **P—KKt3**), and he captured first one Pawn and then another, to secure an easily winning endgame.

Again Euwe made a partial recovery after two draws; and in the 17th game he took excellent advantage of a slight opening slip by Alekhine to establish such a Pawn-majority that nothing could withstand it. At this stage he was making a fine fight; and three more draws ensued, one of them being a really sensational affair (see Part II, Game 52).

With the 21st game came the decisive phase of the match. Alekhine's score stood at 6—4, with 10 draws, or 11 points to 9; and there were 10 games to come. The result was therefore still open. But what followed was an almost complete *débacle* for the title-holder. Alekhine won the 21st and 22nd games, the 23rd was a draw, and Alekhine won the 24th. As his point-score was now 14½—9½, he only required one more win to give him the match. Already Euwe's soundness and equanimity seemed to have deserted him, and at no time in the 25th game did he appear likely to save even half a point. He carried play over the adjournment, though in a hopeless position, but resigned on his 44th move, bringing his short tenure of the Championship to an end.

In accordance with what had been arranged, the remaining five games were played, though they could have no bearing on the match. The first two of them were drawn, in 30 and 28 moves respectively. In the 28th Alekhine, adopting for a change a form of the *Réti-Zukertort Opening*, took advantage of his opponent's bad policy in offering an exchange of Queens to force a passed Pawn and secure his resignation on the 37th move. Of the 29th and 30th games it need only be said that Alekhine played as one for whom tension had been relaxed, carrying neither beyond adjournment-time. Thus Euwe had the barren satisfaction of winning " the bye " by a majority of one point.

The final score was: Alekhine 11 wins, Euwe 6, drawn 13, or 17½-12½ in Alekhine's favour.

It will be interesting to see (as it cannot yet be seen at the moment of writing) what effect Dr. Alekhine's victory in the return match will have on the situation as regards the Chess Championship of the World. On the surface it would appear as though the title-holder is again in the position of a dictator concerning whom he shall next play. He has not so far, as Dr. Euwe did, recognised the authority of the F.I.D.E. to tell him who shall be his challenger in his next match. Therefore, if he agrees to meet Salo Flohr in 1939, it will be an act of grace on his part. If he preferred, as so many friends of chess would like, to play that return match with Señor Capablanca, which has so long been talked about and written about in vain, he could do so; but there is nothing that can compel him.

The state of affairs, it must be confessed, is very unsatisfactory. Perhaps something may happen in the near future to improve it. We can only hope so. There is a suggestion already of a third match between the two recent antagonists in 1939. That would no doubt be an interesting event. But there are the claims of other would-be challengers for the title to be considered. Must they go on waiting, in the first place to see what happens in a third Alekhine-Euwe encounter? And then—well, it is impossible to say what.

It should be plain that some qualifying and eliminating system is required, in view of the number of aspirants to the World title. The F.I.D.E. missed its chance at Stockholm of at least making trial of one qualifying tournament without a strain on its own admittedly inadequate resources. Such a policy puts the loyalty of players towards the International body to a severe test, and it would hardly be a legitimate ground of complaint if the Masters were again, at some convenient meeting together, to take charge of Championship affairs.

The London Rules of 1922, whether or not they can be regarded as satisfactory in the regulation of World Championship matches, left the question of selection of a challenger untouched, except to such an extent as has been mentioned on p. 49. By them the challenger must be able to find financial guarantees; but he need not have proved himself to be the most worthy claimant, in chess ability, to the right of playing in a challenge-match.

The advocates of a series of eliminating matches, as in theory at least there is in the boxing world, rather fail to appreciate the difference made by the length of time required for chess and boxing matches. There is alleged to be an objection on the part of the masters to the idea of an eliminating tournament. It is rather to be doubted whether this is true; and in any case such a tournament is a practical possibility, if the funds are forthcoming, which a series of matches does not appear to be.

The example of the Ostend Championship Tournament of 1907 is worth remembering. It had the fortunate result of making a match between Drs. Lasker and Tarrasch inevitable. Now that Tournament was brought about by private enterprise, there being at that date no international organisation to be consulted in the case. There is today the F.I.D.E.; but it has declined to sponsor the scheme put before it by private enterprise. Must that be the end of the matter?

It cannot be the *end*. The duration of a bad position may be long. But here at least perpetual check is not a possibility.

Postscript.—Since the termination of the recent match two announcements have been made which, if confirmed, will have an important bearing on the situation.

In the first place, it is stated that Dr. Alekhine has declined a challenge by Salo Flohr to defend the World Championship title against him in 1940; and, in the second, Dr. Alekhine is said to have expressed a view that Señor Capablanca should be his next opponent. As the Champion is under engagement to visit South America in the present year, 1938, and as Argentina and Uruguay combined are reported to be willing to put up a large sum (nearly £3,000 is the figure mentioned) for a match Alekhine-Capablanca, it really looks as if the return encounter between these two Grand Masters might at length be in sight.

CHAPTER IV

THE MASTERS

THE name " master " is a very comprehensive term as applied to chessplayers, and there are so many grades of masters that there has grown up a sort of rough classification of them, which few of them are prepared to recognise without qualification.

The World Master's position cannot be disputed, since he gains his title by winning the Championship. Thus there are at present one World Master and three ex-World Masters. Below them, but including them, come the Grand Masters, winners of an International Masters' Tournament recognised as being of the first class, or who have been near enough to winning to make it impossible to deny them the adjective Grand.

After this differentiation becomes difficult. To have been admitted to a first-class International Masters' Tournament is a *cachet*, which perhaps entitles competitors to be considered near-Grand Masters. But then there is the International Tournament not entirely first-class, including a player or players taken in to make up the requisite number. There is also the mixed Masters' Tournament in which a considerable proportion of the entry is drawn from the country in which the tournament is played; and lower still is the national masters' tournament, held to decide who is master—champion is the more suitable word—of his own country.

The World Championship class among chessplayers, however, only comprises actual winners of the Championship title and those who have been permitted to challenge them. Chance has, to a certain extent, larger than is just, decided who may take his place among the challengers. There are not a few names that can be mentioned as obviously suitable in a challengers' list—*e.g.*, those of Pillsbury, Maróczy, Rubinstein, Nimzovitch (all of whom reached the stage of issuing a challenge), Kolisch, Mason, Teichmann, Weiss, Duras, Burn, Spielmann, Bernstein (some of whom, however, had no ambition to challenge)—and doubtless other names might be added, of which the bearers were as fully gifted at chess as some of those who succeeded in obtaining challenge matches.

Chance, and the individual circumstances of the players, too, influenced their admission to the circle of contestants for the World Championship. But it is extraordinary from what a variety of professions or callings great chessplayers have come or in which at one time or another in their lives they have been engaged. A random selection must suffice, as details are often lacking. Ruy Lopez was an ecclesiastic, Philidor a musician, Deschapelles in youth a soldier, William Lewis was employed in commerce, as also was M'Donnell. Staunton was best known, outside chess, for his edition of Shakespeare, Saint-Amant was a wine-merchant, Anderssen a teacher of mathematics, Morphy a lawyer, Kolisch a writer and private secretary, who developed into a banker and millionaire, Steinitz was trained to be a rabbi, as was Rubinstein after him, Zukertort was a doctor of medicine, Blackburne was brought up to trade, Mason began, according to his own account, as a newspaper-boy. Lasker is a mathematician and a student of philosophy, Capablanca a diplomatist, Alekhine a doctor of law, and Euwe a mathematician. There was a chess master, Harmonist, who danced at the Opera House in Vienna, and we have met one who was a professional "strong man."

In Russian chess today the Soviet system is producing players from every trade and craft. But the game has gradually been freed from social barriers since in the early Nineteenth Century it ceased to be mainly a pastime of the nobility and gentry, patrons of a few players infinitely more gifted than themselves. It tended for a time to be rather a preserve of the professional classes —in the general, not the special sense of the word "professional" —but it has rapidly become democratised, a process to which no end is visible. All to the good of the game, provided that the enthusiastic patron does not die out, for Masters may be born, but they must live !

It would be a delicate task to say what manner of men chess masters are outside their actual playing of chess and their other employment in the world; and in the case of those that are still with us it is best unattempted. The past shows them in infinite variety. To name only a few, Deschapelles was so great a boaster that, if it were not otherwise established, we could hardly believe him a really great chessplayer. Staunton, too, suffered from excessive self-esteem, which led him, however, rather to depreciate others than, like Deschapelles, to boast of his own achievements, but he was sensitive to supposed slights on account of his illegitimate birth, and in later life much troubled with bad health. In private life he is said to have been of a most agreeable character. Anderssen was genial, free from jealousy, a chivalrous opponent, and never tired of the game. Morphy, on the contrary, tired of it early, or tired at least of its players. He was in many ways unfortunate, and it has been declared, with some reason, that his greatest misfortune was to have been born well-off. Disease, not originally mental, was the final curse which fell upon a gallant and over-sensitive young man. To some extent Cecil de Vere's case was like Morphy's, though he was not born with money, but inherited it later, and his fatal illness was consumption, ending what might have been a brilliant career before he was thirty.

Steinitz, the greatest of all chessplayers up to his time (or since, according to one whom many hold greater still, Dr. Lasker), was far from being a typical player of the game, if such a type exists. Starting from the other extreme to Morphy, he had all to make in life, and as far as his ambition carried him he made it. He conquered by brain power what he lacked otherwise, and there was more in the jest than appears, that he "invented" chess. He elevated it from a game into a science. His great rival, Zukertort, displayed it as an art, which was in keeping with his abnormally high-strung nature.

But the great Steinitz could not be called either a pleasant or a happy man. He was obstinate, autocratic, and when opposed bitter in the extreme. Staunton had dipped his pen in gall, but Steinitz's medium was vitriol. Doubtless many of the attacks on him were cruel (chiefly, strange to say, from men of his own race), but in abuse he outdid them all. Had he not been a supreme chess master, it is difficult to imagine what he might have become. Certainly no rabbi such as his father had wished him to be. A journalist perhaps ; but then he was a journalist, as well as a chess master.

Blackburne will always be remembered with affection in his own country, and probably was always so regarded in the many other lands he visited. He was a "good mixer." (It is impossible not to recall the thought of alcohol here, but Blackburne showed how a chessplayer *could* drink, poor Mason, on the other hand, how one chessplayer *would* drink.) He was a very entertaining companion, who had picked up much in life besides skill at chess, though it was to that he owed it that he became famous, as he could hardly have done in the commercial career on the low rungs of which he started.

Gunsberg might have begun life in England with an inferiority complex, for he was a foreigner, rather insignificant in appearance, and with no great force of personality. But somehow he did not. The other foreign masters in London were grudging in their recognition of his talent, and he had not the proper tact to conciliate potential enemies. Yet in his often unguarded remarks he was never actuated by malice, but only by a sly humour which many failed to understand. He was modest about his own chess powers, at least as he grew older, and prided himself rather on what he did for the game in his very numerous columns and by his organising abilities. He liked the amateurs more than the other masters, and had many amiable characteristics. Somehow in age he never seemed a man who had won the International Masters' Tournament at Hamburg in 1885 above so many eminent players.

Two very contrasting characters were Carl Schlechter and David Janowski. In the former all who ever met him were bound to recognise a man of modest charm and extreme good nature. Had he not died in 1918, at the age of only forty-six, he might well have aspired to a challenge match for the Championship, of which his encounter with Lasker in 1910 was a foretaste only, but his disposition was not such as to make him put himself forward. His chess was a reflection of his natural self. He thought that the equitable result of a well-played game was a draw, and the frequency with which he attained that result gained for him the name, which had been bestowed on another Viennese, Berthold Englisch, before him, and now seems to have been earned by the young Czecho-Slovakian, Salo Flohr—the name of "drawing master." At the same time Schlechter could let himself go, when he produced some of the most brilliant games in chess history, which belied the foolish charge that he was *merely* a positional player.

Of Janowski, Polish Jew by origin and French by adoption, it was said that he knew well how to attack, but not when to attack, and also that of possible results he dreaded the draw. This was the outcome of an aggressive nature, which, coupled as it was with a strong belief in his own powers, was constantly in his life involving him in feuds with other masters. Yet the present writer can testify that he could be an affable companion, who when he last met him in Paris, unhappily already suffering from the illness which caused his end not long after, discussed men and matters, especially in the chess world, wittily, trenchantly—and somewhat dogmatically.

Dr. Siegbert Tarrasch was a standing example of the possibility of a man being at the same time a Grand Master at chess and highly efficient in another profession, for he never neglected his medical practice to give up excessive time to the game. It is superfluous to say how great he was at chess. His record and his writings attest that. For the fame of German chess he did more—apart from Lasker, who left Germany early—than any player before or since; but, not being an "Aryan," he was treated with ingratitude in the end, and died in exile. It is curious to think that during the War his chess writings were tinged with ultra-patriotism on behalf of a country which was to cast him off a few years later.* He was perhaps rather apt to let personal prejudice influence his pen, but he felt strongly, and lacked not courage to express his feelings. He adhered to his views, in chess above all, against the opinion of no matter how eminent other authorities. And many of those views have prevailed. Some, such as on the merits of the *Tarrasch Defence* in the *Queen's Gambit Declined*, have been rejected and restored to favour among players more than once. At the present moment that defence's supporters are in a minority, but time may yet bring it back, as a fighting method with which to meet the ever recurring *Q.G.D.*

After all, it has not proved possible to consider even such few chess masters as have just been considered outside their chess, for that entered so deeply into their lives that it obscured what else was in them. No doubt living masters would give scope for the pen of a Rev. G. A. MacDonnell, of *Chess Life Pictures*, and other writings always entertaining but not always trustworthy. Such gossip, however, is not the intention here. All that was desired was to show the diversity of temperament behind the players, which comes out in their play and helps sometimes to explain it. Its study, even if more details were obtainable, would not help us to predict what a certain master will do in a particular situation. We are all complexes, and now one, now another part of a multiple personality takes control. Even a "chess machine," such as Capablanca was once declared to be, has an occasional aberration.

If all great masters could become "machines," by eliminating every mistake from their play, the interest of chess for its watchers or followers in print would undoubtedly be much diminished. Schlechter, Capablanca, Flohr—to name only three great masters—have all produced, when met by an opponent bent simply on avoiding errors, a number of games that by the amateur (and by other masters) are voted dull. The subject of the perfect game and mistakes has already been alluded to in our first chapter, and an examination of the games in Part II will reveal how much of the thrill in them is due to the fact that one or both of the players made a slip, offering the possibility of a hostile combination or positional manœuvre.

A distinction, however, must be drawn between a mistake due

* I had some controversy in print with Dr. Tarrasch during the War over his depreciation of English chessplayers. But when I met him at Hastings in the autumn of 1922 any bitterness was forgotten. Chess was a bond which defied national resentments to break it. In fact we never alluded to the dead controversy.

to oversight as to consequences of a move and a theoretical error in the opening, which may be due to personal preference or prejudice of the player. Steinitz is the great example of the faddist in the openings, persisting in clinging to lines of play which he well knew other masters condemned. This, again, is different from the "once only" move, if we may so call it, such as Alekhine in particular is apt to introduce into an opening. It is in its way deliberately inferior, but calculated by its complexity to take the opponent out of his depth. For instance, in the Alekhine-Euwe match of 1935 Alekhine in the 7th and 9th games against Euwe's *French Defence* sprang surprises which succeeded in their object:

(1) 1 **P—K4, P—K3**; 2 **P—Q4, P—Q4**; 3 **Kt—QB3, B—Kt5**; 4 **B—K2, P × P**; 5 **P—QR3, B—K2**; 6 **Kt × P, Kt—QB3**; 7 **P—KKt4**.

(2) 1 **P—K4, P—K3**; 2 **P—Q4, P—Q4**; 3 **Kt—QB3, B—Kt5**; 4 **Q—Kt4**.

Not mistakes, speculations, it may be said. And still more properly perhaps may that be said of another of Alekhine's lines against the *French Defence*, in the famous game which he won from Nimzovitch in the Bled Tournament of 1931:

(3) 1 **P—K4, P—K3**; 2 **P—Q4, P—Q4**; 3 **Kt—QB3, B—Kt5**; 4 **Kt—K2, P × P**; 5 **P—QR3, B × Kt ch**; 6 **Kt × B, P—KB4**; 7 **P—B3**.

All these speculations of Alekhine were successful against the so-called "Winawer variation" of the *French* (though Winawer was not the actual inventor of the move), 3.., **B—Kt5**. But they have not destroyed the credit of the variation. They have merely pointed out some dangers in playing it if one has not explored the bypaths as well as the main road.

The subject of the Masters' treatment of the openings will be resumed in the next chapter. Here it has only been introduced in connection with the launching of a surprise move, which may be inferior against the best possible play, and therefore verges on a mistake—while at the same time being a touch of genius. Annotators are apt to mark such moves ! ?; it is the easiest way out of a difficulty for the critic.

It sometimes appears as if what we have most to thank the Masters for is their mistakes. Not the occasional gross blunders, though those, too, are comforting to the lesser player as showing that his own frailty is not a mere sign of "rabbitry"; but the errors that make possible subsequent brilliancies. The much dreaded death by the draw, which was supposed some time ago to be menacing chess, is just a bogey so long as Homer can nod and a World Champion be guilty of a slip.

Eugène Znosko-Borovsky has written on "How not to play Chess." We have cause to be grateful to the Masters who now and then illustrate the art.

CHAPTER V

THE INFLUENCE OF THE MASTERS

WHAT is sometimes called fashion in chess is a tribute to the skill of a great master in handling the game, and is very marked throughout chess history. It is most noticeable in the openings, because there one can definitely set oneself to imitate what seems admirable in the master's play. For this reason the " theory " of the openings has always been fluid, and perhaps will always be so, in spite of the present-day stereotyping of the Queen's side *débuts*, against which the reaction is only very slight, though the protests of a disgusted few are not lacking in vigour.*

Nothing shows the ascendancy of 1 **P—Q4** better than the records of all the matches in which Alekhine has engaged, notably his two matches with Capablanca in 1927 and with Euwe in 1936. In the first of these there was one game that began with **P—K4**; in the other 7, and one *English Opening*. This was out of a total of 66 games, all the rest of which began with 1 **P—Q4.** The openings in Championship matches generally have been fully dealt with in the accounts of the matches, and it suffices to point out that in the Steinitz-Lasker encounter of 1894 1 **P—K4** was played eleven times, and 1 **P—Q4** only eight. Speaking roughly, we may date the beginning of the modern vogue for 1 **P—Q4** from 1921, when Capablanca beat Lasker.

Now it may be supposed that in Grand Masters' chess, as in amateur chess, too, 1 **P—K4** would be played far more often if there were a belief that the answer would be 1.., **P—K4.** But the *Ruy Lopez* still continues to act as a scarecrow for Black. In 1935 Alekhine was allowed by Euwe to play the *Lopez* against him once only (the game ending in a draw), though its evasion by the *French Defence* on four occasions was very unprofitable to Euwe, who drew one game and lost 3.

Therefore Alekhine, Capablanca and Euwe (we name them in alphabetical order) may be said to have established the fashion of 1 **P—Q4.** Previous to their joint era, it will be remembered by those who are old enough, 1 **P—K4,** and especially the *Ruy Lopez*, were fashionable, while once (but very few can remember

* " Will there ever come a day," wrote my friend the late Clarence S. Howell three years ago, " when this absurdly dull opening [1 **P—Q4, P—Q4;** 2 **P—QB4**] is barred? The QP openings have taken all the romance out of chess."

this save by having read of it) Gambits were the mode. Steinitz came to England, having learnt in the Gambit school of Vienna, and there had to be a revolution in him before he set out to revolutionise chess.

The influence of fashion in opening play is easy to understand. In the later game, apart from the endgame, which defies fashion, a master's influence is much more subtle. The ordinary player cannot well imitate a master's style without having his genius. Who, for instance, could imitate Lasker? One can follow the precepts of Tarrasch or Nimzovitch, indeed, since both set them out so clearly in their writings, but no new Tarrasch or Nimzovitch has been produced thereby.

Steinitz had the widest influence of all masters, past or present. But he had a task of enormous difficulty in making that influence prevail. He came on the scene at a time when rushing tactics against the hostile King's position were the rage, and in his early period used such tactics himself. In fact, he was not yet Steinitz the thinker. That development came about through his introduction to London. English chess, thanks to Staunton, who was first of all positional players, had acquired a sense of " position " to an extent beyond the chess of other countries. (Such is the opinion of Dr. Lasker, and therefore hardly to be questioned.) Through his contact with it Steinitz learnt to become a teacher.

In his *Chess Manual* Lasker thus sums up the ideas of Steinitz in practical play: " Steinitz strove to transform small advantages that rapidly disappear into small advantages that endure, and thus to accumulate them. . . . In defence, conversely, Steinitz carefully avoided creating lasting weaknesses, unless forced to do so by his opponent."

In itself positional play was not calculated to attract the average amateur; but Steinitz's defeat of so brilliant a combinational genius as Zukertort, coupled with the rationality of his written teachings on the subject of chess, could not fail to make students of the game think, with the consequence that judgment of position has come to be the mark of the expert.

Why, then, was Steinitz beaten by Lasker before the advance of years had furnished a sufficient explanation of his defeat? The Doctor suggests as the reason that he himself was a *player*, and Steinitz a *thinker*. This is not a perfectly clear antithesis; but Lasker goes on to express what appears to him to have been lacking in Steinitz's theories. Steinitz, he says, did not speak of the strategy which a player should follow who feels that he is neither attacker nor defender; when the position is a *balanced* one, in fact. What is necessary then, for the player, is to maintain the co-operation of his pieces, which have to be supported according to their value, changing in proportion to the degree of activity they exhibit. The total value of the pieces is not the sum of their separate values, but their co-operative value as they interact.

It is easy to see the mathematical mind behind an explanation such as this, not so easy to see why a master so minded should ever, logically, be beaten—except, of course, through the accidents which attend the playing of chess. But there is a mental element which is not usually reckoned among these accidents, and that is the speculative faculty. In the higher mathematics of chess speculation is not dispensed with. Otherwise all that would be necessary to make the perfect player would be (in addition to the "chess brain") a thorough acquaintance with the theory of the openings, an ability to apply an already thought-out system to the middle game, and a complete knowledge of endings, which are after all reducible to formula.

So chess could conceivably be reduced to a pure science, and speculation abolished. But as an art it would cease to exist. It is speculation, that is imagination, which makes it an art.

But speculation, it may be objected, is gambling. True, and the man with an imagination does gamble. Therefore, all Grand Masters at chess, since they could not be such without imagination, have gambled; when they have been wise, choosing the right opponents against whom to gamble. Steinitz, for instance, often gambled against Tchigorin; he did not so do against Lasker. Alekhine's gamblings against Bogoljuboff have been mentioned; his play against Capablanca in 1927 had shown no such hardihood, and had he continued to play as he did then, when he won his title, there are many who think he would not have lost it eight years later.

This is not to say that some of Alekhine's speculations against Euwe in 1935 were not brilliantly successful. As far as the opening is concerned, we have mentioned two of them in the last chapter. Another, not so successful, may be seen in Part II, Game 46. We must therefore go back, and allow that the two equations, speculation = imagination and speculation = gambling, are not precisely parallel. In other words, "gambling" is a slippery term.

We have, however, strayed from the subject of the influence of the Masters. Now it is curious that the founders of "schools" of chess have not always been the greatest Masters. Steinitz, indeed, introduced the Modern School. But Lasker, as he was a pupil of no particular school, so cannot be said to have founded any. He is too subtle for imitation, the subtlest indeed of all who have ever become great at chess. Also the intrusion of his philosophical ideas into his chess-writings has lessened their appeal to many.

Nor has Capablanca founded a school, though to a certain extent both Flohr and Fine may be said to have sat at his feet, in that they aim at being unbeatable, and in this respect have already proved themselves apt learners. The drawback to invincibility is that, when two players meet who both make it their aim, they appear at least to be too willing to acquiesce in a draw, and without a fair proportion of won games complete success is not to be attained. One example will suffice. In the Cologne Tournament of 1898 Schlechter was the only one of the sixteen competitors who did not lose a single game, but his score of 4 won games and 11 draws brought him no more than a tie for fifth and sixth prizes with Steinitz, who lost 4 games.

The common complaint against Schlechter's play was that it was normally too "static," and the same has been said about Capablanca and, among the younger masters, Flohr and Fine. The complaint is somewhat impertinent, in view of what these "static" masters have achieved, but it is intelligible. The appeal made by the "dynamic" Alekhine is very natural. But that anyone should claim to belong to the school of Alekhine is another matter. Alekhine's countless innovations in the openings —some of them rather happy revivals than actual novelties—are for all to follow who so wish. If, however, the followers lack the Master's brain, they cannot follow him very far.

Recently* Alekhine has written of "a curious psychological weakness" in his youthful chess, "the impression that I could always, or nearly always, when in a bad position, conjure up some unexpected combination to extricate me from my difficulties." This weakness, he said, he had to work hard subsequently to eradicate, if he has ever eradicated it. The confession is illuminating. Those who have followed Alekhine's play throughout his career have suspected, or rather more than suspected, this weakness. It is part of the make-up of a dynamic player. But those who aspire to emulating the style are apt to forget that the conjuring feats of an Alekhine cannot be learnt by observation; and he admits them to have been frequently failures.

The whole question of dynamic *versus* static play, however, is somewhat absurd. One thing which is certain is that it does not mean unsound *versus* sound play, We are not entitled to say that Euwe headed a reaction against dynamism because by his superior soundness he defeated Alekhine in their match of 1935. In what school, then, are we to put the young Russian players of today ? The fallacy of using labels was illustrated in Morphy's

* In the magazine *Chess* for August, 1937.

time, when some looked on him as the combinational genius, others as an essentially solid and analytical player.

It has been said above that the teachings of Tarrasch and Nimzovitch, clear as they were, have produced no new Tarrasch or Nimzovitch. We may revert briefly to this point. Rubinstein is said, on his way to mastership, to have devoted particular study to the works of Tarrasch, and there is no reason to doubt it. Nevertheless, he did not become a second Tarrasch, but the first Rubinstein. With him, of course, it was a case of one master absorbing and transforming the spirit of another. Had Rubinstein continued in good health, and been more fortunate in his circumstances, it is impossible to guess what might have happened. But at least he would be still Rubinstein, not merely Tarrasch's pupil.

The ordinary student of Tarrasch may derive much good from his study, but he cannot well set himself up to be a pupil. Possibly there are at the present day more professed pupils of Nimzovitch than of Tarrasch, and some of them do not hesitate to acclaim him as the greatest of all chess teachers. He made it easier for them to profess themselves of his school by his invention of a new terminology—almost a jargon, like that of the modern problemists. Now as to his eminence as a player there can be no question. Whether he is the best of masters for amateurs to follow is certainly more doubtful.

Some time ago, when exactly it is difficult to say, somebody introduced into chess the term, "the hyper-modern school." The adjective is neither Greek nor Latin nor comely. But it gained currency, as expressing a tendency which, according to its admirers, was to transform chess. Its most brilliant living exponent is Dr. S. G. Tartakover, to whom all who know him will forgive anything, even if it were he who compounded the word "hyper-modern." But where is the school now, apart from the Doctor? Some of its precepts, indeed, have impressed themselves on the memory, such as that about "the avoidance of contact in the centre." We see much of this avoidance today, but so we should have done in the time and games of the Rev. John Owen, who was at the height of his fame in 1862.

As for the exaltation into a doctrine of the fianchetto development of the Bishops, which was another "hyper-modern" mark, this was always a feature of the Indian game of chess, and came into European chess largely through the contact of John Cochrane with "the Brahmin" and other players in India towards the middle of the Nineteenth Century. The memory of the connection is preserved in the names of the *King's Indian* and *Queen's Indian Defences* today.

One must not, however, blame too severely those who claim to be introducing a new style into the playing of chess, on the ground that a hundred or more years ago the style may have been new but now it certainly is not. All innovation is in a sense revival, though it may not be conscious. Once, or more probably a dozen times, there was a great vogue among women, on account of its supposed novelty, for much-flounced skirts, widening downwards from the waist. But it was discovered that the ladies of prehistoric Crete had exactly the same fashion. So, too, the athletic girls of today are in their costumes not unlike the bull-fighting maidens in the arena of the royal palace of Minos.

In chess it is often impossible to say when a certain line of play originated, though it can often be proved that it is much older than the name attached to it would indicate. For example, *Alekhine's Defence* has been traced back to Allgaier in 1811; *Nimzovitch's Defence* (1 **P—K4, Kt—QB3**) was played by Deschapelles in Paris in 1821; the Möller Attack in the *Giuoco Piano* is mentioned by Greco in the Seventeenth Century. But certainly it is the influence of the later master, or sometimes of a prominent amateur, which sets the fashion for the line of play. For the fashion, that is all very well. It is questionable, however, whether there has not been far too much renaming of variations, especially on the Continent, ignoring older claims, even when the original discoverer has not been so long dead that an injustice to him does not matter.

The influence of the masters on the openings is always to be welcomed as tending to establish the right lines of play, often after many attempts (see, for instance, Part II, Game 47), so that they are making " theory " for others to follow. Every Championship match produces some contribution to the theory, however limited may be the range of openings employed in it. If the enthusiasts for variety in the openings had their way we should lose one of the most valuable features of these matches. The attempt to force such variety upon chess masters has never been successful. A classical example of its failure was exhibited in the Gambit Tournament of April, 1914, at Baden, near Vienna, where the chief lesson to be learnt was how the *King's Gambit*, though accepted in the letter, may be evaded in the spirit.

Grand Masters, playing in matches for the World Championship, will never be persuaded to regard themselves as called on to provide the chess public with " turns." They do entertain, as well as instruct; but not unreasonably they choose how they shall do so, while keeping their main object in view, which is to win the match.

PART II

ILLUSTRATIVE GAMES

GAME 1

SAINT-AMANT v. STAUNTON

PARIS, *November* 21, 1843

(MATCH, 5TH GAME)

SICILIAN DEFENCE

White.	*Black.*
SAINT-AMANT	STAUNTON
1 **P—K4**	**P—QB4**
2 **P—KB4**	

A regular continuation at this time. M'Donnell employed it against Labourdonnais in many of their match-games in 1834. Morphy, in an annotation on the games, called it " a line of play radically bad." It is now practically obsolete, Nimzovitch being perhaps the last of recent masters to adopt it.

P—K3

The answer preferred by Labourdonnais. In Nimzovitch-Capablanca, Berlin, 1928, the continuation was 2.., **Kt—QB3**; 3 **P—Q3**, **P—KKt3**; 4 **P—B4** (typical of Nimzovitch), **B—Kt2**; 5 **Kt—QB3**, **P—Q3**.

3 **Kt—KB3**	**Kt—QB3**
4 **P—B3**	**P—Q4**
5 **P—K5**	

M'Donnell's move, to which Labourdonnais's reply was 5.., **P—B3**. Staunton has other ideas.

Q—Kt3

6 **B—Q3**

Saint-Amant says in *Le Palamède* that this move was much criticised; but he had seen Labourdonnais (as first player) make it, as did Mouret regularly.

B—Q2

7 **B—B2**	**R—B1**
8 **Castles**	**Kt—R3**
9 **P—KR3**	**B—K2**
10 **K—R2**	**P—B4**

An effective counter to White's threat of 11 **P—KKt4**.

11 **P—R3**

Better was 11 **P—QR4**, says Saint-Amant.

P—QR4

12 **P—QR4**	**Kt—B2**
13 **P—Q4**	**P—R3**
14 **R—K1**	

By the threat of **B × P** this prevents Black's contemplated **P—Kt4**, but only for a time.

P—Kt3

15 **Kt—R3**	**P × P**
16 **Kt × P**	

Not 16 **P × P**, because then **Kt—Kt5**.

Kt × Kt

17 **P × Kt**	**P—Kt4**
18 **Kt—Kt5**	

As Black will obviously not oblige with a double capture, this is not good, White having a permanent weakness on QKt5.

B × Kt

19 **P × B**	**R—B5 ?**
20 **B—Q3 !**	**R—B1**

Since Black clearly cannot here play **R × P** (21 **B—K3**), his 19th move is shown to have been a loss of time—rare for Staunton, as his opponent remarks.

21 **B—K2**	**P × P**
22 **R—B1**	

Why not **B × P** at once? Black's Kt now comes into powerful action.

		Kt—Kt4
23	**B × P**	**Kt—K5**
24	**R—B1**	**R × R**
25	**Q × R**	**K—Q2**
26	**Q—K3**	**B—Kt4**
27	**B—Q3**	**R—KKt1**
28	**B × Kt**	

White apparently must remove this Kt, but the P which takes its place is a future menace.

		QP × B
29	**B × B**	**P × B**

Position after 29.., **P × B**:

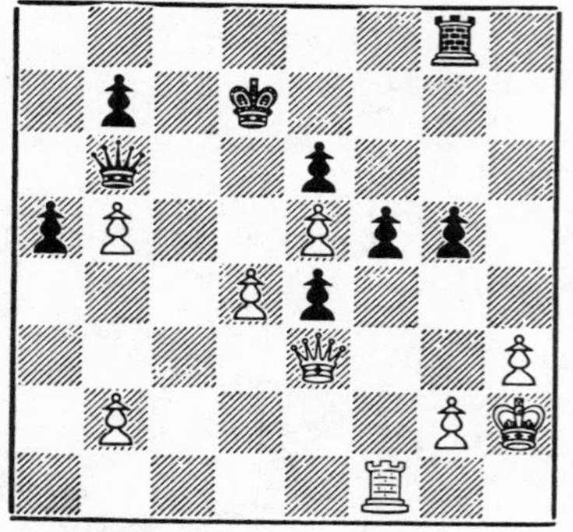

30 **Q—QKt3**

Saint-Amant claims at least an equal game for White with this. Black's next move is terribly hard to meet, but apparently it *could* have been met.

P—Kt5

31 **R—Q1 ?**

31 **R × P** is Saint-Amant's suggestion in *Le Palamède*, though he ventures on no analysis. It is certainly immensely superior to the text-move. Black's best reply is 31.., **P—Kt6 ch !**; 32 **K—R1, P × R** (**Q × QP ?**; 33 **R—B7 ch, K—Q1**; 34 **Q—B2, Q × KP**; 35 **P—Kt6,** and what can Black do ?); 33 **Q—B7 ch, K—B1**; 34 **Q × R ch, K—B2.** Now White has a choice of two lines: (1) 35 **Q—Kt7 ch, K—B1** (**K—Kt1 ?**, 36 **Q × P, Q × QP**; 37 **P—K6** dis. ch and wins); where he must apparently be content with perpetual check, since after 36 **Q—B8 ch, K—B2**; 37 **Q—B5 ch ?, Q × Q**; 38 **P × Q, P—K6** wins for Black. (2) 35 **Q—B4 ch,** the outcome of which is very hard to demonstrate; but White cannot lose and may even be said to stand to win. [Acknowledgment is due to Mr. H. E. Atkins for much appreciated aid in this analysis.]

		P × P
32	**Q × P**	**Q—Q1**

"The latter portion of this game," says Staunton, "is conducted with remarkable caution and skill by both parties."

33 **P—Q5 !**

Ingeniously preventing **R—R1,** for then 34 **P × P ch.**

		K—B1
34	**Q—B3 ch**	**K—Kt1**
35	**P—Q6**	**P—B5**
36	**Q—B5**	**P—K6**
37	**Q—B2**	**Q—R5 ch**
38	**K—Kt1**	**R—QB1**

White threatens **Q—B7 ch.**

39 **Q—K2 ?**

Fatal, leaving a forced mate. After 39 **P—Q7, R × Q**; 40 **P—Q8 = Q ch, Q × Q.** 40 **R × Q ch,** though White would not have a good game, says Saint-Amant, there would still be a fight left. Not much of a fight, however, for **K—B2** would compel 41 **R—Q1,** and then White's Q-side P's fall.

R—R1

White resigns.

Total duration of the game, 9½ hrs.

GAME 2

SAINT-AMANT v. STAUNTON

PARIS, *December* 6, 1843

(MATCH, 13TH GAME)

QUEEN'S GAMBIT DECLINED

	White.	*Black.*
	SAINT-AMANT	STAUNTON
1	**P—Q4**	**P—K3**
2	**P—QB4**	**P—Q4**
3	**P—K3**	**Kt—KB3**
4	**Kt—QB3**	**P—B4**
5	**Kt—B3**	**Kt—B3**

After the strangeness in modern eyes of the opening in the preceding game, this is indeed like an opening of today—one form of the *Tarrasch Defence*. Saint-Amant's next move, too, finds its place in the modern "book," with the continuation, which Staunton does not adopt, 6 **P—QR3, P—QR3;** 7 **QP × P, B × P;** 8 **P—QKt4, B—Q3** (**B—R2** has also been tried by the present writer). See also Game No. 8, note on move 6.

6	**P—QR3**	**B—K2**
7	**B—Q3**	**Castles**

Neither player tries to gain a tempo by making the opponent's KB move again with **QP × P.**

8	**Castles**	**P—QKt3**

This is claimed as a new idea of Staunton's in the close game.

9	**P—QKt3**	**B—Kt2**
10	**BP × P**	

Saint-Amant commends this after Black's B has gone to Kt2 and can no longer be developed at K3. The closing of the B's diagonal in such a position is nowadays almost a matter of course.

		KP × P
11	**B—Kt2**	**BP × P**

Black follows his opponent's lead.

12	**KP × P**	**B—Q3**

Now this B has lost a tempo. **R—K1** is worth consideration.

13	**R—K1**	**P—KR3**

Hardly necessary, for 14 **Kt—KKt5** is no serious threat. **R—K1** still looks good enough.

14	**R—QB1**	**R—B1**
15	**R—B2**	**R—B2**
16	**QR—K2**	**Q—B1**
17	**P—R3**	**Kt—Q1**
18	**Q—Q2**	**P—R3**
19	**P—QKt4**	**Kt—K3**
20	**B—B5**	**Kt—K5**

Kieseritzky and other experts in Paris suggested that with **B—B5** Black could now have obtained the better game; but Staunton continued to think his actual move superior.

21	**Kt × Kt**	**P × Kt**

Now comes the decisive moment of the game.

Position after 21.., **P × Kt**:

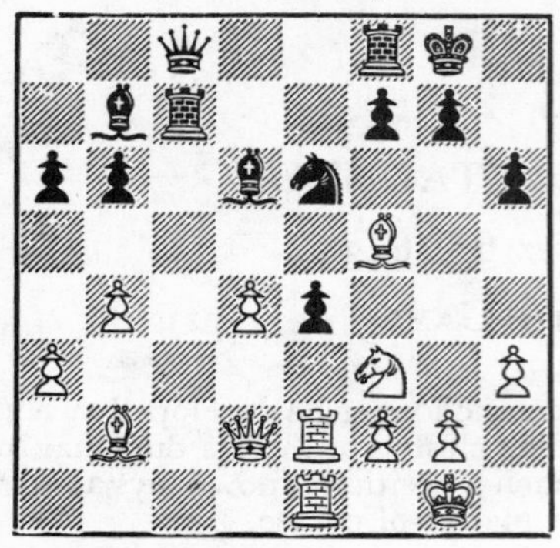

22 **P—Q5**

Black was prepared to meet 22 **B × P** with **B × B**; 23 **R × B**, **R—B7**. But Saint-Amant (or at least the anonymous commentator in *Le Palamède*) is very pleased with this and the following moves, which he says were hailed as "a Labourdonnais attack."

P × Kt ?

A grave miscalculation, says Staunton. At this point he should have played **B—Kt5**, followed by **P × Kt**, with an excellent game.

23 **R × Kt !**

"Divinely played," exclaims *Le Palamède*. White wins a piece by force.

Q—Q1

24 **B—B6 !**

The most wonderful in a series of brilliant moves, says the French commentator; and Staunton allows that it is a remarkably ingenious *coup*.

P × B

25 **R × B**

Here the spectators apparently broke out into enthusiastic applause. If Black captures the R, of course, 26 **Q × P** leads to mate in 2.

	K—Kt2
26 **R × Q**	**R × R**
27 **B—K4**	**P × P**
28 **Q—B4**	**R—B5**
29 **Q—Kt4 ch**	**K—B1**
30 **Q—R5**	**K—K2**

Black would have been well advised to resign now—or indeed on his 26th move. Another piece goes.

31 **P—Q6 ch**	**K × P**
32 **B × B**	**K—B2**
33 **B × RP**	**Resigns**

Saint-Amant had the satisfaction of winning the most brilliant game of the match; but after winning it the score was 9-3 against him, with one draw, and Staunton required only two more victories.

GAME 3

ANDERSSEN v. STEINITZ

LONDON, *July* 21, 1866

(MATCH, 3rd GAME)

EVANS GAMBIT

	White.	*Black.*
	ANDERSSEN	STEINITZ
1	**P—K4**	**P—K4**
2	**Kt—KB3**	**Kt—QB3**
3	**B—B4**	**B—B4**
4	**P—QKt4**	

Anderssen had first met the *Evans Gambit,* in serious play at least, in Paris in December, 1858, when as Black he defended it against Morphy in the opening game of their match. In the present encounter he showed his belief in it for White by adopting it six times out of a possible seven.

		B × P
5	**P—B3**	**B—B4**

Anderssen against Morphy had taken the line 5.., **B—R4** (the standard retreat for the B); 6 **P—Q4, P × P;** 7 **Castles, Kt—B3** —the last move being one that he had condemned in some analysis published a few years previously. But that is not an unparalleled instance in the practice of the masters, either old or new.

6	**P—Q4**	**P × P**
7	**Castles**	**P—Q6**

This is still marked ! in text-books, for example in *Modern Chess Openings.* With 7.., **P—Q3;** **8 P × P, B—Kt3** there would have been a transposition into the " normal position " in the *Evans.*

8 **Q × P ?**

Again Anderssen plays contrary to analysis of his own, published in the *Berliner Schachzeitung* in 1851, and to his usual practice. As Staunton notes in *The Chess World,* he played formerly 8 **Kt—Kt5** with good results. By the immediate capture of the P he places his Q on an unfavourable square for attacking purposes.

		P—Q3
9	**B—KKt5**	**KKt—K2**
10	**QKt—Q2**	**P—KR3**
11	**B—R4**	**Castles**

Black has consequently been able to castle early, and it is very difficult for White to make up for his P minus.

12	**Kt—Kt3**	**B—Kt3**
13	**P—KR3**	**B—K3**
14	**QR—Q1**	**Q—Q2**
15	**B—Q5**	

Staunton remarks that Anderssen's play so far has been " sadly deficient in the vigour and decision so conspicuous in his games formerly." Yet, apart from his 8th move, he has done nothing amiss; a fact which emphasizes the error of that move.

		Kt—Kt3
16	**B—Kt3**	**QR—K1**
17	**P—B4**	**B × B**

Anderssen had affirmed his belief in the strength of his B at Q5 by supporting it there with his last move; and Steinitz shows his agreement with the view by exchanging the B off now.

18	**KP × B**	**QKt—K4**
19	**Kt × Kt**	**Kt × Kt**
20	**Q—QB3**	**Kt—Kt3**
21	**P—B5**	

A new and more interesting phase of the game begins, with Anderssen showing considerable vigour. He now wins back the Gambit P.

		P × P
22	**Kt × P**	**Q—B4**
23	**Kt × P**	**R—K7**
24	**P—Q6**	**P × P**
25	**Kt × P**	**Q—K3**
26	**P—QR4**	**B—Q1**
27	**Q—B5**	

This, followed by the capture of Black's QRP, was blamed as loss of time, very valuable to Black. But see the final note.

Position after 27 **Q—B5**:

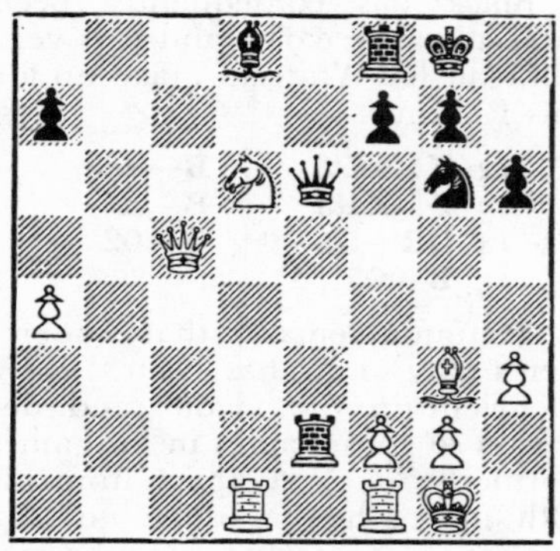

P—B4

Staunton is here struck with admiration for the play of Steinitz, who in the latter part of this game " exhibits a power of combination and a fertility of resource which his most fervent supporters had not supposed him to possess."

28	**Q × RP**	**P—B5**
29	**B—R2**	**Kt—R5**
30	**Q—Kt7**	**Q—Kt3**
31	**R—Q4 ?**	

" Worse than useless," comments Staunton, who allows, however, that Anderssen has made " a gallant fight for many an hour." (The time limit, it must be remembered, was 20 moves in two hours.) Staunton gives no alternative move. Löwenthal suggests 31 **Q—Q5 ch,** but supplies no continuation.

Very likely Anderssen was short of time, and so overlooked his opponent's reply to the text-move. Löwenthal's suggestion is good, and seems to give White superior chances against any but the best moves. If (31 **Q—Q5 ch**) **K—R2;** 32 **Q—Q3,** and Black cannot avoid exchange of **Q5.** Better is **K—R1;** 32 **Kt—B7 ch, K—R2;** and if now 33 **Q—Q3, R—K5.** The continuation might be 34 **P—Kt4, B—K2** (**P × P i.p.;** 35 **B × P** frees White's game); 35 **Kt—Q6, B × Kt;** 36 **Q × B, Kt—B6 ch;** 37 **K—R1, R—B3.** Black appears to maintain his attack as a set-off for the loss of his QRP.

		B—Kt3 !
32	**QR—Q1**	

If 32 **R—Kt4, B × P ch;** 33 **R × B, R × R;** 34 **K × R, Q—B7 ch** and wins. If 32 **Q—Q5 ch, K—R1;** and White has not the resources as in the previous note.

		R—K3
33	**P—R5**	**B—B4**

If Black accepts the offer of the RP, the White Kt gets away to

B4. Steinitz prefers to keep the pressure on the Kt; but he has no time to take it. . . .

34 **P—R6** **R—K2**

For if now **B × Kt** there follows 35 **P—R7, R—K2;** 36 **P queens.** Or 35.., **P—B6;** 36 **P—Kt3,** with the same threat.

35 **Q—Q5 ch** **K—R1**
36 **P—R7**

If 36 **Kt—Kt7, R—Q2 !** wins at once. The menace of mate on his Kt2 is an enduring one, and, though he rescues his Kt by his P-sacrifice now, it takes him 5 more moves to free his Q from the defence by exchanging her.

		B × P
37	**KR—K1**	**R × R ch**
38	**R × R**	**K—R2**
39	**Q—K4**	**R—B3**
40	**Kt—Kt5**	**R—K3**
41	**Q × Q ch**	**R × Q**
42	**Kt × B**	**R × P ch**

Kt—B6 ch; 43 **K—B1, Kt × B ch** (**Kt × R ?;** 44 **K × Kt, R × P;** 45 **B × P**); 44 **K—K2, P—B6 ch;** 45 **P × P, R—K3 ch;** 46 **K—Q1, R × R ch;** 47 **K × R, Kt × P ch** is obviously inferior. As it is, Black comes out a P ahead in a Kt-and-P ending. He wins; but it is not clear that he should have done so. See moves 51 and 62.

43	**K—R1**	**R × B ch**
44	**K × R**	**Kt—B6 ch**
45	**K—Kt2**	**Kt × R ch**
46	**K—B1**	**Kt—Q6**
47	**Kt—B6**	**K—Kt3**
48	**K—K2**	**Kt—B4**
49	**K—B3**	**Kt—K3**
50	**Kt—K5 ch**	**K—B4**
51	**Kt—Q3**	

This is a natural-looking move; but at the time it was suggested that **Kt—B4** was better. From B4 the Kt would have more scope. Against the text-move Black plays what is equivalent to a waiting-move, to force White to shift his Kt again. It is a matter of very elaborate calculation.

		P—Kt3
52	**Kt—K1**	**Kt—Q5 ch**
53	**K—Kt2**	**K—K5**
54	**K—B1**	**P—B6**

White's Kt is reduced to impotence.

55	**K—Kt1**	**P—Kt4**
56	**K—R2**	**P—R4**
57	**K—Kt3**	**Kt—B4 ch**
58	**K—R2**	**P—Kt5**
59	**P × P**	**P × P**
60	**K—Kt1**	**K—Q5**
61	**Kt—B2 ch**	**K—Q6**
62	**Kt—R3 ?**	

It has been thought by some analysts that White here missed a chance of drawing by 62 **Kt—Kt4 ch.** But after **K—K7;** 63 **Kt—Q5, P—Kt6;** 64 **Kt—B4 ch, K—K8;** 65 **Kt—Kt2 ch, P × Kt;** 66 **P × P, Kt—K6;** 67 **P—Kt4,** Black plays **K—K7 !** (we have to thank Mr. H. E. Atkins for pointing out this move); 68 **P—Kt5, K—B6;** 69 **P—Kt6, Kt—B4** and wins. Anderssen, therefore, does not throw away the game at this late point. His last chance of saving it was on move 51.

		P—Kt6
63	**Kt—Kt5**	**P—Kt7**

The report of the game in *The Transactions of the B.C.A.* concludes here merely " and wins." White has none but losing moves—*e.g.*, 64 **K—R2, K—K7;** 65 **K—Kt1, K—K8;** 66 **Kt—R3** (66 **Kt—B3, Kt—Kt6**), **Kt—K6;** 67 **Kt—Kt1, Kt—Kt5;** 68 **Kt—R3, Kt × P;**

69 **Kt—B2 ch, K—Q7.** Or 64 **Kt—R3, Kt—Kt6;** 65 **P × Kt** (forced), **K—K7,** etc.

A wonderfully interesting struggle, of which the memory ill deserves the neglect that has befallen it. Anderssen's errors evidently were not so serious as they were supposed to be when the game was played. Even his 31st move, though markedly inferior to what he might have done, did not, as assumed, necessarily cost him the game. As for his 27th move, considerable doubt is thrown on the validity of the charge of loss of time. The winning of Black's QRP, properly followed up, need not have led to defeat.

GAME 4

STEINITZ v. ANDERSSEN

London, *July* 30, 1866

(Match, 8th Game)

SALVIO GAMBIT

	White.	*Black.*
	Steinitz	Anderssen
1	**P—K4**	**P—K4**
2	**P—KB4**	**P × P**
3	**Kt—KB3**	**P—KKt4**
4	**B—B4**	**P—Kt5**
5	**Kt—K5**	

The move which constitutes the *Salvio Gambit*, now given scant space in the books. Steinitz's belief in it, at this period in his career, is shown by the fact that he played it four times in the match with Anderssen, winning three games and losing the present one.

		Q—R5 ch
6	**K—B1**	

So far the play is as given by Salvio early in the Seventeenth Century, but it was not new even then. Anderssen's reply, in all four games, was 6.., **Kt—KR3,** of which Staunton wrote in *The Chess World*: "By many good players the modification of this defence known as the *Cochrane Gambit* [6.., **P—B6**] is much preferred to the *Salvio* proper." It was not until much later that the move 6.., **Kt—QB3** was shown to kill the *Salvio*.

		Kt—KR3
7	**P—Q4**	**P—Q3**

On this the Rev. W. Wayte remarked that "its inferiority was shown a hundred years ago, yet Anderssen played it every time with his eyes open." 7.., **P—B6** was the approved variation, from which Cochrane got his idea of advancing the P a move earlier.

8	**Kt—Q3**	**P—B6**
9	**P—KKt3**	**Q—K2**

In the 2nd game Anderssen had played 9.., **Q—R6 ch ?**; 10 **K—K1, Q—R4,** and was completely out-generalled.

10	**Kt—B3**	

10 **K—B2,** threatening **P—KR3,** was the usual move. Steinitz introduced a novelty with 10 **Kt—B2** in the 4th game, but preferred the text-move in this and the 10th games.

		B—K3
11	**P—Q5**	

For this he substituted 11 **B—Kt3** in the 10th game.

		B—B1
12	**P—K5 ?**	

Clearly intending the following Kt-sacrifice, which he can hardly have made on the spur of the moment, seeing that the match-score was at the time only 4-3 in his favour. The young Steinitz, however, was very different from the mature Steinitz of the "Modern School," which he founded in England.

	P × P
13 **Kt × P**	**Q × Kt**
14 **B—B4**	**Q—Kt2**

Q—R4, as suggested by Löwenthal in his comments on the match, does not threaten much.

15 **Kt—Kt5**	**B—Q3**

White has certainly a strong attack for the piece sacrificed; and, rather than play **Kt—R3,** Black offers to give up the Exchange. But after 16 **B × B, P × B;** 17 **Kt—B7 ch, K—Q1;** 18 **Kt × R, Kt—B4** Black would be the attacking party. Steinitz therefore refuses the offer.

16 **Q—K1 ch**	**K—Q1**
17 **B × B**	**P × B**
18 **Q—Kt4**	**Kt—B4**
19 **B—Q3**	**Kt—QR3**
20 **Q—R3**	**Kt—B4**
21 **B × Kt**	

White's attack has vanished, and he must make this capture. But he probably did not expect his opponent's reply.

Position after 21 **B × Kt:**

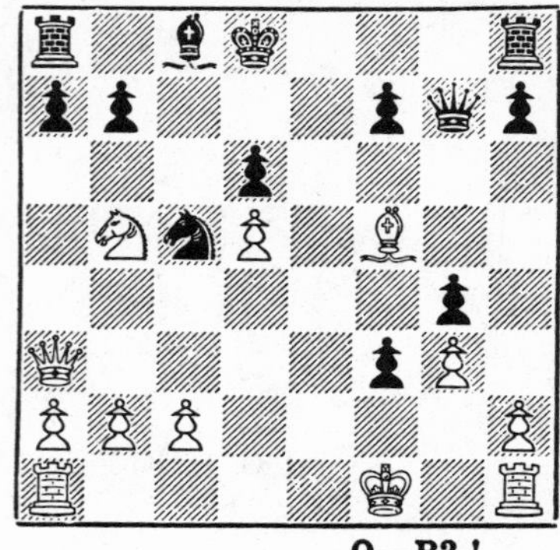

Q—R3 !

With a double menace—22.., **Q—R6 ch** (which White's reply meets, as the K would move to make room for the KR), and 22.., **Q—Q7,** which can indeed be stopped, but only to allow the other line to be fatal.

22 **B—Q3**	**R—K1**
23 **P—R4**	**Q—Q7**
24 **R—KKt1**	**R—K7 !**

White resigns.

Anderssen made the score level with this game. But his opponent, at thirty years of age, had still traces of the Steinitz of the Café Romer days in Vienna, where he had striven after "brilliancies"; and the older master was not too hard put to it to show that such ambition may lead to disaster. Nevertheless the game is interesting, if only as a period-piece.

GAME 5

ANDERSSEN v. STEINITZ

LONDON, *August* 1866

(MATCH, 13TH GAME)

RUY LOPEZ

	White.	*Black.*
	ANDERSSEN	STEINITZ
1	**P—K4**	**P—K4**
2	**Kt—KB3**	**Kt—QB3**
3	**B—Kt5**	**Kt—B3**

When he played the *Ruy Lopez* against Morphy, in their match of 1858, Anderssen had been met by the defence named after his opponent. In the one game in the match where Morphy opened with the *Ruy Lopez* Anderssen adopted the *Berlin Defence,* which he considered the best. Steinitz also shared Anderssen's view, until he championed 3.., **P—Q3** so strongly that it became known as his. Dr. Lasker has always advocated the *Berlin,* but it is nevertheless quite out of favour nowadays.

4	**P—Q3**	**P—Q3**
5	**B × Kt ch**	

It is superficially curious that while this capture is esteemed good in the *Steinitz Defence Deferred* (3 **B—Kt5, P—QR3**; 4 **B—R4, P—Q3**; 5 **B × Kt ch**), here it meets only with condemnation. But the difference is not very subtle; Black has here an extra piece developed.

5	...	**P × B**
6	**P—KR3**	

Apparently disliking the idea of his Kt being pinned. But he weakens his castling position, which turns out a most important factor in the attack for which Steinitz at once prepares.

6	...	**P—Kt3**
7	**Kt—B3**	**B—KKt2**
8	**Castles**	**Castles**
9	**B—Kt5**	**P—KR3**
10	**B—K3**	**P—B4**

Stopping the opening up of the centre by 11 **P—Q4,** which would free White's game.

11	**R—Kt1**	

The object of this and the next move appears to be to obtain an open file for the R; but White does nothing with it. A line suggested by Lasker is **Kt—K2,** followed by **P—B3** and ultimately **P—Q4,** to gain mobility.

11	...	**Kt—K1**
12	**P—QKt4**	**P × P**
13	**R × P**	**P—QB4**
14	**R—R4 ?**	

The R goes out of play. Far better was 14 **R—Kt1,** holding the open file.

14	...	**B—Q2**
15	**R—R3**	**P—B4**
16	**Q—Kt1**	**K—R1**
17	**Q—Kt7**	**P—QR4**
18	**R—Kt1**	**P—R5**

Locking in the R before proceeding with his attack with the K-side P's.

Position after 18.., **P—R5**:

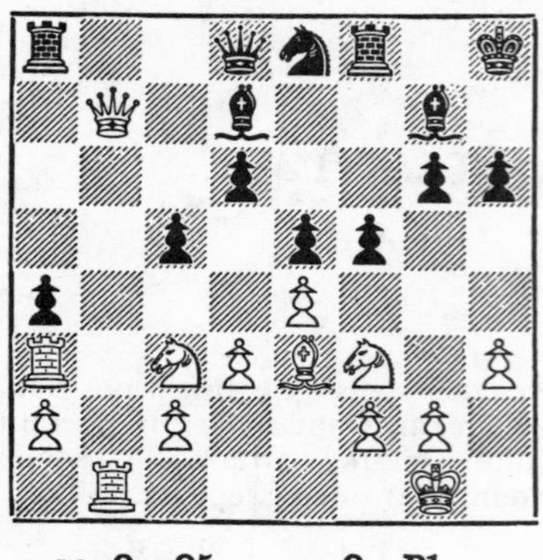

19 **Q—Q5** **Q—B1**
20 **R—Kt6**

"The imprudence of White's plan of action," remarks Staunton, "is already obvious."

R—R2
21 **K—R2** **P—KB5**
22 **B—Q2** **P—Kt4**
23 **Q—B4** **Q—Q1**
24 **R—Kt1** **Kt—B3**
25 **K—Kt1** **Kt—R2**
26 **K—B1**

White's manœuvres are forced upon him by Black's changing threats. He played 21 **K—R2** to meet the veiled attack on the KRP, and started to bring his R back from Kt7 to the defence. He played 25 **K—Kt1** to escape the menace of Black's Kt at B3; and now he runs for the centre, to make room for his Kt at Kt1—all in vain.

P—R4
27 **Kt—Kt1** **P—Kt5**
28 **P × P** **P × P**
29 **P—B3** **Q—R5**
30 **Kt—Q1** **Kt—Kt4**
31 **B—K1** **Q—R7**
32 **P—Q4**

At last, and now of course useless.

KtP × P
33 **KtP × P** **Kt—R6**
34 **B—B2** **Kt × Kt**
35 **P × BP** **Q—R6 ch**
36 **K—K1**

If 36 **K × Kt, R—KKt 1.**

Kt × P ch
37 **R × Kt** **Q × R**
38 **Kt—B3** **P × P**
39 **B × P** **R—QB2**
40 **Kt—Q5** **R × B**
41 **Q × R** **Q × P ch**
42 **K—B2** **R—B1**
43 **Kt—B7** **Q—K6 ch**

White resigns.

Commenting on this game in his *Chess Manual*, Dr. Lasker says that in the present match the germs of Steinitz's theory of play are already discernible: the transformation of small advantages that disappear into small advantages that endure, and their accumulation.

Anderssen's play in the game, however, is of a kind that facilitates the accumulation of advantages by an adversary.

GAME 6

STEINITZ v. BLACKBURNE

London, *February* 22, 1876

(Championship Match, 3rd Game)

KIESERITZKY GAMBIT

	White.	*Black.*
	Steinitz	Blackburne
1	**P—K4**	**P—K4**
2	**P—KB4**	**P × P**
3	**Kt—KB3**	**P—KKt4**
4	**P—KR4**	**P—Kt5**
5	**Kt—K5**	**Kt—KB3**
6	**B—B4**	**P—Q4**
7	**P × P**	**B—Kt2**

7.., **B—Q3**; 8 **Castles** would have led to that later invention, the *Rice Gambit*, of which Blackburne used to speak scornfully as " Tapioca "!

8	**P—Q4**	**Castles**

With 8.., **Kt—R4**; 9 **Kt—QB3, Castles**; 10 **Kt—K2** (10 **Kt—K4** is a subsequent improvement), **P—QB4**; 11 **P—B3, P × P**; 12 **P × P, Kt—Q2**; 13 **Kt × Kt, B × Kt** we have the game Steinitz-Zukertort, Vienna, 1882. The advantage there is Black's.

9	**B × P**	**Kt × P**
10	**B × Kt**	**Q × B**
11	**Castles**	**P—QB4**
12	**Kt—QB3**	

Steinitz played the *Kieseritzky* in this game partly in order to test this move, which he thought was an innovation, but afterwards found to be given in a footnote in the 5th edition of the *Handbuch*. He considered that White must win back the P sacrificed, with about an equal position.

		Q × P ch
13	**Q × Q**	**P × Q**
14	**Kt—Q5**	**Kt—B3**
15	**Kt × Kt**	**P × Kt**
16	**Kt—K7 ch**	**K—R1**
17	**Kt × P**	

White has won back the P, and Black has a scattered Q-side. But Black has the two B's; and Zukertort pronounces his game the better.

		B—Kt2
18	**Kt—K5**	**QR—B1**
19	**R—B2**	**B—K5**
20	**R—Q1**	**P—B4**
21	**Kt—Q3**	

If 21 **R × P**, there might follow **QR—K1**; 22 **R—R4, B × Kt**; 23 **R × B, P × R**; 24 **B × B ch, K—Kt1** and Black should win (Steinitz's analysis).

		KR—K1
22	**R—K2**	**K—Kt1**
23	**Kt—K1**	**K—B2**
24	**B—Kt3**	

Position after 24.., **B—Kt3**:

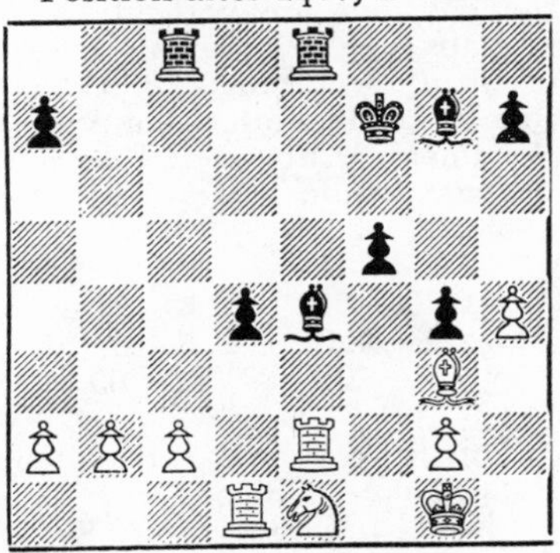

R—K3 !

Steinitz calls this "the initiation of a finely conceived scheme," which he admits he completely overlooked.

25 **B—B2**

25 **K—B1** was better, but even then Black would reply **B × BP.**

	B × BP
26 **R × R**	

Not, of course, 26 **R × B, R × Kt ch !**

	B × R
27 **R—Q6**	**K—K2 ?**

Blackburne, in evolving his scheme, had run himself short of time, and he now failed to see that by **B—K4,** threatening **P—Kt6,** he could win the Exchange for a P. Steinitz says that there was nothing better for White than (27.., **B—K4**) 28 **R × P,** when very hard work might secure a draw.

28 **R—QR6**	**R—B2**
29 **K—B1**	**R—Q2**
30 **R—R3**	**K—K3**

The game was adjourned at this point, and Steinitz claims that the positions are perfectly level, perhaps even in his favour, in spite of the P to the bad, Black's Q-side P's being scattered and weak. We imagine, however, that most players would take Black for choice.

31 **Kt—Q3**	**B—B1**
32 **R—R5**	**B—B7**
33 **K—K2**	**K—B3 ?**

This is very weak, and all but loses offhand. Blackburne is said to have anticipated 34 **K—Q2, B × Kt;** 35 **K × B,** when he could play 35.., **K—Kt3.** But the one line which his K must avoid is the long black diagonal. He can go to K2.

34 **R—R6 ch**

It is curious that Steinitz did not see at once the manœuvre which his opponent allowed him to bring off next move.

	K—Kt2 ?

Quite incomprehensible, and no doubt one of the moves which inspired the remarks about Blackburne's inferior play after the adjournment in this match (see p. 20). 34.., **K—K2** was now compulsory.

35 **R × P**	**R × R**
36 **B × P ch**	**K—B2**
37 **B × R**	**B—Q3**

The ending is not devoid of interest, though there can only be one result to it.

38 **B—K3**	**K—K3**
39 **K—Q2**	**B × Kt**

Many would be tempted to retain the two B's, in hope of a harder fight.

40 **K × B**	**K—Q4**
41 **P—R4**	**P—B5**
42 **B—B2**	**P—Kt6**
43 **B—Kt1**	**B—Kt5**
44 **K—K2**	**B—R4**
45 **K—B3**	**K—B5**
46 **K × P**	**B—B2 ch**
47 **K—Kt5**	**B—Q1 ch**
48 **K—Kt4**	**B—B2**
49 **B—K3**	**B—K4**
50 **P—QR5**	**K—Kt4**
51 **P—Kt4**	**B—Q3**
52 **B—B5**	**B—K4**

The exchange of B's would leave White with a very simple win.

53 **K—B5** **B—B6**
54 **P—R5** **K—R3**
55 **K—K6**

" And after some more moves," says the record, " Black resigned."

The game is no doubt disappointing, owing to the tremendous falling-off in the play after the adjournment. Up to that point, however, it certainly seems to deserve inclusion among championship games of the older days.

GAME 7

STEINITZ v. ZUKERTORT

New York, *January* 13, 1886

(Championship Match, 2nd Game)

SCOTCH GAME

	White.	*Black.*
	Steinitz	Zukertort
1	**P—K4**	**P—K4**
2	**Kt—KB3**	**Kt—QB3**
3	**P—Q4**	**P × P**
4	**Kt × P**	**Kt—B3**

Hoffer states in his notes to the game that this move was introduced by Dr. E. von Schmidt and was revived in a consultation game in 1876, Zukertort and Blackburne *v.* Steinitz and Potter, since when Zukertort frequently adopted it. It is still the standard line, on such rare occasions as the *Scotch* is now seen.

5	**Kt—QB3**	**B—Kt5**
6	**Kt × Kt**	**KtP × Kt**
7	**B—Q3**	

Analysts of the period preferred L. Paulsen's move 7 **Q—Q4** and, if **Q—K2**, either 8 **P—B3** or 8 **B—KKt5.** But the text-move came to stay.

P—Q4

In a game Maróczy *v.* Bogoljuboff, Dresden, 1936, there was played **P—Q3; 8 Castles, Kt—Kt5** (an innovation in place of the older **Q—K2**); 9 **P—KR3, Kt—K4.**

8	**P × P**	**P × P**
9	**Castles**	**Castles**
10	**B—KKt5**	

Hoffer pronounced this move questionable, as the B has to retire later, and suggests 10 **B—Q2.** The pin-move, however, has been favoured by many masters since Steinitz.

P—B3

The alternative **B × Kt,** though it leaves White with two B's *v.* B and Kt, has been adopted by Rubinstein, *e.g.*, against Maróczy, Carlsbad, 1929.

11 **Kt—K2**

11 **Q—B3, B—K2;** 12 **QR—K1, R—Kt1;** 13 **Kt—Q1** may be White's best line.

		B—Q3
12	**Kt—Kt3**	**P—KR3**
13	**B—Q2**	

This, said contemporary analysts, is loss of time. Having pinned, White should now play 13 **B × Kt.** If 13 **B—K3, Kt—Kt5** comes in, as in the game.

Kt—Kt5 !

Threatening, if 14 **P—KR3, Kt × P;** 15 **K × Kt, Q—R5;** 16 **Q—B3, P—KB4,** with an irresistible attack. White must therefore play as he does.

14	**B—K2**	**Q—R5**
15	**B × Kt**	**B × B**
16	**Q—B1**	

If 16 **P—KB3, B—Q2**; 17 **P—KB4, QR—K1** Black has a decided advantage in position.

B—K7

Minckwitz, in his book of the match, calls this a fine move, whereas Hoffer says it neutralises Black's positional advantage !

17 **R—K1** **B—R3**
18 **B—B3**

A palpable threat (19 **B × P**), which is easily countered. Perhaps 18 **P—KB4** is best.

P—KB4
19 **R—K6** **QR—Q1**
20 **Q—Q2** **P—Q5**
21 **B—R5**

If 21 **R × B**, then **P × B**, 22 **Q—Q1, P—B5**; 23 **Kt—K4, P—B6** is crushing.

R—Q2
22 **R × B** **R × R**
23 **B—Kt4** **Q—B3**

This is a mistake, of which White fails to take advantage. **QR—B3** was correct.

24 **R—Q1**

A counter-error. 24 **Kt × P, R—Q2**; 25 **B × R, Q × Kt !**; 26 **B—R3** would have left White a P ahead, though with little prospect of more than a draw.

R—Q4
25 **B × R** **Q × B**
26 **Kt—R5**

Steinitz was growing short of time, and this and the succeeding move look natural; but the result is that Black improves his position. 26 **P—KB4** has its points, but opens a dangerous diagonal for the Black Q.

Q—K1
27 **Kt—B4** **R—K4**
28 **P—KR4** **P—B4**
29 **P—R5**

29 **P—QKt4** was a move suggested, with a view to isolating the QP. The complications then arising, however, from 29.., **P—Kt4** are not easy to work out under a time-limit, asserting itself urgently at this moment.

R—K5

Position after 29.., **R—K5** :

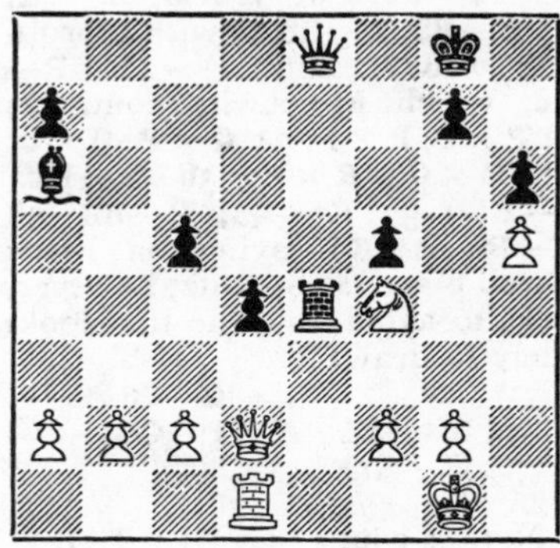

30 **P—QB3**

This was Steinitz's last move before his second hour expired, and the decision to be made was a hard one, both **P—KKt3** and **P—QKt3** (no longer **P—QKt4**) being plausible alternatives. Possibly **P—KKt3** was best, to forestall 30.., **Q—K4**.

Q—Kt1

Zukertort was not much better off as regards his clock, or he might have preferred **Q—K4,** and if 31 **Kt—Q3, Q—Q3**, where Schallopp gives the continuation 32 **P—B3, R—K6**; 33 **Kt—B2, R × KBP**; 34 **P × R, Q—Kt6 ch**; 35 **K—R1, B—Kt2**—and leaves it. White has only 36 **Kt—K4**, whereafter **Q × P ch** appears conclusive.

31 **P—KKt3**

If now 31 **Kt—Q3, R—R5;** 32 **P—KKt3, R × P;** 33 **Kt × P, Q—R1.**

Q—K4

32 **Kt—Kt6**

Against 32 **P—B3** Black had two possible lines: (1) 32.., **R—K7,** commended by Hoffer, who gives the continuation 33 **Kt × R, B × Kt;** 34 **P—KB4, Q—K5;** 35 **R—K1, P—Q6;** 36 **R × B, P × R;** 37 **K—B2, Q—R8,** "with a probable draw"; and (2) 32.., **R—K6,** which Minckwitz continues 33 **P × P, P × P;** 34 **Q × P, Q × Q;** 35 **R × Q, R × P;** 36 **K—Kt2, B—Kt2;** 37 **Kt—Q5; R—K6;** 38 **K—B2, R—K4,** saying that Black is well placed. Steinitz, however, seeks to avoid any line that looks likely to draw.

	Q—Q3
33 **Kt—B4**	**P—Q6**
34 **P—Kt3**	

Not, of course, 35 **Kt × P, B × Kt;** 36 **Q × B, R—K8 ch.**

	P—B5
35 **R—Kt1**	**K—R2**
36 **K—R2 ?**	

Steinitz himself later said that 36 **K—Kt2** was his right move. Hoffer suggests 36 **P × P,** and Minckwitz 36 **R—Kt2,** followed by **P × P.** The text-move is a singularly unfortunate choice, creating a weakness on KB2, of which Black at once takes advantage.

Q—QKt3

Threatening (if, *e.g.*, 37 **P—QKt4**) **R—K7 !;** 38 **Kt × R, Q × P ch** etc. So White must undo his last move.

37 **K—Kt1**	**B—Kt2**
38 **R—Kt2**	**Q—QB3**
39 **P—B3**	

Forced, to cut off Black's Q from Kt7 and R8.

Q—B4 ch.

40 **Q—B2**

If 40 **K—Kt2, R—K6,** while **40 K—R2** leads to a mate by **R—K7 ch;** 41 **Kt × R, Q—B7 ch;** 42 **K—R3, Q—B8 ch;** 43 **K—R2, Q × P** etc.

R—K8 ch

41 **K—R2 ?**

This allows Zukertort to finish elegantly. It is indeed difficult to understand why Steinitz twice within six moves prefers **K—R2** to **K—Kt2.** With 41 **K—Kt2** here his game does not appear lost. The obvious rejoinder is 41.., **R—K6,** and White's natural continuation is 42 **Kt—K6.** Perhaps Steinitz feared now 42.., **B × P ch;** but Minckwitz, not hampered by analysing under a time-limit, works this out in favour of White: 43 **Q × B, R × Kt;** 44 **P × P, R—K6;** 45 **Q—Q5, Q—B2** (if **R—K7 ch,** then 46 **R × R, P × R;** 47 **Q × Q, P—K8=Q;** 48 **Q × P ch**); 46 **Q × P ch, K—Kt1;** 47 **Q—Kt6; Q—K4;** 48 **R—Kt5, Q—B2** 49 **R—Q5** and wins. What tells against Black is the weakness of his KBP. But clearly there are numerous alternative lines for Black. For instance, at the outset, he may play, instead of 41.., **R—K6,** 41.., **Q × Q ch.** After 42 **R × Q, R—QB8;** 43 **P × P, R × P,** who will claim that the position is in White's favour ? The threat 44 **R—Kt2,** to be followed by **R—Kt 8** and **Kt—Kt6,** is easily parried.

	Q × Q ch
42 **R × Q**	**B × P ! !**
43 **P—KKt4**	

If 43 **R × B,** then **P—Q7** and the P queens. And after 43 **Kt—Kt2, B × Kt;** 44 **K × B, P × P;**

45 **P × P, R—QB8**; 46 **P—B4, R—B7**; 47 **K—B1, P—Q7**; 48 **K—K2, P—Q8=Q ch** etc. The text-move is sheer desperation, and Black disregards it.

		B—K7
44	**Kt—Kt2**	**P—Q7**
45	**Kt—K3**	**P × P**
46	**P × P**	**B × P**

White resigns.

A most interesting game and, despite the errors on both sides, a fine example of championship chess. The influence of the clock is very apparent, especially in the case of Steinitz.

Times: Steinitz 3 hr. 20 min.; Zukertort, 2 hr. 36 min.

GAME 8

ZUKERTORT v. STEINITZ

St. Louis, *February* 5, 1886

(Championship Match, 7th Game)

QUEEN'S GAMBIT DECLINED

	White.	*Black.*
	Zukertort	Steinitz
1	**P—Q4**	**P—Q4**
2	**P—QB4**	**P—K3**

In the 1st, 3rd and 5th games Steinitz played **P—QB3** (nowadays known as the *Slav Defence*, and immensely popular among masters), followed by **B—B4**—in the 5th game with the interposition of 3.., **Kt—B3.** Hoffer wrote of 2.., **P—QB3** that it was "not considered in accordance with the recognised defence in the opening."

3	**Kt—QB3**	**Kt—KB3**
4	**P—K3**	

Not until the 15th game of the match did Zukertort play 4 **B—Kt5,** the attack of which Pillsbury was later to demonstrate the force, and to which his name was given. He tried it again in the 17th game (see Game 10) and in the 19th.

P—B4

Now we have a variation of the *Tarrasch Defence*, though it was not so called in 1886. Hoffer speaks of the move as "a side-path from the beaten track" in place of 4.., **B—K2,** followed by the Q's fianchetto.

5	**Kt—B3**	**Kt—B3**
6	**P—QR3**	

The same critic disapproves of this as giving up the advantage of the first move.

White, he says, could have played 6 **QP × P, B × P;** 7 **P × P,** leaving Black an isolated P, whereas he now remains with an isolated P himself. But it is possible to attach too much importance to the presence of an isolated P. For Black in the *Tarrasch Defence*, for instance, such a P may be, as Maróczy has observed, either very weak or very strong.

		QP × P
7	**B × P**	**P × P**
8	**P × P**	**B—K2**
9	**Castles**	**Castles**
10	**B—K3**	**B—Q2**
11	**Q—Q3**	

With 11 **P—Q5** Zukertort could have got rid of his isolated P, and after **P × P;** 12 **Kt × P, Kt × Kt;** 13 **B × Kt** he would have had a level game. But he was not a player (nor, to do him justice, was Steinitz) who was contented with variations seeming to promise mere equality. The question is whether he could hope for more out of the position.

		R—B1
12	**QR—B1**	**Q—R4**
13	**B—R2**	

White could still play **P—Q5,** if he suspected his opponent of wishing to transfer his Q to the K-side.

But Steinitz's idea was rather an attack on the isolated P—which rendered it all the more advisable for White to get rid of it.

KR—Q1

14 **KR—K1**

This R is not doing much here, and would be better at Q1; see move 17.

B—K1

15 **B—Kt1**

It is easy to mistake the time when one has the attack; and Zukertort appears to labour under that impression now. His centre, however, is compromised beyond recovery, so he makes a demonstration against the hostile K-side. Unfortunately it only leads to a strengthening of Black's position.

P—KKt3

16 **Q—K2** **B—B1**

17 **KR—Q1** **B—Kt2**

All has fitted in beautifully for Black, another piece now bearing on the isolated P.

18 **B—R2**

Moves 14 and 17, and 15 and 18 have been two serious losses of tempo for White; and he could not afford them.

Kt—K2

19 **Q—Q2**

More natural seems 19 **R—Q2**, with a view to doubling R's on the Q-file; and the Q here is confronted by a Black R.

Q—R3

This alone of Black's moves lacks adequate explanation, unless it was to avoid 20 **Kt—K4**, **Q × Q**; 21 **Kt × Kt ch**, **B × Kt**; 22 **B × Q.** But 19.., **Q—R4** (the move which the " gallery " of the day expected) would equally have avoided that.

20 **B—Kt5** **Kt—B4**

21 **P—KKt4 ?**

Had White played 20 **P—R3**, instead of his actual move, this would now have been good. As it is, Black refutes it with a temporary sacrifice, which he immediately recovers, and is left with a much superior game. White's proper course, according to Dr. Lasker (*Chess Manual*), was 21 **Q—K1**, in order to try for **P—Q5.**

Position after 21 **P—KKt4 :**

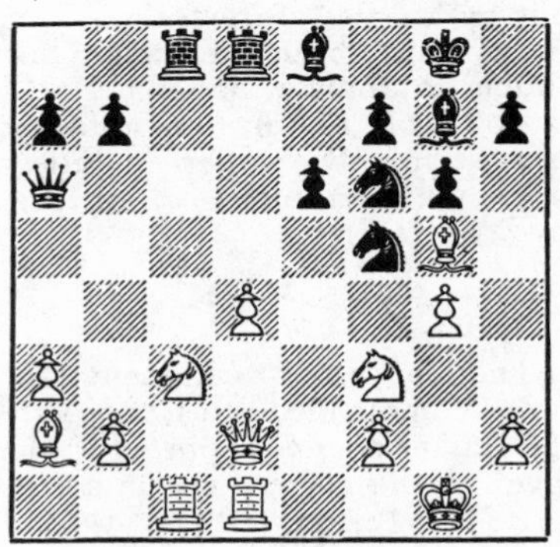

QKt × P !

This is certainly spectacular, and was successful. But it did not force an absolute win; see next note.

22 **Kt × Kt** **P—K4**

23 **Kt—Q5**

This leads to wholesale exchanges and simplification in Black's favour. Comparatively better is 23 **Q—K2, P × Kt;**

24 **Q × Q, P × Q;** 25 **Kt—Q5, R × R;** 26 **R × R.** But Black then has a very strong, though isolated, passed P.

	R × R
24 **Q × R**	

Or 24 **Kt × Kt ch, B × Kt;** 24 **Q × R, P × Kt,** which is still better for Black.

	P × Kt
25 **R × P**	**Kt × Kt**
26 **R × Kt**	

If 26 **B × R, B × R;** 27 **B × Kt, Q—K7** comes in with deadly effect.

	R × R
27 **B × R**	**Q—K7**

Simplification has been carried out by a series of moves which it must have been anything but simple to analyse, and Black's Q is now able to turn to profit by her seemingly rather pointless manœuvre on move 19—helped by White's 21st

28 **P—R3**	**P—KR3**

Though other commentators have commended this as best, Dr. Lasker does not approve. He gives as the correct continuation 28.., **B × P;** 29 **Q—B5, Q—Q8 ch;** 30 **K—R2, B—K4 ch;** 31 **K—Kt2, Q × B ch;** 32 **Q × Q, B—B3** " and wins methodically by means of his P plus." Now Minckwitz in 1886 had considered 28.., **B × P,** but judged it much inferior to Steinitz's actual move, on account of the answer 29 **Q—B8**—taking the analysis no further. The position is by no means clear. After 29 **Q—B8, Q—Q8 ch;** 30 **K—R2, B—K4 ch;** 31 **P—B4,** Black has to proceed with care. But by 31.., **Q—Q7 ch;** 32 **B—Kt2** (anything else is worse), **B × P ch;** 33 **B × B, Q × QB ch;** 34 **K—R1, Q—K6** Black has an ending to be won eventually.

29 **B—QB4 ?**

If 29 **QB × P, B × B;** 30 **Q × B,** of course **Q—Q8 ch,** winning a piece. If 29 **Q—Q2, Q × Q;** 30 **B × Q, B × P;** 31 **B × KtP, B × P;** 32 **B—R6, B—B4** (Black must guard his passed P); 33 **B × P, P—B3;** 34 **B—Q2,** Black has his passed P still, it is true, but with all four B's on the board it is hardly possible to demonstrate how he is to go about a win. In his notes Lasker gives 29 **B—K3** as White's correct move, not carrying the matter further. There might follow 29.., **B × P;** 30 **Q—Kt1 !, K—Kt2** (31 **Q × P ch** is threatened); 31 **B × KtP.** Or 29.., **Q—Kt4;** 30 **Q—B8, B × P;** 31 **B × KtP, B × P;** 32 **B × QRP**—in either case with a draw. The text-move loses.

	Q—B6
30 **Q—K3**	**Q—Q8 ch**
31 **K—R2**	

If 31 **B—B1, B—Kt4.**

	B—QB3
32 **B—K7**	

Now there is no resource. If 32 **B × P, B × B;** 33 **Q × B,** then **Q—R8 ch;** 34 **K—Kt3, Q—Kt8 ch,** and whichever way White moves Black wins the Q.

	B—K4 ch
33 **P—B4**	

33 **Q × B, Q—R8 ch;** 34 **K—Kt3, Q—Kt7 ch;** 34 **K—R4, Q × BP ch;** 35 **Q—Kt3, P—Kt4 ch** etc.

	B × P ch
34 **Q × B**	**Q—R8 ch**
35 **K—Kt3**	**Q—Kt8 ch**

White resigns.

As before, if 35 **K—R4,** Q checks (at K8 this time), and White's Q is lost.

A pretty finish. But the fact that White, after indifferent and time-losing moves, still apparently on his 29th move had a chance of saving the game, argues that Black must somewhere have failed to make the most of his position; and only his 28th move seems to provide the clue.

Times: Zukertort, 2 hr. 5 min.; Steinitz, 2 hr. 10 min.

GAME 9

ZUKERTORT v. STEINITZ

St. Louis, *February* 10, 1886

(Championship Match, 9th Game)

QUEEN'S GAMBIT DECLINED

	White.	*Black.*
	Zukertort	Steinitz
1	**P—Q4**	**P—Q4**
2	**P—QB4**	**P—K3**
3	**Kt—QB3**	**Kt—KB3**
4	**Kt—B3**	

Varying from the 4 **P—K3** of the 7th game; and Black sees to it that there is no mere transposition of moves, by a deferred acceptance of the Gambit, which is more common in modern days than it was in 1886, though usually after 2.., **P—QB3**, not **P—K3**.

P × P

5 **P—K3**

Did Zukertort, one may wonder, give much consideration to the 5 **Q—R4 ch** of Reshevsky-Fine at Nottingham, 1936?

P—B4

The move that has long been commended as productive of equality in the opening.

6	**B × P**	**P × P**
7	**P × P**	

Undeterred by what happened in the 7th game, Zukertort again allows himself to have an isolated P on the Q-file, though here he could easily have avoided it by 7 **Q × P.** But he still less than in the 7th game desires opening simplifications. He was now only one game ahead in the score.

		B—K2
8	**Castles**	**Castles**
9	**Q—K2**	**QKt—Q2**
10	**B—Kt3**	

This early decision in favour of Kt3, not Q3, before the B is attacked, does not please Hoffer. It is always a moot point.

		Kt—Kt3
11	**B—KB4**	**QKt—Q4**
12	**B—Kt3**	**Q—R4**

Again preparing pressure on the isolated P.

13	**QR—B1**	**B—Q2**
14	**Kt—K5**	**KR—Q1**
15	**Q—B3**	

15 **P—B4** would have given more scope to the QB, as Hoffer remarks. But Zukertort had an idea where he wanted his QB.

B—K1

16 **B—KR4**

Threatening 17 **Kt × Kt, Kt × Kt;** 18 **B × Kt, B × B;** 19 **B × KtP, QR—Kt1;** 18 **B—B6 !,** winning a P. Black must therefore exchange Kts first, which relieves the isolation of White's QP.

		Kt × Kt
17	**P × Kt**	**Q—B2**
18	**KR—K1**	**QR—B1**
19	**Q—Q3**	

He must guard against 19.., **R × P.** It is only questionable which was the best way to do so. He had numerous choices—*e.g.*, **R—B2, B—B2,** and **B—Kt3.**

The last (and if 19.., **B—Q3**, 20 **P—B4**) looks best. But the text-move is not bad, if properly followed up.

Kt—Q4

20 **B × B**

Here comes another important question. Without setting undue store by what an eminent American player used to call "the double-Bishop racket," we may ask why this useful weapon should be given up voluntarily. In two moves White now exchanges off both his B's, when he need not lose either. By 20 **B—Kt3** he could keep both, and Black dare not answer 20.., **Kt × P**, for obvious reasons.

Q × B

21 **B × Kt** **R × B**
22 **P—QB4**

It is desirable, no doubt, to dislodge the Black R before it becomes established by **P—QKt4**; but White gives himself "hanging P's," and is in consequence practically forced to make a desperate diversion.

KR—Q1

23 **R—K3** **Q—Q3**
24 **R—Q1** **P—B3**

Position after 24.., **P—B3**:

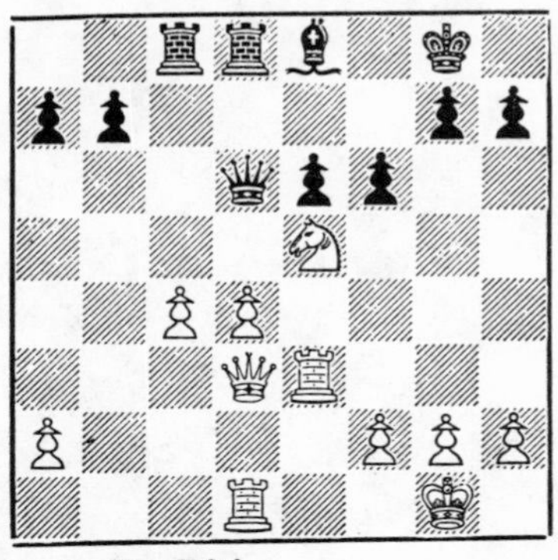

25 **R—R3 !**

An offer of a Kt, which Steinitz, being as usual short of time, declines. In any case he was wise—*e.g.*, 25.., **P × Kt**; 26 **Q × P ch, K—B1**; 27 **R—KKt3** (27 **R—B3 ch, B—B2**; 28 **Q—R8 ch, K—K2**; 29 **Q × P, R—B1**; 30 **P—KR4** could be met with **P—K5,** when Black should be able to extricate himself with his piece ahead), **R—Q2**; 28 **Q—R8 ch, K—K2**; 29 **Q—R4 ch, K—B2**; 30 **Q—R7,** and Black cannot escape the draw. If (instead of 27.., **R—Q2**) 27.., **R—B2,** then 28 **Q—R8 ch, K—K2**; 29 **R × P ch, B—B2**; 30 **Q—R4 ch** (better than 30 **Q—R5, R—KB1**), and again Black cannot escape the draw. Lastly, if 27.., **B—B2,** then 28 **R × P, R—B2**; 29 **Q—R8 ch, K—K2**; 30 **Q—R4 ch,** the variation being now the same as the preceding. This analysis is mainly Schallopp's, and seems to show that by taking the Kt Black could just manage to draw.

Unfortunately for Zukertort, when his offer is refused his diversion on the K-side fails, and his hanging P's become an anxiety again.

P—KR3

26 **Kt—Kt4** **Q—B5**
27 **Kt—K3** **B—R5 !**

A clever sequel to his previous move, driving the R off the first rank, as it must continue to protect the QP; and the vacation of the first rank prevents him freeing his position on move 30.

28 **R—B3** **Q—Q3**
29 **R—Q2** **B—B3**
30 **R—Kt3**

He cannot play 30 **P—Q5,** for then **P × P**; 31 **P × P, B × P,** threatening mate on the rank if 32 **Kt × B.** But, in view of Black's next move, 30 **R—R3** was much better.

	P—B4
31 **R—Kt6**	**B—K5**
32 **Q—Kt3**	**K—R2**
33 **P—B5**	

The R is trapped, so White must counter at all costs.

	R × P
34 **R × P**	

If 34 **Q × KP, Q × Q;** 35 **R × Q, R—B8 ch,** and whichever way White covers disaster follows, Black having a terrible threat of **B—Q4.**

	R—B8 ch
35 **Kt—Q1**	

35 **Kt—B1, Q—B5;** 36 **R—Q1, Q—Kt5;** 37 **P—B3** would be answered simply by **B × P.**

	Q—B5
36 **Q—Kt2**	

Or 36 **Q—K3, Q × Q;** 37 **P × Q, B—B7.**

	R—Kt8
37 **Q—B3**	**R—QB1**
38 **R × B**	

Of course he cannot play 38 **Q × R, Q × R.** But neither does the text-move prolong the game.

	Q × R

White resigns.

The influence of White's weakness on his first rank is very marked in this ending, which Steinitz plays in his most incisive style.

Times: Zukertort, 1 hr. 55 min.; Steinitz, 2 hr. 12 min.

GAME 10

ZUKERTORT v. STEINITZ

New Orleans, *March* 19, 1886

(Championship Match, 17th Game)

QUEEN'S GAMBIT DECLINED

White.	*Black.*
Zukertort	Steinitz
1 **P—Q4**	**P—Q4**
2 **P—QB4**	**P—K3**
3 **Kt—QB3**	**Kt—KB3**
4 **B—Kt5**	

The *Pillsbury Attack*, as it came later to be called. It was the line chosen by Zukertort in the 15th game, which was drawn in 49 moves.

B—K2

In the 15th game Steinitz played the inferior **P—B4,** with the continuation 5 **BP × P, KP × P;** 6 **B × Kt, P × B;** 7 **P—K3, B—K3;** 8 **Q—Kt3, Q—Q2;** 9 **B—Kt5, Kt—B3**—a somewhat bizarre opening.

5 **Kt—B3**	**Castles**
6 **P—K3**	

In the 19th game of the match Zukertort (by then a shattered man) played 6 **P—B5 ?**, and after **P—QKt3;** 7 **P—QKt4, P × P;** 8 **QP × P, P—QR4;** 9 **P—QR3, P—Q5** Steinitz had a speedy victory.

P × P

In this variation this capture is not in harmony with modern ideas, as helping White's development. Nor, for that matter, was it approved at the time of the match, when the commentators generally gave **P—QKt3** as best.

7 **B × P**	**QKt—Q2**
8 **Castles**	**P—B4 ?**

It is strange how Steinitz mismanages the opening in this game. In the cramped position of his pieces it was clearly not the right policy for him to open the Q-file for a White R, which is the effect of this move. It also makes the manœuvre at move 10 loss of time.

9 **Q—K2**	**P—KR3**
10 **B—R4**	**Kt—Kt3 ?**

Hoffer in *The Field* suggests 10.., **P × P,** followed by 11.., **Kt—Kt3,** as at least diminishing Black's disadvantage.

11 **P × P**	**B × P**
12 **KR—Q1**	**QKt—Q2**

Black has little option, as if **B—Q2,** then 13 **B—QKt5** (**B × B;** 14 **Q × B, Q—B2;** 15 **B × Kt, P × B;** 16 **Kt—K4**). Other moves are worse. White has now a very superior position, and maintains the pressure well for another 15 moves, and indeed beyond.

13 **P—K4**	**B—K2**
14 **P—K5**	**Kt—K1**
15 **B—KKt3**	**Q—Kt3**
16 **P—QR3**	**P—QR4**
17 **QR—B1**	**Kt—B4**
18 **B—B4**	

A good alternative to this transfer of the B to K3 is 18 **Kt—Q4,** followed by **P—B4.** It is interesting to watch how Zukertort proposed to take advantage of his positional superiority.

		B—Q2
19	**B—K3**	**B—QB3**
20	**Kt—Q4**	**R—Q1**
21	**KKt—Kt5**	

One might have expected the initiation of K-side attack here by 21 **P—B4;** but White has concentrated for operations on the other wing and now threatens 22 **Kt—R4,** winning a piece.

		R × R ch
22	**R × R**	**B × Kt**
23	**Kt × B**	**Q—B3**

The loss of a piece was still threatened by 24 **P—QKt4**—a move which in any case is coming.

24	**P—QKt4**	**P × P**
25	**P × P**	**Kt—Q2 ?**

This move should have lost an already seriously compromised game. **Kt—R3** was the only salvation.

Position after 25.., **Kt—Q2 :**

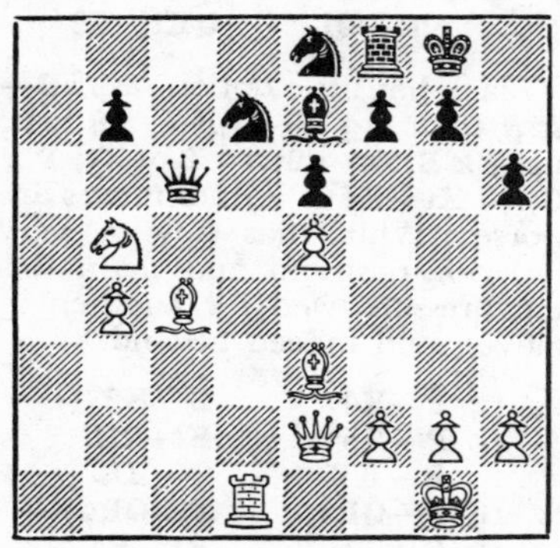

26 **Kt—Q4 !**

Winning, as the game actually went, the Exchange for a P; but it should have been the Exchange without compensation.

Q—K5

If 26.., **Q—B1** (a move which would have been playable after 25.., **Kt—R3**), then 27 **R—QB1** with the threat of 28 **Kt × P** etc. 27.., **Kt—B2** is unavailing without the support of the other Kt, and any move of the Q still leaves the same threat on. It is really astonishing that Steinitz managed to save this game.

27	**Kt × P**	**Kt × P**
28	**Kt × R ?**	

White is too eager to win the Exchange. He should first have played 28 **B—Q5,** and if **Q × P;** 29 **Kt × R, B × Kt** he can continue with 30 **QB × P, P × B;** 31 **Q × Kt,** with the clear Exchange to the good.

		Kt × B
29	**Kt—Q7**	**B × P**
30	**Q—Q3**	

Hoffer gives 30 **R—Q4** as decisive, "forcing the exchange of Q's, when it is more than probable that Black's QKtP would fall." Black would indeed have no choice but 30.., **Q—Kt8 ch;** 31 **Q—Q1, Q × Q ch;** 32 **R × Q,** in order to prevent the loss of a piece.

		Q—Kt5
31	**P—R3**	**Q—K3**
32	**R—Kt1**	**Kt × B**
33	**Q × Kt ?**	

White here misses a fairly sure win. 33 **R × B** would leave Black the task of extricating his Kt from K6. If **Kt—Q4,** then 34 **R × P, Q—QB3;** 35 **Q—Kt1.** Or 34.., **Q—K8 ch;** 35 **Q—B1.** As Zukertort was not short of time (see times below) we may suppose that it was match-strain which caused him to err. The present game contributed not a little to his breakdown; or perhaps it should be said that his play in it was symptomatic of the coming breakdown.

		Q × Kt
34	**R × B**	**Q—Q8 ch**
35	**K—R2**	**Q—Q3 ch**
36	**Q—B4**	

"Obviously," comments Hoffer, "the only chance to try for a win is 36 **R—B4,** followed by 37 **P—Kt3.**" But what *winning* chance can there be after 36 **R—B4, P—KKt4;** 37 **P—Kt3, P × R;** 38 **Q × Kt ch, K—Kt2 ?** The win is present no more, though a fight remains.

		K—B1
37	**Q × Q ch**	**Kt × Q**
38	**K—Kt3**	

38 **R—Kt6** would of course accomplish nothing. The Black K comes up to the Kt in any case.

		K—K2
39	**K—B4**	**K—K3**
40	**P—R4**	**K—Q4**
41	**P—Kt4**	**P—QKt4**
42	**R—Kt1**	**K—B4**
43	**R—B1 ch**	**K—Q4**
44	**K—K3**	**Kt—B5 ch**
45	**K—K2**	**P—Kt5**
46	**R—QKt1**	**K—B4**
47	**P—B4**	**Kt—R6**
48	**R—B1 ch**	**K—Q5**
49	**R—B7**	**P—Kt6**
50	**R—Kt7**	**K—B6**
51	**R—B7 ch**	**K—Q5**

He dare not risk 51 . ., **K—Kt7;** 52 **R × P, K—R2,** for then 53 **R × P, P—Kt7;** 54 **R—Kt7, P—Kt8=Q;** 55 **R × Q, Kt × R;** 56 **P—R5 !**

52	**R—Kt7**

Draw agreed.

Despite Steinitz's poor play in the opening and Zukertort's lapses later, the game is well worth study. Of the 5 drawn games in the match it is the most interesting.

Times: Zukertort 1 hr. 35 min.; Steinitz 2 hr. 35 min.

After this game Zukertort lost the 18th in 40 moves, the 19th in 29, and the 20th and last in 19.

GAME 11

STEINITZ v. TCHIGORIN

HAVANA, *January* 22, 1889

(CHAMPIONSHIP [FIRST] MATCH, 2ND GAME)

QUEEN'S PAWN GAME

	White.	*Black.*
	STEINITZ	TCHIGORIN
1	**Kt—KB3**	**P—Q4**
2	**P—Q4**	**B—Kt5**

This game was headed *Irregular Opening* at the time when it was played. The text-move had been played before by St. Petersburg (represented by Tchigorin and Schiffers) in the correspondence match with the British Chess Club in 1886-7.

3 **Kt—K5**

As played in the correspondence match, on Bird's advice, though Hoffer and D. Y. Mills would have preferred 3 **QKt—Q2** or even 3 **P—K3.**

B—R4

4 **Q—Q3**

The British Chess Club continued boldly 4 **P—KKt4, B—Kt3;** 5 **P—KR4,** and ultimately lost.

Q—B1

Thwarting White's plan of 5 **Q—KR3,** followed by a K-side advance, and so making **Q—Q3** a wasted move; see move 8.

5	**P—QB4**	**P—KB3**
6	**Kt—KB3**	**P—K3**
7	**Kt—B3**	**B—Kt3**
8	**Q—Q1**	**P—B3**
9	**P—K3**	**B—Q3**
10	**B—Q2**	**Kt—K2**
11	**R—B1**	**Kt—Q2**

This looks as if it were intended to facilitate **P—K4.**

12	**Kt—KR4**	**P—KB4**

But this is not in harmony with a central advance, and provokes a reply which Hoffer calls "unusually bold for Mr. Steinitz." Steinitz, however, could be bold enough when he chose.

13	**P—KKt4**	**Kt—B3**
14	**P—KR3**	**Kt—K5**
15	**B—Q3**	**BP × P ?**

The result of this is a loss of a P. Black can hardly have expected to get 15 **RP × P ?, Kt × P !** 15.., **B—KB2** seems to be his best move in the circumstances. Now his position goes from bad to worse.

16	**Kt × B**	**Kt(K2) × Kt**
17	**B × Kt**	**P × B**
18	**Kt × P**	**B—K2**
19	**P × P**	**P—K4**
20	**P—Q5**	**Q—Q2**
21	**B—B3**	**R—Q1**
22	**R—R5 !**	**P × P**
23	**P × P**	

Position after 23 **P × P**:

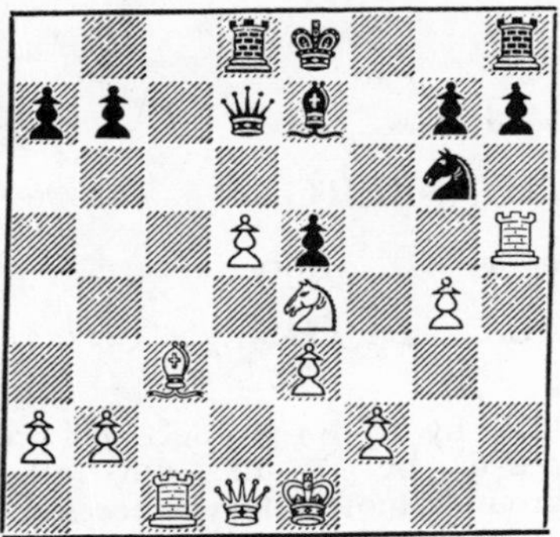

Castles

Not **Q × QP,** for then 24 **Q × Q, R × Q;** 25 **P—B4.** The problem presented by White's QP is insoluble for Black.

24 **P—Q6 !** **Q—K3**

If **B × P,** then would follow 25 **Q—Kt3 ch, Q—B2** (otherwise 26 **R—Q1** would be very unpleasant); 26 **Kt × B, Q × Q;** 27 **P × Q, R × Kt;** 28 **B—Kt4** etc. Or 26.., **R × Kt;** 27 **B—Kt4.** Black, however, has an alternative (suggested to Hoffer by Dr. Carl Schmid, of Dresden) 24.., **Kt—R5,** and if 25 **Q—Kt3 ch, K—R1;** 26 **P × B, Kt—B6 ch;** 27 **K—B1, Q—Q6 ch;** 28 **K—Kt2, Q × Kt.** White would do better to turn this by 25 **P × B** and only if **Q × KP;** 26 **Q—Kt3 ch.**

25	**Q—Kt3**	**Q × Q**
26	**P × Q**	**B × P ?**

Now this costs Black the Exchange. 26.., **B—R5** would have set White a much more difficult task, as 27 **B × P** would be premature. Probably 27 **K—K2** would be best.

27	**Kt × B**	**R × Kt**
28	**B—Kt4**	**R—Kt3**
29	**B × R**	**K × B**
30	**R—B8 ch**	**K—B2**
31	**R—B7 ch**	**K—B3**
32	**R—B5 ch**	**K—K3**
33	**R(B5)—B7**	

White has a comparatively simple ending to play, but does not wish, of course, to lose both his QKtP's, which would follow if he now continued 33 **R × KKtP.**

		R—Kt5
34	**R × QKtP**	**R × KKtP**
35	**R × KtP**	**R—Kt4**
36	**R × KRP**	**K—B4**
37	**P—B3**	**R—Kt7**
38	**R—R6**	**Resigns**

The struggle is clearly hopeless.

GAME 12

STEINITZ v. GUNSBERG

New York, *December* 18, 1890

(Championship Match, 5th Game)

QUEEN'S GAMBIT ACCEPTED

	White.	*Black.*
	Steinitz	Gunsberg
1	**P—Q4**	**P—Q4**
2	**P—QB4**	**P × P**

Gunsberg was partial to the acceptance of the *Queen's Gambit* at this period, though only doing so twice in the present match. On White's reply see the following game.

3	**P—K3**	**P—K4**

" Quite in the old style," comments Steinitz, " as played already by Labourdonnais and M'Donnell." But in their days the answer was always 4 **B × P.**

4	**P × P**	**Q × Q ch**
5	**K × Q**	**Kt—QB3**
6	**B × P**	**Kt × P**
7	**B—Kt5 ch**	

Steinitz says that his object was to stop the retreat **Kt—QB3,** but that 7 **B—K2** was probably better.

		P—B3
8	**B—K2**	**B—K3**
9	**Kt—QB3**	**Castles ch**
10	**K—B2**	**Kt—B3**
11	**Kt—B3**	

It is strange to see Steinitz delaying the liberation of his QB, by **P—K4** at once or preceded by **P—B3.** On other grounds, too, **P—K4** was necessary.

		QKt—Kt5
12	**R—B1**	**B—B4 ch**
13	**K—Kt3**	**Kt—Q2**

This is called by Steinitz a very fine move, forcing the gain of a P. White now plays **P—K4** in vain.

14	**P—K4**	**Kt—B4 ch**
15	**K—B2**	**Kt(B4) × P**
16	**Kt—KR4**	**Kt× Kt dis. ch**
17	**K × Kt**	**B—K3**
18	**P—B4**	**Kt—B3**
19	**P—B5**	**B—Q4**
20	**P—KKt4 ?**	

The Kt should return to KB3, as Black's next move shows.

		B—K2
21	**K—B2**	**B—K5 ch**
22	**K—Kt3**	**Kt—Q2**

Black repeats the manœuvre of his 13th move.

23	**P—Kt5**	**P—B3**
24	**B—Kt4 ?**	

Still refusing to develop his QB. But his game is in any case hopeless. His K-side attack is illusory.

		Kt—B4 ch
25	**K—R3**	

Position after 25 **K—R3:**

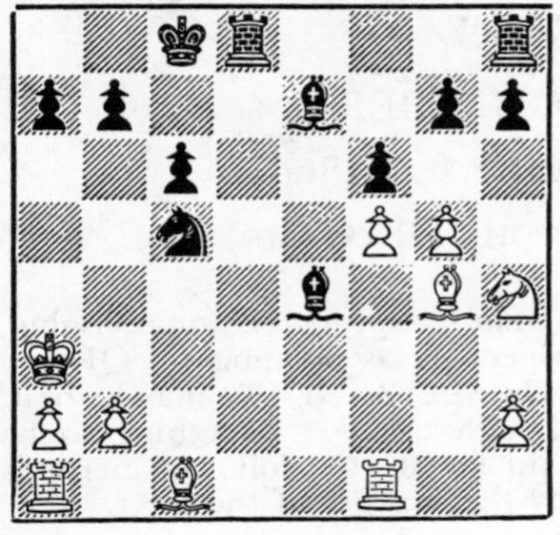

	R—Q6 ch
26 **P—Kt3**	**Kt—R5 dis.ch**
27 **K × Kt**	**R—Q5 ch**
28 **P—Kt4**	**R × P ch**

White resigns.

For whichever way the K moves mate in 2 follows. As an example of Steinitz's chess this game is, of course, entirely unworthy. But it is a good example of Gunsberg's skill when his opponent gave him the chance to show it.

GAME 13

STEINITZ v. GUNSBERG

New York, *December* 22, 1890

(Championship Match, 7th Game)

QUEEN'S GAMBIT ACCEPTED

	White.	*Black.*
	Steinitz	Gunsberg
1	**P—Q4**	**P—Q4**
2	**P—QB4**	**P × P**
3	**Kt—KB3**	

This time Steinitz plays the best move for White; practically the only move ever adopted in these days of a revival of the *Gambit Accepted.*

		Kt—KB3
4	**P—K3**	**P—K3**
5	**B × P**	**B—Kt5 ch**

Modern theory gives 5.., **P—B4,** leading to an even game. The text-move brings about a superficial resemblance to the "Bogoljuboff variation" in the *Queen's Pawn Game*; but here White has his KB developed and is not threatened with doubled P's on the QB file—if that is to be considered a threat.

6 **Kt—B3**

6 **QKt—Q2** is, as in analogous positions, a strong alternative.

		Castles
7	**Castles**	**P—QKt3**

See Steinitz's note on move 7 in the following game, though the position there is somewhat different.

8	**Kt—K5**	**B—Kt2**
9	**Q—Kt3**	**B × Kt**

The capture is inadvisable, especially as opening up QR3 to White's QB. **B—K2** may be best, though there is something to be said for **B—Q3,** followed perhaps by the capture of the KKt.

10	**P × B**	**B—Q4**

Why give up this strong B, when there is the developing move **Kt—B3** available?

11	**B × B**	**P × B**
12	**B—R3**	**R—K1**
13	**P—QB4**	**P—B4**

A good retort.

14	**QR—B1**	**Kt—K5**

But now Black should simplify by exchanging off P's, followed by **Q—Q4.**

15	**KR—Q1**	**BP × P**
16	**KP × P**	**P—B3**

Position after 16.., **P—B3:**

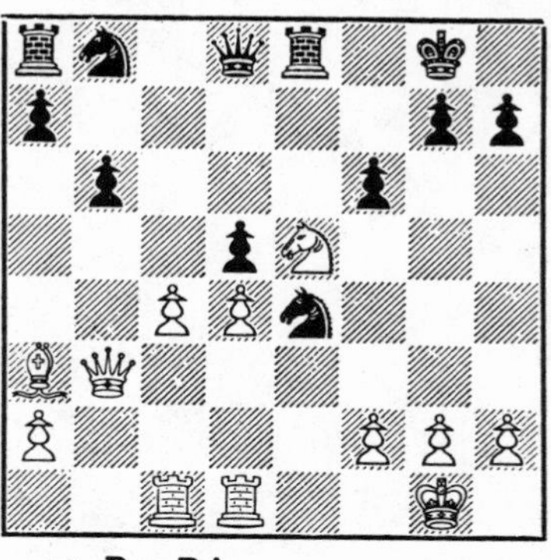

17 **P × P !**

Black cannot have suspected danger in the centre. But his undeveloped Q-side should have warned him against moves like his last, of which White takes the fullest advantage.

	P × Kt
18 **P—Q6 dis. ch**	**K—R1**
19 **Q—Q5**	**Kt × BP**

If Black had played **P × P,** Steinitz says that he would here have replied 20 **R × P,** not 20 **Q × R,** on account of **Kt × BP.**

20 **R—Q2**

Refusing to expose his K to a check by Q at B3. If in reply to the text-move **Kt—R6 ch,** then 21 **P × Kt, Q—Kt4 ch;** 22 **R—Kt2, Q—K6 ch;** 23 **K—R1, Q × B** (or **Kt—Q2**); 24 **QR—KKt1,** with a winning attack. This is C. E. Ranken's analysis in *The British Chess Magazine*.

	Kt—Q2
21 **R × Kt**	**Kt—B3**
22 **R × Kt !**	**P × R**

If **Q × R** the answer is the same.

23 **P—Q7**	**R—KKt1**
24 **P × P**	**R—Kt4**

P × P; 25 **B—Kt2** is still worse for Black.

25 **Q × R**	**Q × Q**
26 **R—B8 ch**	**R—Kt1**
27 **R × Q**	**R × R**
28 **P—K6**	**Resigns**

An admirable ending on Steinitz's part. The game is an extraordinary contrast to the preceding game, with the same opening.

GAME 14

STEINITZ v. GUNSBERG

New York, *January* 7, 1891

(Championship Match, 13th Game)

ZUKERTORT'S OPENING (QUEEN'S PAWN)

	White.	*Black.*
	Steinitz	Gunsberg
1	**Kt—KB3**	**Kt—KB3**
2	**P—Q4**	**P—K3**
3	**P—K3**	**B—Kt5 ch**

The game has become a *Queen's Pawn,* with the "Bogoljuboff variation," except that White has here played **P—K3** instead of **P—QB4.** Consequently he can now interpose his QBP. But whether it was his best move is doubtful. 4 **QKt—Q2** may be better, as Steinitz later suggested.

4	**P—B3**	**B—K2**
5	**B—K2**	**Castles**
6	**Castles**	**P—Q4**
7	**P—QB4**	**P—QKt3**

Steinitz says that he never looked upon this move with favour, in spite of its adoption by most European masters. It may be regarded as a belated *Queen's Indian Defence,* a rare procedure where White has played **P—QB4.**

8	**Kt—B3**	**B—Kt2**
9	**P × P**	**P × P**
10	**Kt—K5**	**KKt—Q2 ?**

Too slow. Steinitz commends **QKt—Q2,** followed by **R—K1** and **Kt—B1.**

11	**P—B4**	**Kt × Kt**
12	**BP × Kt**	

The position suggests that White will develop a vigorous K-side attack. But it is actually on the Q-side that White brings pressure to bear.

		P—QB3
13	**B—Q2**	**B—R3**
14	**B × B**	**Kt × B**
15	**Q—R4**	**Kt—Kt1**
16	**QR—B1**	**P—B3**

With his inferior development, Black creates a diversion away from the Q-side. He is much handicapped, however, by the tying up of that side.

17	**P × P**	**B × P**
18	**Kt—K2**	**R—K1**
19	**R—KB3**	**Q—K2**
20	**QR—B1**	**R—QB1**
21	**B—Kt4**	**Q—K3**

If **P—B4,** Steinitz gives 22 **Q—Kt3, R—Q1;** 23 **P × P, P × P;** 24 **Kt—B4 (P × B ?;** 25 **Kt × P !).** It is hard to find even a plausible move for Black; but perhaps **Q—K1** might have been tried. The text-move brings White's Kt into the game.

22	**Kt—B4**	**Q—K5**
23	**Kt—R5**	**Kt—Q2**
24	**Q—R6 !**	

A move of much subtlety, of which the meaning is not at once apparent.

		Q—K1
25	**R—R3**	**B—Kt4**
26	**K—R1**	**Kt—B3**

Not, of course, **B × P**; 27 **R—K1**, for which White's last move provided. But Steinitz suggests 26.., **B—R3**, followed by **Kt—B1**.

27 **Kt × Kt ch** **P × Kt**

If **B × Kt**, then 28 **R × B**, **P × R**; 29 **Q—Kt7**, winning offhand.

Position after 27.., **P × Kt**:

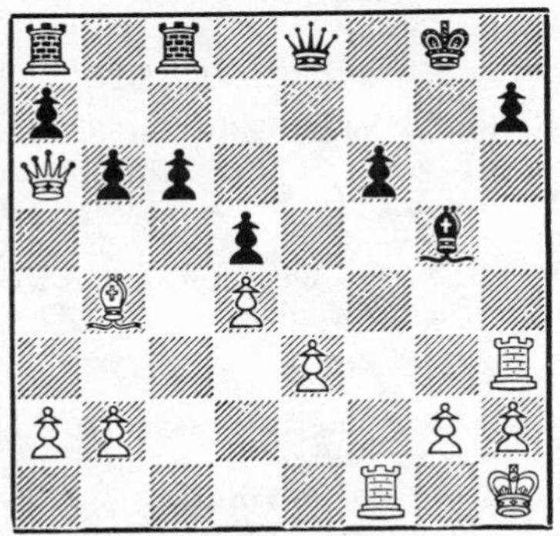

28 **Q—Kt7**

Now this move comes in with deadly effect.

	Q—Kt3
29 **Q—Q7**	**K—R1**
30 **B—K7**	**R—KKt1**

Black is paralysed, and this appearance of a counter-threat has nothing real in it. Two P's must fall.

31 **Q × BP**	**QR—QB1**
32 **Q × QP**	**R—Kt2**
33 **B—Kt4**	**Q—Q6**
34 **Q—B3**	**R—B7**
35 **B—B3**	**R—K2**
36 **P—K4**	

Steinitz is pleased with this move of his. It is "the best way of getting rid of the adverse attack, as White has sufficient to win in the ending, and the KP could not be saved anyhow."

	Q × KP
37 **P—Q5**	**Q—Kt3**
38 **R—Kt3**	**R—KB2**
39 **P—Q6**	

Not 39 **R × B, Q × R**; 39 **B × P ch, R × B**. White must guard against the mate by R on his back rank. 39 **P—KR4** is bad on account of **Q—R3**.

P—KR3 ?

This cuts off the resource just mentioned. But in face of the threat 40 **Q—R8 ch** the game was practically over.

40 **P—KR4** **Resigns**

We have here a good example of Steinitz in his "modern" style, devoid of all sensationalism.

GAME 15

TCHIGORIN v. STEINITZ

HAVANA, *January* 1, 1892

(CHAMPIONSHIP [SECOND] MATCH, 1ST GAME)

EVANS GAMBIT

White.	*Black.*
TCHIGORIN	STEINITZ
1 **P—K4**	**P—K4**
2 **Kt—KB3**	**Kt—QB3**
3 **B—B4**	**B—B4**
4 **P—QKt4**	

Tchigorin and Steinitz played 19 match-games with the Russian master as White in the *Evans*—8 in their first match, 8 in the second, one by cable, and two in tournament. Tchigorin won 11 of these and drew 4.

	B × P
5 **P—B3**	**B—R4**
6 **Castles**	**P—Q3**
7 **P—Q4**	**B—KKt5**

This move was tried again by Steinitz in the 3rd and 5th games of the match. In the 7th he adopted the *Sanders-Alapin Defence* (**B—Q2**), but in the 13th, 15th, and 17th he went back to the text-move. Though a natural-looking manœuvre, it has not won approval. In the *Lasker Defence* it comes in after 7.., **B—Kt3;** 8 **B—R3, P × P;** 9 **P × P.**

8 **B—QKt5**

So Tchigorin played also in the 3rd, 5th and 13th games, but in the 15th he substituted 8 **Q—R4,** and play continued **P × P;** 9 **P × P, P—QR3;** 10 **B—Q5, B—Kt3;** 11 **B × Kt ch, P × B;** 12 **Q × P ch, B—Q2;** 13 **Q—B2, Kt—K2.** Tchigorin thus regained the gambit P; but he forfeited his attack. He won the game, however.

	P × P
9 **P × P**	**B—Q2**

This is practically forced, as 9.., **B × Kt;** 10 **P × B, P—QR3;** 11 **B × Kt ch, P × B;** 12 **Q—R4** or 9.., **P—QR3;** 10 **B × Kt ch, P × B;** 11 **Q—R4** would mean the loss of a P for Black.

10 **B—Kt2**	**QKt—K2**

If this is possible, says Hoffer, Steinitz's defence is an improvement, as it avoids having to play the QKt later to R4, where it is inactive. But Steinitz, as the result of the present game, abandoned the move and played instead 10.., **Kt—B3**

11 **B × B ch**	**Q × B**
12 **Kt—R3**	**Kt—R3**

Now **Kt—B3** would be met by 13 **P—K5.**

13 **Kt—B4**	**B—Kt3**
14 **P—QR4**	**P—QB3**

This turns out ill; but after 14.., **P—QR3;** 15 **Kt × B, P × Kt** Black's Q-side would be very weak.

15 **P—K5**	**P—Q4**

Letting White's QKt into so commanding a position as Q6 seems to damn the variation, if this move is compulsory. The alternative 15.., **P × P;** 16 **KKt × P,** however, is also exceedingly uncomfortable.

16 **Kt—Q6 ch** **K—B1**
17 **B—R3** **K—Kt1**

Steinitz is perhaps in too great a hurry to get his K off the black diagonal. If **KKt—B4** is playable at all, it must be now. But could Tchigorin then have made his sacrifice a move earlier ? 18 **Kt × BP, K × Kt(R—KKt1;** 19 **KKt—Kt5)**; 19 **P—K6 ch, K × P;** 20 **Kt—K5, Q—B1;** 21 **R—K1** is the same as the actual game, with the omission of White's 18 **R—Kt1,** which is not essential to the combination. See note on the 27th move.

18 **R—Kt1** **KKt—B4**

Having moved his K off the hostile B's diagonal, Black has now the option of **QKt—B4,** preventing White's sacrifice; from which it seems clear that he had no suspicion of what was coming. Against **QKt—B4** White would have had to proceed in a different way, perhaps by 19 **P—K6,** which looks very promising.

Position after 18.., **KKt—B4:**

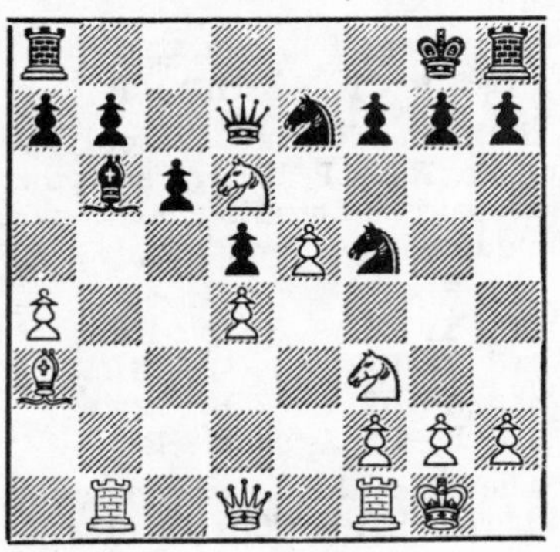

19 **Kt × BP !** **K × Kt**
20 **P—K6 ch** **K × P**
21 **Kt—K5 !** **Q—B1**
22 **R—K1** **K—B3**
23 **Q—R5** **P—Kt3**

White threatens 24 **Kt—Kt4** mate.

24 **B × Kt ch** **K × B**

If **Kt × B,** then 25 **Q—R4 ch, P—Kt4;** 26 **Kt—Kt4 ch, K—B2;** 27 **Q × KtP** and wins.

25 **Kt × KtP dbl.ch** **K—B3**
26 **Kt × R** **B × P**

If **Q × Kt;** 27 **P—Kt4** wins.

27 **R—Kt3**

In the variation mentioned in the note on move 17 this R would be standing on R1 and could go to R3.

Q—Q2
28 **R—KB3** **R × Kt**
29 **P—Kt4** **R—KKt1**
30 **Q—R6 ch** **R—Kt3**
31 **R × Kt ch** **Resigns**

For if **Q × R,** then 32 **Q—B8 ch,** wins the Q, as well as forcing a speedy mate.

Hoffer rightly remarks that "Tchigorin's conduct of this game is of the highest order." But Steinitz handicapped himself by a shaky defence in the opening, which was promptly punished.

GAME 16

STEINITZ v. TCHIGORIN

HAVANA, *January* 7, 1892

(CHAMPIONSHIP [SECOND] MATCH, 4TH GAME)

RUY LOPEZ

	White. STEINITZ	*Black.* TCHIGORIN
1	**P—K4**	**P—K4**
2	**Kt—KB3**	**Kt—QB3**
3	**B—Kt5**	**Kt—B3**
4	**P—Q3**	**P—Q3**
5	**P—B3**	**P—KKt3**
6	**QKt—Q2**	**B—Kt2**
7	**Kt—B1**	**Castles**

This form of the *Berlin Defence* to the *Lopez*, with White's pianissimo development and Black's K-side fianchetto, was well known to both the players. They adopted it in the 2nd game of this match. The standard example in the books is Steinitz-Rosenthal in the London Tournament of 1883, a game which Steinitz lost, but not through the opening.

8 **B—R4**

In the 2nd game of the match Steinitz played **Kt—K3** at once, as he had played also against Rosenthal. He says of the text-move that he made it with a view of keeping the B for an eventual K-side attack, and in order to be able to play **Q—K2** without being liable to having the B exchanged. If 8 **Q—K2, B—Q2;** 9 **B—R4, Kt—Q5;** 10 **P × Kt, B × B;** 11 **P × P, P × P;** 12 **Kt × P, B—Kt4,** Black, though a P behind, has a strong attack.

Kt—Q2

The manœuvre **Kt—Q2—B4—K3** is slow. Black, having practically a move in hand in a variation of the *Morphy Defence* to the *Lopez* (minus **P—QR3**), might venture on 8.., **P—Q4.** If 9 **B × Kt, P × B;** 10 **Kt × P,** then **R—K1,** and again Black has a strong attack.

9 **Kt—K3**

9 **P—KR4** was probably premature, says Steinitz, being answered by **P—KR3.**

		Kt—B4
10	**B—B2**	**Kt—K3**
11	**P—KR4 !**	**Kt—K2**

If now **P—KR3,** there might follow 12 **P—R5, P—KKt4;** 13 **Kt—B5,** with good prospects for White.

12	**P—R5**	**P—Q4**
13	**RP × P**	**BP × P**

Both Steinitz and Hoffer pronounce **RP × P** better; and the latter says that after the text-move the game is lost for Black.

14	**P × P**	**Kt × P**
15	**Kt × Kt**	**Q × Kt**
16	**B—Kt3**	**Q—B3**
17	**Q—K2**	**B—Q2**
18	**B—K3**	**K—R1**

The pin of the Kt was no doubt embarrassing, but this puts the K on a very bad square. The best defence seems to be 18.., **R—B2,** and if necessary **B—R1.**

19	**Castles QR**	**QR—K1**
20	**Q—B1**	

Preparing for the final assault, and also removing the Q from a file that will soon be opened.

P—QR4

Better was **Kt—B5,** with a view to **Kt—R4.**

21 **P—Q4** **P × P**

If now **Kt—B5,** Steinitz gives 22 **P—R4** as best. He did not want his KB dislodged.

22 **Kt × P**

Position after 22 **Kt × P:**

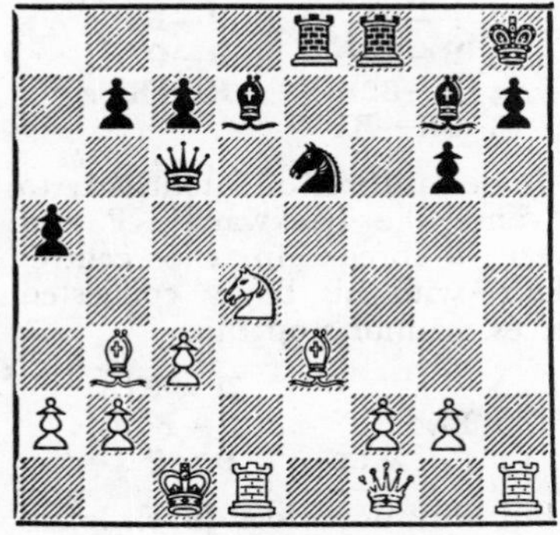

B × Kt

If **Kt × Kt,** the crash comes at once by 23 **R × P ch, K × R;** 24 **Q—R1 ch.** But 22.., **Q—K5** only varies the catastrophe, for then 23 **B—B2;** and no other move of the Q is of any avail.

23 **R × B !** **Kt × R**

Perhaps only reckoning on 24 **B × Kt ch,** when he could cover with **R—B3.** But White's threats are too numerous to cope with, beginning with **Q—Q3.**

24 **R × P ch !**

The first move in a forced mate in 7.

K × R
25 **Q—R. ch** **K—Kt2**

25.., **B—R6;** 26 **Q × B ch** would spin the mate out to 7 moves.

26 **B—R6 ch** **K—B3**

K—R1 would allow mate in 2.

27 **Q—R4 ch** **K—K4**
28 **Q × Kt ch** **Resigns**

There is only 28.., **K—B4;** 29 **Q—B4** mate.

Hoffer, who detested the Modern School of his day, allows that this is "a very beautiful game, played in Mr. Steinitz's happiest old style."

GAME 17

STEINITZ v. TCHIGORIN

HAVANA, *February*, 1892

(CHAMPIONSHIP [SECOND] MATCH, 18TH GAME)

QUEEN'S PAWN GAME (DUTCH DEFENCE)

	White. STEINITZ	*Black.* TCHIGORIN
1	**Kt—KB3**	**P—KB4**
2	**P—Q4**	**P—K3**
3	**P—B4**	**Kt—KB3**
4	**Kt—B3**	**B—K2**
5	**P—Q5**	

Unorthodox, and apparently new at this stage. Its object is said to be to impede Black's development; see note on the 8th move.

		P × P
6	**P × P**	**Castles**
7	**P—KKt3**	

The B at KKt2, says Steinitz, will have a more commanding post than elsewhere. It may be noted that the K's fianchetto against the *Dutch Defence* enjoys considerable favour today; but not in conjunction with Steinitz's **P—Q5.**

		P—Q3
8	**B—Kt2**	**QKt—Q2**

Steinitz comments now on Black's difficulty in developing his Q-side pieces. He suggests here **P—B3**; or else **R—K1**, followed by **B—B1** and **P—KKt3.**

9	**Castles**	**Kt—K4**
10	**Kt—Q4**	**Kt—Kt3**
11	**Q—B2**	

A far-seeing move, which attains its primary object 14 moves later, but also aims at clearing the first rank for the use of the QR.

		Kt—K1
12	**P—B4**	**B—B3**
13	**B—K3**	**B—Q2**
14	**B—B2**	**Kt—K2**
15	**QR—K1**	

A declaration of intentions; to advance the backward KP and make a break in the centre. Black, with his badly congested pieces, cannot stop this.

		B × Kt
16	**B × B**	**P—B4**
17	**P × P i.p.**	**B × P**

But why now does Black leave himself with a weak isolated P? After 17.., **P × P** he would have time to shift his QR off the White KB's long diagonal.

18	**P—K4**	**Q—Q2**
19	**Kt—Q5**	**Kt × Kt**
20	**P × Kt**	

Once more Steinitz has a P fixed at Q5; but now in addition he commands the open K-file.

		B—Kt4
21	**R—B3**	**Kt—B2**

To prevent 22 **R—K6.** But, as will be seen, the move fails in its object. It should have been preceded by 21.., **R—B1,** and if 22 **R—B3** then **R × R.** White could not in that case both dislodge the Kt and hold the K-file.

22 **R—B3** **Kt—R3**

Not, of course, **QR—B1**; 23 **R—QB1.**

23 **R(B3)—K3**

With a double threat, at K6 and K7, Black would have done better to reply 23.., **QR—K1,** as White cannot then exchange off R's and capture the KBP, because a mate is left on.

KR—K1 ?

24 **R—K6** **Kt—B2**

Q—KB2 is the only way to prevent the loss of the BP. Black clearly cannot have seen the full implication of his apparent gain of the Exchange!

Position after 24.., **Kt—B2:**

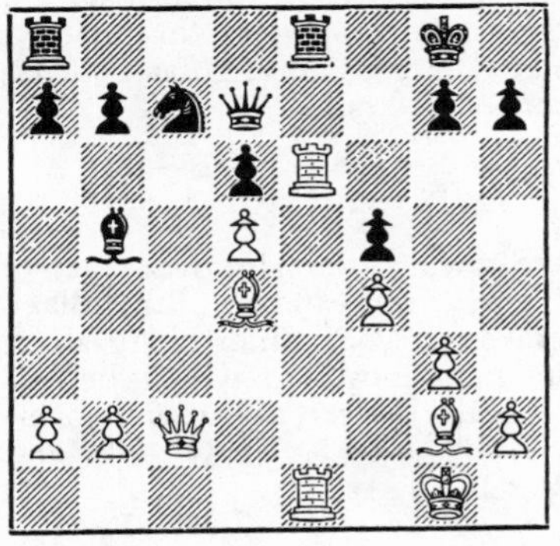

25 **Q × P** **Kt × R**
26 **P × Kt** **Q—K2**
27 **Q × B** **QR—B1**
28 **Q × P** **R—B2**
29 **Q—K4** **KR—QB1**
30 **B—QB3** **R—B5**
31 **Q—Q3** **P—QR4**
32 **R—Q1**

The trap 32 **B × RP, Q—R2 ch** was too simple!

Q—R2 ch

33 **K—R1** **R(B5)—B2**
34 **Q × P** **P—R4**

Rather illusory is this provision of a flight-square for the K.

35 **B—K4**

Steinitz here misses a quicker win, which was shown by A. C. Vasquez: 35 **Q—Q8 ch, K—R2** (**R × Q**; 36 **R × R ch** would only make it quicker still); 36 **B—K4 ch, P—Kt3**; 37 **B × P ch, K × B**; 38 **Q—Kt5 ch, K—R2**; 39 **Q × P ch, K—Kt1**; 40 **Q—R8** mate. But Steinitz also brings off a pretty finish, with some help from his opponent.

R—K1

36 **Q—K5** **R—B4**
37 **R—Q5** **R × R**
38 **B × R** **R—K2**

Q—K2 would also hold up the P-advance, and would stop White's sacrifice of his Q; but the game would still be won for White by 39 **Q × RP.**

39 **Q × P ch** **R × Q**
40 **P—K7 dis. ch** **K—R2**
41 **B—K4 ch** **Resigns**

This game shows Steinitz again in his best form—not without a seeming eccentricity in the opening.

GAME 18

LASKER v. STEINITZ

NEW YORK, *March* 21-22, 1894
(CHAMPIONSHIP [FIRST] MATCH, 3RD GAME)

RUY LOPEZ

	White.	*Black.*
	LASKER	STEINITZ
1	**P—K4**	**P—K4**
2	**Kt—KB3**	**Kt—QB3**
3	**B—Kt5**	**P—Q3**

The present match threw considerable light upon this, the *Steinitz Defence*, as the title-holder played it when he had to meet the *Ruy Lopez*, in the 1st, 3rd, 5th, 7th, and 9th games. He wrote in a note on the move in the 1st game that the revival of this defence met with much opposition, but he had seen nothing as yet to vitiate the equalising effect it possessed, in his opinion. His ill-success with it, however, in the match tended for a time to discredit it.

4	**P—Q4**	**B—Q2**
5	**Kt—B3**	**KKt—K2**

" An important key-move to this defence," wrote Steinitz, " which I first adopted in my match against Gunsberg." Other masters, in adopting the *Steinitz Defence*, have rejected this move in favour of **Kt—B3.**

6 **B—QB4**

" Novel," remarks Steinitz; " White threatens attack by **Kt—KKt5.**" The question is whether he can afford the virtual loss of a move. In the 7th game (which follows) Lasker substituted 6 **B—K3.** Tchigorin had played 6 **B—Kt5** in the 11th game of his match against Steinitz in 1892.

		P × P
7	**Kt × P**	**Kt × Kt**
8	**Q × Kt**	**Kt—B3**
9	**Q—K3**	**Kt—K4**

In the 5th game Steinitz played instead the better 9.., **B—K3,** and after 10 **Kt—Q5, B—K2;** 11 **B—Q2, Castles**—as he did also against the same opponent in the St. Petersburg Quadrangular Tournament of 1895.

10	**B—Kt3**	**B—K3**
11	**P—B4 !**	

Showing the disadvantage of Black's 9th move. But Black makes it worse than he need by his next move, to which he has several better alternatives, including **Kt—Kt5, Kt—Q2,** and **B × B.**

		Kt—B5 ?
12	**Q—Kt3**	**Kt—Kt3**

The fifth move with the Kt, in consequence of which White is much ahead in development.

13	**B—K3**	**P—QB3**

This move has been called " a forced weakening " (of the QP); but why is it forced ? Black can play 13.., **B × B,** and after 14 **RP × B, Kt—Q2.** He would be uncomfortable, but without the burden of having to defend the QP.

14	**P—B5**	**B × B**
15	**RP × B**	**Kt—Q2**
16	**B—B4**	**Q—B2**
17	**P—Kt4**	**P—B3**
18	**Kt—K2**	**Kt—K4**
19	**Kt—Q4**	**Q—Kt3**
20	**P—B3**	**Castles**

Black's dilatory tactics have brought him to a pass whence his only chance of salvation is a furious counter-attack, in which he displays extreme ingenuity and persistence.

21	**Kt—K6**	**R—Q2**
22	**B—K3**	**Q—Kt4**

Lasker calls this a grand conception on the part of his opponent. It leads to the surrender of a piece, and possibly of two.

23	**R × P**	**P—QKt3**
24	**R—R8 ch**	**K—Kt2**
25	**R × B**	**R × R**
26	**Kt × R**	

Position after 26 **Kt × R**:

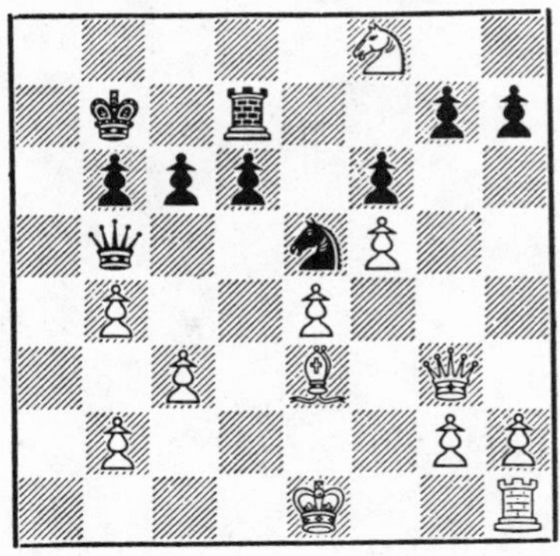

Q—Q6 !

The point of Steinitz's combination, offering the sacrifice of his R for a draw by perpetual check. It remains to be seen whether the perpetual check is really there.

27 **R—B1**

Lasker declined the offer, showing that he thought it sound, or that the line was so difficult in over-the-board play (at 15 moves an hour) that it was better to refuse. But James Mason and the other Irish master, W. H. K. Pollock, with the advantage of extra study of the position after the game had been played, both maintained that White after 27 **Kt × R** could escape the draw. Mason's analysis runs: 27 **Kt × R, Q—Kt8 ch**; 28 **K—Q2 !, Q × P ch**; 29 **K—Q1, Q—Kt6 ch**; 30 **K—K2, Q—B5 ch**; 31 **K—B2, Q—R7 ch**; 32 **K—B1, Q—B5 ch**; 33 **K—K1, Q × P ch**; 34 **B—Q2, Q—R8 ch**; 35 **K—K2,** when Black has nothing better than **Q × R,** leaving him a piece down. There seem to be no plausible alternatives for Black (*e.g.*, 31.., **Kt—Q6 ch** fails against **32 K—Kt1**); and if so Mason has proved his case.

		Q—B7
28	**B—Q2**	**R—K2**

Steinitz afterwards expressed the opinion that Black could at least have drawn by 28.., **Kt—B5**; if 29 **Q—B4, R—Q1**; 30 **Kt—K6, R—QR1**; 31 **K—K2, R—R7** "with a powerful attack." White's game certainly presents extraordinary difficulties.

29	**Kt—K6**	**Q × P ch**
30	**Q—K3**	**Q × KtP**
31	**P—Kt3**	**R—K1**
32	**Q—K2**	**Q—R6**

Q—Q4 would be met by 33 **P—B4.**

33	**K—Q1**	**R—QR1**
34	**R—B2**	**R—R7**

35	**P—Kt5**	**P—B4**
36	**Kt × KtP**	**P—Q4**
37	**K—B1**	**Q—Q6**

If instead **Kt—Q6 ch,** then 38 **K—Kt1, R—Kt7 ch;** 39 **K—R1,** and the White K is out of danger. But after the exchange of Q's, best line as it may be for Black, White's extra piece must prevail.

38	**Q × Q**	**Kt × Q ch**
39	**K—Kt1**	**R—Kt7 ch**
40	**K—R1**	**R × P**
41	**R—B3**	**P—B5**
42	**Kt—K8**	**Kt—Kt5 !**
43	**R—Kt3 !**	**R—R6 ch**
44	**K—Kt1**	**R—Kt6 ch**
45	**K—B1**	**Kt—Q6 ch**
46	**R × Kt**	**P × R**
47	**Kt × P**	**R × KtP**
48	**Kt—K8**	

The correctness of Lasker's decision to fight the ending with B and Kt against R was questioned, notably by Mason. But Black's P's are very weak.

If 49 **Kt × RP,** then **P—Q5.**

		K—B3
49	**P—B6**	**P—Q5**
50	**Kt—Kt7**	**P × P**
51	**B × P**	**R—Kt4 ?**

This is *hara-kiri.* 51.., **K—Q2** would have made it much more difficult for White.

52	**P—B7**	**Resigns**

There is only **R—Kt8 ch;** 53 **K—Q2, R—KB8,** when White replies 54 **Kt—K6.**

A magnificent game. Handicapped by his opening, Steinitz makes a tremendous fight, to which the few slight lapses on both sides only add piquancy.

GAME 19

LASKER v. STEINITZ

New York, *April* 3, 1894

(Championship [First] Match, 7th Game)

RUY LOPEZ

White.	*Black.*
Lasker	Steinitz

(*First* 5 *moves as in preceding game.*)

6 **B—K3** **Kt—Kt3**

Some critics condemn this move, mainly on the general principle that Kt3 is not a good square for a Kt—which is probably too sweeping an assertion. But possibly here 7.., **Kt × P,** with a view to exchanges and the posting of the KKt on QB3, is the soundest line if Black is aiming at a draw—which was not Steinitz's intention.

7 **Q—Q2** **B—K2**
8 **Castles QR** **P—QR3**
9 **B—K2** **P × P**
10 **Kt × P** **Kt × Kt**
11 **Q × Kt** **B—KB3**
12 **Q—Q2** **B—B3**

This, too, does not please some of the commentators, though there seems to be no valid reason against it.

13 **Kt—Q5** **Castles**
14 **P—KKt4**

Blamed as "premature." Lasker's idea was perhaps to begin a K-side attack without a preliminary **P—KB3** or **P—KR3** when he might want to advance one of those P's to the 4th, not the 3rd. Steinitz, however, evolves a plan to refute that idea.

R—K1

15 **P—Kt5**

Hoffer commends 15 **Kt × B ch, Q × Kt;** 16 **P—KB3,** which certainly looks stronger.

B × Kt

16 **Q × B**

The explanation of this, rather than 16 **KP × B,** is difficult. White now loses two P's, without any compensation unless his opponent helps him.

R—K4

17 **Q—Q2**

The alternative 17 **Q × KtP** would be fatal.

B × P

18 **P—KB4** **R × P**
19 **P × B** **Q—K2 !**

With this move the game should be won for Black, who recovers his piece and is two P's up. But Lasker, after mismanaging the opening, begins now to play in very different style, taking many risks, as was legitimate in the position, to induce errors by his opponent.

20 **QR—B1** **R × B**
21 **B—B4** **Kt—R1 ?**

21.., **R—KB1** (and if 22 **P—KR4, Q—K4**) was much to be

preferred. The Kt is now condemned to remain where it is for the rest of the game.

22 **P—KR4** **P—B3**

Position after 22.., **P—B3:**

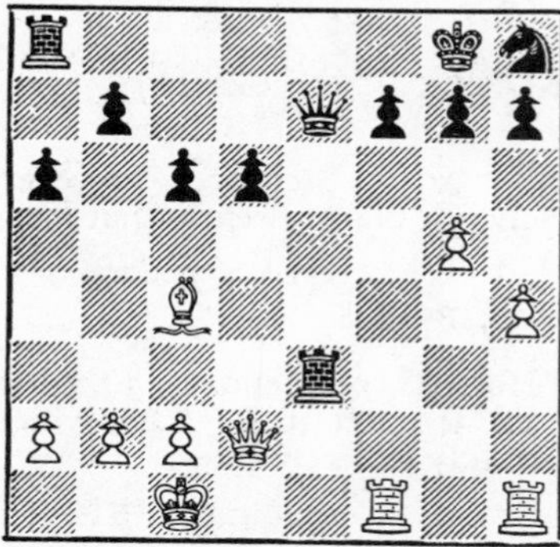

23 **P—Kt6 !**

Obviously White must strike at once; and the fact that his scheme was not sound does not detract from its merits. There was no sound attack. This at least gave Black the greatest opportunity for error.

P—Q4

The flaw was that by 23.., **P × P;** 24 **P—R5, P—KKt4;** 25 **P—R6, P × P !;** 26 **KR × P, R—K1** the attack is brought to a standstill, owing to the threat of a check on the rank. But Black was no doubt playing under time-pressure, a fearful handicap in such a position. Besides, the move he makes should be sufficient if correctly followed up.

24 **P × RP ch** **K × P**
25 **B—Q3 ch** **K—Kt1**
26 **P—R5** **R—K1**

This is not as menacing as in the variation in the preceding note. The defensive **R—Kt6** was to be preferred.

27 **P—R6** **P—KKt3**
28 **P—R7 ch** **K—Kt2**
29 **K—Kt1**

The object of this and the following move is first to get the K off the same diagonal with the Q (so as to prevent a possible pin) and then to provide him with a flight-square at R2.

Q—K4
30 **P—R3** **P—QB4**

The 30th move, completing the second hour. Perhaps more time for reflection might have decided Steinitz in favour of **R—K3,** with a view to **P—KB4.** But the text-move is very reasonable.

31 **Q—B2** **P—B5**
32 **Q—R4**

32 **B × KtP, P × B;** 33 **Q—R4** failed on account of **Kt—B2;** 34 **P—R8=Q ch, R × Q;** 35 **R × Kt ch, K × R.**

P—B3

Lasker said afterwards that he expected 32.., **K—B1,** to which his answer would have been 33 **B—B5,** with good chances of a draw. Presumably, if **P × B,** there would follow 34 **QR—Kt1** (for if **Kt—Kt3;** 35 **R × Kt** etc.).

33 **B—B5 !** **K—B2**

Now **P × B;** 34 **KR—Kt1** would lead to much the same variation as actually occurred. But Black should have played 33.., **R—KKt6,** when the case is by no means clear.

34 **KR—Kt1** **P × B**

Why does Steinitz, having first rejected the offer of the B, accept it now? He must have come to the conclusion that he could capture and win. Nor can it be said that he was unduly sanguine, provided he could avoid errors.

35 **Q—R5 ch** **K—K2**
36 **R—Kt8** **K—Q3**

If **K—Q1**, Pollock gives 37 **K—R2 !**, **R—K8**; 38 **Q × R ch**, **Q × Q**; 39 **R × R**. But Black has no reason to play 37.., **R—K8** when he has 37.., **Q—K3**. Against that move White's 38 **R × P** can be met by **R—K4**. To 38 **R(B1)—KKt1**, however, there seems no valid reply. Therefore Black's 36 . ., **K—Q3** was right.

37 **R × P** **Q—K3**
38 **R × R** **Q × R(K1)**
39 **R × BP ch** **K—B4 ?**

K—B2 was imperative, though it loses a P at once.

40 **Q—R6** **R—K2**
41 **Q—R2** **Q—Q2 ?**

Giving White the opportunity to finish quickly. 41.., **R—K3** was Black's last chance. If then 42 **Q—B7 ch**, **Q—B3** (forced); 43 **Q × Q ch**, **R × Q**; 44 **R—B8**, **Kt—Kt3**; 45 **R—KKt8**, **R—B2** would leave White nothing but 46 **P—R8=Q**, **Kt × Q**; 47 **R × Kt**, with a draw to struggle for.

42 **Q—Kt1 ch** **P—Q5**
43 **Q—Kt5 ch** **Q—Q4**
44 **R—B5** **Q × R**
45 **Q × Q ch** **K—Q3**
46 **Q—B6 ch** **Resigns**

Much the same can be said of this as of the preceding game, except that it is Lasker here who goes wrong early. The resulting struggle is again magnificent.

GAME 20

LASKER v. STEINITZ

PHILADELPHIA, *April* 21, 1894

(CHAMPIONSHIP [FIRST] MATCH, 11TH GAME)

QUEEN'S GAMBIT DECLINED

	White. LASKER	*Black.* STEINITZ
1	**P—Q4**	**P—Q4**
2	**P—QB4**	**P—K3**
3	**Kt—QB3**	**Kt—KB3**
4	**Kt—B3**	**B—K2**
5	**P—K3**	

5 **B—B4** is a common alternative, but among modern masters the young American R. Fine has advocated the text-move. 5 **B—Kt5** might, or might not, transpose into the Pillsbury variation.

		Castles
6	**B—Q3**	**P—B4**

Against Fine at Zandvoort, 1936, Tartakover played 6.., **P—QKt3**, and after 7 **Castles, B—Kt2**; 8 **P—QKt3, P—B4.** Against the same opponent at Nottingham, 1936, Lasker played 6.., **P × P**; 7 **B × P, P—B4.** About the text-move Mason says that Steinitz " plays the opening very badly," and after the exchange of Q's has the inferior position. This seems too sweeping a statement. Black's errors rather come later.

7	**QP × P**	**P × P**
8	**B × P**	**Q × Q ch**
9	**K × Q**	**Kt—B3**
10	**P—QR3**	**B × P**
11	**P—QKt4**	**B—Kt3**

This presumably is preparatory to his 14th move; but the B would be better placed at K2.

12	**K—K2**	**B—Q2**
13	**B—Kt3**	**QR—B1**
14	**B—Kt2**	**P—QR4 ?**

Not a good manœuvre, leading to an uncomfortable disarrangement of his minor pieces. In particular Black should have prevented the dislodging of his QKt, which yields up his K4 to White.

15	**P—Kt5**	**Kt—K2**
16	**Kt—K5**	**B—K1**
17	**P—QR4**	**B—B2**
18	**Kt—B4**	**B—Q2**

Otherwise White will play 19 **B—R3.**

19	**QR—QB1**	**QKt—Q4**
20	**Kt × Kt**	**Kt × Kt**

Hoffer suggests as a lesser evil 20.., **P × Kt**; 21 **Kt—Q2, B—K3**; 22 **B × Kt, P × B,** with chances of a draw. It is doubtful whether White would have played 22 **B × Kt.**

21	**Kt—K5**	**B × Kt**
22	**B × B**	**P—B3**

Position after 22.., **P—B3**:

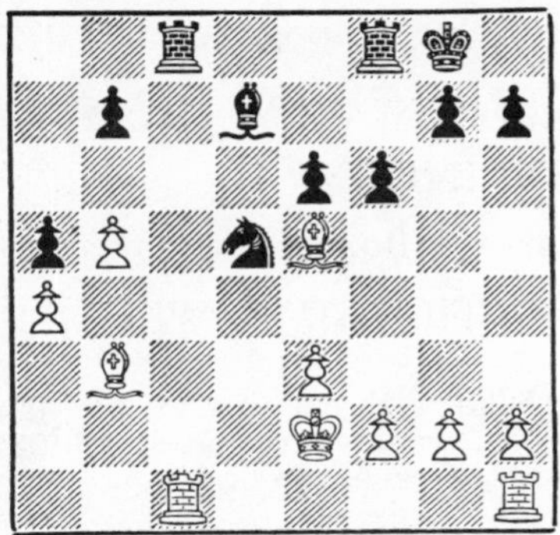

23 **P—K4 !**

A very powerful move. If in reply **Kt—K2,** then 24 **B—B7, R—R1;** 25 **KR—Q1.**

	P × B
24 **P × Kt**	**K—B2**
25 **KR—Q1**	**K—K2 ?**

This is certainly unwise. Black's best line is 25.., **R × R;** 26 **R × R, R—B1;** and if 27 **P × P ch, K—K2;** 28 **R × R, B × R;** 29 **K—K3, B × P.** Here Mason considers a draw the likely result. Lasker, however, gives the following analysis to show that he should win: 30 **B × B, K × B;** 31 **K—K4, P—QKt3;** 32 **P—R4, P—Kt3;** 33 **P—R5, K—Q3;** 34 **P × P, P × P;** 35 **P—Kt4, K—K3;** 36 **P—B3, K—Q3;** 37 **P—B4, P × P;** 38 **K × P, K—K3;** 39 **K—Kt5, K—B2,** 40 **K—R6, K—B3;** 41 **K—R7, K—Kt4;** 42 **K—Kt7, K × P;** 43 **K × P, K—B5;** 44 **K—B6, K—K5;** 45 **K—K6, K—Q5;** 46 **K—Q6, K—B5;** 47 **K—B6, K—Kt5;** 48 **K × P, K × P;** 49 **K—B5** and wins. A very instructive Pawn-ending.

26 **P—Q6 ch**	**K—B3**
27 **K—K3**	**R × R**
28 **R × R**	**R—B1**
29 **R × R**	**B × R**
30 **B—B2**	**K—B2 ?**

Steinitz's sealed move at the adjournment. He was apparently under the impression that his opponent could not take the KRP; but if so it was a strange delusion for so great a master. The right move was 30.., **P—KKt3,** when Lasker would have had another problem to solve like that in the last note.

31 **B × P**	**P—KKt3**
32 **K—K4**	**K—B3**

Black cannot now play **K—Kt2,** on account of 33 **K × P, K × B;** 34 **K—B6,** followed by 35 **K—K7** and 38 **P—Q7.** He is forced therefore to let the White B go.

33 **P—Kt4**	**P—Kt4**
34 **K—B3**	**K—B2**
35 **B—K4**	**K—K1**
36 **P—R4**	**K—Q2**
37 **P—R5**	**K—K1**
38 **K—K3**	**Resigns**

Sooner or later White will play **B—B6 !** and then attack Black's KP with his K again. Since the adjournment the position has been hopeless for Black.

GAME 21

LASKER v. STEINITZ

MONTREAL, *May* 5, 1894

(CHAMPIONSHIP [FIRST] MATCH, 13TH GAME)

RUY LOPEZ

	White.	*Black.*
	LASKER	STEINITZ
1	**P—K4**	**P—K4**
2	**Kt—KB3**	**Kt—QB3**
3	**B—Kt5**	**P—QR3**

A move very rarely made by Steinitz in the *Lopez*. In this case his choice of it is attended by a very happy result for him, Lasker's handling of the *Exchange Variation* being, for him, weak.

4	**B × Kt**	**QP × B**
5	**P—Q4**	**P × P**
6	**Q × P**	**Q × Q**
7	**Kt × Q**	**P—QB4**

Hoffer comments that this is best, but that the game should only be drawn; a somewhat dogmatic statement, inspired presumably by the early disappearance of the Q's.

8	**Kt—K2**	**B—Q2**
9	**QKt—B3**	

Fourteen years later, against Tarrasch at Düsseldorf, Lasker played here **P—QKt3** and, after **B—Kt2** and **Kt—Q2**, on his 14th move castled on the Q-side, which seems to be the right policy in view of Black's Pawn-majority on that wing.

		Castles
10	**B—B4**	**B—B3**

White's threat was 11 **Kt—Q5**, which would have forced **B—Q3**, with an exchange of B's.

11 **Castles KR**

This puts White's K on the wrong side of the board, theoretically, and seems therefore to show that his 9th move was not well-considered, or that he should have followed it with 10 **B—Q2** and then **Castles QR**.

		Kt—B3
12	**P—B3**	**B—K2**
13	**Kt—Kt3**	**P—KKt3**
14	**KR—K1**	

Lasker says that he should have played this R to Q1 to dispute the possession of the Q-file; or else 14 **B—Kt5**, and if **P—KR3**, then 15 **B—K3**. 14 **KR—Q1** looks best.

		Kt—Q2
15	**Kt—Q1**	

Lasker took 40 mins. to consider this move. He did not like the threat of 15.., **B—B3**; 16 **P—K5**, **B—Kt2**; 17 **R—K2**, **KR—K1**; 18 **QR—K1**, **Kt—B1**, when Black's position would clearly be superior. But his actual move gives Black time to prepare for complete domination of the Q-file. The choice is hard. 15 **QR—Q1** merits attention, for then **B—B3** could be met by 16 **KKt—K2**, the Kt being of no service on Kt3.

		Kt—Kt3
16	**Kt—B1**	**R—Q2**
17	**B—K3**	**KR—Q1**
18	**P—QKt3**	**P—B5 !**

Defeating White's plan of blocking Black's 4 P's on the Q-side with his own 3, which was what happened in the game against Tarrasch in 1908. But White could have replied 19 **Kt—B2**, to be followed by **QR—Q1**.

19	**B × Kt**	**P × B**
20	**P × P**	**B—Kt5 !**

Black wishes to induce **P—B3**, so as to unguard the square Q6 for occupation by his R.

21	**P—B3**	**B—B4 ch**
22	**K—R1**	**R—Q6**
23	**R—B1**	**P—QR4**

This is rather a strange interlude in some very forceful play. The move appears merely to mark time. **B—R6** looks much stronger, with the possible continuation (suggested by Pillsbury) 24 **Kt—KB2, R—Q7**; 25 **Kt × R, R × Kt**; 26 **Kt—R3, B × R**; 27 **R × B, P—B3.**

24 **Kt(Q1)—K3**

Position after 24 **Kt—K3:**

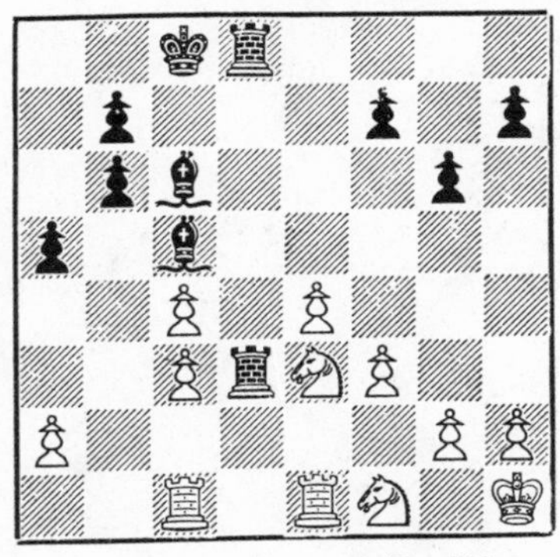

P—B4

Ostensibly offering a second P—which it would be fatal for White to accept. But White has the resource 25 **Kt—Q5 !**, and it is hard to guess why he rejected it.

25	**P × P**	**P × P**
26	**P—KR3**	

If 26 **Kt × P, R × KBP !**; 27 **Kt(B5)—Kt3, R—B7.** Or 27 **Kt—K7 ch, B × Kt**; 28 **P × R, B × P ch**; 29 **K—Kt1, B—B4 ch**; 30 **Kt—K3, R—Q7**; 31 **K—B1, R × KRP.** White is tied up, and Black's two B's are very powerful.

		R—Kt1
27	**Kt—Q5**	

If now 27 **Kt × P, R × KBP** is still more effective.

		B × Kt
28	**P × B**	**R × QP**
29	**QR—Q1**	

This move is no longer good. Lasker was pressed for time. He suggested afterwards that 29 **P—Kt4**, (if) **R—Q6**; 30 **K—Kt2, P—R4**; 31 **KR—Q1, R × R**; 32 **R × R, P × P**; 33 **BP × P, P × P**; 34 **P—KR4** might have given him some chance of a draw.

		R × R
30	**R × R**	**P—B5 !**
31	**K—R2**	

White is fatally shut in. 31 **Kt—R2** would be answered by **P—KR4**, and 31 **Kt—Q2** by **R—Q1.** Nor can the R leave the first rank.

		R—K1
32	**P—QR4**	**K—B2**
33	**P—R4**	**K—B3**
34	**P—B4**	**B—Kt5**
35	**K—R3**	**R—K8**
36	**R × R**	**B × R**
37	**K—Kt4**	**K—B4**
38	**K × P**	**K × P**
39	**K—K4**	

If 39 **P—R5, K—Q6,** and Black wins with his Q-side Pawns.

		B × P
40	**P—Kt3**	**B—Q1**
41	**Kt—K3 ch**	

The Kt has re-entered the game, but can do nothing to save it.

		K—Kt5
42	**K—Q3**	**K × P**
43	**K—B2**	**K—Kt4**
44	**P—B4**	**K—B4**
45	**P—B5**	**K—Q3**
46	**P—Kt4**	**P—Kt4**
47	**Kt—Q1**	**K—K4**
48	**Kt—B3**	**P—Kt5**
49	**Kt—R4**	**K—Q5**
50	**Kt—Kt2**	**P—Kt4**
51	**K—Kt3**	**B—K2**
52	**P—Kt5**	**P—R5 ch**
53	**Kt × P**	**P × Kt ch**
54	**K × P**	**K—K4**

K—B5 is the quickest line.

55	**K—Kt3**	**K × P**

White resigns.

Steinitz's play in this game is like that of his best period.

GAME 22

STEINITZ v. LASKER

MONTREAL, *May* 8, 1894

(CHAMPIONSHIP [FIRST] MATCH, 14TH GAME)

QUEEN'S GAMBIT DECLINED

White. STEINITZ	*Black.* LASKER
1 **P—Q4**	**P—Q4**
2 **P—QB4**	**P—K3**
3 **Kt—QB3**	**P—QB3**

This move, so fashionable today, though generally played one step earlier in the opening, was seriously questioned in 1894. We get here a form of the normal *Slav Defence*, a name then unknown in the books.

4 **P—K3**	**Kt—B3**
5 **Kt—B3**	**B—Q3**
6 **B—Q3**	**QKt—Q2**
7 **Castles**	**Castles**
8 **P—K4**	**P × KP**
9 **Kt × P**	**Kt × Kt**
10 **B × Kt**	

All so far, with transpositions, appears in *Modern Chess Openings*, p. 139, col. 78, the example chosen there being Grünfeld-Bogoljuboff, Berlin, 1926. Bogoljuboff played the " modern " 10.., **P—QB4**, with the continuation 11 **B—B2, Q—B2**; 12 **Q—Q3, P—B4**, which did not yield him a good game.

	P—KR3
11 **B—B2**	**P—KB4**

Lasker said of this that, though it weakens the K-side, it paves the way for a strong attack.

12 **R—K1**	**Kt—B3**
13 **B—Q2**	**B—Q2**
14 **B—B3**	**Q—B2**
15 **Kt—K5**	**B—K1**
16 **Q—Q3**	**P—KKt4**

Black is committed to attack on this wing, as his general development is less logical than White's; and he does not wish to allow 17 **P—B4.**

17 **Q—R3**	**Q—Kt2**
18 **QR—Q1**	**P—Kt5 ?**

Not good, for the White Q goes to a better square. Lasker explains that he thought he could continue with 19.., **Q—Kt4**, seeing too late that the answer would be 20 **Kt × KtP !** He should have played, he says, 18.., **B—R4**, and if 19 **R—Q2, QR—K1.**

19 **Q—K3**	**B—R4**

Position after 19.., **B—R4:**

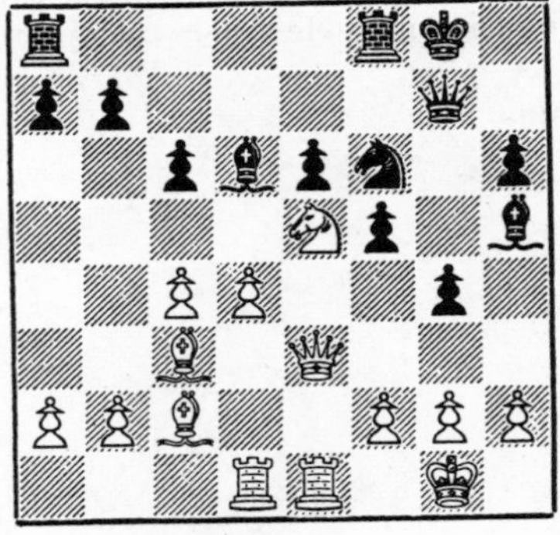

20 **Kt × BP !**

White gets his blow in first, through Black missing his chance to play **QR—K1**. The result is to give White an ending with two P's for the Exchange; for it does not seem that Black can profitably vary his next few moves.

		B × P ch
21	**K × B**	**P—Kt6 ch**
22	**Q × P**	**Q × Q ch**
23	**P × Q**	**B × R**
24	**B × B**	**P × Kt**
25	**R × P**	**Kt—K5**

26 **P—Q5** is threatened, and so Black is compelled to give up another P. The alternative 25.., **Kt—Kt5 ch**; 26 **B × Kt, P × B**; 27 **R × BP** is clearly worse.

26	**R × BP**	**Kt × B**
27	**P × Kt**	**K—Kt2**

Far inferior to **QR—K1**, says Lasker, as White could hardly take the KRP, owing to the close confinement of his K.

28	**R—R6**	**R—B2**
29	**P—B5**	

White makes a first slight slip. He should have played 29 **K—Kt1**.

R—Q1 ?

Lasker's sealed move at the adjournment. He misses the opportunity of **R—K2**, preventing White's K from coming into the game.

30	**K—Kt1**	**R—K2**
31	**K—B2**	**R—QKt1**
32	**B—Kt3**	**QR—K1**
33	**B—B4**	**R—QKt1**
34	**B—Q3**	**P—R4**
35	**K—B3**	**R—Kt7**
36	**B × P !**	

A move requiring very accurate analysis.

		R—KB2
37	**K—K4**	**R—K7 ch**
38	**K—Q3**	**R × KtP**
39	**R—Kt6 ch**	**K—B1**
40	**B—K4**	**R—Kt8**

Obviously he cannot take the RP.

41	**P—Q5**	**R—KKt2**
42	**R × R**	**K × R**
43	**P—B6**	**K—B3**
44	**P—B7**	**R × P ch**
45	**K—Q4**	**R—Kt1**
46	**P—Q6**	**Resigns**

For if **K—K3**, 47 **B—Q6 ch**; and otherwise 47 **P—Q7**.

Steinitz played with admirable vigour at the beginning of the Montreal series of games in this match. So far he had scored a draw and two successive wins in three games.

GAME 23

STEINITZ v. LASKER

MONTREAL, *May* 17, 1894

(CHAMPIONSHIP [FIRST] MATCH, 16TH GAME)

QUEEN'S GAMBIT DECLINED

White.	*Black.*
STEINITZ	LASKER
1 **P—Q4**	**P—Q4**
2 **P—QB4**	**P—K3**
3 **Kt—QB3**	**Kt—KB3**
4 **B—Kt5**	**B—K2**
5 **Kt—B3**	**QKt—Q2**
6 **P—K3**	**Castles**
7 **P—B5**	

This move, generally considered admissible in such a position only after Black has played **P—QR3** (as Euwe used it in the 8th and 10th games against Alekhine in 1935), was played by Steinitz in the 12th game. In the 18th he played the better 7 **R—B1.**

Kt—K5

In the 12th game Lasker had replied **P—B3.** The new move is said to have " startled the spectators " in Montreal.

8 **Kt × Kt**	**P × Kt**
9 **B × B**	**Q × B**
10 **Kt—Q2**	**Kt—B3**
11 **Kt—B4**	

11 **Q—B2, P—K4;** 12 **Kt × P, P × P;** 13 **Kt × Kt ch, Q × Kt** would be favourable to Black.

P—QKt3

This is the move that tests White's variation.

12 **P—QKt4**	**Kt—Q4**
13 **Q—Kt1**	

There does not appear to be a good alternative; for if 13 **P—QR3, P—QR4 !**

P—B4

14 **Kt—K5**

The Kt has now a commanding post, and according to some of the critics should not have left it next move.

P—QR4

15 **Kt—B6**

If this is wrong, however, what is the right move? The QKtP is doubly attacked.

Q—Kt4

16 **P—KR4** **Q—B3**

Position after 16.., **Q—B3:**

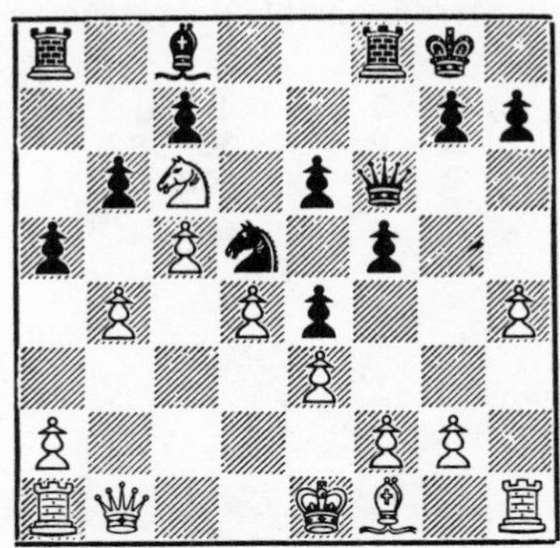

17 **BP × P**

The situation is now very interesting, and the complications which ensue are difficult to analyse. White could have prevented Black's next move by 17 **P—Kt3.** But there was then 17.., **B—Kt2** to be considered. White's precarious Q-side is proving a considerable embarrassment to him.

P—B5

Rather bold, comments Hoffer. But the " boldness " seems justified by the comparative developments of the two sides.

18 **Q × P** **P × KP**
19 **P—B3** **B—Kt2**
20 **P—Kt5**

20 **Kt × P ?, R × Kt !;** 21 **P × R, Kt—Kt5** would give Black a speedy victory.

B × Kt
21 **P × B** **P × P**
22 **B—Q3** **Q—R3**

Threatening **R—B5.**

23 **P—Kt3** **QR—B1**
24 **R—QB1** **R—QB2**
25 **Castles** **R—Q1**
26 **P—B4** **Q—Kt3**

Offering a Pawn-sacrifice, which White must accept, in order to win a more valuable P three moves later.

27 **Q × Q** **P × Q**
28 **B × P** **Kt—K2**
29 **B—K4** **KR × P**
30 **B—B3** **Kt—B4**
31 **KR—K1** **K—B2**
32 **R—Kt1** **Kt × KtP**
33 **R × KtP** **Kt—B4**
34 **R—Kt7** **R × R**
35 **P × R** **R—Kt5**
36 **R—QB1**

Mason gives 36 **B—K4** as a probable draw.

Kt—Q5
37 **K—Kt2 ?**

This loses. 37 **R—B7 ch,** followed by 38 **B—K4,** seems still to save the game. After the text-move Black must win, but the manner in which he does so is instructive.

R—Kt7 ch
38 **K—Kt3** **R × KtP**
39 **B × R** **Kt—K7 ch**
40 **K—B3** **Kt × R**
41 **K × P** **Kt × P**
42 **K—Q4** **K—B3**
43 **K—B5** **Kt—B6**
44 **K—B4** **Kt—K7**
45 **K—Kt5** **Kt × P**
46 **K × P** **Kt—Kt3**
47 **P—R5** **Kt—B5**
48 **B—B3** **K—B4**
49 **K—Kt4** **P—K4**
50 **K—B3** **P—K5**
51 **B—Q1** **P—K6**
52 **B—B3** **K—Kt4**
53 **K—B2** **K—R5**
54 **K—Q1** **K—Kt6**

White resigns.

Wherever the B goes, Black answers **K—B7.**

GAME 24

STEINITZ v. LASKER

MOSCOW, *January* 14, 1897

(CHAMPIONSHIP [SECOND] MATCH, 17TH GAME)

QUEEN'S GAMBIT DECLINED

	White.	*Black.*
	STEINITZ	LASKER
1	**P—Q4**	**P—Q4**
2	**P—QB4**	**P—K3**
3	**Kt—QB3**	**Kt—KB3**
4	**B—Kt5**	**B—K2**
5	**P—K3**	**Castles**
6	**Q—Kt3**	

One of Steinitz's eccentricities which did not find favour with later players.

		QKt—Q2
7	**Kt—B3**	**P—B3**
8	**B—Q3**	

This loss of time with the B has little to recommend it. With his Q misplaced, however, White cannot so well play 8 **R—B1** or **R—Q1** as if the Q stood at B2, on account of the reply **Kt—K5.** Perhaps there is nothing better than 8 **P × P, KP × P;** 9 **B—Q3.**

		P × P
9	**B × P**	**P—Kt4**

Lasker's procedure is on the lines of the later *Meran Variation,* with the addition of the moves **B—K2** and **Castles** for Black, and **B—KKt5** and **Q—Kt3** for White.

10	**B—K2 ?**	**P—QR3**
11	**P—QR4**	

This invites Black's next move. If White had contemplated it, his 10th move should surely have been **B—Q3.** Now at least he should prevent his Kt having to shut his QR in, playing 11 **R—Q1** or **QB1.**

		P—Kt5
12	**Kt—QKt1**	**P—B4**
13	**QKt—Q2**	**B—Kt2**
14	**P—R5**	

White's aim is to isolate Black's QKtP; but Black obviously does not mind that. 14 **Castles** is preferable, to allow his KKt freedom.

		P × P
15	**P × P**	**Kt—Q4**
16	**B—K3**	**B—Q3**
17	**Kt—B4**	**B—B2**
18	**B—Kt5**	**P—B3**
19	**B—Q2**	**Q—K2**
20	**Kt—K3**	**QR—Kt1**

Defeating White's strenuous efforts to win the QKtP, for of course if 21 **Kt × Kt, B × Kt,** and the P is doubly protected again.

21	**B—B4**	**KR—Q1**
22	**Castles**	**Kt—B1**
23	**KR—K1**	**Q—B2**
24	**Kt—B1**	

White abandons designs on the QKtP and withdraws this Kt to the defence.

		K—R1
25	**Kt—Kt3**	**B × Kt**
26	**RP × B**	**Kt—KKt3**
27	**Q—Q3**	**R—Q3**
28	**R—K2**	**B—B1**

The point of this is not clear; but the end of the second hour was approaching.

29 **Kt—K1** **Q—Q2**

Position after 29.., **Q—Q2**:

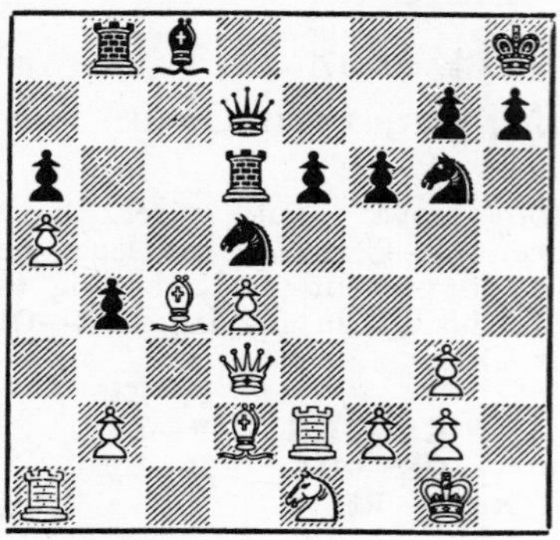

30 **Kt—B2**

30 **P—B4** was suggested. But it does not stop 30.., **P—K4**, White's Q being in a perilous position behind the QP, whilst his K-side would be completely disorganised.

		P—K4 !
31	**QR—K1**	**B—Kt2**
32	**Q—Kt3**	

If 32 **P × P, Kt × P**; 33 **Q—Kt3, B—B3** is still worse for White.

		B—B3 !
33	**Kt × P**	**Kt × Kt**
34	**B × Kt**	**R × P**
35	**Q—QB3**	**B × P**

Threatening **Q—R6.**

36	**K × B**	**Q—B3 ch**
37	**R—K4**	

37 **Q—B3** would allow **Kt—R5 ch**; 38 **P × Kt, R—Kt5 ch.** Any other move would lose both B's.

		R × R
38	**R × R**	**Q × R ch**
39	**K—Kt1**	**Q—Kt2**
40	**B—B5**	**R—Q1 !**

Not 40.., **Q × P**; 41 **Q × Q, R × Q**; 42 **B × P.** Black must keep up the offensive, and retain his QRP as long as possible.

41	**B—K2**	**P—K5**
42	**P—QKt4**	**Kt—K4**
43	**B—K3**	**Kt—Q6**
44	**B—Kt6**	**R—QB1**
45	**Q—Q4**	**P—R3**
46	**K—R2**	**Kt—K4**
47	**Q—Q1**	**R—B6**
48	**Q—Q6**	**Kt—B6 ch**
49	**K—Kt2**	**Q—KB2 !**
50	**P—Kt4**	

If 50 **B × P, Q—R4** wins at once.

		Q—R7
51	**B—B1**	**Kt—R5 ch**
52	**K—Kt1**	**R—B8**
53	**B—K3**	**Kt—B6 ch**
54	**K—Kt2**	**R × B**
55	**Q × RP**	

If 55 **K × R**, a forced mate follows in 5 moves. By the text-move White at least prolongs the game.

		R—Kt8 ch
56	**K—R3**	**Q—Q4**

To guard against 57 **Q—R8 ch** and 58 **Q × P ch.**

57	**Q—B8 ch**	**K—R2**
58	**P—R6**	**R—R8 ch**
59	**K—Kt2**	**Kt—R5 ch**

White resigns

If 60 **K × R, Q—Q8 ch**; 62 **K—R2, Q—B6**; 63 **Q—B5 ch, Kt × Q**; 63 **P × Kt, P—R4 !** and White cannot avoid an ultimate mate even if he queens his RP. If 60 **K—Kt3, Q—K4 ch**; 61 **B—B4, R—R6 ch**; 62 **K × R, Q × B**, and again White can only sacrifice his Q unavailingly.

In his last game for the World Championship Steinitz has made a splendid fight against odds imposed by himself in the opening.

GAME 25

MARSHALL v. LASKER

NEW YORK, *January* 26, 1907
(CHAMPIONSHIP MATCH, 1ST GAME)

RUY LOPEZ

	White.	*Black.*
	MARSHALL	LASKER
1	**P—K4**	**P—K4**
2	**Kt—KB3**	**Kt—QB3**
3	**B—Kt5**	**Kt—B3**

Lasker's favourite *Berlin Defence*. Compare Game 31.

4	**P—Q4**	**P × P**
5	**Castles**	**B—K2**
6	**P—K5**	**Kt—K5**
7	**Kt × P**	**Castles**

An older line of play (Anderssen's) was 7.., **Kt × Kt;** 8 **Q × Kt, Kt—B4,** followed by **Castles.**

8	**Kt—B5**	**P—Q4**
9	**B × Kt**	

9 **Kt × B ch, Kt × Kt;** 10 **P—KB3, Kt—QB4;** 11 **P—QKt4, Kt—K3;** 12 **P—KB4, P—KB4;** 13 **B—R4,** as in Zukertort-Tchigorin, Berlin, 1881, seems a preferable course.

9		**P × B**
10	**Kt × B ch**	**Q × Kt**

The analysts of the day disagreed as to who had the better game at this stage. Teichmann speaks of White's threat of **P—KB3,** followed by **P—QKt3** and **B—R3;** but this obviously is not an immediate threat, and Black easily guards against it, at the same time preparing a subtle sacrifice.

11	**R—K1**	**Q—R5**
12	**B—K3**	

Hoffer strongly advocates **P—KB3** at once.

12		**P—B3**
13	**P—KB3**	

Position after 13 **P—KB3:**

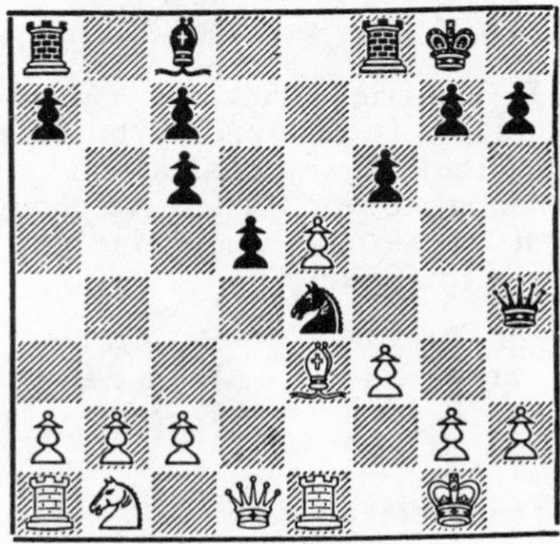

P × P !

Lasker at the beginning of this match, indeed for the greater part of it, seems actuated by a "superiority-complex." That is not to say that this sacrifice is not perfectly sound.

14	**P × Kt**	**P—Q5**
15	**P—KKt3**	

If 15 **B—Q2,** then **B—Kt5;** 16 **Q—B1, R—B7;** 17 **B—Kt5, R × P ch;** 18 **K × R, B—R6 ch,** with a forced mate to follow. If 15 **B—B1,** then **Q—B7 ch;** 16 **K—R1, B—Kt5** etc. The B therefore cannot be saved. But White can play 15 **Q—Q2, P × B;** 16 **Q × P** without serious disadvantage, if indeed any.

Q—B3

Here Lasker misses a quick win by **Q—R6,** when again White cannot save his B, nor in this case the game. If 16 **B—B2,** then **R × B;** 17 **K × R, Q × RP ch;** 18 **K—B3, P—KR4** etc. If 16 **B—Q2, R—B7.** And if 16 **B × P, B—Kt5 !;** 17 **Q—Q2, P × B** with a crushing attack.

16 **B × P**	**P × B**
17 **R—B1**	**Q × R ch**
18 **Q × Q**	**R × Q ch**
19 **K × R**	**R—Kt1**

In material Black has gained nothing. It remains for him to show that his positional advantage is enough to win. There is a good deal of cat-and-mouse business about this ending.

20 **P—Kt3**	**R—Kt4**
21 **P—B4**	**R—KR4**
22 **K—Kt1**	**P—B4**
23 **Kt—Q2**	

Developed at last !

	K—B2
24 **R—B1 ch**	**K—K2**
25 **P—QR3**	**R—R3**
26 **P—KR4**	**R—R3**
27 **R—R1**	**B—Kt5**
28 **K—B2**	**K—K3**
29 **K—Kt2**	

If 29 **Kt—B3,** to avoid the loss of a tempo, Black captures and follows up with **K—K4.**

	K—K4
30 **P—R4**	**R—KB3**
31 **R—K1**	**P—Q6**
32 **R—KB1**	

After the exchange of R's White will obviously be at a great disadvantage. But Black is threatening in any case to get a terrible bind on the position.

	K—Q5
33 **R × R**	**P × R**
34 **K—B2**	**P—B3**
35 **P—QR5**	**P—QR3**
36 **Kt—B1**	**K × P**

By scientific strangulation White has been compelled to give up a P, and he might now resign.

37 **K—K1**	**B—K7**
38 **Kt—Q2 ch**	**K—K6**
39 **Kt—Kt1**	**P—B4**
40 **Kt—Q2**	**P—R4**
41 **Kt—Kt1**	**K—B6**
42 **Kt—B3**	**K × P**
43 **Kt—R4**	**P—B5**
44 **Kt × P**	**P—B6**
45 **Kt—K4 ch**	**K—B5**
46 **Kt—Q6**	**P—B4**

A final reserve move with a P, compelling White to make some move which loses outright—*e.g.*, if **Kt—Kt7,** then **K—K6.**

White resigns.

GAME 26

LASKER v. TARRASCH

MUNICH, *September* 1, 1908

(CHAMPIONSHIP MATCH, 5TH GAME)

RUY LOPEZ

	White.	*Black.*
	LASKER	TARRASCH
1	**P—K4**	**P—K4**
2	**Kt—KB3**	**Kt—QB3**
3	**B—Kt5**	**P—QR3**
4	**B—R4**	**Kt—B3**
5	**Castles**	**B—K2**

The quiet continuation, as opposed to the aggressive **Kt × P,** which is to be seen in Games 32 and 46.

6	**R—K1**	**P—QKt4**
7	**B—Kt3**	**P—Q3**
8	**P—B3**	**Kt—QR4**
9	**B—B2**	**P—B4**
10	**P—Q4**	

The present match did much to establish the popularity of this move against the formerly more favoured 10 **P—Q3.**

		Q—B2
11	**QKt—Q2**	**Kt—B3**
12	**P—KR3**	**Castles**
13	**Kt—B1**	

13 **P—Q5,** before this move, was thought to close up the game too much; but it has later had the preference over the text-move, which sacrifices a P temporarily. White's 12th move, too, has been discarded as unnecessary.

		BP × P
14	**P × P**	**QKt × P**
15	**Kt × Kt**	**P × Kt**
16	**B—Kt5**	

In the 3rd game of the match Lasker played the inferior 16 **Kt—Kt3,** allowing the reply **Kt—Q2,** which he here prevents. But the Russian analyst Malkin gives 16 **R—K2** as best, and if **Q—Kt3,** 17 **Q—Q3.**

		P—R3

Two years later a correspondence game, W. H. Gunston *v.* Rev. E. Griffiths, threw some new light on this variation by the substitution of 16.., **Q—B4** for the text-move. The continuation was 17 **B—KR4** (17 **Q—Q2, R—R2;** 18 **QR—B1, Kt × P,** winning another P), **B—K3;** 18 **R—QB1, Q—Kt5;** 19 **P—QKt3, P—Q4;** 20 **B × Kt, B × B;** 21 **P × P, B—Q2.** Black has given back the P, but retains his two B's against B and Kt.

17	**B—KR4**	**Q—Kt3**

This is not now good. Schlechter suggests **B—K3,** for then 18 **Q—Q3** can be answered by **B—B5.**

18	**Q—Q3**	**P—Kt4**

A more than doubtful move, in view of White's at present masked attack. **P—Kt3** is necessary.

19	**B—KKt3**	**B—K3**
20	**QR—Q1**	**KR—B1**
21	**B—Kt1**	**Kt—Q2**

Position after 21.., **Kt—Q2**:

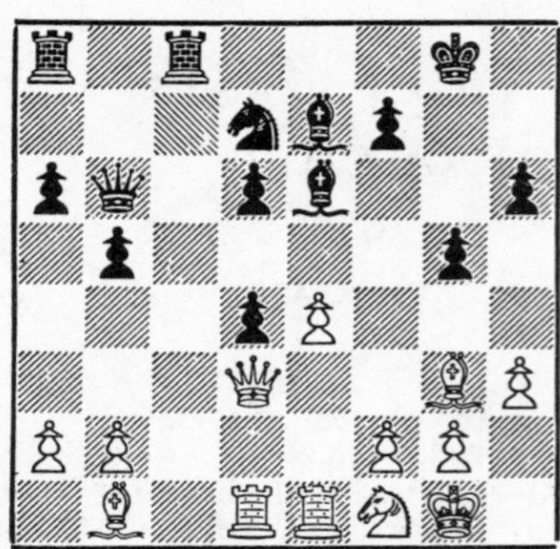

22 **P—K5 !**

When he can at last regain the P he sacrificed, Lasker plays instead a decisive move, which in conjunction with the following Q-moves admits of no effective reply.

		Kt—B1
23	**Q—KB3**	**P—Q4**
24	**Q—R5**	**K—Kt2**
25	**P—B4**	

Another heavy blow. Black's defence crumbles rapidly.

		P—B4
26	**P × P i.p. ch**	**B × P**
27	**P × P**	**P × P**
28	**B—K5**	**P—Q6 dis. ch**
29	**K—R1**	**Kt—Kt3**
30	**Q × P**	**B—B2**
31	**Kt—Kt3**	

After being in reserve for 18 moves the Kt comes into the game again with a strong threat.

		B × B
32	**R × B**	**R—R1**
33	**B × P**	**R—QR2**
34	**QR—K1**	**K—B1**
35	**B × Kt**	**Q × B**
36	**Q—K3**	**R—B2**
37	**Kt—B5**	**Q—QB3**

37 **R—K8 ch** was threatened. But the removal of the Q allows another deadly threat.

38	**Q—Kt5**	**Resigns**

This and the 16th games are decidedly the most attractive of the match.

GAME 27

TARRASCH v. LASKER

MUNICH, *September* 30, 1908

(CHAMPIONSHIP MATCH, 16TH GAME)

FOUR KNIGHTS GAME

	White.	*Black.*
	TARRASCH	LASKER
1	**P—K4**	**P—K4**
2	**Kt—KB3**	**Kt—QB3**
3	**B—Kt5**	**Kt—B3**
4	**Kt—B3**	**B—Kt5**
5	**Castles**	**Castles**
6	**P—Q3**	**P—Q3**
7	**B—Kt5**	**B—K3**

A new move, in place of the more usual **B × Kt,** for which see the next two games.

8	**P—Q4**	**P × P**
9	**Kt × P**	**P—KR3**
10	**B—KR4**	

10 **QB × Kt, Q × B;** 11 **Kt × Kt, P × Kt;** 12 **B × P** would win a P. But by 12.., **R—Kt1;** 13 **Q—Q3, B—R4;** 14 **Kt—Q1, R—Kt5** White would have obtained a game not to Lasker's liking.

Kt—K4

The opening move of a sacrificial combination.

Position after 10.., **Kt—K4:**

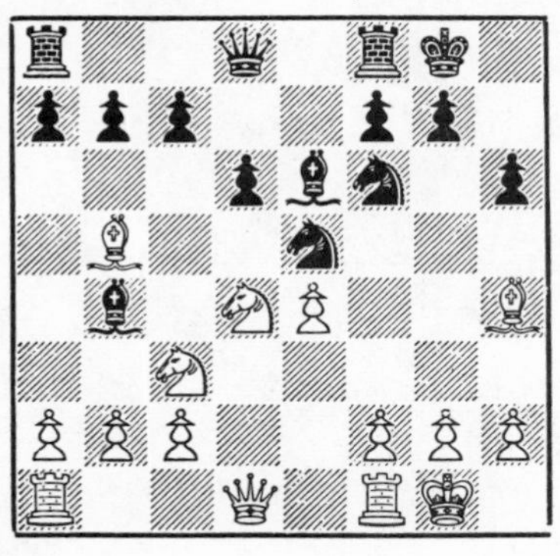

11	**P—B4**	**B—QB4**
12	**B × Kt**	

In a note upon this move later Tarrasch gave as best 12 **K—R1, Kt—Kt3;** 13 **B × Kt, Q × B;** 14 **KKt—K2.** So also Teichmann. Hoffer, on the other hand, suggested 13 **P—B5.** Yet another alternative is 13 **Kt—K2.** The line initiated by the text-move wins two minor pieces for a R, but White has much the more difficult game to play.

		Q × B
13	**P × Kt**	**Q × P**
14	**Kt—K2**	**B—KKt5**
15	**R—B3**	

White's weak point is the position of his KB, making impossible both 15 **P—B3** and 15 **K—R1,** on account of the reply **KB × Kt.**

		B × R
16	**P × B**	**P—B4**

A good move: but there is a good answer to it.

17 **Q—Q3**

Not 17 **P × P, R × P;** 18 **K—R1, R—R4;** 19 **Q—KKt1, R—KB1;** 20 **R—KB1, B × Kt;** 21 **Kt × B, R—B5;** 22 **P—B3, R × Kt;** 23 **P × R, Q × B** (Lasker). Black would be a P to the good, with the better position.

		P—B3
18	**B—B4 ch**	**K—R1**
19	**K—R1**	**P—QKt4**
20	**B—Kt3**	**P × P**
21	**Q × KP**	**Q × Q**
22	**P × Q**	**QR—K1**

23 **Kt × BP** **R × P**
24 **Kt—Kt3** **QR—K1**
25 **R—Q1** **R—B7**
26 **Kt—Q4 ? ?**

A terrible mistake, under time-pressure (from which both players were suffering). It cannot, however, be said that White throws away the game by it, as he had a very inferior position, with his Kt on B6 completely out of play. 26 **P—QR3** seems his only safe move.

B × Kt

White resigns.

Naturally the B cannot be captured.

GAME 28

JANOWSKI v. LASKER

PARIS, *May* 17-18, 1909

(EXHIBITION MATCH, 3RD GAME)

FOUR KNIGHTS GAME

	White.	*Black.*
	JANOWSKI	LASKER
1	**P—K4**	**P—K4**
2	**Kt—KB3**	**Kt—QB3**
3	**Kt—B3**	**Kt—B3**
4	**B—Kt5**	**B—Kt5**
5	**Castles**	**Castles**
6	**P—Q3**	**P—Q3**
7	**B—Kt5**	**B × Kt**

See the preceding game.

8 **P × B** **Kt—K2**

A defence which went out of favour on account of the strength of the reply 9 **Kt—R4,** as played, for instance, by Janowski against Spielmann, Nuremberg, 1906. Now, however, Janowski selects a continuation which Lasker calls "almost the loss of a move."

9 **B—QB4** **B—K3**

This is not the correct reply to show the truth of the criticism just quoted. 9.., **Kt—Kt3** is the right move, for which see the following game.

10 **B—Kt3** **B × B**

The object of Black's previous move, no doubt; but why this haste to exchange B's? **Kt—Kt3** still seems good.

11	**RP × B**	**Kt—Q2**
12	**P—Q4**	**P—KB3**
13	**B—K3**	**Kt—KKt3**

Now this move, so strong at an earlier stage, is much less effective. It allows the continuation 14 **P × P, BP × P** or **Kt(Q2) × P;** 15 **Q—Q5 ch,** winning Black's QKtP—which the great analyst George Marco, of the *Wiener Schachzeitung*, declared to be White's best line. Janowski did not play it; and Marco asks whether he, as perhaps also Lasker, believed that the surrender of the QKtP was correct. But if so Black must have some compensation to show for it. After 14 (**P × P**), **BP × P;** 15 **Q—Q5 ch, K—R1** White does not immediately capture the P (which permits the counter 16.., **R × Kt**), but plays 16 **Kt—Kt5,** followed by **Q × KtP.** If 14.., **Kt(Q2) × P;** 15 **Q—Q5 ch, R—B2;** 16 **Kt × Kt, Kt × Kt** White proceeds with the capture. In neither case does Black appear to have value for the lost P.

Position after 13.., **Kt—KKt3:**

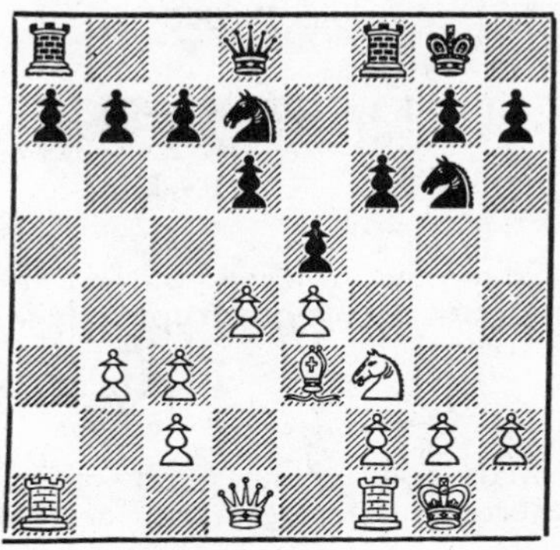

14	**Q—Q3**	**K—R1**
15	**Kt—Q2**	**P—QB3**
16	**P—KB4**	**P × BP**
17	**B × P**	**Q—K2**
18	**B—Kt3**	**KR—K1**
19	**QR—K1**	**Kt—Kt3**

To stop 20 **Kt—B4**, on the way through **K3** to **B5**.

20	**P—R4**	**Kt—KB1**

Otherwise White by 21 **P—R5** could gain a tempo to play 22 **P—R6**.

21	**P—B4**	**QR—Q1**
22	**Kt—B3**	**Q—KB2**
23	**P—Q5**	**Kt(Kt3)—Q2**
24	**Kt—Q4**	**Q—Kt3**

Black will gain nothing by **Kt—B4**; 25 **Q—KB3**.

25	**Kt—B5**	**Kt—K4**
26	**B × Kt**	

White is relying on his positional advantage, which makes the apparent weakness of his KP of no importance. Black has no time to double his R's.

		R × B
27	**R—K3**	**R—Q2**
28	**Q—K2 !**	**Q—K1**

He cannot allow the Q to be attacked by 29 **P—R5**.

29	**Q—Kt4**	**P—KKt3**
30	**Kt—Kt3**	**R—KB2**

The plausible **P—KB4** is met by 31 **Q—B4**.

31	**R(K3)—KB3**	**Kt—Q2**
32	**R—B4**	**R(B2)—K2**
33	**Q—B3**	**P—KR4**
34	**P—Kt4**	

The way in which the KP is protected from a quadruple attack is noteworthy.

		R—Kt2
35	**Q—B3**	**P—KKt4**

Black's only chance is, obviously, to break through to attack on the K-side; but it is a desperate venture.

36	**R—B5**	**P × P**
37	**Kt × P**	**Q × Kt**

If **R—Kt3**, there follows 38 **Kt × P, Kt × Kt**; 39 **R × Kt, R × R**; 40 **R × R**, (if) **Q—R4**; 41 **R—B5**. Black therefore sells the Q for what he can get—R and Kt, which proves inadequate when White counter-sacrifices Q for two R's.

38	**R × Q ch**	**R × R**
39	**Q—KR3**	**K—Kt1**
40	**R—B4**	**R(R4)—Kt4**
41	**R × RP**	**R × P ch**
42	**Q × R**	**Kt—K4**
43	**Q × R ch**	**K × Q**
44	**K—B2**	**Kt × P**

Superficially, with a P for the Exchange, Black might look to have a chance to draw. In reality there is no fight left.

45	**R—R3**	**Kt—K4**
46	**K—K3**	**P—R4**
47	**P × P**	**Kt—B5 ch**
48	**K—B4**	**Kt × P**
49	**R—R3**	**Resigns**

There is no parry to the threat of 50 **R—QB3**.

The manner in which Janowski profits by his opponent's opening errors merits all praise, even if Marco's claim of a better line for him on the 14th move is right. The game being one in an exhibition match, Lasker perhaps did not put so much work into it as if it had been for his championship title. But, as Janowski had already won the 2nd game in a series of 4, it can hardly be supposed that Lasker was careless whether he won or lost.

The object here, however, has been to show an aspirant for the world championship title in his best form.

GAME 29

JANOWSKI v. LASKER

PARIS, *October* 21, 1909

(CHAMPIONSHIP [FIRST] MATCH, 2ND GAME)

FOUR KNIGHTS GAME

White.	*Black.*
JANOWSKI	LASKER

(*First* 8 *moves as in preceding game.*)

9 **B—QB4** **Kt—Kt3 !**

See the preceding game. The contrast is very instructive.

10 **Kt—R4** **Kt—B5**

Lasker, who uses this game as an example in his *Chess Manual*, marks this move with a !

11 **B × QKt**

Lasker suggests 11 **B—Kt3** (not 11 **Q—Q2, Kt × KP**), for if **P—KR3,** then 12 **B × QKt; P × B;** 13 **Kt—Kt6.**

P × B

12 **Kt—B3** **B—Kt5**

13 **P—KR3**

Better is 13 **Q—Q2,** inviting White to open the KKt-file at his peril.

B—R4

14 **R—Kt1** **P—QKt3**

15 **Q—Q2** **B × Kt**

16 **P × B**

Now Black has opened the file; but White's position has been weakened by the advance of the KRP.

Kt—R4

17 **K—R2** **Q—B3**

18 **R—Kt1** **QR—K1**

19 **P—Q4**

19.., **R—K4** was threatened.

K—R1

20 **R—QKt5** **Q—R3**

Many players would no doubt choose here **P—B4,** to prevent White from doubling R's on the KKt-file; but Lasker's line is more subtle, allowing the doubling because he calculates on being able to turn the resulting position to his advantage.

21 **QR—Kt5** **P—KB3**

22 **QR—Kt4**

Position after 22 **QR—Kt4;**

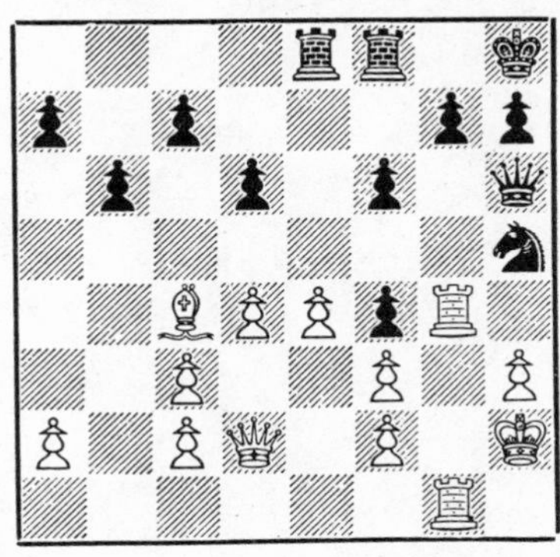

P—Kt3 !

The situation is very interesting. White has great force on an open file, an apparently impregnable centre, and a B in full control of a long diagonal. But Black's advantage, says Lasker, consists in White's inability to open lines of his own accord; and his task is therefore to select the most favourable time to open lines himself.

23 **B—Q3**

The B proves singularly ineffective in this game. The text-move is a deterrent against 23.., **P—KB4.** But Black is biding his time for that move, after the B has moved again to defend other threats.

	R—K2
24 **P—B4**	**Kt—Kt2 !**
25 **P—B3**	

25 **Q × P, Q × Q;** 26 **R × Q, Kt—K3** would be decisively in Black's favour.

Kt—K3

Threatening **Kt—Kt4,** and thus forcing the B to go to the defence of two weak P's—when the KBP makes its advance.

26 **B—B1**	**P—KB4**
27 **QR—Kt2**	**R—B3**

See the next note.

28 **B—Q3**	**P—KKt4**

Now the threat is **Q × P ch;** 29 **K × Q, R—R3** mate.

29 **R—KR1**	**P—Kt5**
30 **B—K2**	**Kt—Kt4**
31 **BP × P**	

Equivalent to resignation. But there is no means of prolonging the game.

	P—B6
32 **R—Kt3**	**P × B**

White resigns.

The game throughout is an admirable exhibition of Lasker's style. The handling of the Kt is in particular a display of chess genius. On Janowski's part there was no absolute " blunder "; he was simply outplayed.

GAME 30

JANOWSKI v. LASKER

Paris, *November* 9, 1909

(Championship [First] Match, 10th Game)

SICILIAN DEFENCE

White.	*Black.*
Janowski	Lasker
1 **P—K4**	**P—QB4**
2 **Kt—QB3**	**Kt—QB3**
3 **Kt—B3**	**P—KKt3**
4 **P—Q4**	**P × P**
5 **Kt × P**	**B—Kt2**
6 **B—K3**	

So far the same as Lasker-Napier, Cambridge Springs, 1904, which continued 6.., **P—Q3;** 7 **P—KR3, Kt—B3;** 8 **P—KKt4** and developed into an extraordinary game.

	Kt—B3
7 **B—K2**	**Castles**
8 **Q—Q2**	

Maróczy's 8 **Kt—Kt3** would prevent 8.., **P—Q4,** which 8 **Castles** and the text-move both allow. At the time of the match 8 **Q—Q2, P—Q4** was held to be favourable to White; but Lasker's opinion to the contrary is endorsed by that great *Sicilian* expert, Professor Albert Becker, in his monograph on the opening.

	P—Q4
9 **P × P**	

If 9 **Kt × Kt, P × Kt;** 10 **P—K5,** Black gets a good game with **Kt—Kt5.**

	Kt × P
10 **QKt × Kt**	**Q × Kt**
11 **B—B3**	

This is a natural move, but is possibly not so strong as 11 **Kt × Kt,** followed, if **Q × Kt,** by 12 **Castles KR** and 13 **B—B3.** Or if 11.., **P × Kt,** then 12 **Q × Q, P × Q;** 13 **Castles QR.**

	Q—B5
12 **P—QKt3**	

Janowski still holds back from **Kt × Kt,** though it looks now the proper sequel to his last move. With the text-move he lands himself into needless difficulties. His harassing of the Black Q fails to drive her to a bad square, and he is faced with two problems, how to find time for castling, and how to get rid of the pin on his QR before Black plays **R—Q1.** There is no solution to both.

	Q—R3
13 **B—K2**	**Q—R6**
14 **P—QB3**	**R—Q1**

Position after 14.., **R—Q1**

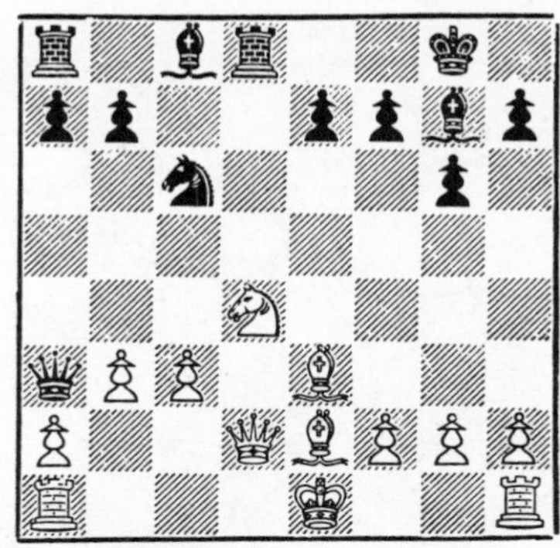

15 **R—Q1**

This loses the QRP without compensation. He might have tried 15 **Q—B1, Kt × Kt;** 16 **P × Kt, Q × Q ch;** 17 **R × Q, B × P;** 18 **B × B, R × B;** 19 **B—B3,** a line where he has at least some positional compensation for a lost P.

		P—K4
16	**Kt—Kt5**	**R × Q**
17	**Kt × Q**	**R × P**
18	**Kt—Kt5**	**B—B4**
19	**B—QB4**	**Kt—R4**
20	**B—Q5**	**B—B7**

A terrible stroke, for if **R—QB1, B × P.** But by giving up the Exchange White gets nothing beyond an easily parried threat.

21	**Castles**	**B × R**
22	**R × B**	**R—Q1**
23	**P—Kt3**	

Now White threatens 24 **B × P ch** etc., having had to make a preliminary move to stop a mate on his first rank. But a little better was 23 **P—R3,** which did not unguard his KB3.

		Kt—B3
24	**P—QB4**	**Kt—Q5**
25	**Kt—B3**	

It is difficult to see why White did not play 25 **Kt × Kt, P × Kt;** 26 **B × P, B × B;** 27 **R × B**—though that would only have prolonged, not saved, the game.

		R—Kt7
26	**Kt—K4**	**R × KtP**
27	**B—Kt5**	

27 **Kt—B5** would again have made a longer fight of it, though after 27.., **R—Kt7;** 28 **B × Kt, P × B;** 29 **B × P,** White would have a very strong passed P to contend against as well as the odds of the Exchange.

		Kt—B6 ch
28	**K—Kt2**	**Kt × B**
29	**Kt × Kt**	**R—Q2**

White resigns.

Lasker is not so highly tried in this as in the preceding game, but from the 8th move onwards his play is above criticism.

GAME 31

SCHLECHTER v. LASKER

VIENNA, *January* 21-24, 1910
(CHAMPIONSHIP MATCH, 5TH GAME)

RUY LOPEZ

White.	*Black.*
SCHLECHTER	LASKER
1 **P—K4**	**P—K4**
2 **Kt—KB3**	**Kt—QB3**
3 **B—Kt5**	**Kt—B3**

The *Ruy Lopez* was played 7 times in the 10 games of the match; 3 times by Schlechter, 4 by Lasker. This was the only one of the 7 games with a decisive result. Lasker defended in the 1st and 3rd games as he did here, while Schlechter always employed the *Morphy Defence*.

4 **Castles**	**P—Q3**
5 **P—Q4**	

As in the 1st game, where it was followed by 6 **R—K1**. In the 3rd Schlechter played **R—K1** first.

	B—Q2
6 **Kt—B3**	

Schlechter omits **R—K1** in the opening here. Lasker also played the text-move in his 12th match game against Capablanca in 1921, but after 6.., **B—K2** followed it with 7 **R—K1**.

	B—K2
7 **B—Kt5**	**Castles**

In the St. Petersburg Tournament the previous year Lasker had played against both Dr. O. S. Bernstein and E. Cohn, 7.., **P × P**; 8 **Kt × P, Castles.**

8 **P × P**

Schlechter, in a note to the game, gave as best 8 **KB × Kt, B × B**; 9 **P × P**. If now **P × P**, then 10 **Kt × P, B × P**; 11 **Q—K2**. If 9.., **Kt × P**, then 10 **Kt × Kt, B × Kt**; 11 **B × B, Q × B**; 12 **P × P, Q × P**; 13 **Q × Q, P × Q**; 14 **Kt—Q4**. In both cases White has some advantage.

	QKt × P
9 **B × B**	**KKt × B**
10 **B × B**	**Kt × Kt ch**
11 **Q × Kt**	**Q × B**

The game certainly looks destined to end in a draw; but its interest arises later, after a start not promising much interest.

12 **Kt—Q5**	**Q—Q1**
13 **QR—Q1**	

13 **Q—B3** was much stronger, says Schlechter.

	R—K1
14 **KR—K1**	**Kt—Kt3**
15 **Q—B3**	**Kt × Kt**
16 **R × Kt**	**R—K3**
17 **R—Q3**	

The fencing for position now begins, with just a shade of initial advantage for White.

	Q—K2
18 **R—Kt3**	**R—Kt3**

Not **P—KB4**, because of 19 **Q—Kt3.**

19 **KR—K3**	**R—K1**
20 **P—KR3**	**K—B1**

The beginning of a remarkable manœuvre with the K, which is crossing the board, so as to help in the defence of the Q-side.

21	**R × R**	**RP × R**
22	**Q—Kt4**	**P—QB3**

Black can hardly avoid this weakening of his QP. *E.g.*, **P—Kt3;** 23 **Q—R3, P—R4** would set up other weaknesses, which White might exploit by a "minority attack" with the Q-side P's, such as he actually got.

23	**Q—R3**	**P—R3**
24	**Q—Kt3**	**R—Q1**
25	**P—QB4**	

Keeping back Black's QP.

		R—Q2
26	**Q—Q1**	**Q—K4**
27	**Q—Kt4**	**K—K1**
28	**Q—K2**	**K—Q1**
29	**Q—Q2**	**K—B2**

The K's journey is now completed, and the defence of the QP looks adequate. But the problem is about to become one of the defence of the K, not the P.

30	**P—R3**	**R—K2**
31	**P—QKt4**	**P—QKt4**

Lasker sealed this move at the end of the first day's play. He was for the moment in no marked positional inferiority, and indeed, were the Q's off, might hope to get the better endgame chances.

32	**P × P**	**RP × P**
33	**P—Kt3**	**P—Kt4**
34	**K—Kt2**	**R—K1**
35	**Q—Q1**	**P—B3**
36	**Q—Kt3**	**Q—K3**
37	**Q—Q1**	**R—KR1**

As it turns out, this move is not helpful to Black. Instead, **R—QR1** is worth consideration.

38	**P—Kt4**	**Q—B5**

Position after 38.., **Q—B5:**

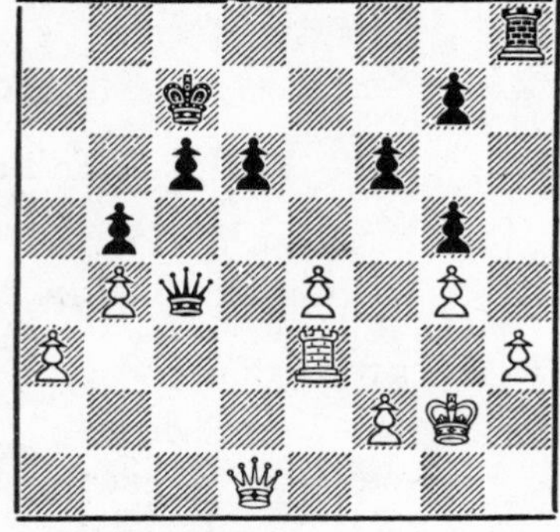

39	**P—QR4**	

A notable effort to break through Black's defence. To do so White strips himself of his Q-side P's.

		Q × KtP
40	**P × P**	**Q × KtP**
41	**R—QKt3**	**Q—R3**
42	**Q—Q4**	

The threat is 43 **Q—Kt2,** followed by **R—R3,** which Black's reply parries, causing the threat to be changed.

		R—K1
43	**R—Kt1**	**R—K4**
44	**Q—Kt4**	**Q—Kt4**

Not **R—Kt4,** for then 45 **Q—B4,** and White penetrates to the 7th rank.

45	**Q—K1**	**Q—Q6**
46	**R—Kt4 !**	**P—QB4**

Has Black a better move here? The Russian master Dr. O. S. Bernstein suggested **R—R4,** to prevent White's occupation of the QR-file. But Black is playing for a win.

47	**R—R4**	**P—B5**
48	**Q—QR1**	

White must give up his KP, as 49 **P—B3** is not playable.

		$Q \times$ **KP ch**
49	**K—R2**	**R—Kt4**

Threatening 50.., **Q—K4 ch,** with an exchange of Q's.

50	**Q—R2 !**	**Q—K4 ch**
51	**K—Kt1**	**Q—K8 ch**
52	**K—R2**	**P—Q4**

One would not think that Black, with his two united passed P's, could lose this game. Schlechter's play is very subtle; but it needed a blunder on his opponent's part to make it completely effective.

53	**R—R8**	**Q—Kt5**
54	**K—Kt2 !**	

This is the subtlest part of White's scheme. It renders innocuous Black's next move, and, in fact, makes it the blunder necessary for White's success.

Q—B4 ? ?

Quite fatal. Black must keep a double guard on the QKt-file. Hoffer gives as a perfectly safe line 54.., **R—Kt1;** 55 **Q—R7 ch, R—Kt2;** 56 **Q—K3, Q—Q3.** Schlechter, however, claimed that by 57 **R—K8,** and if **P—Q5;** 58 **Q—K4,** he still had a strong attack. In his opinion 54.., **R—Kt2** was Black's right move.

55 **Q—R6**

The possibility of this comes from White's previous move. With his K at R2 it could have been met by **Q—Q3 ch.**

R—Kt1

R—Kt2 would have been answered by 56 **Q—K6.**

56	**R—R7 ch**	**K—Q1**
57	**R** $\times$ **P**	**Q—Kt3**
58	**Q—R3**	**K—B1**

White mates in 3 — 59 **Q—B8 ch,** 60 **Q—B5 ch,** and 61 **Q** $\times$ **Q.**

A very fine game apart from Lasker's unfortunate mistake on the 54th move. (It must be mentioned that he was suffering from extreme time-pressure, but for which he claimed later that he might have won the game.) The positional struggle from about the 17th move to that point is of extraordinary interest.

GAME 32

LASKER v. SCHLECHTER

BERLIN, *February* 2-4-5, 1910
(CHAMPIONSHIP MATCH, 8TH GAME)

RUY LOPEZ

	White.	*Black.*
	LASKER	SCHLECHTER
1	**P—K4**	**P—K4**
2	**Kt—KB3**	**Kt—QB3**
3	**B—Kt5**	**P—QR3**
4	**B—R4**	**Kt—B3**
5	**Castles**	**Kt × P**

With regard to this move see Game 46.

6	**P—Q4**	**P—QKt4**
7	**B—Kt3**	**P—Q4**
8	**P—QR4**	

Lasker showed his firm belief in this by playing it on all four possible occasions in the match. When answered by 8.., **R—QKt1** (as in the 4th and 6th games), it gives White, after 9 **RP × P, RP × P,** 10 **P × P,** the preferable development.

QKt × P

This, however, is another story. Schlechter apparently thought that he was innovating when he played the move in the 2nd game of the match; but it was subsequently traced back to Schallopp as early as 1874.

9	**Kt × Kt**	**P × Kt**
10	**P × P**	

In the 2nd game Lasker played 10 **Q × P,** and had to fight hard for a draw with a P down. The main book-variation now is 10 **Kt—B3,** which is attributed to the late Professor Berger, of Graz.

		B—QB4
11	**P—QB3**	**Castles**
12	**BP × P**	**B—Kt3**

Better than **B—Q3,** says Schlechter, for then with 13 **Q—Q3** White would have a good game, whereas against the text-move 13 **Q—Q3** might lead to **B—K3;** 14 **P × P, P—QB4,** when Black is well placed.

13	**Kt—B3**	**B—Kt2**
14	**P × P**	**R × P**
15	**R × R**	**B × R**
16	**R—K1**	**B—Kt2**
17	**Kt—R4**	**Q—B3**

As may be seen from the diagram Black has obtained an excellent game in the defence of the *Lopez*. But there is little scope for complication left, and a draw is foreshadowed already.

Position after 17.., **Q—B3:**

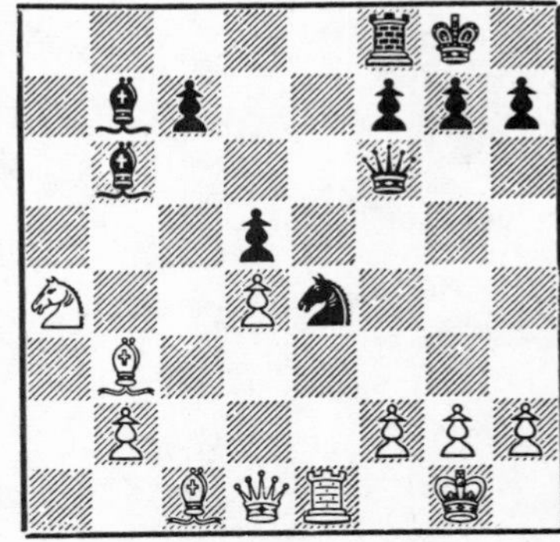

18	**B—K3**	**B—R2**
19	**P—B3**	**Kt—Kt4**
20	**Kt—B5**	**B × Kt**

Black is compelled by the threat of 21 **Kt—Q7** to give up one of his pair of B's. He gets thereby a passed P; but its advance can only be supported by pieces, and consequently threatens little danger.

21	**P × B**	**Kt—K3**
22	**Q—Q3**	**R—Q1**
23	**B—QB2**	**P—Kt3**
24	**P—QKt4**	**P—Q5**
25	**B—B1**	**P—R4**

It was suggested after the game that **B—Q4** may have been better at once.

26	**B—Kt3**	**B—Q4**
27	**B × B**	**R × B**
28	**P—R3**	**R—K4**
29	**R × R**	**Q × R**
30	**K—B2**	**Q—Q4**
31	**P—R4**	**Q—R7 ch**
32	**Q—K2**	**Q—Kt8**
33	**Q—Kt2**	**Q—Q6**
34	**Q—K2**	**Q—Kt6**
35	**B—Q2**	**K—R2**
36	**K—K1**	

Draw agreed.

The last few moves are perfunctory, and indeed the interest of the game lies mainly in the opening. Lasker, commenting on it, declared that at last Schlechter had found a valid defence to the *Ruy Lopez*. Admittedly it is a good drawing defence against a line now seldom seen for White in the *Lopez*. But the game has been included in this book chiefly as an example of sound championship match play, leading to the legitimate result of a draw. Schlechter may be said to have " killed " the variation springing from 10 **P × P** as an aggressive force.

GAME 33

LASKER v. JANOWSKI

BERLIN, *November* 20, 1910

(CHAMPIONSHIP [SECOND] MATCH, 5TH GAME)

QUEEN'S GAMBIT DECLINED

	White.	*Black.*
	LASKER	JANOWSKI
1	**P—Q4**	**P—Q4**
2	**P—QB4**	**P—K3**
3	**Kt—QB3**	**P—QB4**

Janowski believed in the *Tarrasch Defence*, which he also adopted in the 1st and 7th games of this match.

4 **BP × P** **KP × P**

4.., **BP × P** (the *Von Hennig-Schara Gambit*) was not yet dreamed of.

5 **Kt—B3** **B—K3**

The drawback to this move is that it allows White at once to advance **P—K4**, though it is questionable whether that is much to be feared. In the 7th game Janowski played the orthodox 5.., **Kt—QB3**, against which Lasker continued with 6 **B—Kt5**, and not the *Schlechter-Rubinstein Variation*, 6 **P—KKt3**.

6	**P—K4**	**QP × P**
7	**Kt × P**	**Kt—QB3**
8	**B—K3**	**P × P**
9	**Kt × P ?**	

Lasker himself describes this move as "very hazardous." He should have played 9 **B × P**, so as to meet a possible **Q—R4 ch** with **B—B3.**

Q—R4 ch

10 **Kt—B3**

Not 10 **Kt—Q2,** for then **Kt × Kt;** 11 **B × Kt, R—Q1;** 12 **B—B3, B—QKt5.**

Castles

11 **P—QR3**

White is in a fix now, and this does not extricate him, though fortunately for him his opponent fails to see the right reply. There appears to be no saving move for White.

Kt—R3 ?

He should have played 11.., **B—QB4** (much stronger than 11.., **Kt × Kt;** 12 **B × Kt, B—QB4;** 13 **P—QKt4, B × B;** 14 **Q × B, R × Q;** 15 **P × Q,** when Black's advantage is not overwhelming); 12 **P—QKt4, B × Kt;** 13 **B × B, Q—KKt4 !;** 14 **Kt—Kt5, Kt × B;** 15 **Kt × Kt, Q—K4 ch,** and wins. He must have overlooked the possibility of 13.., **Q—KKt4.**

12 **P—QKt4** **Q—K4**

12.., **B × P;** 13 **P × B, Q × P** would have been met by 14 **Q—B1,** threatening 15 **R—R4.**

13 **QKt—Kt5** **Kt—B4**

He might safely have ventured upon 13.., **P—QR3,** for after

14 **Q—B1, P × Kt;** 15 **Kt × Kt, P × Kt;** 16 **Q × P ch, Q—B2** White can do no more.

14 **R—B1** **Kt × B**
15 **P × Kt**

If 15 **Kt × P ch,** says Lasker, **K—B2;** 16 **Kt(Q4)—Kt5 ch, K—Kt3;** 17 **R × Kt ch, P × R;** 18 **Q × R ch, K—Kt2**—and Black is quite safe.

Q × P ch
16 **B—K2** **B—K2**
17 **R—B3**

Position after 17.., **R—B3:**

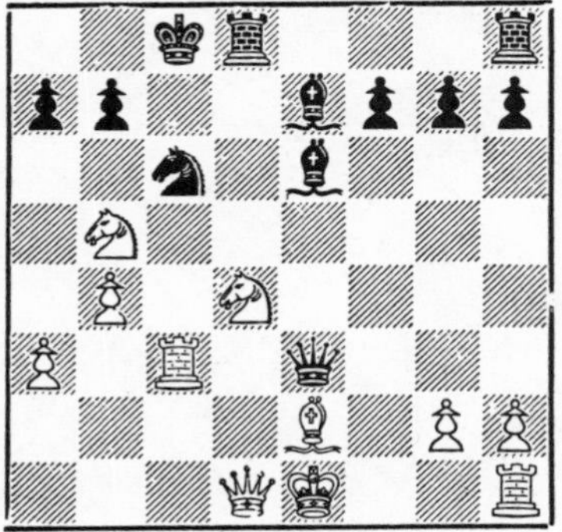

Now comes the turning-point of the game; or the second turning-point if we count as the first Janowski's failure to grasp his opportunity on the 11th move.

B—R5 ch

It was claimed at the time of the match that by 17.., **Q—K4;** 18 **Castles, B—B3;** 19 **Kt × Kt, Q × R;** 20 **Kt(B6) × P ch, K—Kt1;** 21 **Kt × Q, R × Q** Black could have saved himself—the forces after 22 **Kt × R, K × Kt** being level. But, assuming that the analysis gives the best play on both sides (which is not certain), must we say that it is necessary for Black here to "save" himself? The answer depends on what might have happened next move.

18 **P—Kt3** **Q—K5 ?**

Now for what might have happened, as this admittedly lost the game. Black should have played 18.., **Q × R ch !** Lasker writes in his *Chess Manual* of the persistence for many years of the assertion that this would have won, whereas really the issue is problematical. It was assumed that the win came by 18.., **Q × R ch;** 19 **Kt × Q, B—B3;** 20 **Castles, B × Kt ch;** 21 **K moves, B × Kt,** leaving Black with R, B, Kt, and P for his Q. But the assumption was wrong that White should play 20 **Castles.** That move loses, as also does 20 **Q—B1,** because of **B × Kt,** and if 21 **P—Kt5, Kt—K4,** when Black still has too great odds for his Q. The correct line is attributed by Lasker to Tarrasch in his *Moderne Schachpartie*: 20 **Kt (B3)—Kt5 !, B × Kt (Kt × Kt ?;** 21 **Q—B1 ch);** 21 **Kt × B, Kt × Kt;** 22 **K—B2,** when the chances are about even.

19 **Castles** **B—B3**
20 **R × B !**

Destroying the attack at the cost of the Exchange. It is remarkable with what speed the inferior force now wins.

P × R
21 **B—B3** **Q—K4**
22 **Kt × P ch** **K—B2**
23 **Kt(R7) × Kt** **P × Kt**
24 **R × P ch** **K—Kt1**
25 **R—Kt6 ch** **K—B1**

K—R2; 26 **R—Kt7 ch** and mate in 2.

26	**Q—B1 ch**	**K—Q2**
27	**Kt × B**	**P × Kt**
28	**R—Kt7 ch**	**K—K1**
29	**B—B6 ch**	**Resigns**

If **K—B1**, mate in 2 follows.

The loss of this thrilling game was a severe blow to Janowski. Had he won, the score would only have been 2-1 against him, with 2 draws. After losing it he drew the 6th game, and then lost the remaining 5 of the match off the reel.

GAME 34

LASKER v. CAPABLANCA

HAVANA, *March* 20, 1921

(CHAMPIONSHIP MATCH, 2ND GAME)

QUEEN'S GAMBIT DECLINED

	White.	*Black.*
	LASKER	CAPABLANCA
1	**P—Q4**	**P—Q4**
2	**P—QB4**	**P—K3**
3	**Kt—QB3**	**Kt—KB3**
4	**Kt—B3**	

Capablanca, as White, in the 1st game of this match had continued with 4 **B—Kt5,** his regular procedure. Lasker, too, adopted the *Pillsbury Attack* variation in the 4th and 10th games. He still had the option, of course, on move 5 here.

		QKt—Q2
5	**P—K3**	

With the apparent intention of developing his QB at Kt2, the line which the late Amos Burn consistently advocated. But the B ultimately comes out on the K-side after all.

		B—K2
6	**B—Q3**	**Castles**
7	**Castles**	**P × P**
8	**B × P**	**P—B4**
9	**Q—K2**	**P—QR3**
10	**R—Q1**	**P—QKt4**
11	**B—Q3**	

Some of the commentators prefer here **B—Kt3,** so as not to block the Q-file. There being no obvious advantage then in 11.., **P—B5,** though it establishes a Q-side majority, Black's problem would be rather difficult. The complications arising from 11.., **B—Kt2;** 12 **P—K4, P—Kt5;** 13 **P—K5** seem to be in White's favour, while 12.., **P × P;** 13 **KKt × P, Kt—K4** is not here available. Perhaps, however, 13.., **Q—B2** might suffice to hold the position.

		B—Kt2
12	**P—K4**	**P × P**
13	**KKt × P**	**Kt—K4**
14	**Kt—Kt3**	

White elects to let his KB be exchanged off. The variation 14 **B × P, P × B;** 15 **Kt × KP,** (if) **Q × R ch;** 16 **Q × Q, P × Kt;** 17 **Q—Kt3** does not attract him, though he would have a formidable Pawn-majority in addition to his Q to set against R and two minor pieces. But the simple 14 **B—B2** looks best.

		Kt × B
15	**R × Kt**	**Q—B2**
16	**P—K5**	

The alternative is 16 **P—B3;** but that allows **P—QR4** (17 **Kt × KtP ?, Q—Kt3 ch**). 16 **B—Kt5** is bad because of **Kt × P.**

		Kt—Q4
17	**R—Kt3**	**Kt × Kt**
18	**R × Kt**	**Q—Q2**
19	**R—Kt3**	**KR—Q1**
20	**B—R6**	**P—Kt3**
21	**B—K3**	

A stage has been reached in the game where a really forceful move, could it be found, might confirm for White a slight positional advantage, in spite of two enemy B's. But is there such a move on the board? One reasonable objective is to get rid of one of the B's. The text-move threatens to do this by 22 **Kt—B5,** which Black easily prevents. Another objective is the relief of the Q from the defence of the back rank, so that 21 **R—K1** had to be considered.

	Q—Q4
22 **Kt—R5**	

This saves White's previous move from being mere waste of time, for now he can force off a B—Black clearly not being prepared to play **B—QB1.**

	QR—B1
23 **Kt × B**	**Q × Kt**
24 **B—R6**	

To prevent 24.., **Q—K5.**

	Q—Q4
25 **P—Kt3**	**Q—Q5**

Position after 25.., **Q—Q5:**

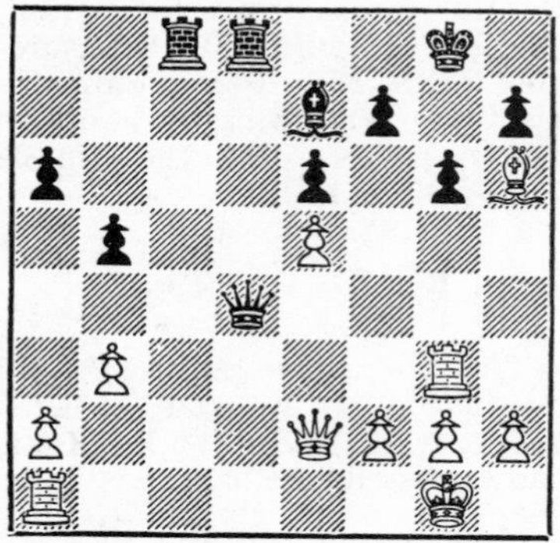

26 **R—KB1**

26 **R—K1, B—Kt5;** 27 **R—KB1** (27 **Q—B3**?, **B × R;** 28 **Q—B6, Q × P ch!**), though it would have drawn Black's B from the defence, would have achieved nothing permanent.

	R—Q4
27 **R—K3**	**B—R6**
28 **P—Kt3**	

Black showed by his last move that he did not consider his B required for the defence. And indeed, if now 28 **Q—B3,** there might follow **R—B8!;** 29 **Q—B6, R × R ch;** 30 **K × R, Q—Q8 ch;** 31 **R—K1, Q—Q6 ch;** 32 **K—Kt1, B—B1;** 33 **B × B** (almost forced), **K × B;** 34 **Q—B4.** For White dare not speculate with 34 **Q—R8 ch** and 35 **Q × P,** or he loses.

	Q—Kt7
29 **R—K1**	

If now **Q—B3,** Black's simplest counter is **B—K2,** and White must defend his menaced P's.

	R—B7
30 **Q—B3**	**B—K2**

Not **Q × RP,** for then 31 **Q—B6, B—B1;** 32 **R—KB3, R—Q2;** 33 **B × B; K × B;** 34 **Q—R8 ch, K—K2;** 35 **Q × P** and White must win.

31 **R(K3)—K2**	**R × R**

Q × RP again loses, for then 32 **R × R, Q × R;** 33 **R—QB1, Q—Q6** (**Q—KB4;** 34 **R—B8 ch, R—Q1;** 35 **Q—B6!, Q—Q6;** 36 **Q—K8 ch** etc.); 34 **R—B8 ch, B—Q1** (**R—Q1;** 35 **Q × Q**); 35 **Q × Q, R × Q,** 36 **B—Kt5** etc.

32 **R × R**	**Q—Kt8 ch**
33 **K—Kt2**	**B—B1**
34 **B—B4**	**P—R3**
35 **P—KR4**	**P—Kt5**
36 **Q—K4**	**Q × Q ch**
37 **R × Q**	**K—Kt2**
38 **R—B4**	**B—B4**
39 **K—B3**	**P—Kt4**

Best. If **P—QR4,** Lasker gives 40 **R—B2, B—Q5;** 41 **R—Q2, B—B6;** 42 **R × R, P × R;** 43 **K—K3** as better for White.

40 **P × P**	**P × P**

Draw agreed.

Times: Lasker 2 hrs. 36 min.; Capablanca 2 hrs. 37 min.

GAME 35

LASKER v. CAPABLANCA

HAVANA, *April* 8-9-10, 1921

(CHAMPIONSHIP MATCH, 10TH GAME)

QUEEN'S GAMBIT DECLINED

	White.	*Black.*
	LASKER	CAPABLANCA
1	**P—Q4**	**P—Q4**
2	**P—QB4**	**P—K3**
3	**Kt—QB3**	**Kt—KB3**
4	**B—Kt5**	**B—K2**
5	**P—K3**	**Castles**
6	**Kt—B3**	**QKt—Q2**
7	**Q—B2**	

So far the moves are the same as in the 4th game of the match. Capablanca, when White, preferred 7 **R—B1,** as he did in his match against Alekhine, playing it invariably when the occasion offered. For Alekhine's practice see Game 38, first note.

P—B4

In the 4th game Capablanca played **P—B3,** which was generally held to be inferior and cramping. But that move was revived in Flohr *v.* Fine, Hastings, 1935-36, where it led to a remarkable game won by Fine. Flohr continued against it 8 **P—QR3** (not, like Lasker in the 4th game, 8 **B—Q3**), **R—K1;** 9 **R—Q1,** and through some indifferent moves by his opponent obtained the superior game, but missed his way later. In his match with Alekhine Capablanca answered 7 **Q—B2** with the text-move.

8 **R—Q1**

The natural move after **Q—B2;** and Q1 is, as Alekhine says, the square on which this R generally stands most effectively. At the same time, when commenting on the 8th game of his match with Capablanca, where he as White had the same position, he stated that he did not like the variation 9 **R—Q1, P—KR3;** 10 **B—R4, Q—R4;** 11 **B—Q3, Kt—Kt3 !**—and he played 8 **BP × P** there, and also in the 10th of the same match.

Q—R4

9 **B—Q3**

In the 7th game of the match, where, with colours reversed, each player had wasted a move in the opening—7 **R—B1, P—B3;** 8 **Q—B2, P—B4;** 9 **R—Q1, Q—R4**—the continuation was now **BP × P.** The text-move proposes to answer 9.., **QP × P** by 10 **B × P ch, Kt × B;** 11 **B × B.** But Black has other ideas.

		P—KR3
10	**B—R4**	**BP × P**
11	**KP × P**	**P × P**
12	**B × P**	**Kt—Kt3**
13	**B—QKt3**	

Sir G. Thomas pointed out that Black could have prevented the retirement of the B to this square by playing his moves in the order 10.., **QP × P;** 11 **B × P, Kt—Kt3;**

for then if 12 **B—QKt3, P—B5.** It is a matter worth consideration whether the B on QKt3 is as strong as it looks.

	B—Q2
14 **Castles**	**QR—B1**

Capablanca seems to have been working according to a plan for a Q-side attack, in which the position of the B on QKt3 suits him well enough. A crisis is now at hand to test theories.

15 **Kt—K5**

A move condemned by some judges at the time as weak. Amos Burn, in *The Field*, gave 15 **Q—K2** as much stronger, getting rid of the pin and stopping Black's **B—Kt4.** Much depends on what is the verdict on the 17th move.

	B—Kt4
16 **KR—K1**	**QKt—Q4**

Position after 16.., **QKt—Q 4:**

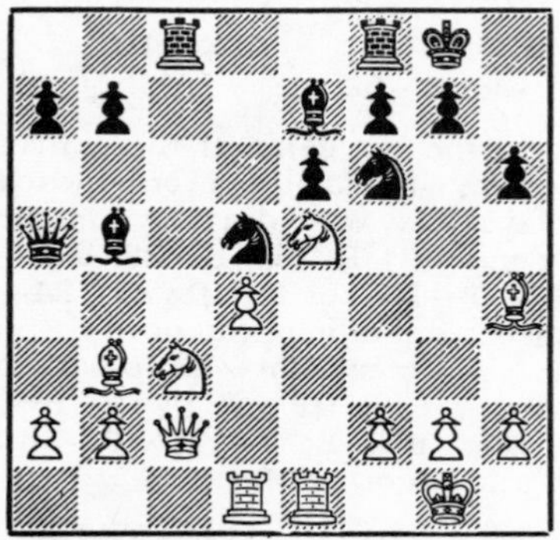

This may be called the most celebrated position in the whole match. The talented young Hungarian player and analyst, Julius Breyer, who died so prematurely in 1921, aged only twenty-eight, claimed that Lasker had a win here by 17 **QB × Kt, B × B;** 18 **B × Kt, P × B;** 19 **Kt—Kt4, B—Q1;** 20 **Q—B5 !** If, instead of 17.., **B × B,** 17.., **Kt × B,** then 18 **Kt—Kt6, KR—K1** (**P × Kt** obviously loses the Exchange and a P); 19 **R × P, P × R;** 20 **B × P ch, K—R2;** 21 **Kt—B8 dbl. ch, K—R1;** 22 **Q—R7 ch, Kt × Q;** 23 **Kt—Kt6** mate.

Lasker in his book on the match gives the first variation as far as 18.., **P × B,** with the continuation 19 **Q—B5** in place of Breyer's **Kt—Kt4,** and says that Black is obviously in great difficulties; *e.g.*, 19.., **B × Kt;** 20 **P × B, B—B3;** 21 **R—K3** or **R—Q4.** He admits that he lost his opportunity here.

17 **KB × Kt**	**Kt × B**
18 **B × B**	**Kt × B**
19 **Q—Kt3**	**B—B3**
20 **Kt × B**	**P × Kt**

Voluntarily separating his Q-side P's in order to hold back White's isolated QP. It is now a question of elaborate play for an endgame advantage.

21 **R—K5**	**Q—Kt3**
22 **Q—B2**	

22 **Q × Q** would have reunited Black's Q-side and given him an open QR file. Nevertheless, White might have had better drawing chances with the Q's off the board—loth as one must be to question Lasker's judgment in such a position.

	KR—Q1
23 **Kt—K2**	

" Here," comments Lasker, " I began to play indifferent chess." The R had gone to K5 to command QB5, and therefore 23 **Kt—R4** was the right move now.

	R—Q4 !
24 **R × R ?**	

This was a still worse move than the last, Lasker says. The right line was 24 **R—K3,** (if) **Kt—B4;** 25 **R—QKt3, Q—Q1;** 26 **R—Kt4,** with threats of **R—B4, R—R4,** or **P—KKt4.**

	BP × R
25 **Q—Q2**	**Kt—B4**
26 **P—QKt3**	

This move could wait. 26 **P—KKt3** is Lasker's own suggestion.

	P—KR4.
27 **P—KR3 ?**	

This only provokes Black's excellent reply, establishing his Kt on B4. 27 **P—KKt3** was now imperative, according to Lasker. 27 **Kt—Kt3** was also suggested.

	P—R5
28 **Q—Q3**	

This and his next 5 moves, leaving his forces in exactly the same position as now, argue a perplexity of mind on White's part as to what he can do. But Black does not stand still while White marks time.

	R—B3
29 **K—B1**	**P—Kt3**
30 **Q—Kt1**	

A move of which Black takes immediate advantage.

	Q—Kt5
31 **K—Kt1**	

Q—Kt2 at once was much better, and the K should not have moved from B1, where he is well placed.

	P—R4
32 **Q—Kt2**	**P—R5**
33 **Q—Q2**	**Q × Q**
34 **R × Q**	**P × P**
35 **P × P**	**R—Kt3**

As a result of White's indecision, Black has now saddled him with another weakness, and the text-move is designed to force **R—Q3** (36 **R—Kt2, R—Kt5**) before Black seizes the open QR file and threatens **R—R8 ch,** which would be conclusive.

36 **R—Q3**	**R—R3**
37 **P—KKt4**	

He must open his KKt2 for his K, as if 37 **R—Q2** (preventing **R—R8 ch; K—R2, R—R7**) then **R—R8,** followed by **R—QKt8.**

	P × P i.p.
38 **P × P**	**R—R7**
39 **Kt—B3**	

39 **K—B2** would tie the Kt, but it is doubtful whether White's case would be worse than after the text-move.

	R—QB7
40 **Kt—Q1**	**Kt—K2**

The Kt's operation on the Q-side, or rather the threat of it, is very powerful.

41 **Kt—K3**	**R—B8 ch**
42 **K—B2**	

Not 32 **R—Q1, R × R ch;** 43 **Kt × R, Kt—B3.**

	Kt—B3
43 **Kt—Q1**	

If instead 43 **K—K2,** then **Kt—Kt5,** 44 **R—Q1** (44 **R—Q2, R—QKt8**), **R—B6;** 45 **R—QKt1,** White has no move to free his Q-side position while Black brings his K up into the game.

	R—Kt8

Lasker points out the trap: 43.., **Kt—Kt5 ?;** 44 **R—Q2, R—Kt8;** 45 **Kt—Kt2, R × Kt ?;** 46 **R × R, Kt—Q6 ch;** 47 **K—K2, Kt × R;** 48 **K—Q2,** and then the Kt has no escape.

44 **K—K2**

Thomas suggests 44 **K—K1, Kt—R4;** 45 **K—Q2, R × P;** 46 **R ×**

R, Kt × R ch; 47 **K—B3,** with very remote chances of a draw.

	R × P
45 **K—K3**	

Naturally not 46 **R × R, Kt × P ch.**

	R—Kt5
46 **Kt—B3**	**Kt—K2**

The P having been won, the Kt returns to the other wing.

47 **Kt—K2**	**Kt—B4 ch**
48 **K—B2**	**P—Kt4**
49 **P—Kt4**	**Kt—Q3**
50 **Kt—Kt1**	**Kt—K5 ch**

Reducing White once more to a position where he can make no effective move to obtain relief.

51 **K—B1**	**R—Kt8 ch**
52 **K—Kt2**	**R—Kt7 ch**
53 **K—B1**	

If 53 **K—B3, R—B7 ch;** 54 **K—K3, R—B8,** followed by **R—KR8** wins another P.

	R—B7 ch
54 **K—K1**	**R—QR7**

The unenterprising character of the play (even on the part of Black) up to the 64th move is explained by the fact that there was a second adjournment in prospect.

55 **K—B1**	**K—Kt2**
56 **R—K3**	**K—Kt3**
57 **R—Q3**	**P—B3**
58 **R—K3**	**K—B2**
59 **R—Q3**	**K—K2**
60 **R—K3**	**K—Q3**
61 **R—Q3**	**R—B7 ch**
62 **K—K1**	**R—KKt7**
63 **K—B1**	**R—QR7**
64 **R—K3**	**P—K4 !**

This was Capablanca's sealed move at the second adjournment. On resumption of the game Lasker took more than three-quarters of an hour over his reply, but might as well have resigned at once, since there is not the faintest chance of saving the game.

65 **R—Q3**	**P × P**
66 **R × P**	**K—B4**
67 **R—Q1**	**P—Q5**
68 **R—B1 ch**	**K—Q4**

White resigns.

Although it is somewhat marred by the time-marking tactics towards the close of the second day's play, the ending is a masterly exhibition of Capablanca's skill in this part of the game. He speaks of it as one of the best efforts of his whole career.

GAME 36

LASKER v. CAPABLANCA

HAVANA, *April* 16-17, 1921

(CHAMPIONSHIP MATCH, 12TH GAME)

RUY LOPEZ

	White. LASKER	*Black.* CAPABLANCA
1	**P—K4**	**P—K4**
2	**Kt—KB3**	**Kt—QB3**
3	**B—Kt5**	**Kt—B3**
4	**Castles**	**P—Q3**
5	**P—Q4**	**B—Q2**
6	**Kt—B3**	**B—K2**
7	**R—K1**	**P × P**
8	**Kt × P**	**Castles**
9	**B—B1**	

In the 3rd game of the match (Capablanca White) and in the 6th, the more usual 9 **B × Kt** was played. Tarrasch advocated the text-move, which avoids exchanges; and Capablanca had played it against A. B. Hodges in the New York Tournament of 1916.

R—K1

In Capablanca - Hodges **Kt × Kt** was played; but that brings the White Q into the game.

10 **P—B3**

A very strong alternative is **P—QKt3.**

B—KB1

11 **B—KKt5** **P—KR3**

12 **B—R4** **P—KKt3**

Capablanca has a liking for the K's fianchetto against the *Ruy Lopez*.

Position after 12.., **P—KKt3:**

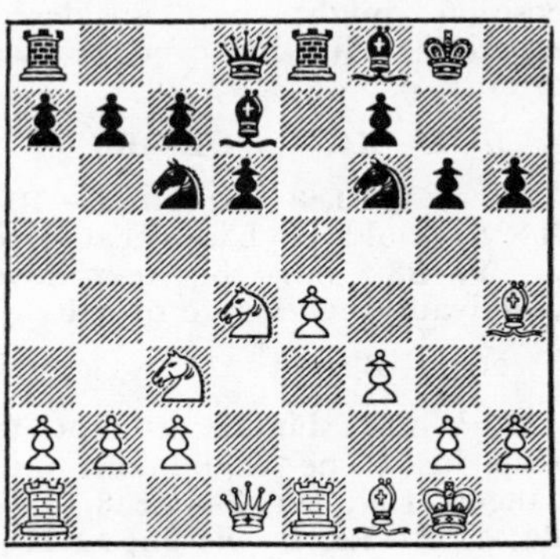

13 **Kt—Q5**

Speculative and interesting, but not, on the whole, in White's favour. Preferable may be 13 **Kt × Kt, P × Kt;** 14 **P—K5, P—KKt4** (not **P × P;** 15 **B × Kt** etc.); 15 **P × Kt, P × B;** 16 **Q—Q4,** where Black's best move seems to be Sir G. Thomas's suggestion, **Q—Kt1.**

B—Kt2

14 **Kt—Kt5**

Tempting, as against the more solid 14 **P—B3.** Lasker, with the score 3—0 in his opponent's favour, is not playing for a draw.

P—Kt4

15 **Kt(Q5) × P**

15 **B × P, P × B,** 16 **Kt(Q5) × P** is defeated by **P—QR3,** and if

17 **Kt × KR, Kt × Kt**; 18 **Kt—B3, Q—Kt3 ch**; 19 **K—R1, Q × P** and wins. If here 18 **Kt × P,** then **B—Kt5 ch** wins a piece at once.

	P × B
16 **Kt × QR**	**Q × Kt**
17 **Kt—B7**	**Q—Q1**
18 **Kt × R**	**Kt × Kt**

The struggle has become the unusual one of two R's against three minor pieces. If White could maintain his extra P, his position might be considered superior. This, however, he fails to do.

19 **R—Kt1**	**B—K3**

19.., **Q—Kt3 ch**; 20 **K—R1, B × P** would be bad because of 21 **P—B3.** But the text-move practically makes sure of a P.

20 **P—B3**

If White should attempt to keep his P he would run into danger—*e.g.*, 20 **P—QKt3, Q—R4**; 21 **P—R4, Q—B4 ch**; 22 **K—R1, B—B6**; 23 **R—K2, Kt—Q5.** Or 20 **P—QR3, B—R7**; 21 **R—R1, Q—Kt3 ch** followed by **Q × P.** Or 20 **P—QB4, Q—R4**; 21 **P—QR3, QB × P,** 22 **B × B, Q—B4 ch** etc.

	QB × P
21 **R—R1**	**B—K3**
22 **Q—Q2**	**P—R3**
23 **Q—KB2**	**P—KR4**

Capablanca took no less than an hour over this move, the object of which is shown by his next. It would be interesting to know what were the alternatives he was considering, or whether it was his coming 25th move that cost him so much thought here.

24 **P—KB4**	**B—R3**
25 **B—K2**	**Kt—B3**

B—Kt5 certainly called for consideration. White could hardly afford to exchange B's.

26 **Q × P**	**Kt × P**
27 **Q × Q ch**	**Kt × Q**
28 **B × QRP**	

Regaining his extra P.

	P—Q4
29 **B—K2**	**B × P**
30 **B × P**	**B—B2**
31 **QR—Q1**	

Draw agreed.

The 31st was Lasker's sealed move, on seeing which Capablanca offered the draw. The ending, had both players been willing to fight it out, might well have been as interesting as the rest of the game. On the ordinary valuation of the chess pieces the differing forces are in White's favour (17 to 15); but that is obviously fallacious here.

GAME 37

CAPABLANCA v. ALEKHINE

BUENOS AIRES, *September*, 21-22, 1927
(CHAMPIONSHIP MATCH, 3RD GAME)

QUEEN'S PAWN GAME

White.	*Black.*
CAPABLANCA	ALEKHINE
1 **P—Q4**	**Kt—KB3**
2 **Kt—KB3**	**P—QKt3**

This was the only occasion in which the *Queen's Indian* was adopted, in a match where the *Queen's Gambit Declined* was the opening in 32 games out of 34.

3 **P—KKt3**	**B—Kt2**
4 **B—Kt2**	**P—B4**

It does not appear that Alekhine had ever before played exactly this form of the defence, in a match-game at least. It is not in favour at the present day.

5 **Castles**	**P × P**
6 **Kt × P**	**B × B**
7 **K × B**	**P—Q4**

Alekhine himself, in his comments on the game, gives either **P—Kt3** or **Q—B1** as better than this.

8 **P—QB4**	**P—K3**

And this he condemns, saying that the simple **P × P** is best. If 9 **Q—R4 ch, Q—Q2**; 10 **Kt—Kt5, Q—B3 ch,** followed by **QKt—Q2.** As the play goes, Black is soon saddled with an isolated QP.

9 **Q—R4 ch**	**Q—Q2**

If **QKt—Q2,** then 10 **P × P** and 11 **R—Q1.**

10 **Kt—Kt5**	**Kt—B3**
11 **P × P**	**P × P**
12 **B—B4**	**R—B1**
13 **R—B1**	**B—B4 ?**

Alekhine puts a double ? against this move, and claims that 13.., **Kt—K5** would have given him excellent chances of equalising the game. 14 **Kt—B7 ch** would then accomplish nothing, because of **R × Kt**; 15 **B × R, Kt—B4**; 16 **Q—KB4, Kt—K3** (and presumably 17 **Q—QR4, Kt—B4**). If 14 **P—QKt4, B—Q3.**

14 **P—QKt4**	**B × KtP**

Getting what compensation he can (R and P for two minor pieces), since 14.., **B—K2** loses the clear Exchange.

15 **R × Kt**	**R × R**
16 **Q × B**	**Kt—K5**
17 **Kt—Q2**	**Kt × Kt**
18 **Q × Kt**	

18 **B × Kt, Q—K2**; 19 **Q—Kt2 !, Q—K5 ch**; 20 **P—B3, Q × KP ch**; 21 **K—Kt1** is suggested by Alekhine as an easier win for White. Certainly Black's ability to Castle prolongs the game.

	Castles
19 **R—Q1**	**R—B4**
20 **Kt—Q4**	**R—K1**
21 **Kt—Kt3**	**QR—B1**
22 **P—K3**	**Q—R5**

Black cannot hold the QP against the threat of an eventual

P—K4, so again looks out for compensation.

23 **Q × P** **R—B7**
24 **R—Q2** **R × P**

Better was **Q × P,** says Alekhine, giving the continuation 25 **Q—Q7, R—KB1;** 26 **R × R, Q × R;** 27 **Kt—Q4, Q—QB4 !;** 28 **Q × P, P—KKt4;** or 28 **B—Q6, Q—Q4 ch.** After the text-move White's command of the board is much fuller.

25 **R × R** **Q × R**
26 **Q—B6** **R—KB1**

Position after 26.., **R—KB1:**

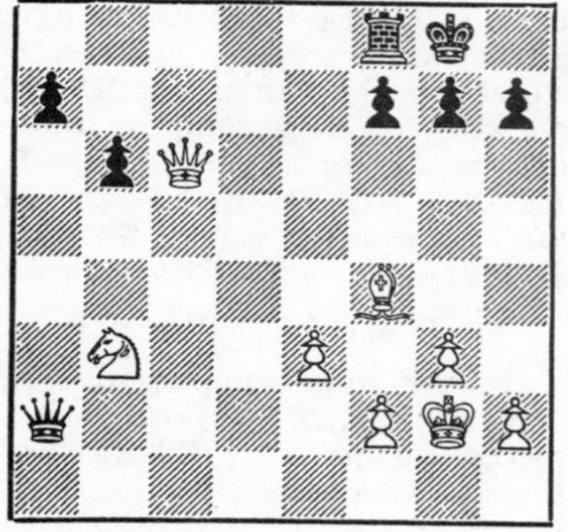

27 **Kt—Q4**

Now White's threats are too numerous to be coped with for long, and Black's worst difficulty lies in getting his Q back for the defence. But first he provides a shelter for his R.

K—R1
28 **B—K5** **P—B3**

He must prevent 29 **B × P ch, K × B;** 30 **Kt—B5 ch,** followed by mate. If **R—KKt1** at once, White plays 29 **P—K4,** cutting off a possible **Q—Q4 ch,** and the continuation might be 29.., **P—B3;** 30 **B × P, Q—B2** (he cannot take the B, for then 31 **Q × P ch, R—Kt2;** 33 **Kt—K6**); 31 **B—K5.** What is Black to do against the threat of 32 **Kt—B5 ?** 31.., **R—KB1** merely strengthens it, and 31.., **Q—K2** is met by 32 **P—B4,** with **Kt—B5** in reserve. There is the alternative line for Black (29.., **R—KKt1;** 29 **P—K4,**) **Q—Kt7,** pinning Kt against B. But then 30 **Kt—B3, Q—R7;** 31 **Kt—Kt5** (threatening 32 **Q—R6**), **P—B3;** 32 **B × P, P—KR3** (**P × B** leads to mate as before); 33 **B—K5 !,** with a new mate-threat at **KR6.** Black is in a complete *Zugzwang*.

29 **Kt—K6** **R—KKt1**
30 **B—Q4** **P—KR3**
31 **P—R4** **Q—Kt8**
32 **Kt × P !** **Q—Kt3**

If **R × Kt,** then 33 **Q × BP, Q—R2;** 34 **Q—B8 ch, Q—Kt1;** 35 **B × R ch** etc.

33 **P—R5** **Q—B2**
34 **Kt—B5** **K—R2**
35 **Q—K4** **R—K1**
36 **Q—B4** **Q—B1**
37 **Kt—Q6** **R—K2**
38 **B × BP** **Q—R1 ch**
39 **P—K4** **R—KKt2**

40 **Q—B5 ch, K—Kt1;** 41 **Q—Kt6 ch** is threatened.

40 **B × R** **K × B**
41 **Kt—B5 ch** **K—B2**
42 **Q—B7 ch** **Resigns**

Mate is forced in 2 moves at the most. A beautiful ending by Capablanca.

GAME 38

CAPABLANCA v. ALEKHINE

BUENOS AIRES, *October* 26, 1927

(CHAMPIONSHIP MATCH, 21ST GAME)

QUEEN'S GAMBIT DECLINED

	White.	*Black.*
	CAPABLANCA	ALEKHINE
1	**P—Q4**	**P—Q4**
2	**P—QB4**	**P—K3**
3	**Kt—QB3**	**Kt—KB3**
4	**B—Kt5**	**QKt—Q2**
5	**P—K3**	**B—K2**
6	**Kt—B3**	**Castles**
7	**R—B1**	

A move played at this stage 13 times by Alekhine and 8 times by Capablanca in the present match; a fact which gave it great vogue. On two occasions only did Alekhine choose in preference 7 **Q—B2.** In his notes on the 12th game (where he played 7 **R—B1**) Alekhine says that 7 **P—QR3** seems to him a trifle stronger, with the view of answering 7.., **P—B4** by 8 **Q—B2** and 9 **R—Q1,** where the R generally stands better. He did not, however, try it against Capablanca.

P—QR3

8 **P—QR3**

Allowing Black to carry out the manœuvre foreshadowed by his last move—**P × P** and **P—Kt4.** An alternative is 8 **P × P, P × P;** 9 **B—Q3,** which seems a sounder line.

P—R3

Once considered a weakening move, but now generally commended at an early stage of the *Queen's Gambit Declined.*

9	**B—R4**	**P × P**
10	**B × P**	**P—QKt4**
11	**B—K2**	**B—Kt2**
12	**Castles**	

White could prevent Black's next move by 12 **P—QKt4,** and Dr. Lasker (*Chess Manual*) says that this would on the whole be advantageous to White. Alekhine, on the other hand, gives 12 **P—QKt4, P—QR4;** 13 **Q—Kt3** (he makes no comment on 13 **Kt × P**), **P × P;** 14 **P × P, P—Kt4;** 15 **B—Kt3, Kt—Q4** in favour of Black.

		P—B4
13	**P × P**	**Kt × P**
14	**Kt—Q4**	**R—B1**
15	**P—QKt4**	

Now this does not seem good, as leaving White's QB4 in the ultimate control of Black. 15 **B—B3,** and if **Q—Kt 3,** 16 **Q—K2** is a natural manœuvre, vacating Q1 for the KR.

QKt—Q2

16 **B—Kt3**

16 **B—B3** could still be played; but there is nothing against the text-move, which was likely to come sooner or later.

Kt—Kt3

17 **Q—Kt3**

In order to answer **Kt—B5** with an eventual **P—QR4,** and also to meet Black's next move.

KKt—Q4

This is still strong, however. Alekhine states his idea to have been 18.., **Kt × Kt;** 19 **R × Kt, B—Q4;** 20 **Q—Kt2, R × R;** 21 **Q × R, Q—R1,** followed by **R—B1.** White's reply is practically forced.

18 **B—B3** **R—B5 !**

Though a Kt is ready to occupy White's weak square it does not do so yet, for then 19 **KR—Q1** with the threat of **P—K4.**

19 **Kt—K4** **Q—B1**
20 **R × R**

Alekhine is inclined to consider this his opponent's decisive error, giving Black complete mastery on the Q-side. He suggests 20 **Q—Kt1,** threatening **Kt** or **B—Q6.** If 20.., **R—Q1,** then 21 **Kt—Q2 !, R × R;** 22 **R × R, Q—R1;** 23 **B—B7.**

Kt × R
21 **R—B1** **Q—R1**

Threatening **Kt × KtP.**

22 **Kt—B3**

Lasker gives 22 **Kt—B5 !, B × Kt;** 23 **P × B, R—B1;** 24 **B—K2** as making a better fight. Alekhine continues this 24.., **R × P;** 25 **B × Kt, Q—QB1,** with a P ahead.

R—B1
23 **Kt × Kt** **B × Kt**
24 **B × B** **Q × B**
25 **P—QR4**

Some diversion is desperately necessary, or else White is gradually strangled; but this creates a new weakness on the Q-side. 25 **P—B3** might be played, with a view to **B—B2.** Then, however, White's centre is very shaky.

B—B3
26 **Kt—B3**

If 26 **R—Q1,** simply **P × P;** 27 **Q × P, Kt—Kt7** etc. Not 26.., **Kt × P;** 27 **P × Kt !, B × Kt;** 28 **Q × Q, B × P ch;** 29 **K—B1, P × Q;** 30 **P × P, P × P;** 31 **R × P.** There is, however, a line which promises better, *viz.* 26 **P × P,** (if) **B × Kt;** 27 **P × B, P × P;** 28 **R—Q1.** No easily demonstrable win is to be found here; but perhaps 26.., **P × P** must be played, holding the position.

Position after 26 **Kt—B3:**

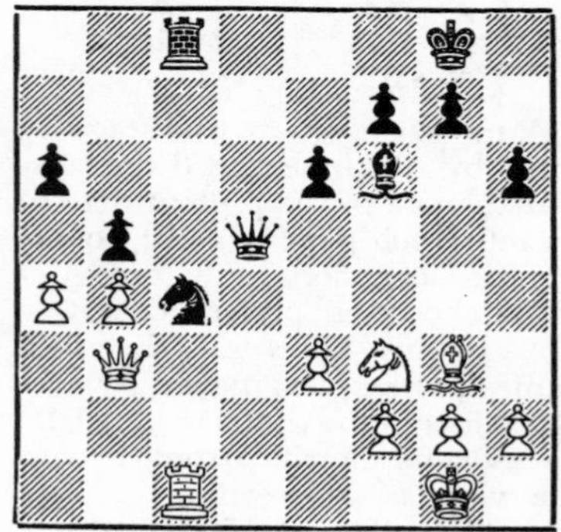

B—Kt7 !

The primary object of this is to enable him to play **P—K4** without closing the B's diagonal. But there is much more in the move. Where is White's R going to?

27 **R—K1**

If 27 **R—Q1,** Black's intention was **P × P;** 28 **Q × P, Kt—Kt3;** 29 **R × Q, Kt × Q;** 30 **R—Q1, Kt—B6;** 31 **R—K1, R—B5;** 32 **B—Q6, Kt—K5;** 33 **B—K7, P—B3;** 34 **R—Kt1, K—B2;** 35 **K—**

B1, B—B6 etc. If 27 **R—Kt1,** then **Kt—R6;** 28 **Q × B, Kt × R;** 29 **Q × Kt, Q—Kt6;** 30 **Q—KB1, P × P;** 31 **P—R3, P—R6.** (If 32 **B—K5** there might follow **P—B3;** 33 **B—R1, Q—B5,** forcing the win.) White has also 27 **R—KB1,** when the continuation would be as in the text.

	R—Q1
28 **P × P**	**P × P**
29 **P—R3**	**P—K4**
30 **R—Kt1**	

If 30 **P—K4, Q—Q6.**

	P—K5
31 **Kt—Q4**	

White has no saving move. *E.g.*, 31 **Kt—K1, Q—Q7;** 32 **Q—B2** (32 **K—B1, R—R1;** 33 **R—Q1, R—R6** and wins), **Q × Q;** 33 **Kt × Q, R—Q7;** 34 **Kt—K1, Kt—R6** and wins. On 31 **Kt—R2, Q—Q6;** 32 **R × B, Q × Q;** 33 **R × Q, R—Q8 ch;** 34 **Kt—B1, Kt—Q7;** 35 **R—R3, Kt × Kt !** etc. This is Alekhine's own analysis. The remaining Kt's move, 31 **Kt—R4,** is obviously worse.

	B × Kt
32 **R—Q1 ?**	

This shortens the game, but 32 **P × B, Q × P** leaves no hope.

	Kt × P

White resigns.

A fine, subtle game, which Alekhine considers only second to the 34th game of the match. Particularly interesting in the opening stage is the way in which Black took advantage of the slight error of judgment 8 **P—QR3.**

GAME 39

ALEKHINE v. CAPABLANCA

BUENOS AIRES, *November* 22-23, 1927

(CHAMPIONSHIP MATCH, 32ND GAME)

QUEEN'S GAMBIT DECLINED

	White.	*Black.*
	ALEKHINE	CAPABLANCA
1	**P—Q4**	**Kt—KB3**
2	**P—QB4**	**P—K3**
3	**Kt—QB3**	**P—Q4**
4	**B—Kt5**	**QKt—Q2**
5	**P—K3**	**P—B3**
6	**P × P**	

One of the three methods of evading the *Cambridge Springs Defence* illustrated in this match (in which there were four examples of the variation itself and five of the variation evaded). The others were 6 **P—QR3** (see the following game) and 6 **B—Q3**, played by Alekhine in the 31st and 33rd games.

6		**KP × P**
7	**B—Q3**	**B—K2**
8	**KKt—K2**	

This seems to have been a new move on the part of Alekhine, who claims for it greater elasticity than the older 8 **Kt—B3** has. He considers 8.., **P—KR3** the best reply to it, when he intended to continue 9 **B—KB4** (not **R4**). Tartakover gives 8.., **Kt—Kt5** as the correct reply.

8		**Castles**
9	**Kt—Kt3**	**Kt—K1**

Now 9.., **P—KR3** could be answered by 10 **P—KR4**!, giving White a well-known attack against the castled K. But an attack is coming in any case, and Black's defence is very difficult.

10	**P—KR4**	**QKt—B3**

Almost the only possible move. 10.., **B × B**; 11 **B × P ch** was obviously fatal; and none of the K-side P's can be moved with safety.

11	**Q—B2**	**B—K3**
12	**Kt—B5**	**B × Kt**

12.., **B—Kt5**, endeavouring to keep both B's, might perhaps be a dangerous weakening of the defensive forces.

13	**B × B**	**Kt—Q3**
14	**B—Q3**	**P—KR3**
15	**B—KB4**	**R—B1 ?**

Only useful in the event of White castling on the Q-side. The move gives White time for a vigorous manœuvre. 15.., **R—K1** would have prevented it, *e.g.*, 16 **P—KKt4, Kt × P**; if 17 **R—KKt1, P—KR4**. If, on the other hand, White played 16 **Castles QR**, then **Kt(B3)—K5** would yield Black a fairly satisfactory game.

16	**P—KKt4 !**	**Kt(B3)—K5**

Not now 16.., **Kt × P**; 17 **B × Kt, Q** or **B × B**; 18 **B—B5**. Black's sacrifice of a P is his best course, and leads to a fighting endgame.

17	**P—Kt5**	**P—KR4**
18	**KB × Kt**	

Dr. Lasker here suggested as best 19 **QB × Kt, Kt × B**; 20 **P—Kt6.** But then, as Alekhine points out, 20.., **B × P.**

		Kt × B
19	**Kt × Kt**	**P × Kt**
20	**Q × KP**	**Q—R4 ch**
21	**K—B1**	**Q—Q4**

Black rightly holds that there are better drawing chances here with the Q's off.

22	**Q × Q**	**P × Q**
23	**K—Kt2**	**R—B7**
24	**KR—QB1 !**	**KR—B1**

Not 24.., **R × P**; 25 **KR—QKt1, R × R**; 26 **R × R, P—QKt3**; 27 **R—QB1,** with a decisive entry of White's R into Black's lines.

25	**R × R**	**R × R**
26	**R—QKt1**	**K—R2**

The endgame proper has now begun. Black had to choose between action on the K-side, as here, or action on the Q-side (26.., **P—Kt4**). The latter would have allowed White quick progress in the centre by **K—Kt3, P—B3,** and **P—K4.**

27	**K—Kt3**	**K—Kt3**
28	**P—B3**	**P—B3 !**

28.., **K—B4** would be bad, because of 29 **P—K4 ch, P × P**; 30 **P × P ch,** and Black cannot capture again. As he plays, Black succeeds in holding up the advance of the KP.

29	**P × P**	**B × P**
30	**P—QR4**	

Alekhine describes this as his "second trump-card"—the release of his R.

		K—B4
31	**P—R5**	**R—K7**

Position after 31.., **R—K7:**

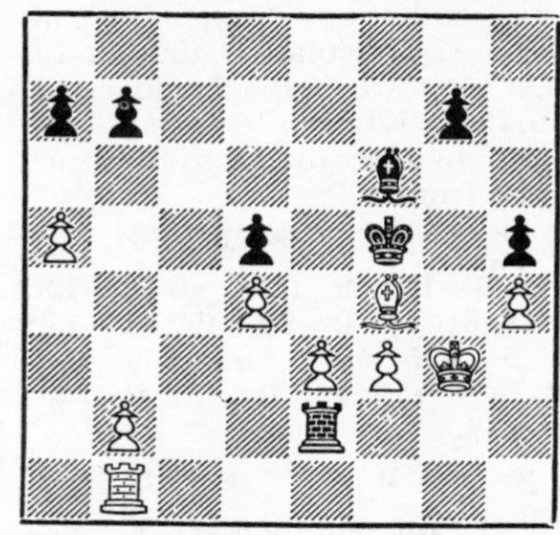

32 **R—QB1 ?**

While some of the critics marked this **!**, Alekhine himself marks it **?** and calls it an unnecessary sacrifice of a P, which makes a win seriously doubtful. It appears that he intended 32 **P—Kt4,** followed by **R—QB1** or **P—Kt5,** but at the last moment became suspicious of Black's 32.. **P—KKt4.** To answer this, however, there was the continuation 33 **P × P, B × KtP** (**P—R5 ch**; 34 **K × P, B × QP**; 35 **R—Q1**); 34 **B × B, K × B**; 35 **P—B4 ch, K—B4**; 36 **K—B3, R—KR7**; 37 **R—KKt1.** It must be admitted that this is not too easy to work out in practical play.

		R × KtP
33	**R—B5**	**K—K3**
34	**P—K4**	**B × QP**

The choice between this and 34.., **P × P** is difficult. After 34.., **P × P**; 35 **P—Q5 ch, K—B4**; 36 **P—Q6 dis. ch, K—K3**; 37 **P × P, R—Kt6 ch**; 38 **K—Kt2, R—Kt7 ch**; 39 **K—R3, R—Kt5**; 40 **R—B8, R × P**; 41 **R—K8 ch, K—Q4**; 42 **R × R, K × R**; 43 **B—Kt5, B—B6**; 44 **P—R6 !, P × P**; 45 **P—Q7, B—R4.** Alekhine gives not 46 **P—Q8=Q,** but 38 **K—Kt2 !** —gaining a move on the hostile

QRP's, and so securing the win. This ending still remains an exercise in calculation, though it is clear that when Black moves his B to B2 or Kt3 White must at once queen, in order to stop the advance of the front RP.

35 **R × P** **B—B6**

If **B—B7 ch,** then 36 **K—R3, R—Kt6;** 37 **R—K5 ch, K—B2;** 36 **B—Kt5** etc. Or 37.., **K—Q2;** 38 **R × P, R × P ch;** 39 **K—Kt4.**

36 **R × P** **P—R3**

If **B—K8 ch,** then 37 **K—R3, R—Kt6;** 38 **R—K5 ch,** and White saves his BP. More difficult was 36.., **P—QKt4;** 37 **P × P i.p., P × P** (now White must stop this P without exchanging R's); 38 **R—Q5, P—QKt4;** 39 **R—Q6 ch, K—K2;** 40 **R—QKt6, P—Kt5;** 41 **K—Kt4,** but the White K's advance should decide the game.

37 **B—B7** **B—K8 ch**

If **R—Kt4,** 38 **R—Kt5.**

38 **K—Kt4** **R—Kt7 ch**
39 **K—R3** **R—KB7**
40 **K—Kt4** **R—Kt7 ch**
41 **K—R3** **R—KB7**

These, of course, are time-gaining moves, as also are some which follow.

42 **P—B4** **R—B6 ch**
43 **K—Kt2** **R—B7 ch**
44 **K—R3** **R—B6 ch**
45 **K—Kt2** **R—B7 ch**
46 **K—Kt1** **R—B7**
47 **B—Kt6** **R—B5 ?**

At last Black makes a mistake, though it is by no means obvious till White demonstrates it. Better was 47.., **B—Kt6;** but 48 **R—K5 ch, K—Q3** (**K—B2;** 49 **P—R5**); 49 **R—KKt5** is still sufficient to win, Alekhine says.

48 **K—Kt2 !**

The point! Black cannot now play **R × P** because of 49 **K—B3, R moves;** 50 **R—K5 ch.** Or 49.., **P—Kt3;** 50 **R—R8, R moves;** 51 **R—K8 ch,** in both cases winning the B.

P—Kt3
49 **R—K5 ch** **K—Q2**
50 **P—R5** **P × P**
51 **K—B3** **P—R5**
52 **R—R5** **R—B6 ch**
53 **K—Kt4**

White must now win, but there is still a little fight left.

R—B5
54 **K—B5**

Not 54 **P—K5, B—Q7;** 55 **R—B5, P—R6 !**

B × P
55 **R—R7 ch**

White does not fall into the trap 55 **B × B, R—B4 ch;** 54 **K—Kt4 ?, R × R;** 55 **K × R, P—R6** and wins. But even there 54 **P—K5, R × B;** 55 **R × P** was a win.

K—B3
56 **B × B** **R—B4 ch**
57 **K—K6** **R × B**
58 **P—B5** **R—R6**
59 **P—B6** **R—KB6**
60 **P—B7** **P—Kt4**

This, curiously, paves the way for White's final slide across the board with a Q.

61 **R—R5** **P—R6**
62 **R—KB5** **R × R**
63 **P × R** **Resigns**

For on 63.., **P—R7** there follows 64 **P—B8=Q, P—R8=Q;** 65 **Q—R8 ch,** winning the Q. See Black's 60th move.

J. H. Blake, annotating the games in *The British Chess Magazine*, calls this " the greatest game of the match." It is marred by some mistakes; but Alekhine only makes one of these, on move 32, and that some annotators hailed as a good move!

GAME 40

ALEKHINE v. CAPABLANCA

BUENOS AIRES, *November* 26-28, 1927

(CHAMPIONSHIP MATCH, 34TH AND LAST GAME)

QUEEN'S GAMBIT DECLINED

White.	*Black.*
ALEKHINE	CAPABLANCA
1 **P—Q4**	**P—Q4**
2 **P—QB4**	**P—K3**
3 **Kt—QB3**	**Kt—KB3**
4 **B—Kt5**	**QKt—Q2**
5 **P—K3**	**P—B3**
6 **P—QR3**	

This method of forestalling the *Cambridge Springs Defence* was employed by Capablanca in the 5th game of the match, where Alekhine expressed his approval of it.

	B—K2
7 **Kt—B3**	**Castles**
8 **B—Q3**	

Alekhine said, concerning the 5th game, that 8 **Q—B2** followed by **R—Q1** was the logical continuation here. Yet he does not play it now.

	P × P
9 **B × P**	**Kt—Q4**
10 **B × B**	**Q × B**
11 **Kt—K4**	

Capablanca as White preferred 11 **R—QB1.** The text-move is stronger.

	KKt—B3
12 **Kt—Kt3**	**P—B4**

Here Maróczy, playing Black against Alekhine, San Remo, 1930, tried 12.., **P—QKt3,** followed by **B—Kt2,** which seems the best line.

13 **Castles**	**Kt—Kt3**

To **P—QKt3** now 14 **P—Q5** is the objection.

14 **B—R2**	**P × P**
15 **Kt × P**	**P—Kt3**

In preparation for **P—K4,** to which at present White could of course reply 16 **QKt—B5.**

16 **R—B1**	**B—Q2**

P—K4 would still be premature, because of 17 **Kt—Kt5.**

17 **Q—K2**	**QR—B1**
18 **P—K4**	**P—K4**
19 **Kt—B3**	**K—Kt2**

Alekhine calls this and his opponent's next move rather careless. Black certainly develops weak spots. He had alternatives in 19.., **B—Kt5,** to be followed by **B × Kt,** and 19.., **R × R;** 20 **R × R, R—B1,** of which the latter seems preferable.

20 **P—R3**	**P—KR3 ?**

Better is 20.., **B—K3.**

Position after 20.., **P—KR3:**

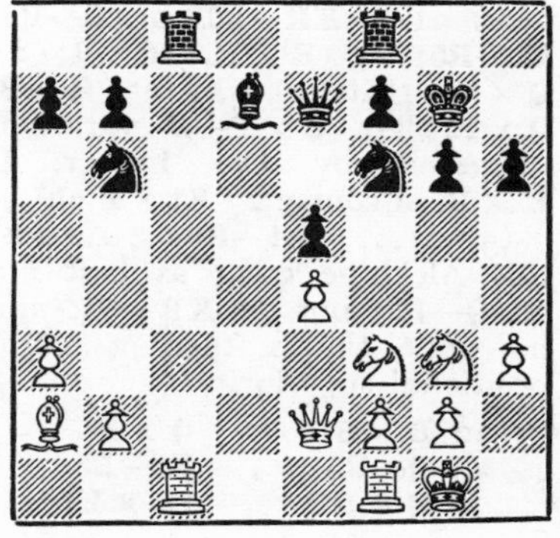

21 **Q—Q2 !**

Very strong, the main threat being 22 **Q—R5,** simultaneously attacking KP and QRP.

B—K3

Black resigns himself to losing a P. He had practically 5 alternative moves, of which 4 are unavailing:

(1) 21.., **B—B3,** which looks natural, but is immediately fatal unless the B goes back next move, as in (2). White replies 22 **Kt—R4 !** with a terrible threat of check at B5. If 22.., **Kt × P,** then 23 either **Kt—B5 ch, P × Kt;** 24 **Kt × P ch,** and Black is mated or loses his Q; *e.g.*, **K—B3;** 25 **Q × P ch, K × Kt;** 26 **P—Kt4** mate. Or 22.., **B × P;** 23 **Q—K3, B—B7;** 24 **R × B, R × R;** 25 **Kt—B5 ch.** Or 22.., **K—Kt1;** 23 **Kt—B5, P × Kt;** 24 **Kt × P, Q—Q2;** 25 **Q × P, Kt—K1;** 26 **R—B3.**

(2) 21.., **B—Kt4;** 22 **Kt—R4, B—Q2;** 23 **Q—R5, Kt × P** (**Kt—R5;** 24 **Q × Kt, B × Q;** 25 **Kt—B5 ch**); 24 **Kt × Kt, Q × Kt;** 25 **Q × P ch, P—B3;** 26 **Q—K7 ch, K—R1;** 27 **R × R, R × R;** 28 **Kt × P.**

(3) 21.., **R × R;** 22 **R × R, R—B1;** 23 **R × R ch, Kt × R;** 24 **Q—B3.** Or 23.., **B × R;** 24 **Q—R5.**

(4) 21.., **KR—K1;** 22 **Q—R5, Kt—R5;** 23 **R × R, R × R;** 24 **Q × RP, Kt(R5) × P;** 25 **Q × P, Q × P;** 26 **B × P**—a variation suggested by Dr. Lasker. If **K × B,** of course 27 **Kt × P ch.**

(5) 21.., **Kt—R5 !** Against this Alekhine gives as best not 22 **Q—R5,** but 22 **KR—Q1,** and he only claims then a slight positional superiority.

22	**B × B**	**Q × B**
23	**Q—R5**	**Kt—B5**
24	**Q × RP**	**Kt × KtP**

If **R—QR1,** then 25 **Q—B5 !**

25	**R × R**	**R × R**
26	**Q × P**	**Kt—B5**
27	**Q—Kt4**	**R—QR1**
28	**R—R1**	**Q—B3 !**

Capablanca makes a fine fight of it. He now threatens **R—R5,** putting both White's RP and KP in danger.

29	**P—QR4**	**Kt × P**
30	**Kt × P**	

Not 30 **Kt × Kt, Q × Kt;** 31 **R—QB1, R—QB1;** 32 **Kt × P, Kt—K6 !;** 33 **Q × Q, R × R ch;** 34 **K—R2, Kt—B8 ch;** 35 **K—Kt1, Kt—Kt6 dis. ch** and wins back the Q (Alekhine).

		Q—Q3
31	**Q × Kt**	**Q × Kt**
32	**R—K1**	**Kt—Q3**
33	**Q—QB1**	**Q—B3**
34	**Kt—K4**	**Kt × Kt**
35	**R × Kt**	

The ending now requires a lot of winning, and, as conducted against such an endgame-expert as Capablanca, is a model, in spite of two opportunities missed (see moves 67 and 70) of winning in quicker time than by the process actually adopted.

R—QKt1

Aiming at **Q—Kt7,** which White prevents, as an exchange of Q's does not suit him at present.

36	**R—K2**	**R—QR1**
37	**R—R2**	**R—R4**
38	**Q—B7**	**Q—R3**
39	**Q—B3 ch**	**K—R2**
40	**R—Q2 !**	**Q—Kt3**

Not **R × P;** 41 **R—Q8** etc.

41 **R—Q7**

This was White's sealed move at the adjournment.

		Q—Kt8 ch
42	**K—R2**	**Q—Kt1 ch**

43 **P—Kt3** **R—KB4**
44 **Q—Q4** **Q—K1 !**

In order to meet 45 **R—Q8** with **R × P ch.**

45 **R—Q5 !** **R—B6**

An exchange of R's would simplify matters for White.

46 **P—R4** **Q—KR1**

On the other hand, an exchange of Q's would still not suit White's book, for then Black's R would get behind the QRP.

47 **Q—Kt6** **Q—R8**
48 **K—Kt2** **R—B3**
49 **Q—Q4 !**

Now White forces the exchange of Q's, when Black's R is in front of, not behind, the QRP.

		Q × Q
50	**R × Q**	**K—Kt2**
51	**P—QR5**	**R—R3**
52	**R—Q5**	**R—QB3**
53	**R—Q4**	**R—R3**
54	**R—R4**	**K—B3**
55	**K—B3**	**K—K4**
56	**K—K3**	**P—R4**
57	**K—Q3**	**K—Q4**
58	**K—B3**	**K—B4**
59	**R—R2**	**K—Kt4**
60	**K—Kt3**	**K—B4**

If **R × P,** naturally 61 **R × R ch, K × R;** 62 **K—B4** etc.

61 **K—B3** **K—Kt4**

It is curious that some published scores of the last two moves give them as 60 **R—Kt2 ch, K—B4;** 61 **R—R2, K—Kt4.** We follow Alekhine's own version. The 60th move was no doubt made against the clock. The point is not of much importance as Black could not play **K × P** without losing at once.

62 **K—Q4** **R—Q3 ch**

Or 62.., **K—Kt5;** 63 **R—R1, K—Kt6;** 64 **K—B5** etc.

63 **K—K5** **R—K3 ch**
64 **K—B4** **K—R3**
65 **K—Kt5** **R—K4 ch**
66 **K—R6** **R—KB4**

Position after 66.., **R—KB4:**

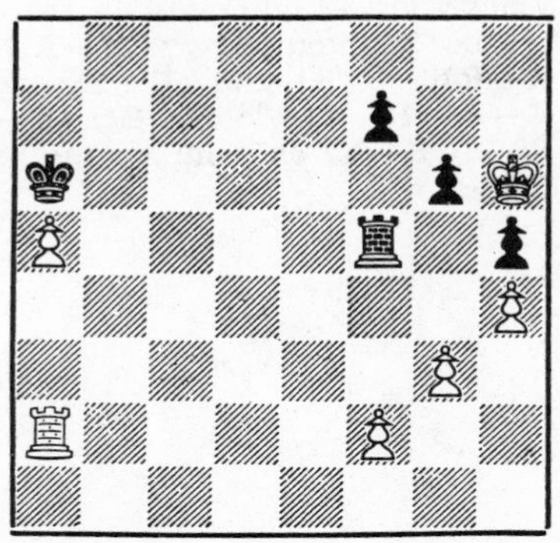

A very unusual position. Alekhine points out that he had a quicker win by 67 **K—Kt7, R—B6;** 68 **K—Kt8, R—B3;** 69 **K—B8, R—B6** (**R—B4;** 70 **P—B4**); 70 **K—Kt7, R—B4;** 71 **P—B4.**

67 **P—B4** **R—B4**
68 **R—R3** **R—B2**
69 **K—Kt7** **R—Q2**
70 **P—B5**

Quicker again was 70 **K—B6, R—B2;** 71 **P—B5, P × P;** 72 **K × P, R—B4 ch;** 73 **K—B6, R—B2;** 74 **R—KB3, K × P;** 75 **R—B5 ch** etc. (Alekhine).

		P × P
71	**K—R6**	**P—B5**
72	**P × P**	**R—Q4**
73	**K—Kt7**	**R—KB4**
74	**R—R4**	**K—Kt4**
75	**R—K4 !**	**K—R3**
76	**K—R6**	

He might also play 76 **K—Kt8, R—B3;** 77 **K—B8, R—B4;**

78 **K—Kt7, K—R2;** 79 **R—K7 ch,** winning the BP.

R × RP

Against **K—R2** Alekhine gives as his line 77 **R—K5, R × P;** 78 **K—Kt5, R—B8;** 79 **K × P, P—B4;** 80 **K—Kt5, P—B5;** 81 **R—KB5, P—B6;** 82 **K—Kt4,** and Black's last P falls. Again there is the manœuvre 77 **K—Kt7, K—R3;** 78 **K—Kt8, R—B3;** 79 **K—B8, R—B4;** 80 **K—Kt7, K—R2;** 81 **R—K7 ch,** winning the P.

77	**R—K5**	**R—R8**
78	**K × P**	**R—KKt8**
79	**R—KKt5**	**R—KR8**
80	**R—KB5**	**K—Kt3**
81	**R × P**	**K—B3**
82	**R—K7**	**Resigns**

This is the game which the winner considered the best in the match. With regard to the two possibilities missed of winning more quickly, the influence of the time-limit must not be forgotten.

GAME 41

BOGOLJUBOFF v. ALEKHINE

HEIDELBERG, *November* 19, 1929

(CHAMPIONSHIP [FIRST] MATCH, 8TH GAME)

QUEEN'S PAWN GAME

White.	*Black.*
BOGOLJUBOFF	ALEKHINE
1 **P—Q4**	**Kt—KB3**
2 **P—QB4**	**P—QKt3**

This was the only *Queen's Indian* of the match. The difference in treatment from that in Game 37 is notable. But there Alekhine was meeting 2 **Kt—KB3,** not 2 **P—QB4,** against which the defence is very rarely played.

3 **Kt—QB3**	**B—Kt2**
4 **P—B3**	

Starting to build a centre, and practically forcing Black's answer.

	P—Q4
5 **P × P**	**Kt × P**
6 **P—K4**	**Kt × Kt**
7 **P × Kt**	**P—K3**

White certainly has his centre; but Black is not seriously incommoded, as he now threatens to disturb it by **P—QB4.**

8 **B—Kt5 ch**	**Kt—Q2**
9 **Kt—K2**	**B—K2**
10 **Castles**	**P—QR3**
11 **B—Q3**	**P—QB4 !**
12 **B—Kt2**	

An error of judgment, based, as J. H. Blake says in a note upon the game, on the preconception that Black must castle on the K-side, which proves fallacious. This **B** would stand better at K3.

	Q—B2
13 **P—KB4 ?**	

This is a more serious error, as Alekhine demonstrates. White should have reckoned by now on the possibility of Black's Q-side castling and a consequent attack on his own K-side, which this weakens. 13 **R—B1** may be his best move.

	Kt—B3
14 **Kt—Kt3**	

He cannot play 14 **P—K5,** because of **Q—B3** etc.; and 14 **Q—Kt1** is scarcely inviting. The text-move, however, provides Black with an immediate target.

	P—KR4
15 **Q—K2**	

The problem is the defence of the KP, weakened two moves ago. **P—R5** is obviously coming, so that the defence must be taken up by the Q. 15 **Q—B2** is defeated by **P—R5,** followed by **P—B5;** 15 **Q—B3** by **P—R5** and if 16 **Kt—K2, P—R6.** There remain only 15 **Q—Kt1** and what is actually played.

	P—R5
16 **Kt—R1**	**Kt—R4**
17 **Q—Kt4**	**Castles QR**

With two of White's minor pieces out of play, this manœuvre

is quite safe. No danger is threatened by 18 **P—Q5, P—B5;** 19 **B—B2,** for then **B—B4 ch** etc. Nor does 18 **P—B5** harm against **K—Kt1;** 19 **BP × P, KBP × P** and if 20 **Q × KP, B—QB1** (not **Kt—B5;** 21 **R × Kt, Q × R;** 22 **Q × B, Q—K6 ch,** 23 **Kt—B2**); 21 **Q—Kt3** (anywhere else is fatal), **Kt—B5;** 22 **Q—B2, P × P;** 23 **P × P, Q × Q;** 24 **B × Q, Kt—K7 ch.**

18 **QR—K1**	**K—Kt1**
19 **P—B5**	**P—K4**
20 **P—Q5**	**P—B5**
21 **B—B2**	**B—B4 ch**
22 **Kt—B2**	

Position after 22 **Kt—B2:**

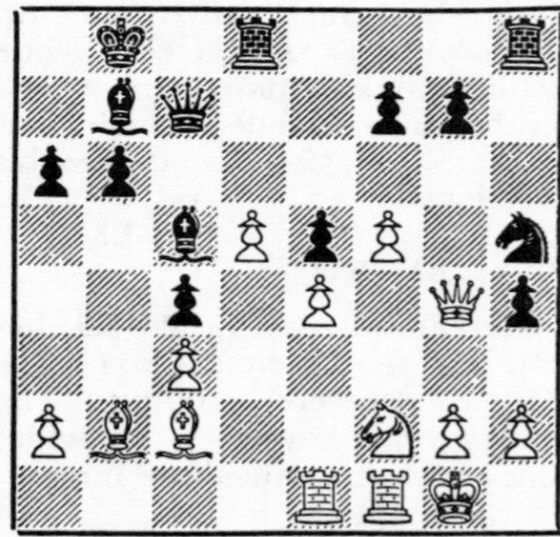

P—Kt3 !

A real masterstroke, whereby both the QR and the long passive QB are brought into action in two consecutive moves; but White's reply is injudicious.

23 **P × P**

B—B1 at once was the only chance of prolonging the game, bringing White's still more passive QB to the defence—though then 23.., **B—QB1** would be a terrible retort.

	QR—Kt1
24 **B—B1**	**B—QB1**
25 **Q—B3**	

Somewhat better would be 25 **Q—K2,** so as to be able to meet Black's next move with **B—K3** without endangering the Q.

	R × P
26 **K—R1**	**Kt—Kt6 ch**
27 **P × Kt**	

If 27 **K—Kt1, B—KKt5** wins the Q.

	P × P dis. ch
28 **Kt—R3**	**B × Kt**
29 **P × B**	**R × P ch**

and mates next move.

Bogoljuboff's mistakes in the opening do not spoil this game as an example of Alekhine's artistry, which here touches perfection.

GAME 42

ALEKHINE v. BOGOLJUBOFF

BERLIN, *October* 10, 1929

(CHAMPIONSHIP [FIRST] MATCH, 13TH GAME)

QUEEN'S GAMBIT DECLINED

	White.	*Black.*
	ALEKHINE	BOGOLJUBOFF
1	**P—Q4**	**P—Q4**
2	**P—QB4**	**P—QB3**
3	**Kt—QB**	**Kt—B3**
4	**B—Kt5**	**P—K3**
5	**Kt—B3**	**QKt—Q2**
6	**P—K3**	

Permitting his opponent to branch into the *Cambridge Springs Defence*, which was four times seen in this match, and was twice evaded by Alekhine, as White, playing 6 **P—K4.** On 6 **P—QR3** see Game 40.

Q—R4

7 **P × P**

So Bogoljuboff played, as White, in the 12th game of the match, each player having previously (9th and 10th games) adopted the " normal " 7 **Kt—Q2.**

Kt × P

8 **Q—Q2**

Bogoljuboff's move in the 12th game, and evidently approved by Alekhine, in place of the older 8 **Q—Kt3** or **Q—B2,** as he adhered to it in his 25th game with Euwe in 1935. The best reply to it is Professor A. Becker's suggestion, 8.., **QKt—Kt3,** which Euwe followed with profit, Alekhine missing the right continuation 9 **Kt × Kt.**

B—Kt5

Though this looks natural, it is inferior to **QKt—B3.**

9	**R—B1**	**Castles**
10	**B—Q3**	**P—KR3**
11	**B—R4**	**P—K4 !**
12	**Castles**	

The first divergence, except for a transposition, from Bogoljuboff-Alekhine, 12th game, where with 12 **P—QR3, B × Kt;** 13 **P × B** Bogoljuboff offered to sacrifice a P. 12 **P × P** would be met by **Kt × Kt;** 13 **P × Kt, B—R6.**

R—K1

13	**P—K4**	**Kt—B5**
14	**B—B4**	**Kt—KKt3**
15	**P—QR3**	

15 **B—KKt3** has been suggested in place of this, as 15.., **P × P;** 16 **Q × P** merely develops White's game. It certainly seems better than the move played.

Kt × B

16 **Kt × Kt** **B—K2**

But this is not correct, for White could have played 17 **P—QKt4** with effect. If then **Q × RP,** the Russian analyst E. Rabinovitch discovered the pretty continuation 18 **R—R1, Q × P;** 19 **B × P ch, K × B;** 20 **Q—R2 ch, K—B3;** 21 **P—B4** and wins. The opening of this game shows what advantages the analyst at home has over the greatest masters sitting at the match-board, with clocks at their side.

17 **Kt—B5** **B—B1**
18 **P—QKt4**

Not now so strong as in Rabinovitch's variation. But Black, being so undeveloped, avoids all complications at this point, and retires his Q for the defence. White's best move may have been 18 **K—R1,** to prepare for **P—B4.**

Q—Q1
19 **Q—R2** **Q—B3**

Position after 19.., **Q—B3**:

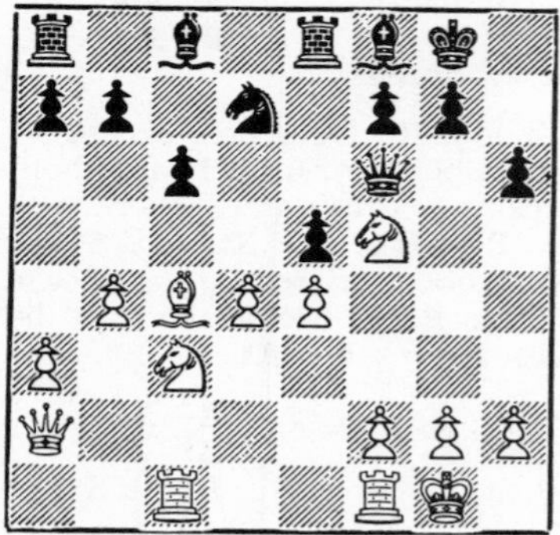

20 **P—Q5**

White's attack has come to a halt, and he had to deal with the threat of 20.., **P × P.** His present territorial advantage cannot be maintained by any than the text-move, and Bogoljuboff proceeds to show that it is illusory, conducting the rest of the game in admirable style.

Kt—Kt3
21 **Kt—K3** **Q—Kt3 !**
22 **B—Kt3**

22 **B—K2** is better, avoiding the necessity of going to a worse square two moves later.

P—QR4
23 **P—Kt5** **P—R5**
24 **B—Q1** **P × QP**
25 **Kt(B3) × QP** **Kt × Kt**
26 **Kt × Kt**

If 26 **P × Kt, Q—Q6** and White's QRP can only be saved at the expense of another P. But now comes a very unpleasant pin.

B—K3
27 **R—B4**

If 27 **B—B3,** Black's best line seems to be **B × Kt;** for if 28 **P × B** (he can hardly play 28 **Q × B, B × P;** 29 **R—R1,** on account of **B—Kt7**), **Q—Q6,** when a P must fall.

KR—B1
28 **R—K1** **B × Kt**
29 **P × B** **Q—Q6**

The threat is carried out at last. If in reply 30 **R × RP, R × R;** 31 **B × R,** Black can win as in the game itself by **Q—K5 !**

30 **R × R** **R × R**
31 **B × P ?**

White now had the option, as Alekhine pointed out afterwards, of 31 **Q—R1, Q × KtP;** 32 **R × P, B—Q3;** 33 **R—K1, Q × P;** 34 **B × P.** But after 34.., **R—R1** he must lose the QRP, and in spite of B's of opposite colours, Black's passed P should decide the issue.

Q—K5 !

The move overlooked by White.

32 **Q—Q2** **Q × B**
33 **P—Q6** **Q—Q5**
34 **Q × Q** **P × Q**

White resigns.

Much of the interest of this game lies in the opening. Nevertheless it is a fine struggle throughout to the 31st move.

GAME 43

BOGOLJUBOFF v. ALEKHINE

AMSTERDAM, *November* 3, 1929

(CHAMPIONSHIP [FIRST] MATCH, 22ND GAME)

RUY LOPEZ

White.	*Black.*
BOGOLJUBOFF	ALEKHINE
1 **P—K4**	**P—K4**
2 **Kt—KB3**	**Kt—QB3**
3 **B—Kt5**	**P—QR3**
4 **B—R4**	**P—Q3**
5 **P—B3**	

The vogue of 5 **B × Kt,** the now popular continuation against the *Steinitz Defence Deferred* to the *Ruy Lopez*, had not yet set in, though Bogoljuboff had been known to play it years earlier.

	B—Q2
6 **P—Q4**	**P—KKt3**

A variation characteristic of Capablanca, but rarely adopted by Alekhine. When followed by (7 **Castles**) **B—Kt2** and **KKt—K2,** it is known as the *Capablanca Defence*.

7 **B—KKt5**

This move was later condemned by Bogoljuboff himself, on the ground that Black's reply opens a good square for his KKt at B2.

	P—B3
8 **B—K3**	**Kt—R3**
9 **Castles**	**B—Kt2**
10 **P—KR3**	

The alternative 10 **P × P** is better, though with 10.., **QP × P** (not 10.., **BP × P;** 11 **B—KKt5,** nor 10.., **Kt × P,** losing control in the centre); 11 **B—B5, Kt—K2 !** the Hungarian master L. Steiner claims that Black has a good game. The text-move creates a weakness later; see Black's 27th move.

	Kt—B2
11 **QKt—Q2**	**Castles**
12 **P × P**	**QP × P**
13 **B—B5**	

This is of no profit, as the B has to go back two moves later.

	R—K1
14 **B—Kt3**	**P—Kt3**
15 **B—K3**	**Q—K2**
16 **Q—K2**	**QKt—Q1**
17 **B—Q5**	

White's design is to weaken his opponent's Q-side, which he achieves to some extent; but Black has a resource.

	B—B3
18 **P—B4**	**B × B**
19 **BP × B**	**P—KB4 !**

A fine counter-stroke, calling off attention temporarily from the Q-side.

20 **Kt—B4**	**Kt—Kt2**
21 **QR—B1**	**QR—Q1**
22 **P—Q6**	

Black threatened **P × P,** and White therefore decides to give up his QP getting in exchange Black's QRP.

	QKt × P
23 **Kt × Kt**	**R × Kt**

Not **Kt × Kt,** because of 24 **B—Kt5,** forcing exchanges and winning Black's QBP.

24 **Q × P** **Q—Q2**

P × P would only gain a P for the moment, Now 25.., **P—B5** is threatened; and also Black is in control of the Q-file.

25 **R—B2** **P—B4**
26 **P—QR4** **P—KB5**
27 **B—Q2** **P—KKt4**

With the threat of **P—Kt5** and an attack which White is badly placed to meet. In consequence White offers an exchange of Q's, though the resulting position is unfavourable to him.

28 **Q—Kt5** **Q × Q**
29 **P × Q** **R—Q6 !**
30 **R—R1**

Not 30 **P—QKt4, P—B5;** 31 **R × P, Kt—Q3** (a move for which Black has just made room). White is doomed to lose a P.

Kt—Q3
31 **R—R6** **R—Kt1**
32 **B—B3**

If 32 **R—B3** Akekhine's intention was to reply **P—B5;** 33 **R × R, P × R;** 34 **R—R3, Kt × KP;** 35 **R × P, R—R1.** If 32 **Kt × KtP,** then **Kt × KtP.**

Kt × KP
33 **B × P** **B × B**
34 **Kt × B** **R—Q8 ch**
35 **K—R2**

Position after 35 **K—R2 :**

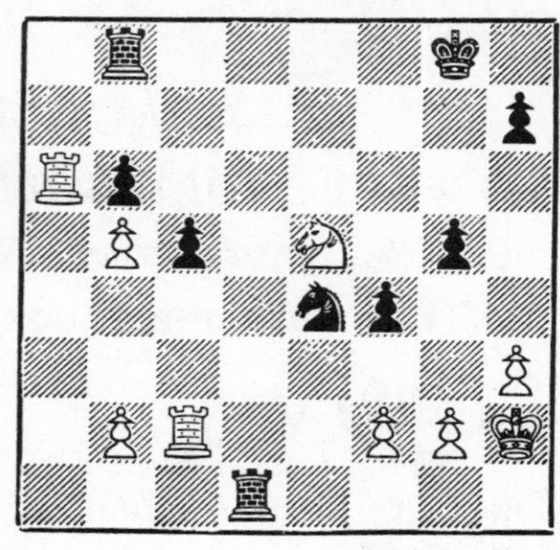

Kt—Q7 !

A beautiful move, which threatens mate by **Kt—B8 ch, Kt—Kt6 dis. ch,** and **R—R8.** The reply 36 **P—KKt3** is unavailing, for then **R—K1;** 37 **P × P, P × P;** 38 **Kt—Kt4, Kt—B6 ch;** 39 **K—Kt2, Kt—R5 ch;** 40 **K—R2, R(K1)—K8,** and only few checks can postpone mate.

36 **P—R4** **R—K1**
37 **Kt—B3**

If 37 **Kt—Kt4,** Dr. Euwe pointed out a mate by **Kt—B8 ch;** 38 **K—R3, P—R4;** 39 **Kt—B6 ch, K—B2;** 40 **P × P, Kt—K6**—and there is no escape.

Kt × Kt ch
38 **P × Kt** **R(K1)—K8**
39 **K—R3** **P—R4**

White resigns.

One of Alekhine's best games.

GAME 44

BOGOLJUBOFF v. ALEKHINE

PFORZHEIM, *April* 25, 1934

(CHAMPIONSHIP [SECOND] MATCH, 9TH GAME)

QUEEN'S PAWN GAME (BENONI COUNTER-GAMBIT)

White.	*Black.*
BOGOLJUBOFF	ALEKHINE
1 **P—Q4**	**P—QB4**

Those many critics who complain of the sameness and dullness of the openings in modern championship matches were silenced on the occasion of this game at least. The *Benoni Counter-Gambit* had for years been out of favour in master-play, because of the advantage which 2 **P—Q5** was supposed to confer on White. Yet Alekhine played it, though knowing that his opponent in his book *D2—d4!* six years before this match had published analysis supporting the claim of advantage for White by 2 **P—Q5**.

2 **P—Q5** **P—K4**

This was not a new move, having been tried by Spielmann and Tartakover among the masters. It is, moreover, merely a transposition.

3 **P—K4** **P—Q3**

Producing a " book " position, of which the standard illustration is Alekhine-Tartakover, Dresden, 1926.

4 **P—KB4**

Here Bogoljuboff departs from the line that he had himself commended, 4 **Kt—QB3** and, if **B—K2**, 5 **P—KKt3**, mentioning the possibility of an eventual **P—KB4**. At this stage the move is an interesting novelty; but Dr. Lasker calls it " useless violence," commending instead 4 **B—Kt5 ch**, **Kt—Q2**; 5 **Kt—QB3**, **Kt—B3**; 6 **KKt—K2**.

P × P

5 **B × P** **Q—R5 ch**

Lasker gives as best **Kt—K2**; 6 **Kt—KB3**, **Kt—Kt3**.

6 **P—Kt3**

6 **B—Kt3 ?**, **Q × P ch**; 7 **B—K2** would be met by **B—B4 !**

Q—K2

7 **Kt—QB3 ?**

Alekhine in a note suggests 7 **Kt—KB3**, when **Q × P ch**; 8 **K—B2** would be dangerous for Black. After his next move Black gets a firm hold on his K4—which explains why he checked on his 5th move and induced 6 **P—Kt3**, circumscribing the White QB's action.

P—KKt4 !

8 **B—K3** **QKt—Q2**

9 **Kt—B3**

Better is 9 **Q—Q2, P—KR3;** 10 **P—KR4.**

	P—KR3
10 **Q—Q2**	

Obviously White must castle on the Q-side, with such menaces against his K-side. But perhaps he has time here for 10 **B—Kt2.**

	KKt—B3
11 **Castles**	**Kt—Kt5**

Kt × KP; 12 **Kt × Kt, Q × Kt** might land Black in troublesome complications.

12 **B—K2**

White should not have given up his QB, even if its only square is Kt1.

	B—Kt2
13 **KR—B1**	**Kt × B**
14 **Q × Kt**	**P—R3**
15 **Kt—KKt1**	**P—Kt4**
16 **QR—K1**	**B—Kt2**
17 **Kt—Q1**	**Castles QR**
18 **B—Kt4**	**K—Kt1**
19 **B × Kt**	

White fears **Kt—K4;** but he now has the disadvantage of contending against a pair of B's when he has an insecure centre to protect.

	R × B
20 **Q—Q2**	

Better 20 **Kt—KB3,** with a view to **Kt—Q2** (Lasker).

	P—KKt5
21 **Kt—K3**	

And here Lasker gives 21 **Q—Kt2,** to be followed by **P—KR3.**

	Q—K4
22 **P—B3**	**P—KR4**
23 **Kt—B5**	**B—KB3**
24 **Q—B4**	**Q × Q**

Black gladly agrees to the exchange of Q's.

25 **P × Q**

Position after 25 **P × Q:**

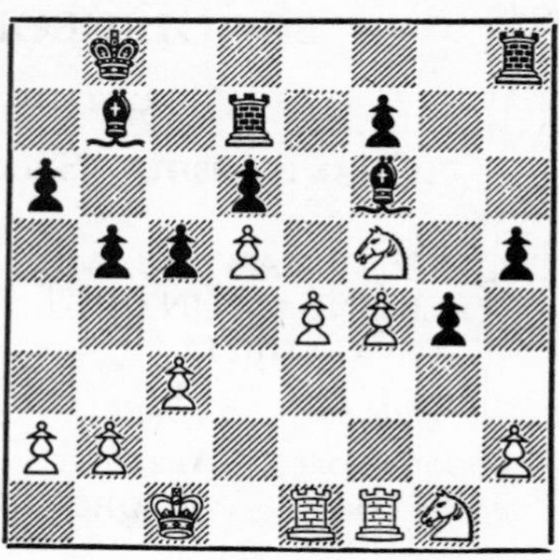

QR—Q1

White's chief asset is his Kt at B5, and with the text-move Black threatens to drive it away by **B—B1,** since White cannot leave it to be exchanged, with a break-up of his P's. Therefore White strives to find another strong square for this Kt. It would have been better to allow its dislodgment and retreat it *via* K3 to B2.

26 **P—B4 ?**	**P × P**
27 **Kt—K3**	**P—B6 !**
28 **P—Kt3**	**B—Q5**
29 **Kt—B4**	

The Kt has reached the intended square. But in the meanwhile the game is lost.

P—B4

This stroke demolishes White's centre completely, and that virtually finishes matters.

30 **P—K5**	**P × P**
31 **P × P**	**QB × P**
32 **R × P**	**QR—KB1**
33 **R × R ch**	**R × R**

34	**P—K6**	**R—K1**
35	**P—K7**	**QB × Kt**
36	**P × B**	**B × Kt**
37	**R × B**	**R × P**
38	**P—KR3**	**P × P**
39	**K—B2**	**P—R7**
40	**R—Kt1 ch**	**R—Kt2**
41	**R—KR1**	**R—Kt7 ch**
42	**K × P**	**R × P**
43	**K—Q3**	**K—B2**
44	**K—K4**	**K—B3**
45	**K—B5**	**P—R4**
46	**K—Kt5**	**P—QR5**

White resigns.

As he might have done nine moves earlier.

The chief interest of this game lies, of course, in the opening; but Alekhine's method of pressing his advantage home is worthy of study.

GAME 45

ALEKHINE v. EUWE

AMSTERDAM, *October* 3, 1935

(CHAMPIONSHIP [FIRST] MATCH, 1ST GAME)

QUEEN'S GAMBIT DECLINED

	White.	*Black.*
	ALEKHINE	EUWE
1	**P—Q4**	**P—Q4**
2	**P—QB4**	**P—QB3**

The first of twelve *Slav Defences* played in this match, seven by Euwe, five by Alekhine. Another is Game 47.

3 **Kt—KB3** **Kt—B3**
4 **Kt—B3**

A method of avoiding the *Meran Variation*, which may come after 4 **P—K3, P—K3;** 5 **Kt—B3** (5 **B—Q3,** as in Reshevsky-Vidmar, Nottingham, 1936, also avoids the *Meran*), **QKt—Q2** (Alekhine as Black in the 8th and 10th games of the match played **P—QR3**); 6 **B—Q3, P × P;** 7 **B × BP, P—QKt4.** See Game 24 for an anticipation in 1896 of Black's procedure in the *Meran*.

P × P

Amounting to a temporary acceptance of the Gambit, which is seen also in the 15th, 19th, 20th, 21st, and 23rd games of the match.

5 **P—QR4**

This was the line followed in the first four of these games, the 23rd varying with 5 **P—K3.** Alekhine played the text-move thrice in his first match with Bogoljuboff, who replied with 5.., **P—K3** in the 1st, with 5.., **B—B4** in the 3rd and 15th games. Capablanca played it in two well-known games in 1931, *v.* A. W. Dake in the New York Tournament, and *v.* Euwe in their 9th match-game.

B—B4

Considered the best. In the 19th game Euwe played 5.., **P—K3**, a move which Bogoljuboff had adopted against Alekhine in their first match, and still persisted with against him at Nottingham last year.

6 **Kt—K5**

Neither player in this match chose the quieter 6 **P—K3,** which found favour at Nottingham, producing some speedy draws (*e.g.*, Lasker-Capablanca and Capablanca-Euwe). Lasker in his *Chess Manual* commends it, saying that after **Kt—R3;** 7 **B × P, Kt—QKt5** the excellent position of the QKt gives Black the chance of a strong fight. The text-move is attributed to the Danish analyst, the late Dr. O. H. Krause, who also suggested 6 **Kt—R4**, played by Alekhine in the 15th game of the match.

QKt—Q2

Bogoljuboff in the 3rd and 5th match-games of 1929 preferred 6.., **P—K3.**

7 **Kt × P(B4)** **Q—B2**

To enable **P—K4.** 7.., **P—K3** would lead to a cramped game, giving White time for 8 **P—B3,** (if) **B—K2;** 9 **P—K4.**

8 **P—KKt3**	**P—K4**

Having secured this advance, Black is destined to conduct a hard defence, with a Kt pinned against his Q, though it is true that many eminent masters have not shunned the task. The crucial point arises on the 11th move for Black.

9 **P × P**	**Kt × P**
10 **B—B4**	**KKt—Q2**
11 **B—Kt2**	**B—K3 ?**

It is curious that Euwe chose this move here, when the merits of 11.., **P—B3** were shown in the game Capablanca-Vidmar, Carlsbad, 1929, and in Capablanca-Dake, New York, two years later. Euwe had played as in the text in his 9th match game against Capablanca in 1931, following Alekhine against Bogoljuboff at San Remo in 1930. Nowadays there is an improvement even on the immediate 11.., **P—B3.** See Game 47.

12 **Kt × Kt**	**Kt × Kt**
13 **Castles**	**B—K2**

In the 9th Capablanca-Euwe game, Euwe had still followed Bogoljuboff-Alekhine, San Remo, with 13.., **Q—R4.** In a comment on the latter game Tartakover suggested 13.., **B—K2** as best, while Alekhine condemned his own 13.., **Q—R4** as "artificial" and said that after 13.., **B—K2 !;** 14 **P—R5, Castles;** 15 **P—R6, P—B3** Black has a fairly satisfactory game. It is to be remarked that Alekhine does not proceed with 14 **P—R5** here.

14 **Q—B2**	

This was the move which Bogoljuboff had played at San Remo against 13.., **Q—R4.** It is good here also, and caused Euwe much deliberation over his reply—40 minutes in fact.

	R—Q1

The pin on the Q is very irksome to Black. He is anxious to get rid of it by **Q—R4,** but hesitates to do so yet. The text-move allows him to answer the threatened 15 **Kt—Kt5** with **Q—Kt1,** without shutting in his R; a threat which made 14.., **P—B3** undesirable.

15 **KR—Q1**	

Now, of course, 15 **Kt—Kt5, Q—Kt1;** 16 **B × Kt, Q × B;** 17 **Kt × P, Q—Kt1** would cost White his Kt.

	Castles
16 **Kt—Kt5**	**R × R ch**

Still he cannot play **Q—R4,** for then 17 **R × R** (17 **B × Kt, P × Kt**), and he cannot recapture with R because of 18 **B × Kt, P × Kt;** 19 **B—B7.** But alternatives to the text-move, which surrenders the open file, are 16.., **Q—Kt1** and **Q—Kt3.** The latter is analysed by V. Ragosin, with the suggested continuation 17 **R × R, R × R;** 18 **B × Kt, P × Kt;** 19 **P—R5** (if 19 **B—B7,** presumably **R—QB1**), **Q—B4;** 20 **Q × Q, B × Q;** 21 **KB × P, P—B3;** 22 **R—QB1, B—B5;** 23 **B—QB3, B × P;** 24 **B × P, R—Q8 ch;** 25 **R × R, B × R,** with drawing chances.

17 **R × R**	**Q—R4**
18 **Kt—Q4**	**B—B1**

If **Kt—Kt3,** then 19 **Kt × B,** and Black's K-side is weak.

Position after 18.., **B—B1**:

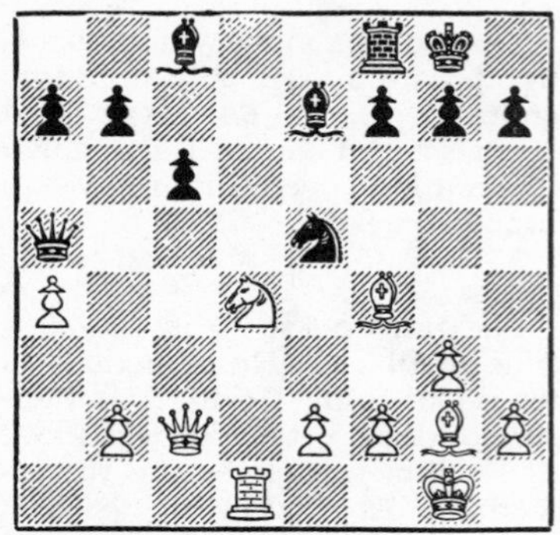

19 **P—QKt4 ! !**

White has command of the board and now produces a fine move, even if it is reminiscent of Capablanca's move with the same P in his 9th match-game with Euwe in 1931. If 19.., **B × P**, there follows 20 **Kt—Kt3, Q—B2**; 21 **Q—K4, B—Q3**; 22 **Q—Q4**, winning a piece. The excursion of **Q—R4** has proved unlucky after all, and there is nothing left but to go back into the pin-position, White's QKtP coming on with great effect.

	Q—B2
20 **P—Kt5**	**P—QB4**
21 **Kt—B5**	**P—B3**

If **B—B3**, his Q3 is left fatally weak. And if 21.., **B × Kt**, then 22 **Q × B, P—B3**; 23 **B—K4, P—KKt3**; 24 **Q—K6 ch, K—Kt2** (**R—B2**; 25 **B—Q5**); 25 **R—Q5** would be decisive.

22 **Kt—K3**	**B—K3**
23 **B—Q5**	**B × B**
24 **R × B**	**Q—R4**

Black is at a loss for a move. If **P—QKt3**, then 25 **Q—K4**. On **R—Q1** might follow 25 **B × Kt, P × B**; 26 **Q—K4**.

25 **Kt—B5**	**Q—K8 ch**
26 **K—Kt2**	**B—Q1**

An alternative is **Kt—Kt3**; 27 **B—K3, P—Kt3**; 28 **R—Q7, R—K1**; 29 **Q—B4 ch, K—B1**; 30 **Q—K6**.

27 **B × Kt**	**P × B**
28 **R—Q7**	**B—B3**

Or **P—KKt3**; 29 **Kt—R6 ch, K—R1**; 30 **R × B, R × R**; 31 **Kt—B7 ch**.

29 **Kt—R6 ch**	**K—R1**
30 **Q × BP**	**Resigns**

White's threat is 31 **Q—Q5**, with a hint of the Lucena mate (" Philidor's legacy "). If 30.., **R—K1**, then 31 **Kt—B7 ch, K—Kt1**; 32 **Q—B4, K—B1**; 33 **Kt—R6** etc.

Times: Alekhine 1 hr. 35 min.; Euwe 2 hr. 25 min.

GAME 46

ALEKHINE v. EUWE

AMSTERDAM, *October* 31-*November* 1

(CHAMPIONSHIP [FIRST] MATCH, 13TH GAME)

RUY LOPEZ

	White.	*Black.*
	ALEKHINE	EUWE
1	**P—K4**	**P—K4**
2	**Kt—KB3**	**Kt—QB3**
3	**B—Kt5**	**P—QR3**
4	**B—R4**	**Kt—B3**
5	**Castles**	**Kt × P**

It is pleasing to see the fighting defence adopted in the only example of the *Ruy Lopez* shown in the match. But Euwe had shown his preference for it before. The more generally favoured 5.., **B—K2** would hardly have been likely to lead to so thrilling a game; and there is a theoretical novelty to come in the attack.

6	**P—Q4**	**P—QKt4**
7	**B—Kt3**	**P—Q4**
8	**P × P**	**B—K3**
9	**P—B3**	**B—K2**

So far all has been normal in this variation, and White now selects an old line, though it has not been played in a serious game for many years, 10 **QKt—Q2,** 10 **B—K3,** and 10 **R—K1** having all had the preference over it.

10	**P—QR4**	**P—Kt5 !**
11	**Kt—Q4**	

Here is the innovation. The book example before was Perlis-Lasker, St. Petersburg, 1909, Perlis continuing with 11 **R—K1, Kt—R4;** 12 **B—B2,** from which he got no advantage after Lasker's **B—Kt5.** Possibly best is 11 **B—K3;** but Alekhine's idea is to attack by means of a Pawn-sacrifice. Since this match what seems to be an improvement has been introduced by H. von Hennig, playing against A. Buraas in the championship of Kiel, 1936, *viz.*, **Kt—Q4** on move 10 instead of on move 11, with the continuation **QKt × P;** 11 **P—B3, Kt—B4;** 12 **B—B2, Kt—B5;** 13 **P—QKt3, Kt—Kt3;** 14 **Kt—Q2, Castles;** 15 **P—KB4.**

		QKt × P
12	**P—KB4**	**Kt—B5**

In his book upon the openings in this match Professor A. Becker says that Black should here have played **B—Kt5,** giving the continuation 13 **Q—B2, Kt—Kt3;** 14 **P—B5, Kt—K4;** 15 **P—R3, P—B4,** with advantage to Black. A question here is whether 14 **P—B5** is White's best. He has the option of 14 **P—R3,** when **P—QB4** could be met by 15 **Kt—B6.**

13 **P—B5**

This move met with considerable criticism, in particular from the Russian annotator N. Rumin, whose suggestion of 13 **Q—K2** has been generally accepted as sound, supported as it was by some elaborate analysis. **Kt—R4, Kt—B4,** and **B—QB4** are all plausible answers, but Rumin claims advantage for White in all. After the last, which has the apparent merit of pinning White's menacing Kt, he gives 14 **B × Kt, P × P !; 15 B—K3 !, P × P;** 16 **R—R2, P × B;** 17 **Kt × B, P × Kt;** 18 **B × B, Kt × B;** 19 **Q—R5 ch** and wins.

	B—B1
14 **Q—K1**	

By the threat of 15 **B × Kt,** winning back the P sacrificed.

	B—Kt2
15 **P × P**	**P—B4 !**

Much stronger than **Castles.** White dare not exchange P's, and does not like 16 **Kt—B2.** He therefore sacrifices again to make another square for his Kt and also draw off Black's B from QB5.

16 **P—B6**	**B × P**
17 **Kt—B5**	**Castles**
18 **P × P**	**R—K1 !**
19 **Q—Kt4**	**Q—B1**

A possibility is **Q—R4,** for if 20 **Q × B, Q × P ch.** Of course, White would not take the B; but if 20 **Q × Q, Kt × Q;** 21 **B—B2, Kt × P,** with a clear P to the good.

20 **B × Kt**	**P—QR4 !**
21 **Q—R3**	**P × B**
22 **Kt—B3**	

Position after 22 **Kt—B3 :**

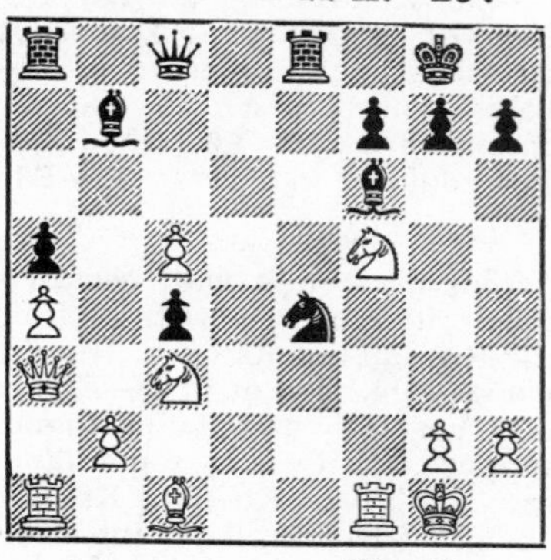

Kt × P

Euwe has a choice here of three continuations, and prefers that with the prettiest possibilities. If now 23 **Kt—Q6, B—Q5 ch;** 24 **K—R1, B × P ch;** 25 **K × B, Q—Kt5 ch;** 26 **K—R1, R—K8,** forcing mate—into which, of course, Alekhine does not fall. Black's other lines are (1) 22.., **Kt × Kt;** 23 **P × Kt, QB × P** (**R—K7;** 24 **R—R2, QB × P;** 25 **R × R, B × R;** 26 **K × B, Q × Kt ch** should also win, though with more difficulty); 24 **K × B** (practically forced), **R—K7 ch;** 25 **K—B3** (the longest fight), **R × P;** 26 **K—Kt3, B—K4 ch;** 27 **B—B4, Q × Kt;** 28 **K × R, B × Kt ch,** and, whether White gives up the Exchange or not, his exposed K's position loses him the game. (2) 22.., **Q × P ch;** 23 **Q × Q, Kt × Q;** 24 **Kt—Q6, B—Q5 ch;** 25 **K—R1,** and Black, having to move his KR and lose the advantage of the two B's, has nothing much to boast about. This alternative may therefore be rejected.

23 **B—K3 !**	**Q—B3**
24 **R—B3**	**Kt—Q6**

R × B; 25 **Kt × R, B—Q5** is already possible.

25 **QR—KB1**	**R × B !**
26 **Kt × R**	**B—Q5**

Now, suggests M. Blümich, **Q—Kt3** may be better, as not letting in White's Q and attacking his R on B3. But as he plays Black wins back the Exchange.

27 **Q—K7**	**Kt—K4**
28 **K—R1**	**Kt × R**
29 **R × Kt**	**R—KB1**
30 **P—R3**	

Threatening **Kt × P,** which was impossible before on account of the reply **Q × R !**

B × Kt(K6)?

This imperils Black's winning chances, when he could safely have given up his threatened P. To S. Flohr is attributed the suggestion 30.., **Q—QKt3**; 31 **Kt × P** (What else is there? If 31 **R—Kt3, Q × P.** If 31 **Kt—Q5, B × Kt**; 32 **Kt × B, Q × P**; 33 **R × P, Q—Kt8 ch**; 34 **K—R2, Q—Kt8 ch** and wins), **Q—Kt5**; 32 **Q × Q, P × Q**; 33 **R—Q3, P × Kt**; 34 **R × B, P—B7 !** etc. A. Brinckmann suggests another line: 30.., **Q—B1**; 31 **QKt—Q5, B × Kt**; 32 **Kt × B, B × P**; 33 **Q—K2, Q—QB4**, Black's advantage being obvious.

After the text-move some positional manœuvring follows. Black is naturally willing to exchange Q's, with a P ahead and B against Kt.

31	**Q × KB**	**Q—K3**
32	**R—Kt3**	**R—K1**
33	**Q—Kt5**	**Q—K4**
34	**Q × Q**	**R × Q**
35	**R—Kt4**	**R—K6**

The passive **R—QB4** does not promise much. Nor does **R—K8 ch**; 36 **K—R2, R—QB8** (threatening 37 **R—B7**), because of 37 **R—Q4**, with the threat of **R—Q7**.

36 **K—Kt1**

The decision was not easy here. 36 **R × P, R × P ch**; 37 **K—Kt1, R—Kt6**; 38 **Kt—K4, R—Kt3**; 39 **R—B7, B—R3**; 40 **Kt—B5, P—R3** (best); 41 **R—R7, B—B5**; 42 **R × RP, R—Kt3**; 43 **Kt—Q7** required careful consideration. If forced, it was good enough, for **R × P** would be answered by 44 **R—R8 ch, K—R2**; 45 **Kt—B8 ch** etc., securing a draw. Nor does Black seem to have any good alternatives after his 37.., **R—Kt6**. He has, however, instead of that, 37.., **R—R3**, when 38 **R—B5** or **7** could be met by **R—QKt3**, and 38 **R—Q4** by **K—B1**. The text-move leads up to a pretty conception on Alekhine's part.

R—Q6

If **B—R3**, then 37 **R—Q4.**

37	**R × P**	**R—Q7**
38	**P—QKt4 !**	**R × P ch**

If **P × P ?**, 39 **R × P** saves White's KKtP and prevents Black's B from moving.

39 **K—B1** **R—Kt7**

Still less now is **P × P** playable.

40 **R—Q4** **P—Kt3**

The relative merits of this and **K—B1** are arguable. White's next move, which he sealed at the adjournment, was an easy choice.

41 **P × P** **R—B7**

If **B—Kt7 ch**; 42 **K—Kt1, B × P**, then 43 **R—Q8 ch, K—Kt2**; 44 **P—R6** and wins !

42	**Kt—Kt5**	**K—Kt2**
43	**K—K1**	

If 43 **R—Q6 ?**, Blümich gives the continuation **B—Kt7 ch**; 44 **K—Kt1, B × P**; 45 **P—R6, R—B1!**; 46 **P—R7, B—B4**; 47 **Kt—B7, B—K5.**

		R—B4
44	**R—Q6**	**B—B3**
45	**P—R6**	

45 **R—Q1, B × Kt**; 46 **P × B, R × P**; 47 **R—R1, R—Kt2**; 48 **P—R6, R—R2** seems to bring a draw nearer. But Alekhine prefers a speculative line, not shutting out remote chances of a win.

		B × Kt
46	**P—R7**	**B—B3**
47	**R × B**	**R—QR4**
48	**R—B7**	**R × P(R5)**
49	**K—Q2**	**P—Kt4**
50	**K—B3**	**P—R4**
51	**K—Kt3**	**R—R8**
52	**K—B4**	**P—Kt5**

Obviously not **R—B8 ch;** 53 **K—Q5, R × R ? ?** But 52.., **K—Kt3** was strong.

53 **P × P** **P × P**
54 **K—Q4** **K—Kt3**
55 **K—K5 ?**

A mistake, of which his opponent fails to take advantage. The right line was 55 **K—K3,** and if **R—R5,** 56 **R—B4 !** The draw is then assured.

P—B3 ch ?

A counter-error which brings the game to what should have been its conclusion in the position after the 44th move. Black's right move was **R—R5,** and then if 56 **R—B4, P—B3 ch.** After 57 **K—Q5, R—R4 ch;** 58 **K—K6, R—R3 ch;** 59 **K—Q5, K—Kt4;** 60 **R—B7, P—B4** and the two passed Pawns win.

56 **K—B4** **R—R5 ch**
57 **K—Kt3** **P—B4**
58 **K—R4**

Threatening 59 **R—B6 ch** and 60 **K—Kt5.**

K—B3

59 **R—QKt7**

Drawn.

Black might try **R—R6,** but then 60 **R—Kt6 ch, K—K2** (**K—K4;** 61 **R—Kt7**); 61 **R—Kt7 ch, K—Q3;** 62 **R—Kt6 ch, K—B2;** 63 **R—B6.** There is no way to avoid the draw.

Times: Alekhine 3 hr. 28 min.; Euwe 3 hr. 26 min.

GAME 47

ALEKHINE v. EUWE

Ermelo, *November* 19, 1935

(Championship [First] Match, 21st Game)

QUEEN'S GAMBIT DECLINED

	White.	*Black.*
	Alekhine	Euwe
1	**P—Q4**	**P—Q4**
2	**P—QB4**	**P—QB3**
3	**Kt—KB3**	**Kt—B3**
4	**Kt—B3**	**P × P**
5	**P—QR4**	**B—B4**
6	**Kt—K5**	**QKt—Q2**
7	**Kt × P(B4)**	**Q—B2**
8	**P—KKt3**	**P—K4**
9	**P × P**	**Kt × P**
10	**B—B4**	**KKt—Q2**
11	**B—Kt2**	

So far the opening is the same as in the 1st and 20th games of the match. For notes see Game 45.

R—Q1

This is Euwe's reply, as Black, to the line which he had previously played as White. In the 20th game Alekhine (Black) played **P—B3,** which he had once—in his notes on his San Remo game against Bogoljuboff—called a loss of time, and after 12 **Castles, R—Q1**; 13 **Q—B1, Q—Kt1 ?,** to which Euwe answered 14 **Kt—K4 !**

A possible alternative to 12.., **R—Q1** in the 20th game was 12.., **B—K3,** with the continuation 13 **Kt × Kt, P × Kt** (Vidmar suggested **Kt × Kt**); 14 **B—K3, B—QB4**; 15 **B × B, Kt × B,** as in Capablanca-Vidmar, Carlsbad, 1929, a game which ended in a draw on the 23rd move.

12	**Q—B1**	**P—B3**
13	**Castles**	**B—K3**

Now Euwe gets this move in, with the preliminary **R—Q1** interposed, which Vidmar did not try at Carlsbad; and for the present at least Black's play in this variation seems standardised.

14	**Kt × Kt**	**Kt × Kt**
15	**P—R5**	

The idea is to follow up with 16 **P—R6, P—QKt3**; 17 **Kt—Kt5,** which Euwe easily prevents, leaving White's RP weak. In the Moscow International Tournament of 1936 G. Lövenfisch against S. Flohr improved on Alekhine's play with 15 **Kt—K4,** and, after **Q—R4,** 16 **B—Q2, B—QKt5**; 17 **B × B, Q × B**; 18 **Q—KB4** (threatening **Kt × P ch**), **Q—K2**; 19 **Q—K3.***

P—QR3

16 **Kt—K4**

This is not so effective now, because of Black's excellent reply, attacking the weak RP.

B—QKt5

17 **Kt—B5** **B—B1**

* In the 1st game of the return-match Euwe, as White, omitting 14 **Kt × Kt, Kt × Kt,** played 14 **Kt—K4,** the continuation being **B—QKt5**; 15 **P—R5, Castles**; 16 **P—R6, P × P ?** (**P—QKt3 !**); 17 **Kt × Kt, Kt × Kt**; 18 **Kt—B5.**

Though it looks like loss of time, obviously right against the threat of (17.., **B—B2**) 18 **B × Kt, P × B**; 19 **Kt × KtP!** And 17.., **B—Q4** would be met with 18 **P—K4, B—B2**; 19 **R—R4!** forcing off Black's KB and securing the Q-side.

18 **B × Kt**

An alternative is 18 **Kt—Kt3,** and if **B—K3,** 18 **Kt—B5** again, which would be tantamount to offering a draw. But Black need not accept, playing 18.., **Q—K2,** followed by castling. White, however, is aiming at a win by attack on the uncastled K. It turns out ill.

P × B

Not **Q × B ?**; 19 **Kt—Q3 !**

19 **P—B4 ?**

Had White refrained from this, could he still, in spite of his 15th move, have saved the game? 19 **Q—QB4** is useless, because of **R—Q5,** as happened a move later. But there is 19 **Q—K3,** against which (as castling is ruinous, and 19.., **B × P**; 20 **R × B !, Q × R**; 21 **Q × P ch, K—B2**; 22 **Q—B4 ch** leads to perpetual check) Black's best seems 19.., **Q—K2.** After 20 **Kt—Kt3,** said W. A. Fairhurst in *The British Chess Magazine*, "Black has certainly the advantage, but probably not enough to win." It is a matter which defies ordinary analysis. Black can castle, and retain his two B's; but his isolated KP is a responsibility to be set against White's QRP.

	B—Q7 !
20 **Q—B4**	**R—Q5**
21 **Q—Kt3**	

Clearly 21 **Kt—K6, Q—B2**; 22 **B × P ch, P × B**; 23 **Q × P ch, Q—Q2** is bad for White.

	P × P
22 **P × P**	**Q—K2**

Position after 22 **P × P**:

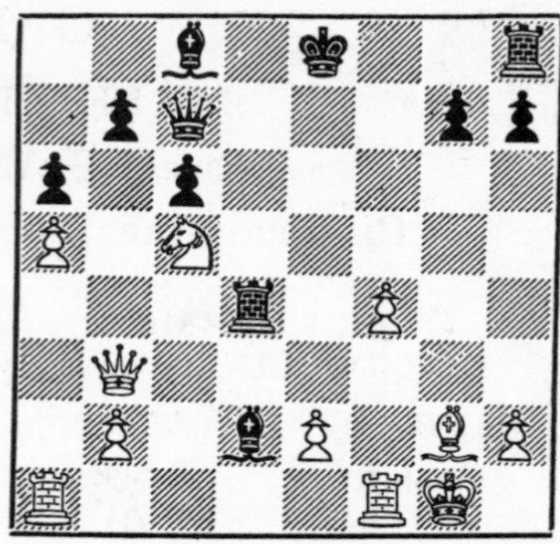

Black has secured his position and can soon castle. To have taken a P, on the other hand, would have been fatal—*e.g.*, 22.., **B × BP**; 23 **Kt—K6, B × Kt**; 24 **Q × B ch, Q—K2** (**K—Q1**; 25 **QR—K1**); 25 **Q—B8 ch, R—Q1**; 26 **B × P ch, P × B**; 27 **Q × P ch, Q—Q2**; 28 **Q—K4 ch** etc. And, of course, if 22.., **B × RP,** simply 23 **Q—K3 ch.**

23 **Kt—Q3**	**B—K3**

There is also **Q × P**; 24 **QR—Q1, B—K6 ch,** 25 **K—R1, R × Kt.**

24 **Q—R3**

If 24 **Q—Q1, B—K6 ch.**

	B—B5
25 **K—R1**	**Q × Q**

Not now **Q × P,** for then 26 **QR—K1,** which shows the object of White's last move, to avoid a check by **B—K6.**

26 **R × Q**	**Castles**

The endgame follows, with Black standing at a considerable advantage, if he has not actually a demonstrable win yet.

27 **R—R4**

Various commentators queried this move, without suggesting an alternative. It threatens 28 **P—Kt3,** but is easily refuted. Possibly 27 **P—B5** is the least harmful resource at White's disposal. But see the next note.

	KR—Q1
28 **R—R3**	

W. A. Fairhurst proposes 28 **R—B3** as holding out longer, for then **B × Kt;** 29 **R × R, R × R;** 20 **R × B, R × R;** 31 **P × R** leaves on the threat of **B—R3—B8;** so that 28.., **KR—Q4** might be the best move at Black's command.

	B × Kt
29 **P × B**	**R—Kt5**

Better than the capture of either of the P's already at his mercy. If White now attempts to protect his KtP he loses more than one P.

30 **R—B2**	**R × KtP**
31 **B—B1**	**R—Q5**
32 **P—B5**	**R—KB5**
33 **R × R**	**B × R**
34 **P—R3**	**B—Q3**

By **R—KB7** Black would have made sure of the KBP, but at the expense of his own QKtP—*e.g.*, 34.., **R—KB7;** 35 **R—R1, B—K4;** 36 **R—Kt1, R × P;** 37 **P—Q4, B × P;** 38 **B—B4 ch, K—B1;** 39 **R × P,** and the game is at least prolonged. No other 35th move for Black seems any better.

35 **R—R1**	**K—B2**
36 **P—Q4**	**K—B3**
37 **R—K1**	**B—Kt5**
38 **R—R1**	

If 38 **R—K5, R—R7.**

	R—Q7
39 **B—B4**	**R × P**
40 **B—K6**	**R—Q1**

Stopping 41 **B—B8.** The game was here adjourned, Alekhine sealing the move 41 **B—Kt3;** but he resigned a hopeless game without any further play.

As is said elsewhere, Alekhine was suffering from ill-health when he played this game. It is nevertheless a very fine struggle, even if Euwe does gain the chief credit out of it. From the point of view of opening-theory it is highly important.

Times not stated.

Postscript.—A new continuation for White on move 17 was introduced at the Semmering-Baden Tournament of 1937, in the games Fine-Capablanca and Eliskases-Capablanca, *viz.*, 17 **B—Q2,** Capablanca replying **B × B** in the first game, **Q—K2** in the second.

GAME 48

EUWE v. ALEKHINE

DELFT, *November* 28, 1935

(CHAMPIONSHIP [FIRST] MATCH, 24TH GAME)

QUEEN'S PAWN GAME
(DUTCH DEFENCE)

	White.	*Black.*
	EUWE	ALEKHINE
1	**P—Q4**	**P—K3**
2	**P—QB4**	

Euwe does not choose by 2 **P—K4** to transpose the opening into a *French Defence*, though he himself had done badly with that as Black, losing three and only drawing one out of four games.

P—KB4

The first of the two *Dutch Defences* in the match. Alekhine had previously tried it against Euwe in the 10th game of their match in 1926-7, which opened with the moves 1 **Kt—KB3, P—K3;** 2 **P—B4, P—KB4;** 3 **P—KKt3** (a *Réti* development for White so far), **Kt—KB3;** 4 **P—Q4, B—Kt5 ch;** 5 **B—Q2, B × B ch.**

3 **P—KKt3** **B—Kt5 ch**

This check followed by retreat to K2 is said to have originated from Russia, being an idea, in the first instance, of the master N. Rumin, who claimed that by inducing 4 **B—Q2** Black causes White to put that B on a wrong square, cutting off the defence of QP by Q. Alternatively, if White plays 4 **Kt—B3,** Black can capture and aim at preventing the undoubling of the P's on the QB file. In the game Kmoch-Yudovitch, Leningrad, 1934, the manœuvre was seen a move later: 3.., **Kt—KB3;** 4 **B—Kt2, B—Kt5 ch;** 5 **B—Q2, B—K2.** Black got a very cramped game then (after 6 **Kt—QB3, Castles;** 7 **Kt—R3, P—Q3**), and Kmoch won a brilliancy prize for his play.

4 **B—Q2** **B—K2**

Q—K2 may be called the natural continuation; but that is not part of the new theory.

5	**B—Kt2**	**Kt—KB3**
6	**Kt—QB3**	**Castles**
7	**Kt—B3**	

7 **Kt—R3,** as played by Kmoch, is commended by Alekhine. Euwe, however, showed his preference for the text-move by repeating it in the 26th game.

Kt—K5

Alekhine, in his notes in the magazine *Chess*, says that this is good only because White cannot answer 7 **Kt × Kt, P × Kt;** 8 **Kt—Q2**—Q2 being occupied by the B. The move therefore is a logical sequel of the manœuvre **B—Kt5 ch—K2,** and imparts its value to the opening of this game. See move 9.

8 **Castles** **B—B3**

This is Alekhine's first thought, which he abandoned in the 26th game for **P—QKt3.** In both games he rejected the *Stonewall*, **P—Q4,** which Kmoch claims as the best move, though other analysts do not agree.

9 **Kt × Kt**

White after all exchanges Kt's! But now, of course, he has a square waiting for his KKt and a prospect of attack. In a game Grünfeld-Spielmann, played in Vienna three days after the present one, the continuation was 9 **Q—B2, Kt × B;** 10 **Q × Kt, P—Q3;** 11 **P—K4, P × P;** 12 **Kt × P, Kt—B3;** 13 **R—Q1, B—Q2,** the end being a draw.

	P × Kt
10 **Kt—K1**	**B × P**

If **P—Q4,** says Alekhine, 11 **B—QB3,** followed by **Kt—B2,** would give White a favourable position. Some of the critics nevertheless commend **P—Q4.**

11 **B × P**	**B × P**

Once more **P—Q4** has its advocates; but Alekhine remarks that it is refuted by 12 **P × P, P × P;** 13 **Q—Kt3.** With the line he chooses he claims that he gets better endgame chances, because of his compact Pawn-position, though his opponent has counter-chances of attack against the compromised K-side.

12 **B × P ch**	**K × B**
13 **Q—B2 ch**	**K—Kt1**
14 **Q × B**	**Kt—B3**
15 **Kt—B3**	

A good alternative is 15 **B—B3, Q—K2;** 16 **P—B4,** and, if **P—Q3,** then 17 **Kt—B3,** with increased attacking threats.

	P—Q3
16 **P—B5!**	**P × P**

The sacrifice cannot well be refused, for **P—Q4** would leave a backward KP and the B blocked in. Nor can Black allow 17 **P × P.**

17 **B—B3**	**Q—K2**
18 **QR—Q1**	**P—QKt3**
19 **Q—B2**	

The attack halts here, or misses direction. Why not 19 **P—KR4?** The Kt will be very powerful at Kt5.

	B—Kt2
20 **Q—Kt6?**	

Alekhine suggests **P—KR4** at this stage, but it could be answered by **Kt—Kt5,** or, he says, by **R—B4,** contemplating the sacrifice of the Exchange if White plays **Kt—Kt5.**

	Q—B2!
21 **Q—Kt5**	

Not 21 **Q—Kt4, QR—Q1;** 22 **Kt—Kt5?, Q × P ch!** and wins. White would be reduced to 22 **R × R,** when **Kt × R;** 23 **Kt—Kt5?, Q—B4** renders White's attack innocuous.

	QR—Q1
22 **P—KR4**	

The force of this is now lost. But 22 **Kt—K5, Q—B4!;** 23 **Q—R4, P—KKt4** is hopeless.

	R × R
23 **R × R**	

Position after 23 **R × R;**

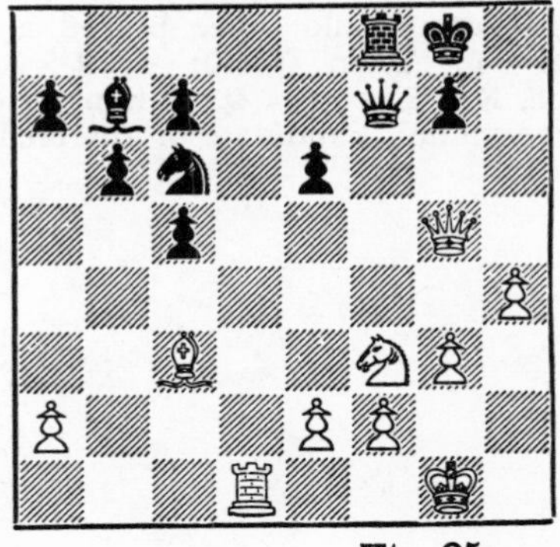

Kt—Q5

Though he holds that this (properly followed up) was good enough to win, Alekhine points out that **Kt—Kt5** is more convincing, for if 24 **B × Kt, P × B** the win is "almost automatic." Another possibility is 23.., **P—K4**, and if 24 **B × P, Kt × B**; 25 **Q × Kt, B × Kt**; 26 **P × B, Q × BP,** though that would leave considerable fight in the game.

24 **B × Kt** **P × B ?**

With **B × Kt** instead, Alekhine claims a win for Black—*e.g.*, 25 **B × BP, P × B**; 26 **P × B; Q × P**; 27 **R—Q2, P—B5,** this passed P being destined to decide the game in Black's favour. But obviously White can still put up a strong resistance; and Flohr wrote of good drawing chances. Very patient analysis would be required to settle the question.

Black had also to consider the line (24.., **B × Kt**) 25 **B × KtP, Q × B**; 26 **Q × Q ch, K × Q**; 27 **R—Q7 ch, R—B2**; 28 **R × R ch, K × R**; 29 **P × B.** But this was less formidable than 25 **B × BP** etc.

25	**R × P**	**B × Kt**
26	**R—KB4**	**Q—R4**
27	**R × R ch ?**	

White should have played 27 **R × B.** Then **Q × Q**; 28 **R × R ch, K × R**; 29 **P × Q** left him with the minor handicap of doubled P's on the Kt file, not as now doubled P's on the B file, which Black can, and does, paralyse.

		K × R
28	**Q—B4 ch**	**Q—B2**
29	**Q × B**	**Q × Q**
30	**P × Q**	**P—K4 !**
31	**K—B1**	**P—QKt4**
32	**K—K2**	**P—B4 ? ?**

The last in a series of mistakes in endgame-play which are, to say the least, uncommon in championship chess. Alekhine himself marks the move with a double query. It gives away the win, which might have been secured by 32.., **P—R4.** Against that 33 **K—K3** would be unavailing, for after **P—Kt5** White has not time for 34 **P—B4, P × P**; 35 **K × P.** His K is outside the "queening square."

33 **K—K3**

Draw agreed; for now White has time for **P—B4, P × P; K × P,** and there is nothing for either side in the position.

Times: Euwe, 1 hr. 50 min.; Alekhine, 2 hr. 50 min.

This game has been described by Alekhine as to him far and away the most dramatic of the match. It may also be considered as to the ordinary amateur the most comforting, as showing how the great masters, too, may err—more than once—in endings not of terrific complexity.

GAME 49

EUWE v. ALEKHINE

ZANDVOORT, *December* 3-4, 1935

(CHAMPIONSHIP [FIRST] MATCH, 26TH GAME)

QUEEN'S PAWN GAME
(DUTCH DEFENCE)

White.	*Black.*
EUWE	ALEKHINE

(*First 7 moves as in preceding game.*)

8 **Castles** **P—QKt3**

Alekhine's second thoughts; see the previous game.

9 **Q—B2**

9 **Kt × Kt, P × Kt;** 10 **Kt—K5, P—Q3 !;** 11 **B × P, P × Kt;** 12 **B × R, P—B3;** 13 **B—B3 !,** threatening 14 **P—Q5,** is maintained by Kmoch to be the best line for White.

B—Kt2

10 **Kt—K5** **Kt × Kt**

In this way Black releases himself from the pin, and the move is much the best at his disposal.

11 **B × Kt**

Not 11 **B × B, Kt × P ch;** 12 **K—R1** (or **Kt2**), **Kt × QP;** 13 **Q—B3, QKt—B3;** 14 **Kt × Kt, P × Kt;** 15 **B × R, Q × B**—and White cannot capture the Kt. So Black has two P's against the Exchange.

B × B

12 **K × B** **Q—B1**

Black has some difficulty in development. 13 **P—Q5** is clearly pending; and **P—Q4,** to stop it, is scarcely in harmony with the previous **P—QKt3.** 12.., **P—Q3** would merely drive the White Kt to the good square Q3. Black is reduced to the latter course next move; but it can then be followed up with **P—K4.**

13 **P—Q5** **P—Q3**
14 **Kt—Q3** **P—K4**
15 **K—R1**

15 **P—B4** has been suggested. It is good when it is played two moves later, and there seems little against it now. It prevents a K-side attack by Black with **P—B5.** The text-move, it is true, holds that back, for if 15.., **P—B5,** than 16 **P × P, P × P;** 17 **R—KKt1.** But it turns out rather otiose, compared with Euwe's play in the rest of the game.

P—B3

16 **Q—Kt3**

Countering the threat of **P × P;** 17 **P × P, Q—B5**

K—R1

17 **P—B4** **P—K5**
18 **Kt—Kt4**

The first of 7 consecutive moves by the Kt ! It makes 19 altogether in the game.

P—B4

From Q5 at least the Kt must be barred.

19 **Kt—B2** **Kt—Q2**
20 **Kt—K3** **B—B3**

Deliberately provocative, instead of the solid **Kt—B3,** which stops all tricks. It is impossible to suppose that Black did not see what might happen.

Position after 20.., **B—B3;**

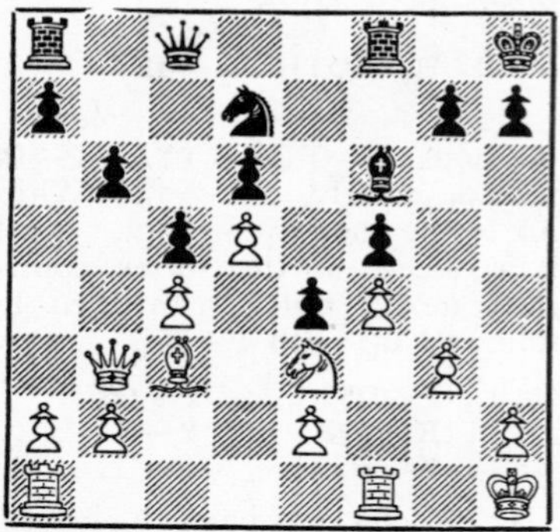

21 **Kt × P**

Euwe accepts the challenge and sacrifices a piece, if it can be called a sacrifice to exchange a B for three P's. The final outcome of it is hardly calculable at the board.

	B × B
22 **Kt × QP**	**Q—Kt1**
23 **Kt × P**	**B—B3**
24 **Kt—Q2 !**	**P—KKt4**

The only chance of attack, and it does not prevent the advance of the KP at once.

25 **P—K4**	**P × P**
26 **P × P**	**B—Q5**

The strong position of this B is some slight compensation for the menacing centre P's.

27 **P—K5**	**Q—K1**
28 **P—K6**	**R—KKt1**

Not **Kt—B3,** because of the answer 29 **Kt—B3.** But Black would now welcome 29 **P × Kt,** replying with **Q—K7 !**

29 **Kt—B3**	**Q—Kt3 !**
30 **R—KKt1 !**	**B × R**
31 **R × B**	**Q—B3 ?**

The cut-and-thrust work has been pretty, but now Black slips. He cannot, of course, play **Q—K5** because of 32 **Q—B3 ch.** He can, however, play **Q—B4,** with drawing chances. White has nothing better than 32 **P × Kt,** when might follow **R × R ch;** 33 **K × R, Q × P(Q2).** A lot of play remains, but Black's R when it comes into action will be very mobile. C. J. S. Purdy also works out a draw if Black plays here 33.., **Q × BP.**

32 **Kt—Kt5 !**	**R—Kt2**

P—KR3 ?; 33 **P × Kt, P × Kt;** 34 **Q—R3 ch, K—Kt2;** 35 **R × P ch** would cost Black his Q.

33 **P × Kt**	**R × P**
34 **Q—K3**	**R—K2**

It is recorded that Alekhine took 51 min. over this move. The most obvious danger threatening is 35 **Q—K5,** and even the text-move only delays this by one move. A defence that had to be considered was 34.., **R—KKt2,** and if 35 **Q—K5, R—KB1.** However, after 36 **Kt—K6, R × R ch;** 37 **K × R,** Black has only **Q × Q;** 38 **P × Q, R—B2;** 39 **P—Q6, K—Kt1,** to which 40 **Kt—B7** appears a conclusive reply.

35 **Kt—K6**	**R—KB1**
36 **Q—K5**	

Kmoch suggests 36 **Q—KKt3** as a safer way of reaching a win.

	Q × Q

R × Kt; 37 **P × R, Q × Q;** 38 **P × Q, R—K1;** 39 **R—K1, R × P;** 40 **K—Kt2** leaves White's K master of the situation, as he cannot be kept away from Q5.

37 **P × Q**	**R—B4**

The opportunity occurs again to lose by **R × Kt**.

38 **R—K1**

A very important question for White arises. Should he play 38 **R—Kt5 ?** If **R × R**; 39 **Kt × R,** Black clearly cannot continue **R × P** because of 40 **Kt—B7 ch.** Black's choice is between three lines, which Kmoch works out thus: (1) 39.., **P—KR3**; 40 **P—Q6, R—KKt2**; 41 **P—K6**— and a P must queen. (2) 39.., **R—KKt2**; 40 **P—Q6, R × Kt**; 41 **P—Q7, R—Kt1**; 42 **P—K6** etc. (3) 39.., **K—Kt2**; 40 **P—Q6, R—Q2 !**; 41 **Kt—K6 ch, K—B2**; 42 **Kt—B4, R—Q1**; 43 **K—Kt2, K—K1**; 44 **K—B3, K—Q2**; 45 **K—K4, K—B3**; 46 **Kt—Q5** and wins. This appears flawless, but under time-pressure was a difficult piece of analysis. White chooses a simpler-looking alternative.

P—KR3

Now Black has to make an important decision. If he plays **K—Kt1,** and White replies 39 **R—Kt1 ch, K—R1** restores the *status quo ante*, with the risk that White may now see the force of **R—Kt5.** If, on the other hand, he plays 39.., **K—B2,** then might follow 40 **Kt—Q8 ch, K—K1**; 41 **R—Kt8 ch.** Interposing loses through exchange of R's and **P—K6.** And if **K—Q2,** then 42 **Kt—B6,** and wins.

Alternatives which would be dismissed were: (1) 38.., **R—K1**; 39 **Kt—B7, R × P**; 40 **R × R, R × R**; 41 **P—Q6, R—K8 ch**; 42 **K—Kt2, R—Q8**; 43 **Kt—Q5.** (2) 38.., **R × Kt**; 39 **P × R, K—Kt1**; 40 **R—K3 !, K—B1**; 41 **R—QR3** etc.

39 **Kt—Q8** **R—B7**

Again Black cannot capture the P and exchange R's because of **Kt—B7 ch.**

40 **P—K6** **R—Q7**
41 **Kt—B6**

This was White's sealed move. He does not, of course, play 41 **P—Q6,** which is answered by **R × QP**; 42 **Kt—B7 ch, R × Kt**; 43 **P × R, K—Kt2,** with a draw in sight.

		R—K1
42	**P—K7**	**P—Kt4**
43	**Kt—Q8**	**K—Kt2**
44	**Kt—Kt7**	**K—B3**
45	**R—K6 ch**	**K—Kt4**
46	**Kt—Q6**	**R × KP**
47	**Kt—K4 ch**	**Resigns**

In spite of Alekhine's speculation, unjustified by the result, on the 20th move, and his slip on the 31st, this is a magnificent game, one of the best in the match. Euwe's play throughout is of the highest order of chess.

Times: Euwe, 2 hr. 45 min.; Alekhine, 2 hr. 40 min.

GAME 50

CAPABLANCA v. ALEKHINE

August 11, 1936

(NOTTINGHAM TOURNAMENT)

QUEEN'S PAWN GAME
(DUTCH DEFENCE)

White.	*Black.*
CAPABLANCA	ALEKHINE
1 **P—Q4**	**P—K3**
2 **Kt—KB3**	**P—KB4**
3 **P—KKt3**	**Kt—KB3**
4 **B—Kt2**	**B—K2**
5 **Castles**	**Castles**
6 **P—B4**	

6 **QKt—Q2** is the alternative suggested by Capablanca.

Kt—K5

This and Black's next move constitute what might very properly be called the "Alekhine variation" in the *Dutch Defence*. He had played it before—*e.g.*, against Flohr at Podebrad, shortly before the Nottingham Tournament; but Flohr, answering with 7 **Kt—K1**, forestalled 7.., **B—B3**, Alekhine playing instead **P—Q4**.

7 **Q—Kt3**

Q—B2 !, says Capablanca; and Fine afterwards played this against Alekhine at Amsterdam in October, interposing, however, 7 **QKt—Q2**.

	B—B3
8 **R—Q1**	**Q—K1**

Q—K2 seems stronger, with a view to meeting the later **Kt—QKt5** with **P—Q3**.

9 **Kt—B3**	**Kt—B3**
10 **Kt—QKt5**	**B—Q1**
11 **Q—B2**	

According to Capablanca's later judgment, 11 **P—Q5** was better, and if **Kt—R4**, then 12 **Q—B2.** As it is, Black gets in the move **P—Q3.**

	P—Q3
12 **P—Q5**	

Alekhine, in the book of the tournament, condemns this, and suggests 12 **P—QR3,** to prevent the loss of another move with the Q. White could follow up with **P—QKt4.**

	Kt—Kt5
13 **Q—Kt3**	**Kt—R3**
14 **P × P**	**QKt—B4**
15 **Q—B2**	**QKt × P**

Now Black has an open K-file to increase his positional superiority.

16 **KKt—Q4**	**Kt × Kt**
17 **Kt × Kt**	**B—B3**
18 **Kt—Kt5 ?**	

A bad move (Capablanca). 19 **B—K3** was necessary.

	Q—K2
19 **B—K3**	**P—QR3**
20 **Kt—Q4**	**B—Q2**
21 **QR—B1**	**QR—K1**
22 **P—QKt4**	**P—QKt3**
23 **Kt—B3**	

It is remarkable that White, though he had lost so many

moves, should still have a game not hopelessly inferior, had he not made this move, when 23 **Q—Kt3** (yet another Q-move!) would have held the position. But the move he actually makes leads, surprisingly, to his victory.

Position after 23 **Kt—B3:**

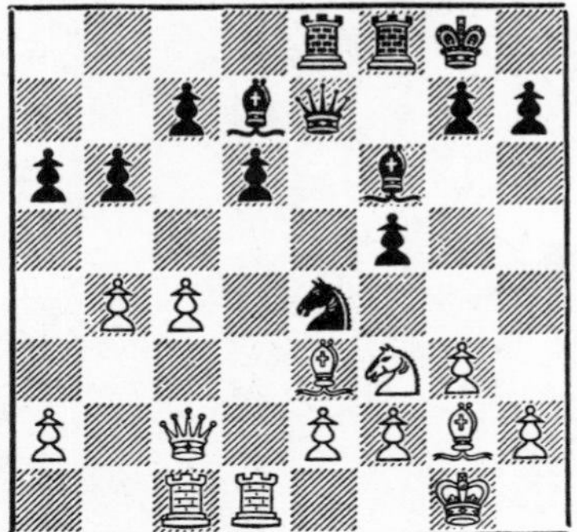

Kt—B6

Against this move Capablanca puts a ?, calling Alekhine's combination incorrect, as winning the Exchange but leaving him with a lost game. See, however, the next note.

24 **R—Q3** **P—B5** ?

This is where Alekhine puts the ?. He thought, he says, to win the double Exchange, whereas he lost three minor pieces for the two R's. He should have played simply **B—QR5;** 25 **Q—Q2, Kt—K5;** 26 **Q—K1, P—KKt4**!, with a positional advantage perhaps decisive.

25 **P × P** **B—B4**
26 **Q—Q2** **B × R**
27 **P × B** **P—B4** ?

Black misses his last chance, which was **Kt—R5.** To this Capablanca gives as his answer 28 **Kt—Kt5**! The threat of 29 **B—B6** is certainly pressing; but **P—Kt4** at least saves the Kt, though the chances of its re-entry into the game are remote. After the text-move Black has no hopes.

28 **R × Kt** **B × R**
29 **Q × B**

Three minor pieces and a P are bound to outweigh two R's in such a position, where White is practically unassailable.

Q—B3
30 **Q × Q** **P × Q**
31 **Kt—Q2** **P—B4**
32 **P—Kt5** **P—QR4**

P × P is obviously bad, for after 33 **P × P** the Kt comes in at B4 with decisive effect. There is, however, another path for the Kt.

33 **Kt—B1** **K—B2**
34 **Kt—Kt3** **K—Kt3**
35 **B—B3** **R—K2**
36 **K—B1** **K—B3**

The end of the second hour.

37 **B—Q2** **K—Kt3**
38 **P—QR4**

This was White's sealed move at the adjournment; but Black resigned ultimately without asking to see it. Capablanca gives as his course of procedure **P—R4—R5,** followed by **B—Kt2—R3, K—Kt2—B3,** and **Kt—B1—K3—Q5.**

There was a dispute over the sealing of a move, owing to some lack of formality in the calling of time at the adjournment, and in consequence the question of continuing the game was held up until the following week. Fortunately the matter had no bearing upon the game itself.

The inclusion of this as an example of Championship Chess, in spite of its not having been played, like most of the preceding games, in a match for the title, is prompted by a desire to illustrate the different conditions imposed on the greatest of masters by tournament-play, notably by the faster time-limit. Moreover, the game, with its faults, is historic. The players' own comments add much interest to its study.

GAME 51

ALEKHINE v. EUWE

ROTTERDAM, *October* 7, 1937

(CHAMPIONSHIP [SECOND] MATCH, 2ND GAME)

QUEEN'S GAMBIT DECLINED

White.	*Black.*
ALEKHINE	EUWE
1 **P—Q4**	**P—Q4**
2 **P—QB4**	**P—QB3**
3 **Kt—KB3**	**Kt—B3**
4 **Kt—B3**	**P × P**

This variation of the *Slav Defence* was a familiar battle-ground for the two masters. See Games 45 and 47 for instance, and compare the 1st game of the present match, wherein Euwe was White.

5 **P—QR4**	**B—B4**
6 **Kt—K5**	**P—K3**

A change from the 6.., **QKt—Q2** so regular in the games between these two, but played by Bogoljuboff in the 3rd and 5th games of his match with Alekhine in 1929.

7 **B—Kt5**

So Alekhine played in the 5th game *v.* Bogoljuboff, the reply being **B—K2**. Euwe has a different continuation.

	B—QKt5
8 **Kt × P(B4)**	**Q—Q4**

This is the point of Euwe's continuation. If now 9 **Kt—K3, Q—R4;** 10 **Q—Kt3, Kt—Q4.** If 9 **Q—Kt3, Kt—R3.** If 9 **P—K3, B—Kt5.**

9 **B × Kt**	**Q × Kt**

If **P × B,** then 10 **Q—Q2, Q × Kt** would lead to the position that actually occurred. But 10 **P—K3** would there be stronger.

10 **Q—Q2**	**P × B**
11 **P—K4**	**Q—Kt6**
12 **P × B**	**Kt—Q2**

Of course not **P × P.**

13 **P × P**	**P × P**
14 **B—K2**	**Castles QR**
15 **Castles KR**	**P—K4**

Forcing open the Q-file, but leaving Black with very weak K-side P's. An alternative is **Kt—B4,** with the possible continuation 16 **Q—K3, Q × KtP;** 17 **P × Kt, Q × Kt;** 18 **Q × P ch, K—Kt1.**

16 **P × P**	**Kt × P**
17 **Q—B1**	**B × Kt**

This splits White's Q-side P's, but exposes Black's K to attack. Euwe, however, did not like the idea of White's **Kt—K4.**

18 **P × B**	**KR—Kt1**
19 **Q—K3**	**K—Kt1**

W. Winter suggests rather 19.., **Q—Q4** and if 20 **P—Kt3, Q—Q7,** with an attempt to exchange Q's while the Black K is a move nearer the centre than he was when the exchange occurred in the actual game.

20 **P—Kt3**	**R—Q2**
21 **QR—Kt1**	**Q—B7**

Position after 21.., **Q—B7**:

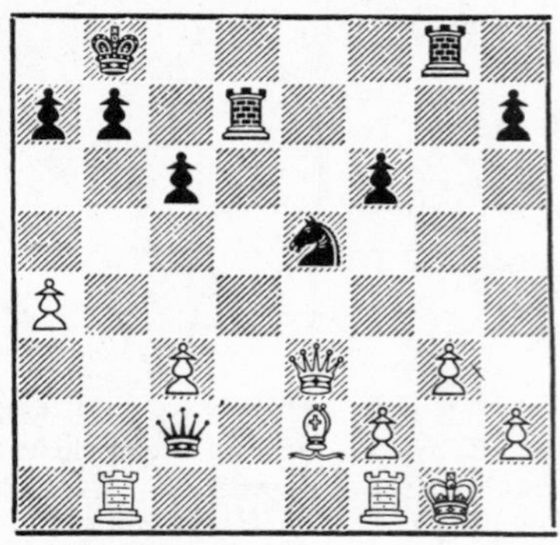

22 **KR—K1**

A clever move preparatory to the endgame, and threatening 23 **P—KB4**, which is not at present possible on account of 23.., **R—Q7**.

Q—Q7

The exchange of Q's is to White's advantage, and therefore **R—Q7** seems preferable. 23 **P—KB4** could then be met by **Kt—Q6**.

23	**Q × Q**	**R × Q**
24	**P—KB4**	**Kt—Kt3**

Now if **Kt—Q6**, there would follow 25 **B × Kt, R × B**; 26 **R—K7**—Black not having two pieces co-operating against White's K-side

25	**B—B4**	**KR—Q1**
26	**R—K6**	**KR—Q3**

Black does not stand to gain by 26.., **R—Q8 ch**; 27 **R × R, R × Rch**, owing to his indefensible KBP.

27	**QR—K1**	**K—B2**
28	**R × R**	**R × R**

Not **K × R**; 29 **B—Kt8**.

29	**P—R4**!	**K—Q2**
30	**K—B2**	**Kt—K2**
31	**K—B3**	**Kt—Q4**

This allows the B more scope. **K—K1** looks less harmful to Black, as his K must cross some time.

32	**B—Q3**	**P—KR3**

32.., **Kt × QBP**; 33 **B × P, Kt × P**; 34 **B—B5 ch** leaves White's RP the controlling factor of the game.

33	**B—B5 ch**	**K—Q1**
34	**K—Kt4**	**Kt—K2**

Now if **Kt × QBP**, 35 **K—R5**.

35	**B—Kt1**	**K—K1**

Winter suggests 35.., **R—Q4**, and if 36 **R—K6, P—R4 ch**, which certainly leaves a fight. But White must ultimately get a passed P on the K-side, it would seem. The text-move loses quickly.

36	**K—R5**	**K—B2**
37	**B—R2 ch**	**K—B1**
38	**K × P**	**R—Q7**

If **Kt—B4 ch**, then 39 **K—Kt6**.

39	**B—K6**	**R—Q6**
40	**P—Kt4**	**R × P**
41	**P—Kt5**	

This was Alekhine's sealed move at the adjournment. Euwe, however, resigned the same day without waiting to see it. He could not but recognise that all was over.

The ending is a true masterpiece on Alekhine's part.

GAME 52

EUWE v. ALEKHINE

EINDHOVEN, *November* 20-21, 1937

(CHAMPIONSHIP [SECOND] MATCH, 19TH GAME)

QUEEN'S PAWN GAME

White.	*Black.*
EUWE	ALEKHINE
1 **P—Q4**	**Kt—KB3**
2 **P—QB4**	**P—K3**
3 **Kt—QB3**	**B—Kt5**

Alekhine had played this, the *Nimzovitch Defence*, in the 22nd game of his first match with Euwe, when after 4 **Q—B2, Kt—B3;** 5 **Kt—B3, P—Q3;** 6 **B—Q2, Castles;** 7 **P—QR3, B × Kt ;** 8 **B × B, Q—K2** a draw was agreed to very early. The present game is a great contrast.

4 **Kt—B3** **Kt—K5**

Alekhine had, in his *Auf dem Wege zur Weltmeisterschaft*, discussing a game Euwe-Alekhine in 1926, called White's 4 **Kt—B3** " this indifferent move." In that game he continued with 4.., **P—QKt3,** and later played **P—Q3.** He now has a totally different plan.

5 **Q—B2**	**P—Q4**
6 **P—K3**	**P—QB4**
7 **B—Q3**	**Kt—KB3**

If this is necessary, the merits of Black's 4th move are doubtful.

8 **BP × P**

This has been queried as freeing Black's game. Instead 8 **P—QR3, B × Kt ch;** 9 **Q × B** looks good. Or simply 8 **Castles.**

	KP × P
9 **P × P**	**B × P**
10 **Castles**	**Kt—B3**
11 **P—K4**	**B—K2**

He cannot play 11.., **P × P;** 12 **Kt × P, Kt × Kt;** 13 **B × Kt+,** while 11.., **P—Q5;** 12 **Kt—K2,** would seem to doom the isolated P to ultimate loss.

12 **P—K5**

The preliminary **P—QR3,** to prevent **Kt—QKt5,** might be met by **P × P;** 13 **Kt × P, Kt × Kt;** 14 **B × Kt, B—Q2,** but Black would still be unable to castle on account of 15 **R—Q1.**

	Kt—KKt5
13 **R—K1**	**Kt—Kt5**
14 **B—Kt5 ch**	**K—B1**

Alekhine's choice of a move here is very interesting. He forgoes castling, with the idea of his 17th move already in his mind. On the other hand, 14.., **B—Q2;** 15 **Q—K2** would have left him most uncomfortable.

15 **Q—K2** **B—QB4**

The fourth move of this B, while the KKt has also moved four times, making in all 10 moves already of the minor pieces—with the QB still at home.

16 **Kt—Q1**	**B—B4**
17 **P—KR3**	

Position after 17 **P—KR3:**

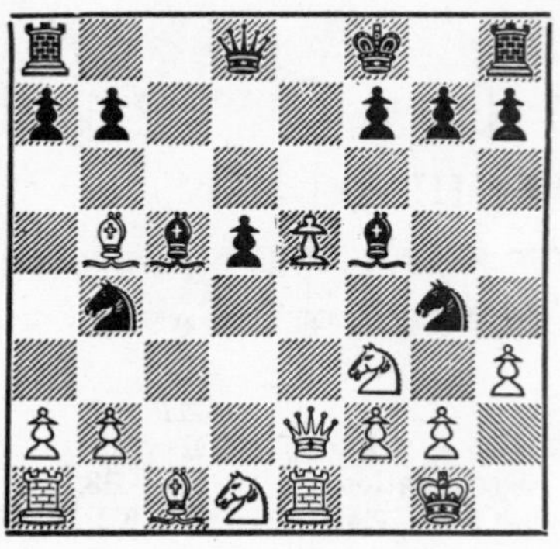

	P—KR4 !
18 **B—Kt5**	

If 18 **P × Kt,** then **P × P;** 19 **Kt—Kt5** (he cannot allow 19 **Kt—Q2, Q—R5**), **Kt—B7;** 20 **Kt—K3, Q × Kt,** with the threat on the R-file to follow. One charm of this combination, of a type more commonly seen for White than for Black, is that the Kt can be left to be taken.

	Q—Kt3
19 **Kt—R4**	

If now 19 **P × Kt, P × P** and if 20 **Kt—R4, P—Kt6.**

	B—K5
20 **P × Kt**	

If White does not capture now he cannot prevent **Kt × KP** without allowing **Kt—B7;** and the latter move the capture does not stop.

	Kt—B7
21 **Kt—QB3**	

Not **R—QB1,** for then **Kt—Q5** wins the B.

	Kt—Q5
22 **Q—B1**	**P × P !**

Again the menace of **P—Kt6** comes in; *e.g.*, 23 **Kt × B, P × Kt;** 24 **B—K2, P—Kt6,** and there is no move to escape heavy loss. But White's next two moves just save him.

23 **Kt—R4**	**Q—B2**
24 **R × B !**	**P × R**
25 **Q—B4**	**R—B1**
26 **R—B1**	**P—QKt3**
27 **Kt × B**	**P × Kt**
28 **B—R6**	**Q × P**

And so Black eventually makes the pieces level again, and arrives at an endgame which he cannot well lose.

29 **B × R**	**Q × B**
30 **Q × QBP ch**	

The alternative 30 **P—KKt3** is not good. Black replies **R × Kt;** 31 **P × R, Q × R ch !** with **Kt—K7 ch** to follow.

	Q × Q
31 **R × Q**	**R × Kt**
32 **R—B4**	**Kt—K7 ch**
33 **K—B1**	**Kt—B5**
34 **K—Kt1**	**P—Kt6**
35 **B—R6**	

White has still a struggle to attain equality—or near enough to it to secure a draw. If, for instance, 35 **R × P, Kt—R6 ch.**

	P × P ch
36 **K × P**	**R—R3**
37 **R × P**	**R × B**
38 **R × Kt**	**R × P**
39 **R—QKt4**	**P—Kt3**
40 **R—Kt7**	**K—Kt2**
41 **K—B3**	**P—Kt4**
42 **P—QKt4**	**K—Kt3**
43 **P—Kt5**	**P—B4**
44 **P—Kt6**	

The quickest way of bringing the game to a standard drawn ending, which 44.., **P × P;** 45 **R × P ch** would produce at once.

R—R6 ch
45 K—B2 P—R3
46 R—Kt8 R—Kt6
47 P—Kt7 K—Kt2

Black must of course stop a check, followed by **P—Kt8=Q**.

48 R—QR8 R × P
49 R × P

Draw agreed.

This is aptly called by Winter in *The Manchester Guardian* "the mystery game of the contest," as Alekhine's defiance of the accepted rules of development actually led to his getting such a position after 17 moves that Euwe had to find the right reply every time to avert disaster.

PART III

MODERN DAY CHESS

by Fred Reinfeld

CHAPTER VI

THE AGE OF BOTVINNIK

On March 24, 1946 the chess world was stunned by the sudden death of the World Champion, Alexander Alekhine. Alekhine had accepted Mikhail Botvinnik's challenge to a championship match and negotiations had been proceeding satisfactorily. Added to natural sorrow over the passing of one of the game's great geniuses, was keen disappointment over the failure of the match to take place.

How was the problem of the title to be solved? There was one living ex-Champion, Dr. Max Euwe, who had wrested the title from Alekhine in 1935 and lost it back to him in 1937. Botvinnik, the current challenger, had to be considered. Although Dr. Euwe was considered by some to have at least a legalistic claim to the title, he took a sportsmanlike attitude and readily agreed to the staging of an open tournament to determine the new titleholder. Dr. Euwe's generous gesture removed the final obstacle to such a contest, which accordingly was scheduled for the spring of 1948.

For the first time in chess history the World Championship had been placed under the jurisdiction of the International Chess Federation. By means of a series of qualifying tournaments held at regular intervals the official challenger would be determined and the World Champion would be called upon to defend his title from time to time. But first it was necessary to establish a new titleholder, and this was the function of the World Championship Tournament of 1948.

Five Grand Masters were deemed to be of the necessary calibre for such a contest. There was Dr. Euwe, of course, the former titleholder; Botvinnik, the official challenger and considered by many the world's strongest player; the brilliant Estonian master, Paul Keres; Vassily Smyslov, second only to Botvinnik among the Soviet Masters; and Sammy Reshevsky, the American Champion.

The selection of these five outstanding masters met with universal approval in the chess world. The feeling was well-nigh unanimous that the entries were the strongest that could have been assembled for the purpose.

While Botvinnik's victory hardly came as a surprise, the ease with which he triumphed was not wholly expected. Certainly there was no element of luck in his victory. He obviously was the best player and played the best chess—so much so that he was mathematically certain of first prize well before the conclusion of the tournament.

There was universal regret that Dr. Euwe, a star of an earlier generation, was clearly outclassed by his younger rivals. Keres and Reshevsky proved rather disappointing, despite occasional flashes of their best style. The passage of time has strengthened that impression, for while they were—and remain—masters of the first rank, they do not have that extra something which characterises players of championship quality.

Young Smyslov—he was then still in his twenties—provided a pleasant surprise by coming in second, a half-point ahead of Keres and Reshevsky. Thereby Smyslov foreshadowed his later victory in the second World Championship match with Botvinnik in 1957.

The winning of this tournament showed Botvinnik at the height of his playing strength. His is a style that cannot be described in a few words without neglecting vitally important nuances. Above all, Botvinnik at the zenith of his career was a fighter. Difficult positions were his special domain, but he was equally at home in patient manoeuvring, brilliant combination play, the cumulative building-up of an overwhelming position from slight, almost impalpable beginnings. Like all the World Champions, he displayed an uncanny skill in the endgame phase.

Three years later, when Botvinnik was 40, he faced his first challenger for the title—David Bronstein. Botvinnik, who had once been the youthful challenger, was now called upon to repulse a brilliant player 13 years his junior. In the ensuing match Bronstein's play was in character—imaginative, bold, even reckless. His weakness, as anticipated, was in the endings and generally speaking in the realm of technique.

Botvinnik, on the other hand, was unrecognisable. He was hesitant, conservative, vacillating. He drew the match, but only with great difficulty. But according to the rules that govern these matches, a tied match leaves the Champion in possession of his title. There was general agreement that Botvinnik had escaped by the skin of his teeth, and only by exerting himself to the utmost and exploiting his greater experience and more polished technique. But he had had a narrow scrape.

Three years later, in 1954, Botvinnik defended his title again, this time against Smyslov, 10 years younger than he. Now 42, Botvinnik showed some traces of his palmy days, but he was manifestly exhausted by the gruelling contest. He was perceptibly nearing exhaustion in the second half of the match and yet, by calling on the last ounce of his reserves, he again tied the match and thus again retained his title. It was clear that Smyslov had won a moral victory, if not an official one, for after the first six games the score had stood 4½-1½ against him. Any player who could overcome such a lead was clearly a fighter of the first rank.

In 1957 the two masters met again for the title. Botvinnik again took an early lead—not so big as in the previous match—but Smyslov soon came back strongly and established a two-point lead that Botvinnik was never able to break. Thus Smyslov became the new Champion by means of a fully earned victory. Botvinnik, it seemed, was a "tired old man." At 45 he no longer had the fighting spirit and stamina of earlier times.

When the two masters began their return match in the following year, therefore, it seemed that Botvinnik would very likely get badly mauled. Yet he started like a lion, winning the first three games in a row. Thereafter, although fatigue soon began to gain visibly on him, he was able to maintain his lead and eventually regain his title.

But a World Champion, like a gladiator in the arena, never gets a respite from wearisome struggle. In 1960 Botvinnik, now 48, had to meet a new challenger in the person of Mikhail Tal, a fiery combinative player of 23. What Bronstein and Smyslov had failed to accomplish, Tal achieved—dynamically and convincingly.

Time after time Tal upset his now elderly opponent with dramatic risks, unexpected sacrifices, outlandish-looking manoeuvres. Botvinnik was on the defensive from the very start, and the seemingly tireless Tal pressed his advantage with unrelenting ferocity. It took the younger master only 21 games to obtain the necessary 12½ points that gave him the title.

Botvinnik's failure was a tragedy, as the downfall of every Champion is a tragedy. But the defeat of every older Champion goes hand in hand with the triumph of a younger Champion. When Tal was asked by an interviewer to name his best game he replied, whimsically perhaps but with basic earnestness, "I haven't played it yet." It is an answer that sums up master chess at its very best.

But the return match for the title in 1961 told an amazingly different story. Astonishingly rejuvenated, though a year older, Botvinnik showed all his old wizardry to win by 13-8: 10 wins, 5 losses, 6 draws. This time it was Tal who was hesitant, nervous, unsure of himself. By disheartening experience he learned the bitter lesson that there is no royal road to championship chess. Once more Botvinnik was World Champion—truly a great achievement, for he has been more active than any other World Champion in defending his title.

GAME 53

BOTVINNIK v. KERES

THE HAGUE, *March* 25, 1948

(WORLD CHESS CHAMPIONSHIP)

QUEEN'S PAWN GAME
(NIMZOVITCH DEFENCE)

White.	*Black.*
BOTVINNIK	KERES
1 **P—Q4**	**Kt—KB3**
2 **P—QB4**	**P—K3**
3 **Kt—QB3**	**B—Kt5**
4 **P—K3**	**Castles**
5 **P—QR3**	**B × Kt ch**
6 **P × B**	**R—K1**

Here Keres begins a series of inferior moves that mount up to a considerable disadvantage. The alternative 6.., **P—B4**; 7 **B—Q3**, **Kt—B3**; 8 **Kt—K2**, **P—Q3**; 9 **Kt—Kt3**, **P—QKt3** as played by the same opponents in the Avro tournament ten years earlier, gives Black much better prospects than he obtains in the present game.

7 **Kt—K2**	**P—K4**
8 **Kt—Kt3**	**P—Q3**
9 **B—K2**	**QKt—Q2**

There was still time for Black to play.., **Kt—B3** (with or without.., **P—B4**) in the hope of keeping White's centre from expanding.

10 **Castles**	**P—B4**
11 **P—B3**	**BP × P?**

A serious positional blunder which straightens out White's Pawns and enables his Queen Bishop to enlarge its scope considerably.

12 **BP × P**	**Kt—Kt3**
13 **B—Kt2**	**P × P?**

The logical sequel to the previous mistake: he opens up the position still more, anticipating **14 P × P**, **P—Q4** with a game of sorts.

Position after 13.., **P × P**:

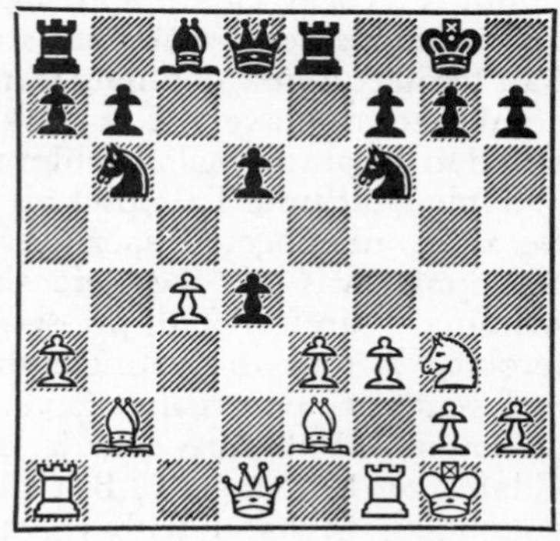

14 **P—K4!**	....

A disconcerting surprise for Black. White prevents.., P—**Q4** for good and prepares to recapture on Queen 4 with a piece, so as to operate on the long diagonal.

14	**B—K3**

Hoping for 15 **Q × P**, **Kt—R5**; 16 **B—B1**, **Q—Kt3**. But again Botvinnik fools him.

15 **R—B1!**	**R—K2**
16 **Q × P**	**Q—B2**

Somewhat better was 16.., **Kt—R5,** restraining the following advance which enables Botvinnik to switch to a devastating King-side attack.

17	**P—B5!**	**P×P**
18	**R×P**	**Q—B5**
19	**B—B1!**	**Q—Kt1**
20	**R—KKt5!**	....

This surprisingly powerful move (threatening **Q×Kt**) leaves Black without recourse, for example 20.., **Kt—K1;** 21 **Kt—R5, P—Kt3;** 22 **B—Kt2** and wins—or 21.., **P—B3;** 22 **Kt×BP ch** etc.

20	....	**QKt—Q2**

Position after 20.., **QKt—Q2:**

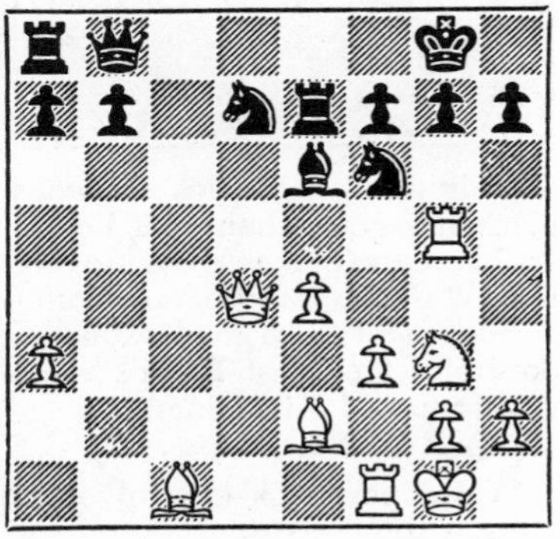

21	**R×P ch!!**	**K×R**
22	**Kt—R5 ch**	**K—Kt3**

Black's situation is hopeless. On 22.., **K—R1** there follows 23 **B—Kt5, Q—KB1;** 24 **Kt×Kt**—or 23 **Kt×Kt, Q—K4;** 25 **B—Kt2!**—with an easy win for White in either case.

Against 22.., **K—Kt1** White wins with 23 **Kt×Kt ch, Kt×Kt;** 24 **Q×Kt** as Black has no defence against the coming **B—KR6.**

Finally, if 22.., **K—B1;** 23 **Kt×Kt, Kt×Kt;** 24 **Q×Kt, K—K1;** 25 **R—Q1** wins.

23	**Q—K3!**	**Resigns**

A strong finish to an exceedingly well played game by Botvinnik.

GAME 54

BOTVINNIK v. EUWE

Moscow, *April* 13, 1948

(World Chess Championship)

QUEEN'S GAMBIT DECLINED

	White.	*Black.*
	Botvinnik	Euwe
1	**P—Q4**	**P—Q4**
2	**Kt—KB3**	**Kt—KB3**
3	**P—B4**	**P—K3**
4	**Kt—B3**	**P—B3**
5	**P—K3**	**QKt—Q2**
6	**B—Q3**	**P×P**
7	**B×BP**	**P—QKt4**

Black is playing the famous Meran Variation, on which a wealth of analysis has been lavished ever since its introduction into master play in 1924. Botvinnik has played an important role in this analysis, and has impartially played the line with the White and Black pieces.

8	**B—Q3**	**P—QR3**
9	**P—K4**	**P—B4**

The characteristic move which starts a tumultuous scramble for control of the centre.

10	**P—K5**	**P×P**
11	**Kt×KtP**	**P×Kt**

The alternative 11.., **Kt×P;** 12 **Kt×Kt, P×Kt;** 13 **Q—B3** also seems to favour White.

12	**P×Kt**	**Q—Kt3**
13	**P×P**	**B×P**
14	**Castles**	**Kt—B4**

Position after 14.., **Kt—B4:**

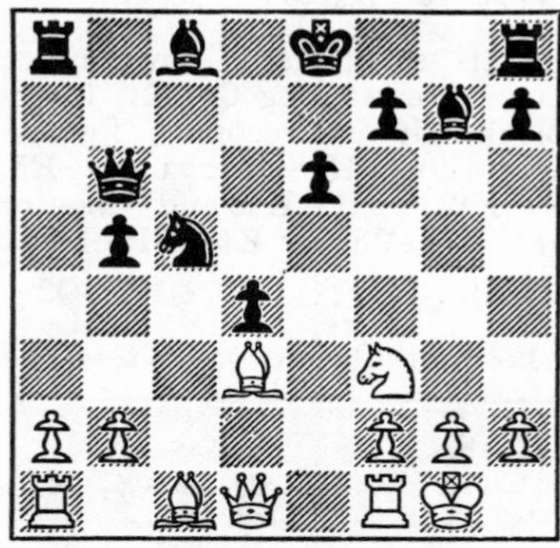

A situation with pros and cons. Black has good chances if he can get his central Pawn mass moving. But White has a more harmonious development and good attacking possibilities against Black's somewhat exposed King-side.

15 **B—KB4!** ....

White plays for control of his King 5 square.

15 .... **B—Kt2**

But not 15.., **Castles?;** 16 **B×P ch!, K×B;** 17 **Kt—Kt5 ch, K—Kt3** (if 17.., **K—Kt1?;** 18 **Q—R5, R—Q1;** 19 **Q×P ch, K—R1;** 20 **B—K5** and White wins); 18 **Q—Kt4** and White's attack should be conclusive.

16 **R—K1** **R—Q1?**

Best seems 16.., **Kt×B;** 17 **Q×Kt, B×Kt;** 18 **Q×B, Castles (K);** 19 **QR—B1, QR—B1;** 20 **Q—KKt3, K—R1;** 21 **P—KR4, R—KKt1** and Black's game is playable.

17 **QR—B1** **R—Q4**

In order to be able to move his Knight without having to fear **B—B7** in reply.

18 **B—K5!** **B×B**

If instead 18.., **Castles;** 19 **Kt—Kt5!** gives White a winning attack, for example 19.., **R×B;** 20 **R×R, B×R;** 21 **Q—R5** forcing mate.

19 **R×B** ....

And now 19.., **Castles** is still a losing move: 20 **Kt—Kt5!, P—B4** (if 20.., **R×R;** 21 **Q—R5** wins on the spot); 21 **Q—R5, Q—B2;** 22 **R×R. B×R;** 23 **R×Kt!** and White wins.

19 .... **R×R**
20 **Kt×R** **Kt×B**

What else? If 20.., **Castles;** 21 **Q—Kt4 ch** wins a Pawn, or if 20.., **R—Kt1;** 21 **B—B1** and White soon wins a Pawn.

21 **Q×Kt** **P—B3**

Black has no good move, for if 21.., **K—K2;** 22 **Q—KKt3** with a winning game for White. Or if 21.., Castles, White wins by 22 **Kt—Q7** or else 22 **Q—KKt3 ch, K—R1;** 23 **R—B7!, Q×R;** 24 **Kt—Kt6 ch** followed by 25 **Q×Q.**

Position after 21.., **P—B3:**

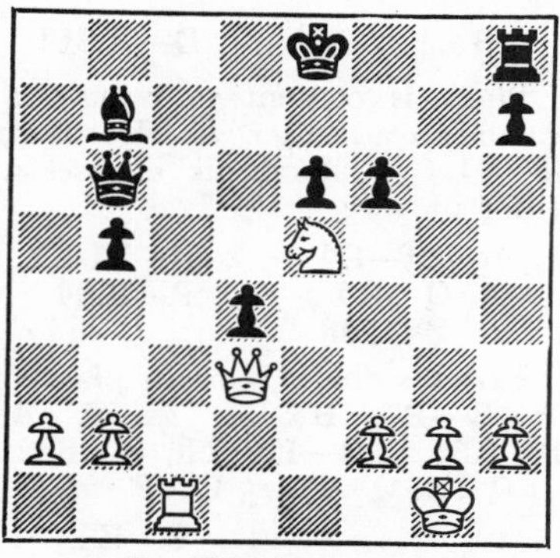

22 **Q—KKt3!!** **P×Kt**

Realising that **Q—Kt7** must be decisive, Black surrenders to the inevitable.

23 **Q—Kt7** **R—B1**
24 **R—B7** **Q×R**

The real beauty of Botvinnik's incisive play appears after 24.., **Q—Q3;** 25 **R×B, P—Q6;** 26 **R—R7!, Q—Q1;** 27 **Q×RP!, P—Q7;** 28 **Q—Kt6 ch** and mate next move.

25 **Q×Q** **B—Q4**
26 **Q×KP** **P—Q6**
27 **Q—K3** **B—B5**
28 **P—QKt3** **R—B2**

If the B retreats, 29 **Q×QP** wins effortlessly. But Botvinnik is in no hurry to take the Bishop.

29 **P—B3** ....

To bring in his King.

29 .... **R—Q2**

Threatens.., **P—Q7.**

30 **Q—Q2** **P—K4**
31 **P×B** **P×P**
32 **K—B2** **K—B2**

Black realizes that 32.., **P—B6;** 33 **Q×BP, P—Q7** is refuted by 34 **Q—B8 ch** and 35 **Q×R ch!** followed by 36 **K—K2.** (This explains White's 29th move.)

33 **K—K3** **K—K3**
34 **Q—Kt4** **R—QB2**
35 **K—Q2** **R—B3**
36 **P—QR4** **Resigns**

Otherwise White's Queen Rook Pawn keeps advancing; while.., **P—B6 ch** can always be answered by **Q×P.** A great game by White.

GAME 55

BOTVINNIK v. BRONSTEIN

Moscow, *April* 8, 1951

(Championship Match, 11th Game)

QUEEN'S PAWN GAME
(QUEEN'S INDIAN DEFENCE)

	White.	*Black.*
	Botvinnik	Bronstein
1	**P—Q4**	**P—K3**
2	**Kt—KB3**	**Kt—KB3**
3	**P—B4**	**P—QKt3**
4	**P—KKt3**	**B—Kt2**
5	**B—Kt2**	**B—K2**
6	**Castles**	**Castles**
7	**P—Kt3**	....

In search of variety, Botvinnik dismisses the more conventional 7 **Kt—B3, Kt—K5** etc.

7	....	**P—Q4**
8	**P×P**	**P×P**
9	**B—Kt2**	**QKt—Q2**
10	**Kt—B3**	**R—K1**
11	**Kt—K5**	**B—KB1**

Black anticipates 12 **P—B4, P—B4** or 12 **Kt—Q3, Kt—K5** with a good game in either event. Instead Botvinnik resorts to a Pawn sacrifice that calls for patient and resourceful play on Bronstein's part.

12	**R—B1?!**	**Kt×Kt**
13	**P×Kt**	**R×P**
14	**Kt—Kt5**	**R—K2**
15	**B×Kt**	**P×B**

Black's King-side has been broken up, but he has the two Bishops and fair mobility. To get a more effective set-up, Botvinnik sacrifices a second Pawn.

16	**P—K4!**	**P×P**
17	**Q—Kt4 ch**	**B—Kt2!**

Not 17.., **K—R1**; 18 **KR—Q1, Q—B1**; 19 **Q—B4** and White has a winning game.

18	**KR—Q1**	....

Position after 18 **KR—Q1**:

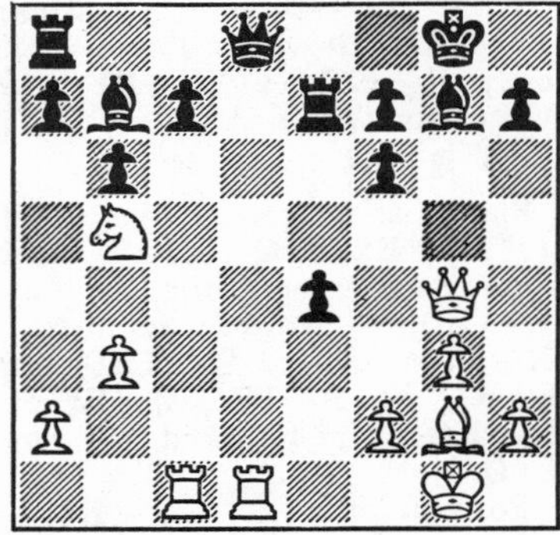

18	....	**Q—KB1!**

Black is content to remain a Pawn ahead after 19 **Kt×BP, R—Q1.** So Botvinnik chooses a different way.

19	**Kt—Q4**	**B—B1**
20	**Q—R4**	**P—KB4**
21	**Kt—B6**	....

Perhaps there is more play in 21 **B—R3, B×Kt**; 22 **R×B, B—K3**; 23 **Q—Kt5 ch, Q—Kt2**; 24 **Q×R, Q×R**; 25 **R×P** etc.

21	....	**R—K1**
22	**B—R3**	**B—KR3!**
23	**R—B2**	**P—K6!**

True to his style, Bronstein switches to counterattack. White's reply is forced, for if 24 **P—B4, P—K7;** 25 **R—K1, Q—Q3** (threatens.., **Q—Q8**); 26 **Kt—K5, Q—Q5 ch;** 27 **K—R1, Q—B7** wins for Black.

24 **P×P** **B×P ch**
25 **K—R1** **B—K3**
26 **B—Kt2** **P—QR4!**

Prevents **Kt/Kt4—Q5,** which would give White good prospects.

27 **B—B3** ....

On 27 **Kt—K7 ch** Black can play 27.., **R×Kt,** for after 28 **B×R** he captures the Bishop with a check—and in fact soon forces checkmate.

27 .... **K—R1!**
28 **Kt—Q4** **QR—Q1!**

Position after 28.., **QR—Q1:**

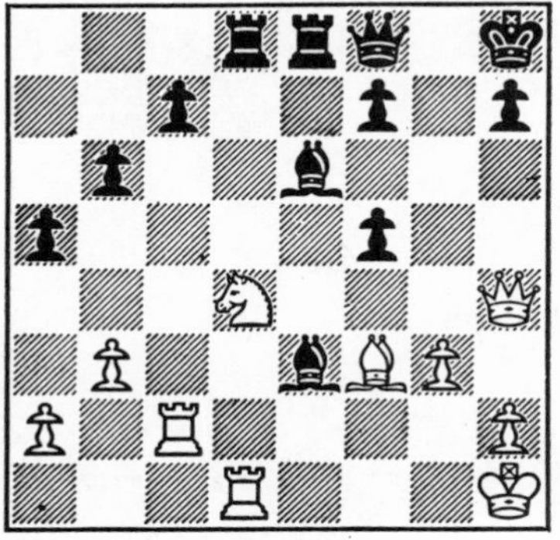

29 **R×P** ....

He can hang on longer with 29 **Q—B6 ch, Q—Kt2;** 30 **Q×Q ch, K×Q;** 31 **Kt×B ch, P×Kt;** 32 **R×P ch, K—B3;** 33 **R×R, R×R;** 34 **R×P** with even material and Bishops on opposite colours. But after 34.., **P—K4!** the ending would nevertheless be won for Black because of his passed Pawn.

29 .... **B—Q4!**

Threatens to win outright with 30.., **B×B ch.** If White plays 30 **B×B, R×B** he cannot meet all the threats, such as.., **R—K5.** And on 30 **R—KB1** Black has a forced win with 30.., **Q—Q3;** 31 **Kt×P, B×B ch;** 32 **R×B, Q—Q8 ch** (not 32.., **Q×R;** 33 **Q—B6 ch** and mate next move); 33 **K—Kt2, R—Q7 ch;** 34 **K—R3, B—Kt4;** 35 **Q—R5, Q—KKt8;** 36 **Q×BP, Q×RP ch!;** 37 **K—Kt4, B—Q1 dis ch;** 38 **Q×R ch!?, K×Q;** 39 **Kt—R6 ch, Q×Kt ch!;** 40 **K×Kt, R—R7 mate.**

30 **R—K1** ....

White threatens 31 **R×B, R×R;** 32 **Q—B6 ch, K—Kt1;** 33 **Q—Kt5 ch** and 34 **Q×R.**

30 .... **Q—Q3!**

Much faster than 30.., **B×Kt;** 31 **Q×B ch, K—Kt1;** 32 **B×B** (forced), **R×R ch** etc.

31 **R—B2** **R—K5!**
32 **B×R** **B×B ch**
33 **Q×B** ....

White struggles to no avail.

33 .... **P×Q**
34 **Kt—B5** **Q—Kt5**

Stronger than 34.., **Q—Q6;** 35 **Kt×B.**

35 **R×B** **R—Q8 ch**
36 **K—Kt2** **R—Q7 ch**

If now 37 **R—K2, R×KR ch;** 38 **R×R, Q—Kt4;** 39 **R—KB2. Q—Q6** and Black wins.

37 **R×R** **Q×R ch**
38 **K—R3** ....

Or 38 **K—Kt1, Q×QRP** and White cannot play 39 **R×P?** because of 39.., **Q—Kt8 ch** etc.

38 .... **Q—KB7!**
39 **K—Kt4** ....

Or 39 **P—KKt4, P—R4** and Black wins easily.

39 .... **P—B3!**

White resigns, as 40.., **P—R4 ch** will win the Knight. Splendidly energetic play by Bronstein.

GAME 56

BRONSTEIN v. BOTVINNIK

Moscow, *April* 10, 1951

(Championship Match, 12th Game)

QUEEN'S PAWN GAME
(DUTCH DEFENCE)

White.	*Black.*
Bronstein	Botvinnik
1 **P—Q4**	**P—K3**
2 **P—QB4**	**P—KB4**
3 **P—K3**	....

One of the curious features of this match was the feeble systems adopted for White against the Dutch Defence. The next move is not calculated to strike terror to Black's heart. Best is 3 **P—KKt3** with the fianchetto of White's King Bishop.

3 .... **Kt—KB3**
4 **Kt—QB3** **P—Q4**
5 **Kt—R3** ....

This avoidance of the more normal (and less adventurous) **Kt—B3** hints at White's subsequent **P—B3** as a preparation for **P—K4.**

5 .... **P—B3**

Botvinnik has his favourite Stonewall formation.

6 **B—Q2** **B—Q3**
7 **Q—B2** **Castles**
8 **Castles** ....

A daring, anti-positional venture from which Bronstein manages to harvest all the obvious disadvantages and none of the hoped-for advantages.

8 .... **Q—K2**
9 **P—B3** **P×P!**

Intending to answer 10 **B×P** with 10.., **P—QKt4;** 11 **B—Kt3, P—QR4** or 11 **B—Q3, Kt—Q4.**

10 **P—K4** **P×P**
11 **Kt×P?** ....

Realizing that after 11 **P×P, P—K4;** 12 **B×P ch, K—R1** Black has an excellent game, Bronstein chooses an all too venturesome alternative.

11 .... **P—QKt4!**

Botvinnik realizes that his subsequent weakness on the black squares will be outweighed by his extra Pawn.

12 **Kt×B** **Q×Kt**

Position after 12.., **Q×Kt:**

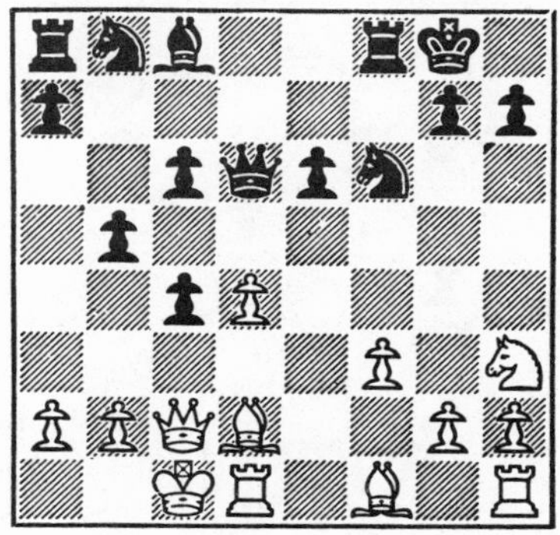

13 **P—B4** ....

Botvinnik has suggested 13 **P—KKt4** here, but that would make no appreciable difference.

13 .... **Kt—R3**

Satisfied with his booty, Botvinnik avoids 13.., **Q×QP** and continues his development.

14 **B—K2** **P—B4!**
15 **B—KB3** **R—Kt1**
16 **B—B3** **Kt—QKt5**

If now 17 **B×Kt, P×B** followed by.., **B—Q2** and.., **KR—B1** and .., **P—Kt6** and Black wins effortlessly. White prefers to give up a second Pawn.

17 **P×P** **Kt×P ch**
18 **K—Kt1** **Kt×B ch**
19 **Q×Kt** **Q×QBP**
20 **KR—K1** **P—KR3**

This prevents White's counterplay by **Kt—Kt5.**

21 **R—K5** **Q—B2**
22 **P—KKt4** **B—Kt2!**
23 **B×B** **R×B**

On 24 **R×KP, Kt×P;** 25 **R—Kt1** Black will play 25.., **Q—B2!;** 26 **R—K2, P—Kt5** with an easy win.

24 **P—Kt5** **Kt—Q4**

Position after 24.., **Kt—Q4:**

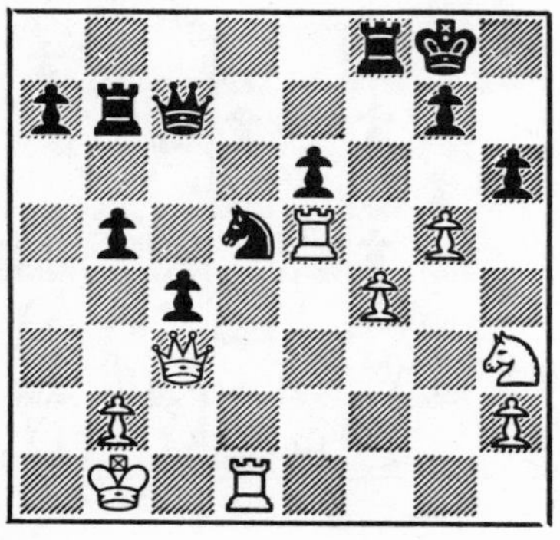

White now decides to give up the Exchange, for 25 **Q—Q4, P—B6;** 26 **R—QB1, Q—B5!;** 27 **Q×Q, P×Q;** 28 **R—B2, KR—Kt1** is ruinous for him.

25 **R(Q1)×Kt** **P×R**
26 **Q—Q4** ....

Or 26 **R×P, P—Kt5** followed by.., **P—B6** etc.

26 .... **P—B6!**

So that if 27 **Q×BP, Q×Q;** 28 **P×Q, P—Kt5** and Black's win is child's play. Or 26 **Q×QP ch, Q—B2!** etc.

27 **P—Kt3** **Q—Q2**
28 **Kt—B2** **P—B7 ch**

And now if 29 **K×P, R—B1 ch** followed by.., **Q—QB2** and Black has a mating attack.

29 **K—B1** **P×P**
30 **R×KtP** **Q—K3**
31 **R—K5** **Q—Q3**
32 **K×P** **R—QB2 ch**
33 **K—Q2** **Q—B4**
34 **Q×Q** ....

Forced. All is lost save honour.

34 .... **R×Q**

Black has an easy end game win now.

35 **Kt—Q3** **R—QB3**
36 **R×P** **P—R3**
37 **P—R4** **R—R3**
38 **P—R5** **R(R3)—KB3**
39 **P—Kt4** **R—B4**
40 **R—Q6** **R(B1)—B3**
Resigns

That Bronstein was able to tie the match despite the liberties he took in several such games is an indication of Botvinnik's undistinguished form in this contest.

GAME 57

BOTVINNIK v. SMYSLOV

Moscow, *April* 10, 1954

(Championship [First] Match, 12th Game)

QUEEN'S GAMBIT DECLINED

White.	*Black.*
Botvinnik	Smyslov
1 **P—Q4**	**P—Q4**
2 **P—QB4**	**P—QB3**

The Slav Defence—a great favourite with Smyslov.

3 **Kt—KB3**	**Kt—B3**
4 **Kt—B3**	**P×P**
5 **P—QR4**	**B—B4**
6 **P—K3**	**P—K3**
7 **B×P**	**B—QKt5**
8 **Castles**	**QKt—Q2**
9 **Kt—R4**	....

This move has two possible objectives: either exchanging Knight for Bishop, obtaining two Bishops against Bishop and Knight—or else forming a new Pawn centre with **P—B3** and **P—K4.** As the game goes, White combines both goals.

9 .... **Castles**

Smyslov avoids 9.., **Kt—K5?** 10 **Kt×B, P×Kt;** 11 **B×P ch!, K×B;** 12 **Q—Kt3 ch** followed by 13 **Q×B** with a won game for White.

Nor do the complications arising from 9.., **B—Kt5** appeal to him, for example 10 **P—B3, Kt—Q4;** 11 **P—KKt3, B—KR6;** 12 **R—B2** and although Black can win a Pawn, White will obtain a very strong initiative.

10 **P—B3** ....

More promising than 10 **Kt×B, P×Kt** etc. when Black has a good hold on his King 5 square.

10	**B—Kt3**
11 **P—K4**	**P—K4**

Counterplay in the centre. The plausible alternative 11.., **Kt×P?,;** 12 **Kt×B, Kt×Kt;** 13 **P×Kt, B×P;** 14 **Kt×R** costs Black a piece.

12 **Kt×B** ....

Botvinnik criticises this move as premature, recommending 12 **P×P!, QKt×P;** 13 **B—K2** when White maintains a vastly superior game—regardless of whether or not Black exchanges Queens—because Black's unfortunate Queen Bishop remains out of play.

12	**RP×Kt**
13 **B—K3**	....

Now too, says Botvinnik, 13 **P×P, QKt×P;** 14 **B—K2** was in order.

13 .... **Q—K2**

Black fails to rise to the occasion. With 13 .., **Q—Kt3!** followed by.., **QR—Q1** he would have had an excellent game because of his pressure in the centre.

14 **Q—K2**	**P×P**
15 **B×QP**	**B—B4**
16 **B×B**	**Q×B ch**
17 **K—R1**	**P—KKt4**

Directed against White's indicated **P—B4** followed by **P—K5.** Now in order to carry out this manoeuvre White will have to weaken his position somewhat.

18 **P—KKt3!** **QR—Q1**

Hoping for 19 **P—B4, P×P;** 20 **P×P, Kt—Kt3;** 21 **B—R2, R—Q5** with counterplay for Black. But White proceeds with great care.

19 **B—R2** **KR—K1**
20 **QR—Q1** **Kt—B1**
21 **R×R** **R×R**
22 **P—K5** **Kt—Q4**
23 **Kt×Kt** ....

More promising than 23 **Kt—K4, Q—K6!** etc.

23 .... **P×Kt**
24 **Q—Q2!** ....

Here 24 **P—B4** is premature because of 24.., **P×P;** 25 **P×P, Q—Q5!**

24 .... **Kt—K3**
25 **P—B4** **P×P**
26 **P×P** **Q—B3?**

After playing with commendable energy Smyslov misses his best chance: 26.., **Q—Q5!**

27 **P—B5** **Kt—B4**
28 **Q—Kt5** **R—Q2?**

This loses quickly. The only move worth considering was 28.., **P—B3**—best answered by 29 **Q—Kt2!**

29 **R—KKt1** **P—B3**
30 **P×P** **Kt—K5**

The move on which Smyslov relied—but Botvinnik has a clever refutation.

Position after 30.., **Kt—K5:**

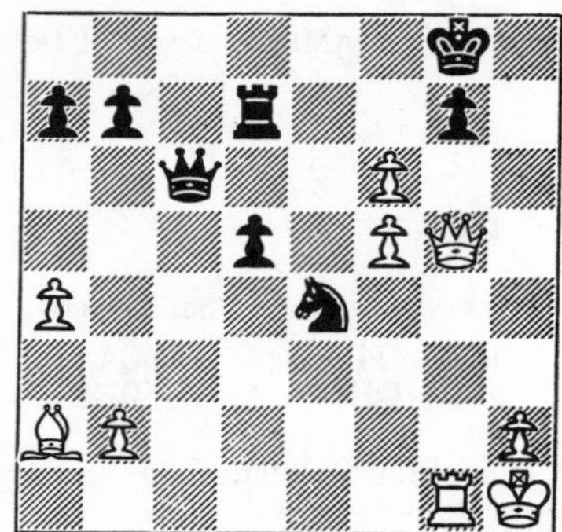

31 **P—B7 ch!** **R×P**
32 **Q—Q8 ch** **K—R2**

Even worse for Black is 32.., **R—B1;** 33 **B×P ch, K—R2;** 34 **R×P ch!, K×R;** 35 **Q—K7 ch** and White wins.

33 **B×P** **Kt—B7 ch**

At least a piece goes, no matter what Black does.

34 **K—Kt2** **Q—B3**
35 **Q×Q** **R×Q**
36 **K×Kt** **R×P ch**
37 **B—B3** **R—B5**
38 **R—Kt4** **Resigns**

A masterly game by Botvinnik.

GAME 58

BOTVINNIK v. SMYSLOV

Moscow, *April* 15, 1954

(Championship [First] Match, 14th Game)

KING'S INDIAN DEFENCE

White.	*Black.*
Botvinnik	Smyslov
1 **P—Q4**	**Kt—KB3**
2 **P—QB4**	**P—KKt3**
3 **P—KKt3**	**B—Kt2**
4 **B—Kt2**	**Castles**
5 **Kt—QB3**	**P—Q3**
6 **Kt—B3**	**QKt—Q2**
7 **Castles**	**P—K4**
8 **P—K4**	**P—B3**
9 **B—K3**	....

More usual is 9 **P—KR3,** to avoid the ensuing complications.

9	**Kt—Kt5**
10 **B—Kt5**	**Q—Kt3!**

Most enterprising—and well calculated too. First point: after 11 **B—K7, R—K1;** 12 **B×P, P×P;** 13 **Kt—QR4, Q—R3** Black has a very promising position and White's looks dis-organised.

11 **P—KR3**	....

Position after 11 **P—KR3:**

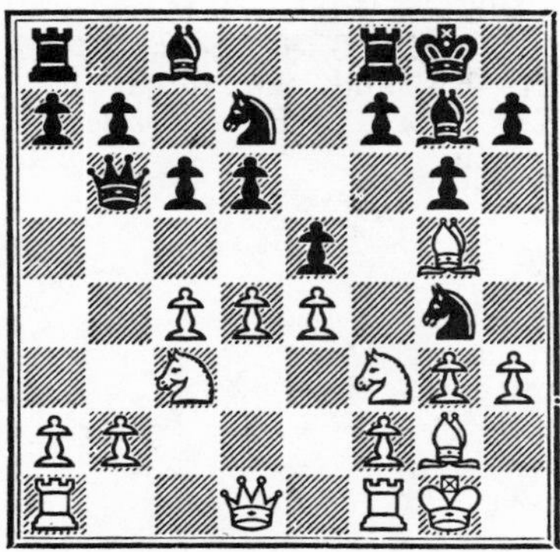

11	**P×P!**

Much stronger than the colourless 11.., **KKt—B3;** 12 **Q—Q2** etc. which leaves White with a fine game.

12 **Kt—QR4**	**Q—R3**
13 **P×Kt**	**P—Kt4**

Necessary to regain the sacrificed piece. Black has to give up the Exchange, but he gets ample counterplay. For example, 14 **P—B5, P×Kt;** 15 **B—K7, P×P!;** 16 **B×R, Kt×B** favours Black—as does 14 **P—B5, P×P;** 15 **Kt×BP, Kt×Kt;** 16 **B—K7, Kt—K3** etc.

14 **Kt×P**	**P×Kt**
15 **Kt×P!?**	**Q×Kt!**
16 **P—K5**	**Q×P**
17 **B×R**	**Kt×P**

White has many ways to go wrong, for example 18 **B—K7, B×P;** 19 **Q—Q5, Q—B1!;** 20 **B×R, B—B6** with a winning attack—or 18 **B—Q5, Q—Kt4!** with the strong threat of.., **Kt—Q6.** Likewise 18 **B—Kt2, B—K3;** 19 **Q×QP, Q×KtP;** 20 **B—B4, Kt—B6 ch** does not look inviting for White.

18 **R—B1**	**Q—Kt5!**
19 **P—R3**	**Q×QKtP**
20 **Q×RP**	....

Position after 20 **Q×RP**:

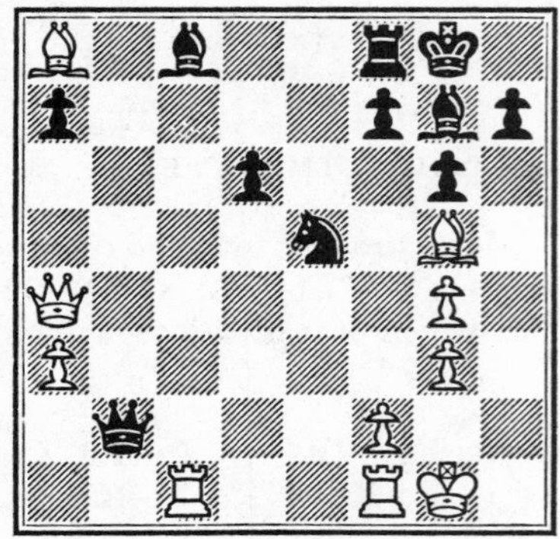

20 .... **B—Kt2!**

To this the best reply was 21 **B×B, Q×B**; 22 **R—B3, Kt—B6 ch**; 23 **R×Kt, Q×R**; 24 **B—K7, R—B1**; 25 **B×P** with about equal chances. Instead, Botvinnik goes sadly astray.

21 **R—Kt1?** ....

Seemingly crushing, but Black has a convincing refutation.

21 .... **Kt—B6 ch**
22 **K—R1** **B×B!**

Botvinnik had expected 22.., **Q×R**; 23 **R×Q, B×B**; 24 **B—K7**. A plausible continuation then would be 24.., **Kt—Q7 dis ch**; 25 **K—Kt1, Kt×R**; 26 **B×R, B×B**; 27 **Q—Kt4** and the Knight is trapped!

23 **R×Q** **Kt×B dis ch!**
24 **K—R2** **Kt—B6 ch**
25 **K—R3** **B×R**

Black is not only ahead in material; he soon builds up a clever mating attack.

26 **Q×P** **B—K5!**

It is important to prevent White's **R—QKt1**.

27 **P—R4** **K—Kt2**
28 **R—Q1** **B—K4**
29 **Q—K7** **R—B1!**

Now White cannot carry out his intention of getting rid of one of the redoubtable Bishops, for 30 **R×P** is answered by 30.., **R—B8!** with the terrible threat of 31.., **R—KR8 ch**; 32 **K—Kt2, Kt—R5** mate (or 32.., **Kt—K8** mate).

30 **P—R5** **R—B7**

Black threatens 31.., **R×P** with 32.., **R—KR7** mate in the offing. Nor will 31 **R—KB1** serve because of 31.., **B—Q6.**

31 **K—Kt2** **Kt—Q5 dis ch**
32 **K—B1** **B—B6**
33 **R—Kt1** **Kt—B3**
Resigns

White is helpless. If for example 34 **Q—K8, B—Q5!**; 35 **Q—K1, Kt—K4** and the threat of.., **Kt×P** or .., **Kt—Q6** decides quickly.

GAME 59

BOTVINNIK v. SMYSLOV

Moscow, *March* 16, 1957

(Championship [Second] Match, 5th Game)

KING'S INDIAN DEFENCE

White.	*Black.*
Botvinnik	Smyslov
1 **P—QB4**	**Kt—KB3**
2 **Kt—QB3**	**P—KKt3**
3 **P—KKt3**	**B—Kt2**
4 **B—Kt2**	**Castles**
5 **P—Q4**	**P—Q3**
6 **Kt—B3**	**B—Kt5**

The object of this unusual move is to continue with.., **B×Kt** in the hope of gaining control of White's Queen 4 square. Botvinnik's alert play parries this plan.

7 **P—KR3**	**B×Kt**
8 **B×B**	**Kt—B3**
9 **B—Kt2**	**Kt—Q2**

Now 10 **P—Q5** will not do because of 10.., **Kt(B3)—K4;** 11 **Q—Kt3, Kt—B4** or 11 **P—Kt3, Kt—B6 ch!**

Another possibility is 10 **B—K3, P—K4;** 11 **P—Q5, Kt—Q5!** and Black has achieved his strategic objective. The sequel might be 12 **B×Kt, P×B;** 13 **Kt—Kt5, P—Q6!** with an excellent game for Black.

10 **P—K3!**	**P—K4**
11 **P—Q5**	....

This is now in order, as.., **Kt—Q5** is ruled out. White has won the war of strategy.

11	**Kt—K2**
12 **P—K4**	**P—KB4**

Here and on the next few moves Black should be thinking of the standard manoeuvre.., **P—QR4** followed by.., **Kt—QB4.**

13 **P—KR4!** ....

A very fine and subtle move. On the face of it, the Pawn move threatens **P—R5** opening up the King Rook file. This consideration induces Black's reply, with the objective of keeping the position closed.

13 .... **P—B5**

For if 14 **P—R5** Black barricades the King-side with 14.., **P—KKt4.**

14 **B—R3!** ....

Now Botvinnik's real intention is revealed. He has opened up a beautiful diagonal for his King Bishop. A real possibility now is 15 **B—K6 ch, K—R1;** 16 **P—R5, P—KKt4** (Black can hardly allow the opening of the King Rook file); 17 **Q—Kt4** and White wins the King Knight Pawn.

14 .... **R—B3**

Black's idea is to answer 15 **B—K6 ch** with 15.., **K—R1;** 16 **Q—Kt4, Kt—KB1** avoiding material loss.

15 **Q—K2**	**B—R3**
16 **B—Q2**	**Kt—QB4?**

Deliberately provoking **P—QKt4,** which Smyslov apparently considers a weakening move. It does not prove so; hence he should have played 16.., **P—R4** as a prelude to .., **Kt—QB4.**

17 **P—QKt4** **P—B6**

By shutting out the possibility of a later .., **P×P** Black deprives himself of potential counterplay. Hence 17.., **Kt—R3;** 18 **P—R3, P—B4** was a preferable alternative.

18 **Q—B1** **B×B ch**
19 **K×B** ....

White's King is perfectly safe here and frees White's Rooks for action.

19 .... **Kt—R3**
20 **P—R3** **P—B3**

Smyslov continues to appraise the situation incorrectly; he hopes to open up the position with.., **P—QKt4,** but the opening of lines can only favour White. Hence 20.., **P—B4** was better.

21 **Q—Q3** **Kt—B2**
22 **QR—QKt1** **R—Kt1**
23 **KR—QB1** **P—QR4**

He sees that 23.., **P—QKt4?** will not do because of 24 **QP×P** and White wins a Pawn.

24 **P—Kt5** **P—B4?**

Now this is bad. There was nothing better than 24.., **P×KtP** or 24.., **P×QP.**

25 **P—Kt6!** ....

Doubtless an unexpected reply. The point is that after 25.., **Kt—R1?;** 26 **Kt—R4** the Black Knight is trapped for the duration. In any event, Black's Queen Rook Pawn is now artificially isolated and must go lost.

Position after 25 **P—Kt6:**

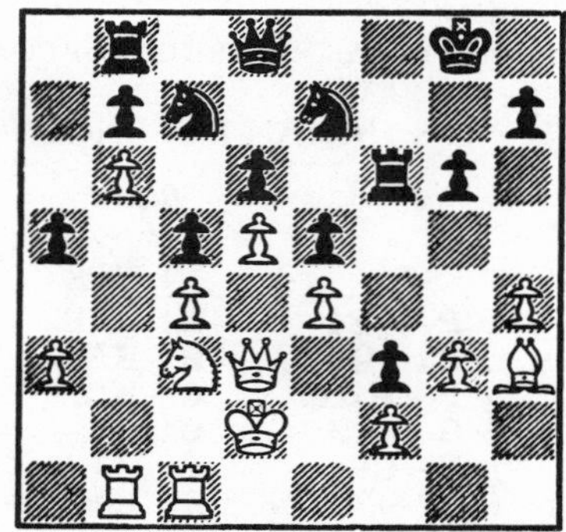

25 .... **Kt—K1**
26 **R—K1** **Kt—Kt2**
27 **R—K3** **Q—KB1**
28 **R—Kt5** **R—R1**
29 **Kt—R4** ....

This prepares for **Q—B3** as well as the following Knight manoeuvre. A good alternative was 29 **B—Kt4** winning the King Bishop Pawn.

29 .... **Q—B2**
30 **Q—B3** **P—R4**
31 **R×RP** **R—Kt1**
32 **Kt—Kt2** **K—R2**
33 **Q—Kt3** **Kt—Kt1**
34 **Kt—Q3** **Kt—R3**

The game has already been decided in White's favour but it takes time to break down Black's position.

35 **R—K1** **Kt—Kt5**
36 **Q—R4** **Q—K2**
37 **K—B2** **R(B3)—B1**
38 **R—R7** **Kt—K1**
39 **B×Kt!** ....

Leaving Black with a weak King Knight Pawn before his other Knight gets to King Bishop 3.

39	....	**P×B**
40	**Q—Kt5**	**Kt—B3**
41	**P—R4**	**K—Kt1**
42	**Q—R5!**	....

White's play on both wings is extremely interesting. Black's last move pointed to 42.., **Q—R2** with a view to 43.., **P—Kt4;** 44 **P×P, Kt×P** and Black at last secures some counterplay. Now if 42.., **Q—R2;** 43 **Q—Q2!** and 43.., **P—Kt4** is ruled out because of 44 **Q×P ch.**

42	....	**Q—Q1**
43	**Kt—Kt2!**	**Kt—Q2**
44	**Kt—Q1!**	....

Position after 44 **Kt—Q1:**

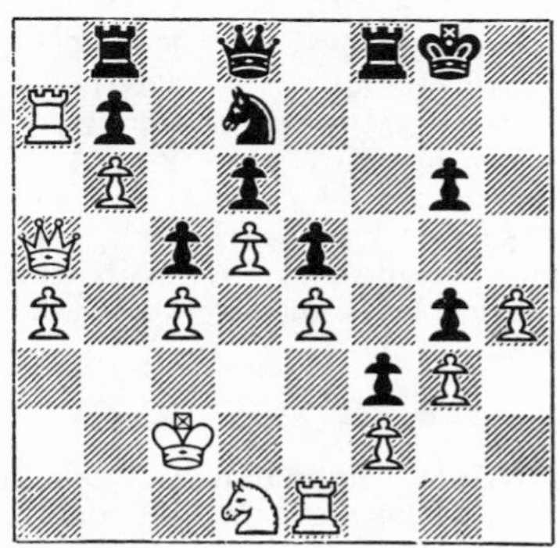

To appreciate the accuracy of Botvinnik's calculations, we must note that after 44.., **Q×P;** 45 **Q×Q, Kt×Q;** 46 **Kt—K3** (threatening **R—QKt1**), **R—R1;** 47 **R×P, Kt×RP;** 48 **Kt×P** White wins with ease. The same is true of 44.., **Kt×P;** 45 **Kt—K3, R—R1;** 46 **R—QKt1, R×R;** 47 **Q×R, Kt—B1;** 48 **Q×KtP** with 49 **Kt×P** in the offing.

44	....	**Kt—B3**
45	**Q—Kt5**	**Q—K2**
46	**P—QR5**	**Q—R2**
47	**K—Q3**	....

Directed against the possibility of 47.., **P—Kt4;** 48 **P×P, Kt×KP** etc.

47	....	**R—B2**
48	**Q—Kt2**	**Kt—R4**
49	**R—Kt1**	**P—Kt4**

Black's desperation is well justified.

50	**P×P**	**QR—KB1**
51	**Q—Q2**	**R—B5?!**

Hoping for 52 **P×R, Kt×P ch** followed by the capture of the King Pawn. Though this would win easily enough for White, Botvinnik prefers to go his own way.

52	**Kt—B3**	**Kt×P?!**
53	**R×Kt**	**Q—R7**

Threatening 54.., **Q×R;** 55 **P×Q, P—B7** etc.

54	**Q—K1**	**Resigns**

A good positional game by Botvinnik.

GAME 60

SMYSLOV v. BOTVINNIK

Moscow, *April*, 1957

(Championship [Second] Match, 20th Game)

FRENCH DEFENCE

White.	*Black.*
Smyslov	Botvinnik
1 **P—K4**	**P—K3**
2 **P—Q4**	**P—Q4**
3 **Kt—QB3**	**B—Kt5**

To have a chance to retain his title, Botvinnik must win this game. Hence he resorts to his favourite defence on which he has relied in many an important contest.

4 **P—K5**	**P—QB4**
5 **P—QR3**	**B×Kt ch**
6 **P×B**	**Q—B2**
7 **Q—Kt4**	**P—B3**

In keeping with his aggressive intentions, Black veers from the customary 7.., **P—B4** in a strained attempt to undermine White's centre. Smyslov reacts in an equally aggressive vein.

8 **Kt—B3 !**	....

Black can now win a Pawn with 8.., **QBP×P**; 9 **B—Kt5 ch !**, **K—B1**; but after 10 **Castles** White has a fine attacking game.

8	**Kt—B3**
9 **Q—Kt3**	**Q—B2**

In order to be able to develop his King Knight. Botvinnik considers the loss of a Pawn a trivial matter, as White is left with a tripled Pawn; still, it would have been better to interpolate 9.., **QBP×P**; 10 **BP×P** before.., **Q—B2.**

10 **QP×P !**	**KKt—K2**
11 **B—Q3**	**P×P**

This leaves Black with a permanently weak centre. More consistent, therefore, was 11.., **Kt—Kt3.**

12 **Kt×P**	**Kt×Kt**
13 **Q×Kt**	**Castles**
14 **Castles**	**Kt—B3**
15 **Q—Kt3**	**P—K4**

At this juncture Black's centre looks imposing, but Smyslov's subtle play soon shows up weaknesses in it.

16 **B—K3**	**B—B4**

White immediately demonstrates the flaw in this natural move.

17 **QR—Kt1 !**	....

Threatens to win a Pawn by 18 **B×B, Q×B**; 19 **R×P.** Black avoids this by exchanging Bishops, which has the drawback of straightening out White's position. Hence 17.., **B—K3**—despite the loss of time involved—was preferable.

17	**B×B**
18 **P×B**	**QR—K1**

Position after 18.., **QR—K1**:

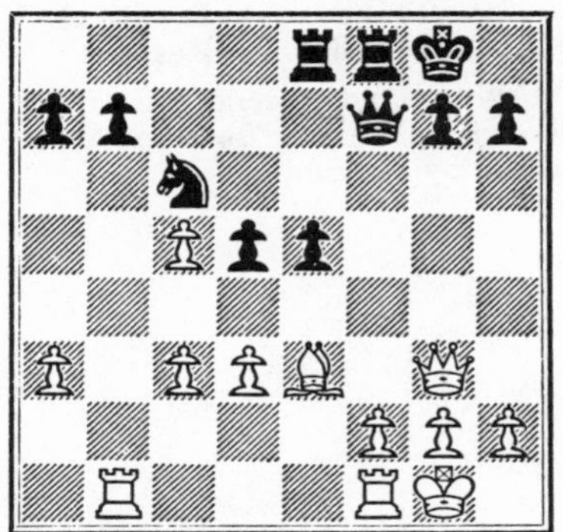

19 **P—KB4!** ....

Forcing a decision in the centre. Black's best course seems 19.., **P—K5**; 20 **P—Q4**, **Kt—R4**; 21 **P—B5**, **Kt—B5**; but after 22 **B—Kt5!** (threatening **P—B6**) White has very promising possibilities on the King-side.

19 .... **Q—B2?**

This move is so weak that one suspects Botvinnik of failing to foresee the fairly obvious sequel.

20	**P×P**	**R×R ch**
21	**R×R**	**Q×P**

Leads into a hopeless endgame, but after 21.., **Kt×P**; 22 **B—Q4!** the threat of **R—B5** is decisive.

22	**Q×Q**	**Kt×Q**
23	**R—Q1**	**K—B2**
24	**P—R3**	**Kt—B3**
25	**B—B4**	....

Smyslov's handling of the whole ending is masterly. Move by move he tightens his grip on the position.

25	....	**R—K2**
26	**B—Q6**	**R—Q2**
27	**R—KB1 ch**	**K—K3**
28	**R—K1 ch**	**K—B2**
29	**K—B2**	....

If Black marks time White will continue with **K—K3** followed by **P—Q4** and **K—Q3** and **P—B4** forcing a passed Pawn and thus increasing his advantage decisively.

29	....	**P—QKt3**
30	**R—QKt1**	**K—K3**
31	**R—Kt5**	**P—Q5**

This only makes matters easier for White; the immediate.., **P×P** is slightly better.

32	**P—B4**	**P×P**

Position after 32.., **P×P**:

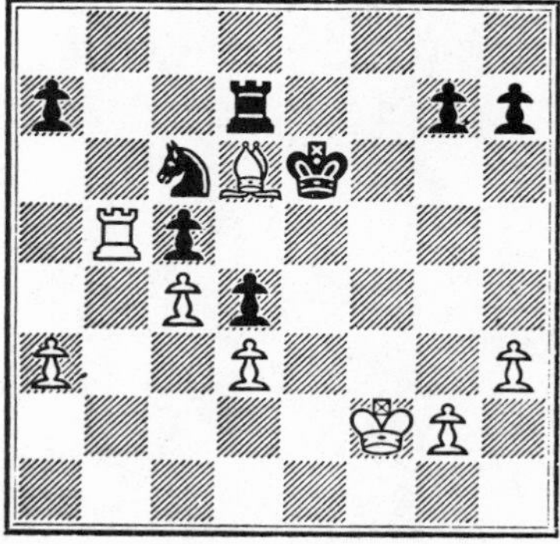

33 **B—R2!** ....

The finest move in the game. White keeps his Bishop on its best diagonal and prepares for an eventual **B—Kt1** that will menace Black's Queen Pawn after White has had time for **R×P**.

33	....	**R—KB2 ch**
34	**K—K2**	**R—K2**

He realises that 34.., **R—B4** is futile because of 35 **P—Kt4**, **R—Kt4**; 36 **B—B4** driving off the Rook.

35	**R×P**	**K—Q2 dis ch**
36	**K—Q2**	**R—K3**

37	**R—KKt5 !**	**P—Kt3**
38	**R—Q5 ch**	**K—B1**
39	**B—Kt1 !**	**R—B3**

He cannot save the Queen Pawn.

40	**B×P**	**Kt×B**
41	**R×Kt**	**R—B7 ch**
42	**K—B3**	**Resigns**

White's advance of his passed Pawns wins easily for him. A fine game by Smyslov.

GAME 61

BOTVINNIK v. SMYSLOV

Moscow, *March* 6th, 1958

(Championship [Third] Match, 2nd Game)

KING'S INDIAN DEFENCE

White.	*Black.*
Botvinnik	Smyslov
1 **P—Q4**	**Kt—KB3**
2 **P—QB4**	**P—KKt3**
3 **Kt—QB3**	**B—Kt2**
4 **P—K4**	**P—Q3**
5 **P—B3**	....

This prepares for **B—K3** without allowing .., **Kt—Kt5** in reply. It also prepares for an eventual **P—KKt4** in conjunction with White's Queen-side castling.

5	**Castles**
6 **B—K3**	**P—QR3**

A hint that Black aims for .., **P—QKt4** in due course as a reaction to White's Queen-side castling.

7 **B—Q3**	....

This move shows a profound understanding of the position. Botvinnik decides to castle on the King-side, taking the sting out of Black's aggressive Queen-side tendencies.

7	**Kt—B3**
8 **KKt—K2**	**R—Kt1**
9 **P—QR3 !**	**Kt—Q2**
10 **B—QKt1**	**Kt—R4**
11 **B—R2**	....

The point of White's last three strange-looking moves is that on .., **P—QKt4** White will exchange Pawns and suddenly open a splendid diagonal for his King Bishop.

11	**P—QKt4?**

Superficial. Much better was 11 .., **P—QB4** with the likely continuation 12 **P—QKt4, Kt—QB3;** 13 **P—Q5, Kt—R2** and while Black's game is cramped, his fianchettoed Bishop is effective and White's King Bishop is the reverse.

12 **P×P**	**P×P**
13 **P—QKt4 !**	**Kt—B5**

This move has been condemned as it leaves Black with a weak Pawn at Queen Bishop 5. However, after a while White secures a potentially formidable passed Queen Rook Pawn. But 13 .., **Kt—QB3;** 14 **B—Q5, Kt—R2;** 15 **P—QR4 !** gives Black an even more pitiable game.

14 **B×Kt**	**P×B**
15 **Castles**	**P—QB3**
16 **Q—Q2**	**Kt—Kt3**

Black can avoid the ensuing exchange of Bishops with 16 .., **R—K1** but after 17 **B—R6, B—R1;** 18 **P—B4** he is left with a miserable position.

17 **B—R6**	**B×B**
18 **Q×B**	**P—B3**
19 **P—QR4**	**Kt—R1**
20 **KR—Kt1**	**P—KB4**

In the face of White's threat to obtain two connected passed Pawns with **P—Q5,** Black vainly strives for counterplay on the King's wing.

21 **Q—K3** **P×P**
22 **P×P** **Kt—B2**
23 **P—Q5** **P×P**
24 **P×P** **B—Kt2**
25 **R—KB1!** ....

Well played. Botvinnik plays to secure control of the open file, and he ignores 25.., **B×P?** because of 26 **Kt×B, Kt×Kt;** 27 **Q—K6 ch**—or 25.., **Kt×P?;** 26 **Q—K6 ch,** and in either case White wins a piece.

25 .... **Q—Q2**
26 **Q—Q4** ....

Guarding his Queen Pawn, but 26 **Q—R7** was possibly even stronger, as White protects the Queen Pawn and threatens to win a piece with **R×R ch.**

26 .... **P—K3**
27 **P×P** **Kt×P**

In the hope of getting his pieces into better play, Smyslov offers a Pawn expecting 28 **Q×BP, P—Q4;** 29 **Q—Kt4, P—Q5** etc. (After 27.., **Q×KP;** 28 **P—Kt5** White wins handily by advancing his passed Pawns.)

28 **Q—Kt4!** ....

Botvinnik prefers to keep up the pressure.

28 .... **KR—K1**
29 **Kt—Q4** **Q—Kt2**
30 **QR—Q1!** ....

Much stronger than 30 **Kt×Kt, Q×Kt** which gives Black some freedom of action.

30 .... **Kt—B2**

Clearly 30.., **Kt×Kt;** 31 **Q×Kt, Q×Q ch;** 32 **R×Q, P—Q4;** 33 **P—Kt5** leaves White with an easily won game.

31 **Q—B4** **R—K4**

Or 31.., **P—Q4;** 32 **Kt(B3)—Kt5, Kt×Kt;** 33 **Kt×Kt, P—Q4;** 34 **Kt—B7** and White wins easily.

Position after 31.., **R—K4:**

32 **Kt—B6!** **B×Kt**
33 **Q×P ch** **P—Q4**
34 **Q×B** **R—Q1**

The real point of White's fine play is that on 34.., **R×P** White continues 35 **Kt×P, R×Kt;** 36 **R×R** and Black cannot play 36.., **Kt×R** because of 37 **Q—K8 ch** forcing mate.

35 **Q—Kt6!** **Q—K2**

Still the same motif: if 35.., **Kt—K3;** 36 **R×P! R(Q1)×R;** 37 **Kt×R, R×Kt;** 38 **Q×Kt ch** forcing mate.

36 **Q—Q4** **Q—Q3**
37 **KR—K1** **QR—K1**
38 **R×R** **R×R**

Or 38.., **Q×R;** 39 **Q×Q, R×Q;** 40 **P—Kt5** and White wins at least another Pawn.

39 **P—Kt5** **Kt—K3**
40 **Q—R7** **P—Q5**
41 **Kt—K4** **Resigns**

If 41.., **R×Kt;** 42 **Q—R8 ch** wins the Rook. And on 41.., **Q—Q1** there follows 42 **P—Kt6!, R×Kt;** 43 **P—Kt7** when the Pawn must queen. A very superior game by Botvinnik.

GAME 62

SMYSLOV v. BOTVINNIK

Moscow, *April* 1, 1958

(Championship [Third] Match, 11th Game)

GRUENFELD DEFENCE

White.	*Black.*
Smyslov	Botvinnik
1 **P—Q4**	**Kt—KB3**
2 **P—QB4**	**P—KKt3**
3 **Kt—QB3**	**P—Q4**
4 **Kt—B3**	**B—Kt2**

Though Smyslov is himself very fond of this defence, he seems to feel no uneasiness about playing against it.

5 **Q—Kt3** **P×P**

Black gives up the centre—not that he has much choice—in the expectation of recovering the lost ground later on by harrying White's Queen.

6 **Q×BP**	**Castles**
7 **P—K4**	**B—Kt5**
8 **B—K3**	**KKt—Q2**
9 **R—Q1**	**Kt—Kt3**

The alternative 9.., **P—K4** is not very promising because of 10 **P—Q5** leaving Black with a position which is anything but alluring.

10 **Q—Kt3**	**Kt—B3**
11 **P—Q5**	**Kt—K4**
12 **B—K2**	**Kt×Kt ch**
13 **P×Kt**	**B—R4**
14 **P—KR4**	....

An interesting innovation which seems more logical than the customary 14 **P—B4** allowing Black to exchange his well-nigh useless Bishop.

14 .... **Q—Q2**

The alternative 14.., **Q—B1** has the merit of guarding Black's Queen Knight Pawn and creating a somewhat more efficient retreat for Black's Knight. On the other hand, the Queen would be consigned to rather a passive status and Black's Rooks would remain disconnected.

15 **P—R4!?** ....

A Pawn offer which Botvinnik declines, for after 15.., **B×Kt ch;** 16 **Q×B, Kt×RP;** 17 **Q—Q4** (threatens to win the Exchange with 18 **B—KR6**), **P—KB3;** 19 **P—B4, B×B;** 20 **K×B** followed by 21 **P—R5** White has a fierce initiative.

15 .... **P—R4**

Now after 16 **B×Kt, P×B;** 17 **Q×P, B×Kt ch;** 18 **P×B, Q×P** White can win a Pawn with 19 **Q×QKtP.** But Smyslov naturally prefers to retain the initiative.

16 **Kt—Kt5** ....

White threatens **Kt×P!**

16 .... **Kt—B1**

Black has parried the threat, but he can never find a good square for this Knight.

17 **B—Q4** ....

Again White has a threat: 18 **B×B, K×B;** 19 **Q—B3 ch, K—Kt1;** 20 **Q×BP** etc.

17 .... **Kt—Q3**

An indirect defence of the Pawn, for if now 18 **B×B, K×B**; 19 **Q—B3 ch, K—Kt1**; 20 **Q×BP, Q×Q**; 21 **Kt×Q, QR—B1**; 22 **Kt—Kt5, Kt×Kt**; 23 **P×Kt, R—B7** and Black has sufficient play for the lost Pawn.

18 **B×B**	**K×B**
19 **Kt—Q4**	....

White has admirably centralised his Knight.

19	**K—Kt1**
20 **KR—Kt1**	**Q—R6**

This shot in the dark turns out badly. The best chance is apparently.., **P—QB4.**

Position after 20.., **Q—R6:**

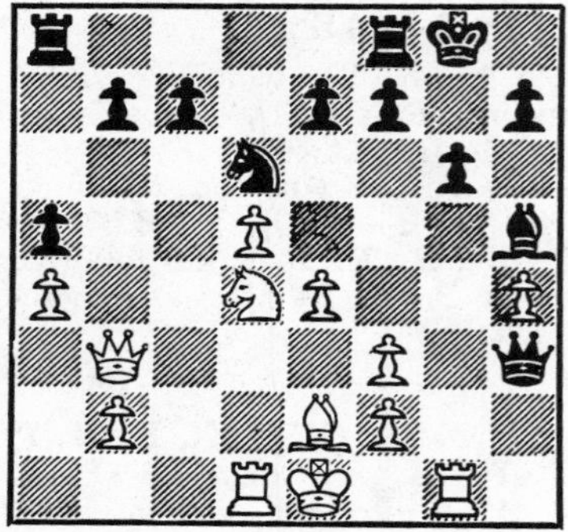

21 **Q—K3!**	....

Leaving Black without a good move, for example 21.., **Q×RP**; 22 **P—K5, Kt—B1**; 23 **Q—R6, P—B4**; 24 **P—B4** with a quick win for White. On 21.., **K—Kt2**; 22 **Q—Kt5** is ruinous for Black.

21	**P—QB4**
22 **P×P e.p.**	**P×P**
23 **Q—Kt5**	....

With the murderous threat of **Q×B.** If Black tries 23.., **K—R1,** he is lost after 24 **Q×KP, QR—Q1**; 25 **Kt×P** etc.

23	**P—QB4**
24 **Kt—B6**	**Resigns**

If Black saves his Bishop with 24.., **K—R1** the reply 25 **Q×KP** is crushing, as his Knight has no moves.

GAME 63
BOTVINNIK v. TAL
Moscow, *March* 26, 1960
(Championship Match, 6th Game)

KING'S INDIAN DEFENCE

	White.	*Black.*
	Botvinnik	Tal
1	**P—QB4**	**Kt—KB3**
2	**Kt—KB3**	**P—KKt3**
3	**P—KKt3**	**B—Kt2**
4	**B—Kt2**	**Castles**
5	**P—Q4**	**P—Q3**
6	**Kt—B3**	**QKt—Q2**
7	**Castles**	**P—K4**
8	**P—K4**	**P—B3**

So far identical with Game 58, in which Botvinnik played 9 **B—K3** provoking 9.., **Kt—Kt5.** Here he prevents the Knight move.

9 **P—KR3** **Q—Kt3**

This somewhat unusual move threatens to win a Pawn, for example 10.., **P×P;** 11 **Kt×P, Kt×P** etc. In addition, the possibility of.., **Q—Kt5** may create an awkward situation for White.

10 **P—Q5** ....

White closes the centre—the easiest way to neutralise the pressure of Black's Bishop on the diagonal.

10 .... **P×P**

True to his aggressive style, Tal dismisses the solid but stodgy alternative 10.., **P—B4** in the hope of operating on the Queen Bishop file later on.

11 **BP×P** **Kt—B4**
12 **Kt—K1** ....

The plausible alternative 12 **Q—B2** has the drawback of allowing 12.., **B—Q2** followed by.., **KR—B1** threatening.., **QKt×P.**

12 .... **B—Q2**
13 **Kt—Q3** **Kt×Kt**
14 **Q×Kt** **KR—B1**
15 **QR—Kt1** ....

Preparing for **B—K3**—but the Rook move gives the alert Tal an idea for an amazing combination.

15 .... **Kt—R4**
16 **B—K3** **Q—Kt5**

Black concentrates on developing pressure along the open Queen Bishop file.

17 **Q—K2** **R—B5**
18 **KR—B1** **QR—QB1**

Tal characteristically courts complications, inviting the curious line 19 **B×P?!, P—B4!;** 20 **P×P, B×P;** 21 **R—R1, P—Kt3!** and Black wins.

19 **K—R2** **P—B4**
20 **P×P** **B×P**
21 **R—QR1** ....

Now it seems that Black must retreat in view of White's threatened **P—KKt4.**

Position after 21 **R—QR1:**

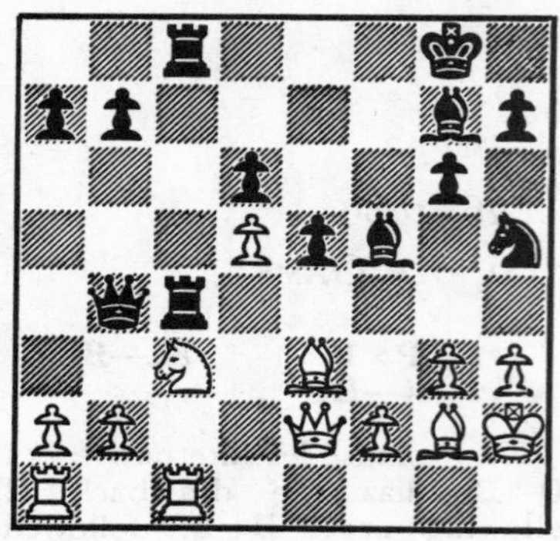

21 .... **Kt—B5?!**

A daring but unsound sacrifice which leaves Botvinnik badly confused.

22 **P×Kt** **P×P**

If now 23 **P—R3, Q—Kt6;** 24 **B×RP, P—Kt3** and White's trapped Bishop will soon be lost.

23 **B—Q2** **Q×P**

So far, so good. Black has two Pawns for the sacrificed piece and threatens to capture the Knight.

24 **QR—Kt1** ....

Botvinnik anticipates 24.., **B×R;** 25 **R×B, Q—B7** (or 25.., **Q—R6;** 26 **R—Kt3** and White preserves a winning advantage); 26 **B—K4** and wins.

24 .... **P—B6?!**

Black should still lose, but this surprise move accomplishes its objective of completely deflecting White from the winning line: 25 **B×P!, B—K4 ch;** 26 **K—Kt2!, B×R;** 27 **R×B, Q—B7;** 28 **R—QB1, Q—Kt7;** 29 **B—Kt4!** The most difficult line then is 29.., **R(B1)—B2;** 30 **B—K6 ch, K—R1;** 31 **Kt—Q1!, Q×P** (31.., **Q—Kt4?** will not do because of 32 **Kt—K3!**); 32 **Q—B3!, K—Kt2** (here 32.., **B—Kt2** loses rapidly because of 33 **R×R, Q×R;** 34 **B—B3!**); 33 **R×R, Q×R;** 34 **B—Kt5!** (with the terrible threat of **B—Q8**), **P—Kt4;** 35 **Kt—K3, Q—B6;** 36 **Q—K2!** and White forces the position after 36.., **P—QR3;** 37 **Kt—Kt4, B—Q5;** 38 **B—R6 ch, K—R1;** 39 **B—Q7!** or 36.., **P—KR3;** 37 **Q×P!, P×B;** 38 **Q—K8!** etc. A beautiful piece of analysis by Hans Kmoch.

25 **R×Q??** **P×Q**
26 **R—Kt3** ....

Having released himself from the diagonal pin, Botvinnik intends to release himself from the other pin by 27 **Kt×P.**

Position after 26 **R—Kt3:**

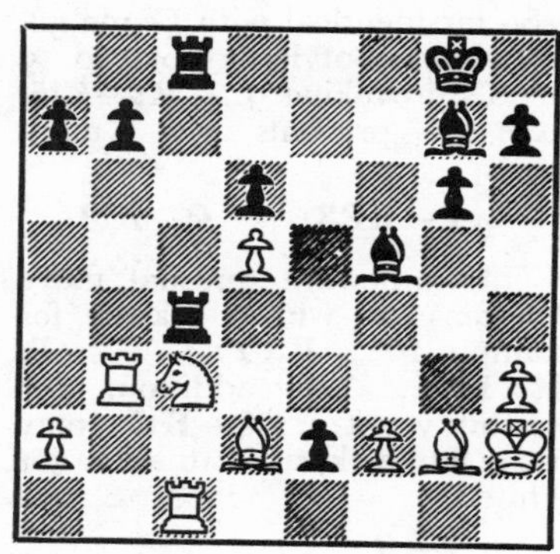

26 .... **R—Q5!**

Now White has a lost game, thanks to the power of Black's seemingly condemned passed Pawn.

27 **B—K1** ....

If 27 **B—K3, R×Kt;** 28 **R(Kt3)×R, R—Q8** and White can resign. Or 27 **R—Kt2,**

R—Q6!; 28 **R(Kt2)—B2, B×Kt**; 29 **R×B, R(B1)×R**; 30 **B×R, R×B** etc.

27 .... **B—K4 ch**
28 **K—Kt1** **B—B5**

Good enough to win, but 28.., **R×Kt!**; 29 **R(Kt3)×R, R—Q8**; 30 **R—B7, B—Kt7** was faster.

29 **Kt×P** ....

He must return the piece, for if instead 29 **R—R1, R×Kt!**; 30 **R×R, R—Q8** wins—or 29 **R(Kt3)—Kt1, B×R(Kt8)**; 30 **R×B, R×Kt!**; 31 **B×R, R—Q8 ch** and wins.

29 .... **R×R**
30 **Kt×R(Q4)** ....

After 30 **Kt×R(B1), R—Q8** wins easily; even 30.., **B×Kt** is good enough, as White dare not play 31 **R×P?** because of 31.., **R—Q8** winning a piece for Black (32 **K—B1, B—Q6 ch**).

30 .... **R×B ch**
31 **B—B1** **B—K5**

Black has come out of the skirmish with a Pawn to the good, and the ending is easily won for him.

32 **Kt—K2** ....

Not 32 **R×P?, B—Q6** and Black wins a piece. The Black Bishops, which played so formidable a role in the middle game, are still powerful.

32 .... **B—K4**
33 **P—B4** ....

On 33 **R×P?, B—Q6** still wins a piece, as the Rook cannot retreat to Knight 2.

33 .... **B—B3**
34 **R×P** **B×P**

On 34.., **B—Q6** White has 35 **K—B2, B—R5 ch**; 36 **K—K3.**

35 **R—QB7** ....

But not 35 **R×QRP?, R×Kt**; 36 **B×R, B—Q5 ch** and wins.

35 .... **B×P**
36 **R×QRP** **B—B5**

At this point 36.., **R×Kt?** would not do because of 37 **R—R8 ch!** and White comes out the Exchange ahead.

37 **R—R8 ch** **K—B2**

Now it seems that White is lost, for if 38 **K—B2?, B—R5 ch** wins a piece for Black.

38 **R—R7 ch** **K—K3**

If Black's King avoids the King file, White keeps checking. If 38.., **B—K2**; 39 **K—B2** saves White, as Black cannot play.., **B—R5 ch.**

39 **R—R3** ....

This holds the position for the time being, as on 39.., **B×Kt** White has 40 **R—K3 ch** and on 39.., **R×Kt**; 40 **B×R, B×B**; 41 **R—K3 ch.**

39 .... **P—Q4!**

The winning Pawn.

40 **K—B2** **B—R5 ch**
41 **K—Kt2** **K—Q3**

Now Black threatens.., **R×Kt ch.**

42 **Kt—Kt3** **B×Kt**
43 **B×B** **P×B**
44 **K×B** **K—Q4**

With Black's King supporting the passed Pawn and with White's King cut off, the ending is easily won for Black.

45 **R—R7** **P—B6**
46 **R—QB7** **K—Q5**
47 **R—Q7 ch** ....

White sealed this move and then resigned without resuming play. The finish might have been 47.., **K—K6;** 48 **R—K7 ch, K—Q7;** 49 **R—Q7 ch, K—B8;** 50 **R×P, P—B7;** 51 **R—QB7, R—K7;** 52 **K—B3, K—Q8;** 53 **R—B8, R—Q7!** followed by the queening of the Pawn.

GAME 64

BOTVINNIK v. TAL

Moscow, *March* 31, 1960

(Championship Match, 8th Game)

BENONI DEFENCE

White.	*Black.*
Botvinnik	Tal
1 **P—Q4**	**Kt—KB3**
2 **P—QB4**	**P—K3**
3 **Kt—KB3**	**P—B4**

The Queen's Indian Defence (3.., **P—QKt3**) is considered to give Black easy equality. But Tal is more interested in complications rather than equality.

4 **P—Q5** **P×P**
5 **P×P** **P—KKt3**

The idea of this defence becomes clear: Black provokes the advance of White's Queen Pawn in order to obtain a clear diagonal for the fianchettoed Bishop.

6 **Kt—B3** **B—Kt2**
7 **B—Kt5** ....

This hampering pin places difficulties in the way of Black's harmonious development of his pieces.

7 .... **Castles**
8 **P—K3** **R—K1**

Driving off the oppressive Bishop may end badly for Black, for example 8.., **P—KR3**; 9 **B—R4**, **P—KKt4**; 10 **B—Kt3**, **Kt—R4**; 11 **B—K5**! Now if 11.., **P—B3??**; 12 **B×Kt**, **R×B**; 13 **P—KKt4** and White wins a piece.

9 **Kt—Q2** ....

Experience shows that this Knight can go to Queen Bishop 4 or King 4 later on, with good effect.

9 .... **P—Q3**
10 **B—K2** **P—QR3**

Since Black will not be allowed to play.., **P—Kt4** (the logical complement to this move), it seems preferable to continue.., **Kt(R3)—B2** etc. As the game actually proceeds, Black's development is inordinately protracted.

11 **P—QR4** **QKt—Q2**
12 **Castles** **Q—B2**
13 **Q—B2** **Kt—Kt3**

Black attacks the Queen Pawn in order to provoke **P—K4**, which would give him the potential occupation of the Queen 5 square. Botvinnik declines the invitation, for if 14 **P—K4?**, **KKt×QP!** and Black wins a Pawn.

14 **B—B3** **P—B5**

Sacrifice or oversight? In any event, White now wins a Pawn by force.

15 **B×Kt!** **B×B**
16 **P—R5** **Kt—Q2**
17 **Kt(B3)—K4** **B—K4**
18 **Q×P** **Q—Q1**
19 **Q—R2** **P—B4**

True to his style, Tal strives for attack; but his Pawn minus and his laggard development should tell against him.

20	**Kt—B3**	**P—KKt4**
21	**Kt—B4**	**P—Kt5**
22	**B—K2**	**Q—B3**
23	**Kt—R4!**	**K—R1**
24	**P—KKt3**	....

Good enough, but Kmoch suggests that the obvious occupation of the open Queen Bishop file would be much more effective; 24 **QR—B1, P—R4;** 25 **Kt(B4)—Kt6** (threatens **R×B!**), **Kt×Kt;** 26 **Kt×Kt, QR—Kt1;** 27 **R—B7!** with a very strong game for White, for example 27.., **B×P?;** 28 **R—Kt1, B—K4;** 29 **R(Kt1)—QB1, Q—B1;** 30 **Q—B4!** and Black's unfortunate Bishop is lost.

Position after 24 **P—KKt3:**

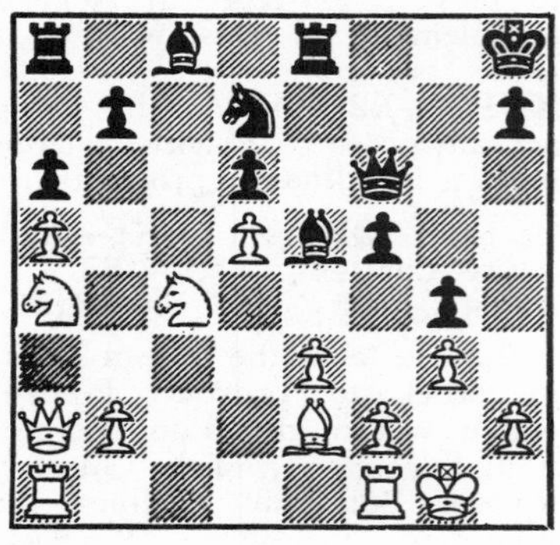

24	....	**P—R4**
25	**P—B4!**	**B—Q5**

The quest for complications continues, 25.., **P×P e.p.** being out of the question because of 26 **R×P** followed by **QR—KB1.**

26	**Q—R3**	**QR—Kt1**

Now White can gain a clearly winning advantage with the obvious 27 **P×B!**, for example 27.., **R×B;** 28 **Q—Q3, R—K2;** 29 **QR—K1** and White's command of the board is decisive—or 27.., **Q×P ch;** 28 **R—B2, R×B;** 29 **Q—QB3!, Q×Q;** 30 **P×Q, R×R;** 31 **K×R, Kt—B3;** 32 **Kt×P, Kt×P;** 33 **P—B4, Kt—K2;** 34 **Kt—Kt6, R—Kt1;** 35 **R—K1** and wins. But Botvinnik is already plagued by acute time pressure, and his play suffers accordingly.

27	**Kt(R4)—Kt6**	**P—R5**
28	**QR—Q1?**	....

Again **P×B** was the right way. Now Black disposes of his King Bishop in a more profitable manner.

28	....	**B×Kt**
29	**P×B**	**Kt—B4!**

Suddenly Black's chances are looking up. If now 30 **Q—B3, Q×Q;** 31 **P×Q, P×P;** 32 **P×P, Kt—K5** and Black regains his Pawn with a decidedly superior ending.

30	**P×P**	**B—Q2!**

Stronger than 30.., **Q×RP;** 31 **Q—B3 ch** followed by 32 **Q—K1.**

31	**Q—B3**	....

This leads to a markedly inferior ending, but against 31 **Kt—Q2** Black proceeds advantageously with 31.., **Kt—R5!**

31	....	**Q×Q**
32	**P×Q**	**B—Kt4!**

A very uncomfortable situation for White, despite his two extra Pawns.

33	**KR—K1**	**Kt—K5**

At this point White can still save himself with 34 **R—Q4!, Kt×P;** 35 **B—Q3** etc. But the time scramble is too much for the players.

34	**R—QB1?**	....

Now Balck wins with 34.., **KR—QB1!;** 35 **Kt—R5, B×B;** 36 **R×B, Kt×P** as White must lose the Exchange (37 **KR—QB2, Kt—K7 ch!**).

34 .... **QR—B1?**

This costs the Queen Knight Pawn, so that White becomes the player who has the winning chances.

35 **Kt—R5!** **B×B**
36 **R×B** **Kt×P**
37 **R×Kt** ....

White must lose the Exchange in any event, and this is the most favourable way.

37 .... **R×R**
38 **Kt×P** **R(K1)×P?**

A superficial move. Black can draw with 38.., **R—QKt1;** 39 **Kt×P, R—Q6!** etc.

39 **R×R** **R×R**
40 **Kt×P** ....

If now 40.., **R—QKt6;** 41 **Kt—B4, K—Kt1** (on 41.., **R—Kt5;** 42 **P—Q6!** and one of the White Pawns must queen); 42 **P—Q6, K—B1;** 43 **P—R5, R—Kt5;** 44 **P—R6!** and one of the three passed Pawns must get through.

40 .... **R—Q6**

Position after 40.., **R—Q6:**

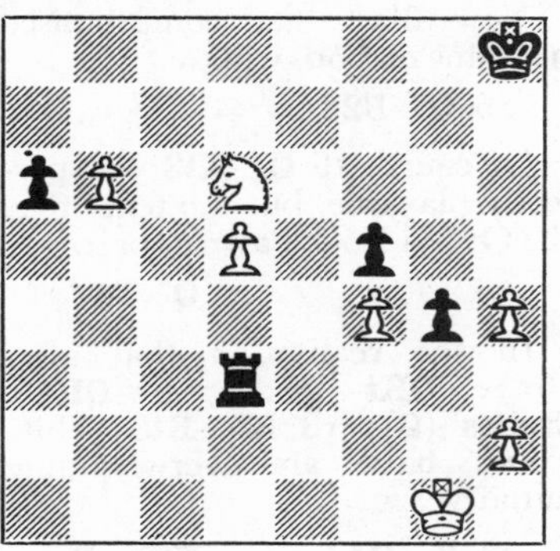

In this position, with the time pressure over, Botvinnik reflected for half an hour before making his sealed move.

41 **Kt—B7 ch!!** **Resigns**

If 41.., **K—R2;** 42 **P—Q6, P—R4;** 43 **P—Kt7, R—QKt6;** 44 **P—Q7** wins.

The most stubborn defence is 41.., **K—Kt2;** 42 **P—Kt7, R—QKt6;** 43 **Kt—Q8, P—R4** (if 43.., **K—B1;** 44 **P—R5!, K—K1;** 45 **P—R6, K×Kt;** 46 **P—R7** and wins—or 43.., **K—B1;** 44 **P—R5!, R—Kt3;** 45 **P—R6, K—Kt1;** 46 **P—Q6, P—R4;** 47 **P—Q7, P—R5;** 48 **Kt—B6** etc.); 44 **P—Q6, P—R5** (if 44.., **K—B1;** 45 **P—R5!, K—K1;** 46 **P—R6!** wins); 45 **P—Q7, P—R6;** 46 **Kt—K6 ch** and wins. An exciting finish to an absorbing game.

GAME 65
BOTVINNIK v. TAL
Moscow, *April*, 1961
(Championship Match, 7th Game)

NIMZOVITCH DEFENCE

White.	*Black.*
Botvinnik	Tal
1 **P—QB4**	**Kt—KB3**
2 **Kt—QB3**	**P—K3**
3 **P—Q4**	**B—Kt5**
4 **P—QR3**	....

The famous Saemisch line, frequently tried in games between these players. White gets rid of the pin at once with a view to building up a formidable Pawn centre.

4	**B×Kt ch**
5 **P×B**	**P—QKt3**

Black should come to a decision as to whether he intends to play .., **P—Q4** or .., **P—Q3**. Tal postpones a decision but derives no advantage thereby.

6 **P—B3**	....

Clearly aiming for **P—K4**.

6	**B—R3**

A fashionable move, albeit one of dubious utility. The alternative 6 .., **P—Q4** has more bite.

7 **P—K4**	**P—Q4**
8 **BP×P !**	....

Botvinnik realises that the loss of castling is of little moment here.

8	**B×B**
9 **K×B**	**P×P**
10 **B—Kt5**	**P—KR3**
11 **Q—R4 ch**	....

A timely interpolation, as 11 .., **Q—Q2**; 12 **Q×Q ch, QKt×Q**; 13 **B×Kt, Kt×B**; 14 **P—K5** gives White a superior ending. In any event, Botvinnik reckons on his opponent's evasion of an early ending.

11	**P—B3**
12 **B—R4 !**	....

Botvinnik indicates his readiness to give up a Pawn, shrewdly foreseeing that Black will compromise his position in his efforts to hold on to his extra material.

12	**P×P**
13 **R—K1**	**P—KKt4**
14 **B—B2**	**Q—K2**
15 **Kt—K2 !**	....

Obviously Black cannot reply 15 .., **P×P??** in view of 16 **Kt—Kt3** and White wins.

15	**P—Kt4**

Now Black has compromised his game on both wings.

16 **Q—B2 !**	....

Of course 16 **Q—Kt3** was perfectly playable, but the text offers the Queen Rook Pawn as bait.

16	**Q×P?!**

In the realisation that after 16 .., **QKt—Q2**; 17 **P—QR4 !, Castles (Q)**; 18 **Kt—Kt3** White would have an overwhelming initiative.

17 **P—R4 !**	**KtP×P**

The alternative 17 .., **KP×P**;

18 **Kt—Kt3 dis ch, K—Q1;** 19 **RP × P** is anything but inviting.

18 **B × P**	**QKt—Q2**
19 **Kt—Kt3**	**Castles (Q)**
20 **Kt × P**	....

Position after 20 **Kt × P:**

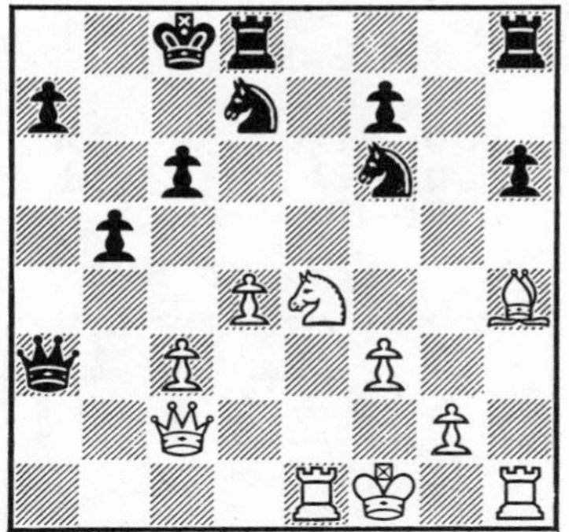

Black is lost. After 20 .., **Kt × Kt;** 21 **Q × Kt** the double threat of **Q × P ch** or **B × R** decides easily.

20	**KR—K1**

Black hopes for 21 **B × Kt, Kt × B;** 22 **Kt × Kt, R × R ch;** 23 **K × R, Q—K2 ch;** 24 **Kt—K4, P—KB4.**

It is true that White can win a piece with 21 **Kt × Kt, R × R ch;** 22 **K × R, Q—R8 ch;** 23 **Q—Q1;** but after 23 .., **Q × P ch** Black can still put up some fight.

Botvinnik finds a much stronger move:

21 **K—B2!!**	**Kt × Kt ch**
22 **P × Kt**	**P—B3**
23 **R—R1**	....

Botvinnik remains a Pawn down but he gets a terrific attack.

23	**Q—K2**
24 **R × P!**	**Q × P**
25 **Q × Q!**	....

White sees that he will maintain a fierce attack despite the exchange of Queens.

25	**R × Q**
26 **R—R8 ch**	**Kt—Kt1**

Or 26 .., **K—B2;** 27 **B—Kt3 ch** and wins.

27 **B—Kt3**	**K—Kt2**
28 **KR—R1**	....

This is the position that Botvinnik was aiming for. He must now win a piece.

28	**R—QB1**
29 **R(R8)—R7 ch!**	

Very fine play.

29	**K—Kt3**
30 **B × Kt!**	....

The point. If 30 .., **R × B;** 31 **R(R1)—R6** mate!

30	**P—Kt5**
31 **B—Q6**	**P × P**
32 **B—B5 ch**	**K—Kt4**
33 **R(R1)—R4!**	**Resigns**

Black is helpless against the coming **R(R7)—R5** mate. A very fine game by Botvinnik.

GAME 66

TAL v. BOTVINNIK

Moscow, *April*, 1961
(Championship Match, 8th Game)

CARO-KANN DEFENCE

White.	*Black.*
Tal	Botvinnik
1 **P—K4**	**P—QB3**
2 **P—Q4**	**P—Q4**
3 **P—K5**	....

This variation, deemed moribund for years, was revived by Tal with remarkable success in his first match with Botvinnik.

3 .... **P—QB4**

Botvinnik veers from the standard 3 .., **B—B4**. The text leads to a variation of the French Defence, with Black a move down.

4 **P×P**	**P—K3**
5 **Q—Kt4**	**Kt—QB3**

Here 5 .., **Kt—Q2** gives Black an easier game.

6 **Kt—KB3**	**Q—B2**
7 **B—QKt5**	**B—Q2**
8 **B×Kt**	**Q×B**
9 **B—K3**	**Kt—R3**

This leads to a difficult game for Black after the obligatory weakening of his Pawn position which now follows. Much better was 9 .., **P—KR4 !** with excellent chances for Black.

10 **B×Kt**	**P×B**
11 **QKt—Q2**	**Q×P**
12 **P—B4**	**Castles**
13 **Castles (K)**	**K—Kt1**
14 **KR—Q1**	**Q—Kt3**
15 **Q—R4**	**P—QR4**
16 **QR—B1**	**R—Kt1**
17 **Kt—Kt3**	....

Position after 17 **Kt—Kt3**:

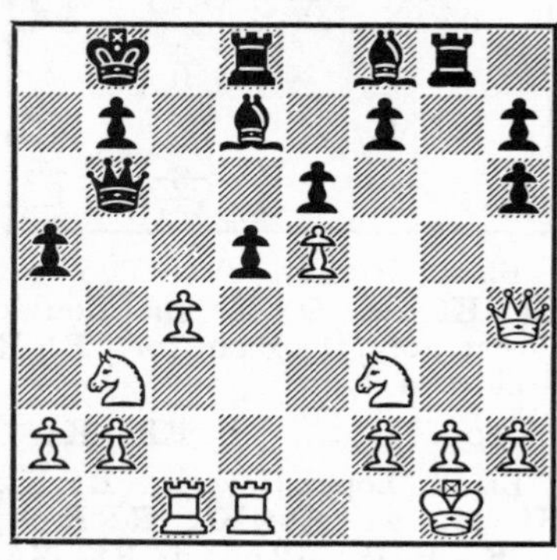

17 .... **P—R5?**

The turning point. Correct was 17 .., **P×P !**; 18 **R×P** (threatening 19 **QR—Q4**), **P—R5 !**; 20 **Kt(Kt3)—Q4** (if 20 **R×P?**, **B—K2 !** wins; or if 20 **Kt—B1**, **B—B4**; 21 **Kt—Q3**, **B—Kt4**; 22 **R×B?**, **Q×R !** and wins), **B—B4** with a good game for Black.

18 **P—B5 !**	**Q—B2**
19 **Kt(Kt3)—Q4**	**R—B1**
20 **P—QKt4**	**P×P e.p.**
21 **P×P**	**Q—Q1**
22 **Q×Q**	**R×Q**

Though the Queens have disappeared, White's pressure persists.

23 **P—QKt4** **R—Kt5**

24 **P—Kt5** **R—B1**

White was threatening to win a piece with 25 **P—B6,** etc.

25 **P—B6** **B—K1**

After 25 .., **P×P;** 26 **P×P, B—K1;** 27 **R—Kt1 ch, K—B2;** 28 **Kt—Kt5 ch!** a likely continuation is 28 .., **K—Q1;** 29 **Kt—R7, R—B2;** 30 **R—Kt8 ch, K—K2;** 31 **Kt—B8 ch** and wins.

26 **R—B2** **B—Kt2**

27 **R—R1!** **B×KP**

This leads to a very fine finish.

28 **Kt×B** **R×Kt**
29 **Kt—Q7 ch!** **Resigns**

Black must choose between 29 .., **K—B2;** 30 **P—Kt6 ch, K** moves; 31 **P×P** and wins—or 29 .., **B×Kt;** 30 **P×B, R—Q1;** 31 **R—B8 ch!** (not 31 **R—R8 ch?, K×R;** 32 **R—B8 ch, K—R2!**), **R×R;** 32 **R—R8 ch!,** etc.